# ADempiere 3.4 ERP Solutions

Design, configure, and implement a robust enterprise resource planning system in your organization by using ADempiere

**Bayu Cahya Pamungkas**

[PACKT PUBLISHING]

BIRMINGHAM - MUMBAI

# ADempiere 3.4 ERP Solutions

Copyright © 2009 Packt Publishing

All rights reserved. No part of this book may be reproduced, stored in a retrieval system, or transmitted in any form or by any means, without the prior written permission of the publisher, except in the case of brief quotations embedded in critical articles or reviews.

Every effort has been made in the preparation of this book to ensure the accuracy of the information presented. However, the information contained in this book is sold without warranty, either express or implied. Neither the author nor Packt Publishing, and its dealers and distributors will be held liable for any damages caused or alleged to be caused directly or indirectly by this book.

Packt Publishing has endeavored to provide trademark information about all of the companies and products mentioned in this book by the appropriate use of capitals. However, Packt Publishing cannot guarantee the accuracy of this information.

First published: December 2009

Production Reference: 1111209

Published by Packt Publishing Ltd.
32 Lincoln Road
Olton
Birmingham, B27 6PA, UK.

ISBN 978-1-847197-26-9

www.packtpub.com

Cover Image by Vinayak Chittar (vinayak.chittar@gmail.com)

# Credits

**Author**
Bayu Cahya Pamungkas

**Reviewers**
Colin Rooney
Heng Sin Low
Praneet Tiwari

**Acquisition Editor**
Sarah Cullington

**Development Editor**
Amey Kanse

**Technical Editors**
Hithesh Uchil
Mayuri Kokate

**Copy Editor**
Leonard D'Silva

**Indexer**
Rekha Nair

**Editorial Team Leader**
Akshara Aware

**Project Team Leader**
Priya Mukherji

**Project Coordinator**
Zainab Bagasrawala

**Proofreader**
Dirk Manuel

**Graphics**
Nilesh Mohite

**Production Coordinator**
Aparna Bhagat

**Cover Work**
Aparna Bhagat

# About the Author

**Bayu Cahya Pamungkas** has experience of working in various financial and manufacturing industries. He is currently employed as a functional consultant on both financial and manufacturing domains for a leading proprietary ERP system. He works on the implementation of project management software for apparel industries and is also involved in the implementation of Electronic Data Interchange (EDI) software. With his experience and background, he established his own consulting company, and implements ADempiere for customers around the world.

Currently, Bayu also teaches and implements ADempiere Libero Manufacturing (a new feature in ADempiere 3.5). He is an official ADempiere committer, and shares his thoughts through his blog at `http://sistematika.web.id`. If you need ADempiere professional services, then you can reach his team at `consulting@sistematika.web.id`

> I would like to thank Jesus Christ, who guides me and who gave me the ability to finish the book, all of the reviewers who gave their invaluable advice, the entire ADempiere community that directly or indirectly supported this ADempiere book, and the people at Packt Publishing who helped me realize this book.
>
> My wife Rossy, and my children Yohanes and Moses—thank you for all your love. It's an honor to have you in my life.

# About the Reviewers

**Colin Rooney** is a founding member of the ADempiere project, and is a strong advocate of Free and Open Source Software and its use by businesses to reduce risk, reduce costs, and be more flexible.

Born in Dublin, Ireland, Colin has been involved in the development and deployment of business information systems since he began his IT career at Germany's Nixdorf Computers, in 1986. From there, Colin embarked on a long career working with many of Europe's biggest multinational companies, on projects in a wide range of business areas—from manufacturing to services, and CRM to accounting.

After sixteen years of living and working in several countries across Europe, in 2002 Colin returned to his native Ireland, from where he now provides a variety technical and business services, primarily based around ADempiere, to clients, via `OpenBiz.ie`.

> Thank you to all of those in the ADempiere community who have helped make ADempiere one of the most popular and best business solutions available today. Thank you also to all of those who have had the wisdom to realize that collaboration and sharing is the way for us all to achieve the most. It takes courage to be the first to step forward, so I thank you all for your enlightenment and bravery.

**Heng Sin Low**, living in the city of Petaling Jaya, Malaysia, is one of the most active committers of the ADempiere ERP project at SourceForge. He has been into software development since 1997, performing business application development for small and big enterprises. He started his software development journey using the once-popular PowerBuilder tool, integrated into the Oracle database. As the world shifted to Java programming, Heng Sin Low shifted his focus to Java, in 2001. Before joining the ADempiere project, he was briefly engaged with the Castor and WebWork open source project. He is now the main maintainer of the ZK web client for ADempiere. His other major contributions include the porting of ADempiere to PostgreSQL.

At the time of writing the book, Sin Low was working at Idalica (M) Sdn Bhd in Malaysia, which is a development subsidiary of Idalica Corporation, USA.

**Praneet Tiwari** holds a Master of Business Administration from the Indian Institute of Management Bangalore, and a Master of Technology in Computer Science from the Indian Institute of Technology Delhi. He has been working on integrating ADempiere with other enterprise class software such as Glassfish, MySQL, and OpenDS. His interest areas include open source software, modeling of fixed income securities, Bioinformatics string algorithms, Abstract Algebra, and Multivariate Analysis. He is currently working with Sun Microsystems. He can be reached at praneet.tiwari@gmail.com and praneet.tiwari@yahoo.com.

> I want to thank my parents for the immense faith they have put in me, and my wife for her boundless patience.

# Table of Contents

| | |
|---|---|
| **Preface** | **1** |
| **Chapter 1: ADempiere Installation** | **9** |
| ADempiere hardware and operating system requirements | 10 |
| Installing the Sun Java Development Kit (JDK) | 10 |
|    Obtaining JDK/JRE | 11 |
|    Installing JDK/JRE | 11 |
|       JDK installation on the ADempiere server computer | 12 |
|       JRE installation on the ADempiere client computer | 13 |
|    Configuring Java system variables and the Windows path | 14 |
|    Verifying system variables and the Windows path | 15 |
| **Installing databases** | **16** |
|    Obtaining PostgreSQL databases | 16 |
|    Installing PostgreSQL databases | 17 |
|    Adding the PostgreSQL path | 17 |
|    Verifying the additional PostgreSQL path | 18 |
|    Configuring PostgreSQL | 19 |
|       Modifying the client authentication configuration file | 19 |
|       Verifying the PostgreSQL configuration file | 20 |
|    Configuring the firewall to allow database connections | 20 |
| **Installing ADempiere on the server side** | **21** |
|    Downloading the ADempiere core installation files | 21 |
|    Downloading the latest ADempiere patch files | 21 |
|       Obtaining the ADempiere application patch files | 22 |
|       Obtaining the ADempiere database migration script | 23 |
|    Verifying the ADempiere binary files | 23 |
|    Extracting the ADempiere core installation files | 25 |
|    Applying the ADempiere application patch files | 25 |
|    Creating an ADempiere PostgreSQL database | 26 |
|       Creating a PostgreSQL new login role | 26 |
|       Creating an ADempiere database | 27 |

*Table of Contents*

| | |
|---|---|
| Configuring the ADempiere server | 27 |
| Importing the initial ADempiere database | 30 |
|     Applying the database migration script | 31 |
| ADempiere server memory management | 32 |
| Starting up the ADempiere application server | 32 |
| **Installing ADempiere on the client side** | **33** |
| Web Start client installation | 34 |
| Verifying the ADempiere client installation | 34 |
| **Reading the ADempiere 3.4.2s release notes** | **35** |
| **Summary** | **36** |
| **Chapter 2: Exploring the ADempiere Client and Performing Tasks** | **37** |
| **The Connection aspect of ADempiere** | **38** |
| Checking the ADempiere client version | 38 |
| The predefined user ID and password | 38 |
| Understanding the Client and System users | 40 |
| Changing our ADempiere server connection | 40 |
| Which ADempiere server are we working on? | 41 |
| **Managing ADempiere client** | **42** |
| Working with the Menu | 43 |
|     Menu Icon | 44 |
|     Accessing menus | 44 |
|     Menu Lookup and creating shortcuts | 45 |
| User preferences | 46 |
|     More on the Cache Window option | 48 |
| Parts of the ADempiere window | 48 |
|     More on Record Info | 49 |
|     OK or Cancel button in the window | 50 |
| Maintaining a log of data changes | 50 |
| Standard window fields | 51 |
|     Client and Organization fields | 51 |
|     Active checkbox fields | 51 |
| **Performing tasks** | **52** |
| Data management | 52 |
| Data navigation | 53 |
| Other tasks | 54 |
| More on Lookup records | 55 |
|     Setting additional search criteria | 56 |
| More examples on the use of Zoom Across | 57 |
| Field context menu | 58 |
|     Zoom | 59 |
|     ReQuery | 59 |
|     **Value preference** | **60** |
| **Summary** | **61** |

## Chapter 3: Exploring Company Structures and the Initial Client Setup — 63

- **Sample apparel company structure** — 64
- **ADempiere company structures** — 65
- **Managing the Chart of accounts template** — 66
  - Exploring the accounting format template files — 67
  - Account editor tools — 68
- **Creating a new ADempiere client** — 70
- **Reviewing your new ADempiere client creation** — 73
  - Setting additional organizations — 74
    - Creating the organization type — 74
    - Creating an additional organization — 74
    - Updating organization information — 75
  - Setting up an additional warehouse — 76
    - Altering the existing default warehouse and locators — 76
    - Adding extra warehouses and locators — 78
  - Re-importing the chart of accounts — 80
    - Import File Loader — 81
    - Import Account — 81
- **Taking a look at the other configuration parts** — 83
  - Accounting schema — 84
  - Calendar Year and Period — 85
    - Creating a new year and periods — 85
    - Opening document types — 85
    - Period Closed error message — 86
  - Accounting processor — 87
    - Automatically posting documents — 87
    - Common errors during manual posting — 88
- **Summary** — 89

## Chapter 4: Setting up Master Data and Knowing its Accounting Configuration — 91

- **Introduction to master data accounting configuration** — 92
  - Example of a Product's accounting configuration — 92
  - The meaning of HQ-14120-_-_-_-_ — 93
  - Account combination — 94
    - Common rules when creating an account combination — 95
    - Creating a new account combination — 95
  - Changing the account combination of the ADempiere default account — 98
    - Account alias — 98
    - Altering the Product Asset default account — 98
- **Managing a Business Partner** — 100
  - Business Partner Group — 100
    - Grouping criteria — 100

| | |
|---|---:|
| Accounting configuration | 101 |
| Creating a new business partner group | 102 |
| **Business Partner** | **103** |
| Registering a new Vendor | 103 |
| Vendor accounting configuration | 105 |
| Registering a new Customer | 105 |
| Customer accounting configuration | 106 |
| **Company financial management** | **106** |
| Managing your bank information | 107 |
| Registering your bank information | 107 |
| Registering a bank account document | 108 |
| Bank account configuration | 108 |
| Managing a Cash Book | 109 |
| Configuring your own cash book | 109 |
| Cash book accounting configuration | 110 |
| Introduction to Charge | 110 |
| Preparing new account combinations for Charge | 111 |
| Creating a new type of Charge | 111 |
| **Using multiple currencies** | **112** |
| Currency | 113 |
| Deactivating unneeded currencies | 113 |
| Currency conversion rate types | 114 |
| Creating a new currency type | 114 |
| Currency rates | 115 |
| Entering new currency rates | 115 |
| Entering reciprocal rates | 116 |
| **Price management** | **116** |
| Managing Price List Schema | 117 |
| Registering a new price list schema | 117 |
| Creating a Price List | 118 |
| Registering a new Price List | 118 |
| Creating a Price List version | 118 |
| **Product management** | **119** |
| Product Type | 119 |
| Product configuration | 120 |
| Creating a Product Category | 121 |
| Product Category accounting configuration | 121 |
| Creating a new Product | 122 |
| Preparing a new unit of measurement | 122 |
| The Product tab | 123 |
| The Purchasing tab | 124 |
| The Price tab | 124 |
| **Summary** | **127** |

## Chapter 5: Procurement Activities — 129
### Introduction to the ADempiere Document — 129
### Working on a Purchase Requisition — 131
#### Creating a Purchase Requisition manually — 131
#### Working with Replenish Reports — 132
- Setting up replenish information — 132
- Setting up the default Price List — 133
- Completing the replenish information — 134
#### Accounting facts — 134
### Working with Purchase Orders — 136
#### Creating a Purchase Order manually — 136
#### Creating a Purchase Order from a Purchase Requisition — 137
- Accounting facts — 138
### Receiving material — 138
#### Receiving materials with a Purchase Order reference — 139
- Accounting facts — 141
#### Receiving material without a Purchase Order reference — 141
#### Posting error — 142
#### Matching a Purchase Order to a Receipt — 143
- Accounting facts — 145
#### Matched Purchase Orders — 145
- Accounting facts — 147
### Managing vendor invoices — 147
#### Invoicing with a Material Receipt reference — 148
- Accounting facts — 150
#### Invoicing without a Material Receipt reference — 150
- Accounting facts — 152
#### Matching an Invoice to Material Receipt documents — 152
#### Evaluating Matched Invoices — 153
- Accounting facts — 154
#### Summary of Material Receipt and Invoice (Vendor) accounting facts — 155
### Making a payment to the vendor — 156
#### Outstanding liabilities — 156
#### Payment Selection — 157
- Creating a list of unpaid invoices — 157
- Creating a payment proposal — 157
- Payment Print/Export — 159
#### Account Payable payments — 160
- Accounting facts — 160
#### Viewing payment allocation — 161
- Accounting facts — 161

## Table of Contents

| | |
|---|---|
| Bank Statement | 162 |
|   Entering Bank Statement information | 162 |
|   Entering a Bank Statement Line | 163 |
|   Accounting facts | 164 |
| Summary of Payment, Allocation, and Bank Statement accounting facts | 164 |
| Cash payment | 165 |
|   Cash Type | 165 |
| Invoice cash payment | 166 |
|   Accounting facts | 166 |
| Cash Payment Allocation | 167 |
|   Accounting facts | 167 |
| Summary of Cash Payment and Cash Allocation accounting facts | 168 |
| **Summary** | **169** |
| **Chapter 6: Landed Costs, Production, and Sales Activities** | **171** |
| **Activating the accounting processor** | **172** |
| **Landed costs** | **172** |
|   Prerequisite configuration | 173 |
|     Entering an additional business partner | 173 |
|     Creating a new account combination | 174 |
|     Setting transportation charges | 174 |
|     Setting a new cost element | 176 |
|     Altering the product cost adjustment default account | 176 |
|     Creating additional Price Lists | 177 |
|   Registering for the transportation charges | 178 |
|     Cost distribution type | 178 |
|     Expected distribution value | 179 |
|     Entering our transportation cost | 179 |
|     Accounting facts | 181 |
| **Manufacturing finished goods—shirts** | **182** |
|   Bill of material (BOM) | 183 |
|     Entering the bill of material information | 183 |
|   Expense type of product as a part of bill of material | 184 |
|     Creating an overhead product category | 184 |
|     Creating labor and electricity products | 185 |
|     Altering the product's default account | 185 |
|     Setting up the product's standard cost | 186 |
|     Registering labor and electricity products into the Shirt's BOM | 187 |
|   Production | 188 |
|     Accounting facts | 189 |
| **Proposal or Quotation document** | **191** |
|   Introduction to Proposal and Quotation | 191 |
|   Setting up a product's sales price | 192 |
|   Entering a Proposal or Quotation document | 193 |

| | |
|---|---|
| **Sales Order** | **195** |
| Proposal conversion to a Standard Order | 196 |
| Examining the resulting standard order document | 196 |
|     Accounting facts | 197 |
| **Shipments** | **198** |
| Generating Shipments | 198 |
| Shipment (Customer) | 199 |
|     Shipment confirmation | 200 |
|     Updating the Shirt Finished Goods standard cost | 201 |
|     Accounting facts | 202 |
| **Generating customer invoices** | **203** |
| Generating invoices using Generate Invoices (manual) | 203 |
| Examining the Invoice (Customer) window | 204 |
|     Accounting facts | 206 |
| **Account receivable payment** | **206** |
| Customer payment | 207 |
|     Accounting facts | 207 |
| Payment allocation | 208 |
| View allocation | 209 |
|     Accounting facts | 210 |
| Void and Reset allocation | 210 |
|     Reset allocation | 211 |
|     Void allocation | 211 |
| Bank statement | 212 |
|     Accounting facts | 213 |
| Summary of Account receivable payment accounting facts | 214 |
| **Managing direct sales** | **214** |
| Preparing cash books | 214 |
| Entering a sales order | 215 |
| Unveiling POS Order transaction workflow | 216 |
| Accounting facts | 216 |
| **Summary** | **217** |
| **Chapter 7: Accounting Information and Configuration** | **219** |
| **Managing ADempiere accounts** | **220** |
| Chart of accounts | 220 |
| A journey through the ADempiere list of accounts | 221 |
| Adding more accounts | 222 |
|     Summary accounts option | 223 |
|     Document Controlled option | 224 |
|     Post Actual, Budget, and Statistical options | 225 |
| **Introducing accounting dimensions** | **226** |

| | |
|---|---|
| **Re-posting a document** | **227** |
| **A walkthrough of the Accounting Schema** | **229** |
|   Exploring the Accounting Schema tab | 229 |
|     GAAP | 230 |
|     Commitment Type | 230 |
|     Accrual- or cash-based accounting | 230 |
|     Costing method and costing level | 231 |
|     Currency | 232 |
|     Periods controlling | 232 |
|     Use Account Alias | 233 |
|     Post Trade Discount | 234 |
|     Post services separately | 236 |
|     Explicit Cost Adjustment | 237 |
|     Allow Negative Posting | 237 |
|     Post if Clearing Equal | 239 |
|   The Account Schema Element tab | 240 |
|     Adding campaign information | 240 |
|     Registering another account schema element | 242 |
|     Deactivating the account schema element | 243 |
|     Avoiding the Intercompany Due From/To journal entries | 244 |
|   The General Ledger and Defaults tabs | 245 |
| **Avoiding Product Inventory Clearing journal entries** | **246** |
|   Prerequisites | 246 |
|   Testing the configuration | 247 |
|     Accounting facts | 247 |
| **Practicing commitment accounting** | **248** |
|   Prerequisites | 248 |
|   Requisition reservation | 249 |
|     Accounting facts | 249 |
|   Purchase Order Commitment and Reservation | 250 |
|     Accounting facts | 250 |
|   Matched Invoices commitment release | 251 |
|     Accounting facts | 251 |
| **General Ledger distribution** | **252** |
|   Concept of GL distribution | 252 |
|     Distribution tab configuration | 252 |
|     Line tab configuration | 254 |
|   Sample of GL distribution case | 255 |
|     Configuring GL distribution | 255 |
|   Sample transactions and accounting facts | 256 |
|     Creating a new account combination | 256 |
|     Creating a new General Ledger Journal transaction | 256 |
| **Product costs information** | **258** |
| **Summary** | **259** |

## Chapter 8: Managing Inventory — 261
### Introducing Product Attributes — 261
#### Attributes for a raw material's product — 263
- Registering color attribute configuration — 263
- Registering the vendor serial number configuration — 264
- Registering additional information (description) — 264
- Registering internal number references (lot number) — 265
- Binding raw material attributes into an Attribute Set — 265
- Registering attributes for a raw material product — 267

#### Example of using raw material product attributes — 268
- Creating a new Purchase Order using a material that uses attributes — 268
- Entering attribute information during Material Receipt — 268

#### Tracking raw material related information using its attribute information — 270
- Tracking using the Attribute Set Instance window — 270
- Defining additional search criteria — 271

#### Attributes for Shirt finished goods products — 272
- Registering size attribute configuration — 273
- Registering a lot number to identify production identity — 274
- Registering the internal number for shipment references — 274
- Creating an Attribute Set for the Shirt product — 275
- Attaching an attribute set to finished goods products — 276

#### Example of using product attributes on the Shirt finished goods product — 277
- Attaching attributes during production activities — 277
- Searching for the Shirt product by its attributes — 279
- Assigning information during shipment activities — 280

### Managing internal use of inventory — 281
#### Creating advertising and promotion types of charge — 282
#### Sample usage of Internal Use inventory — 282
- Accounting facts — 283

#### Tracking inventory transactions — 284

### Managing Physical Inventory — 285
#### Stock counting and reconciliation — 285
- Accounting facts — 287

#### Migrating an existing raw material into ADempiere — 288
- Creating a migration product category — 289
- Creating a migration product — 290
- Setting a product's product costs — 290
- Performing migration activities — 291
- Accounting facts — 292

### Moving Inventory — 292
#### Movement between locations in different warehouses and / or different organizations — 293
- Setting up the In-Transit Material Movement document — 293
- Practising Moving Inventory with confirmation — 295

|   |   |
|---|---|
| Confirming receipt of full material quantity | 295 |
| Accounting facts | 296 |
| Confirmation of receiving with scrapped material | 297 |
| Confirmation of receiving with partial material | 298 |
| Movement among locations in the same warehouse | 299 |
| **Summary** | **300** |
| **Chapter 9: ADempiere Workflow** | **303** |
| Knowing the General workflow—a step-by-step guide | 303 |
| Example of general workflow | 304 |
| Constructing our own general workflow | 304 |
| Attaching general workflow to a menu | 305 |
| **Understanding ADempiere workflow** | **306** |
| Knowing the workflow for an ADempiere document | 306 |
| Activity/Node flow | 309 |
| Setting up transition among Activities/Nodes | 309 |
| Node's Action | 310 |
| Node's workflow responsible | 311 |
| Responsible Type | 311 |
| Setting up a new workflow responsible | 312 |
| **Document process workflow** | **312** |
| Setting up User Choice actions | 313 |
| Finding the person with approval rights | 314 |
| Sample of approval workflow implementation | 316 |
| Initiating a requisition document | 316 |
| Approving the requisition document | 316 |
| Monitoring workflow progression | 317 |
| Cancelling a workflow in progress | 318 |
| Setting up E-mail actions | 318 |
| Activating the e-mail feature | 319 |
| Setting up e-mail for end users | 319 |
| Setting up a mail template | 320 |
| Altering workflow configuration | 320 |
| Testing the e-mail notification configuration | 321 |
| Setting up an application process's action | 322 |
| Finding the internal ADempiere process identity name | 322 |
| Identifying a parameter for a certain ADempiere processes | 323 |
| Additional workflow configuration | 324 |
| Testing the application process configuration | 325 |
| Setting up a Variable's action | 326 |
| Configuring the set attribute action | 327 |
| Testing the set variable workflow | 328 |
| **Document value workflow** | **329** |
| Setting up a new mail template | 329 |
| Defining configuration | 330 |

| | |
|---|---:|
| Testing the document value workflow | 332 |
| Document value logic format | 333 |
|     Document and Evaluation Value | 333 |
|     Operator | 334 |
| Multiple logic | 334 |
| SQL document value logic format | 335 |
| **Summary** | **335** |
| **Chapter 10: Reporting Management** | **337** |
| Introduction to the ADempiere standard printing feature | 338 |
|   Accessing the Report button | 338 |
|     Working with the Drill down feature | 339 |
|     Working with the Drill across feature | 339 |
|   Printing a report | 340 |
|     Introducing print format templates | 340 |
|     Sending e-mail, archiving reports, and exporting | 342 |
|   How the ADempiere window finds its print format templates | 343 |
|     Purchase Order and Sales Order | 343 |
|     Invoice | 343 |
|     Payment | 344 |
|     Shipment (Customer) and Material Receipt | 345 |
| **Customizing Reports** | **345** |
|   Creating new print format templates | 346 |
|     Duplicate Order Line print format | 347 |
|     Duplicate Order Header print format | 347 |
|     Setting the purchase order default print format | 348 |
|   Altering the logo | 349 |
|   Altering another header layout | 350 |
|   Altering the detailed purchase order layout | 352 |
| **Financial Reporting** | **353** |
|   Working with the Report Line Set window | 354 |
|   Working with the Report Column Set window | 355 |
|   Creating a Financial Report | 357 |
|     Enabling the List Sources option | 358 |
| **Reporting Hierarchy** | **359** |
|   Configuring a specific financial report | 359 |
|     Setting up a new summary product | 360 |
|     Setting up a Summary of Products Tree | 360 |
|     Setting Tree Maintenance | 361 |
|     Verifying the Summary of Products Tree | 361 |
|     Setting up the Summary of certain products reporting hierarchy | 362 |
|     Testing our sample reporting hierarchy reports | 363 |
|   More details on the summary financial report | 364 |
|     Setting up a new summary business partner | 364 |
|     Setting up a Summary of BP Tree | 365 |

| | |
|---|---|
| Setting Tree Maintenance | 365 |
| Verifying the Summary of BP Tree | 366 |
| Setting up a more specific reporting hierarchy | 366 |
| Executing a more specific financial report | 366 |
| **Info window** | **367** |
| **Integration with JasperReports** | **367** |
| **Summary** | **368** |
| **Chapter 11: Importing Data** | **369** |
| **ADempiere's import mechanism** | **370** |
| Determining the Import Loader Format | 370 |
| Preparing the data source | 373 |
| Loading data with the Import File Loader | 373 |
| Import activities | 373 |
| **Import the Business Partner information** | **374** |
| Creating the BPartner Import Loader Format | 374 |
| Preparing the Business Partner data files | 375 |
| Loading the Business Partner data | 376 |
| Importing the Business Partner data | 377 |
| Import Error Message sample | 377 |
| **Importing Products** | **378** |
| Creating the Product Import Loader Format | 378 |
| Preparing Product data files | 379 |
| Loading Product data | 379 |
| Importing Product data | 380 |
| **Importing currency rates** | **380** |
| Creating the Daily currency rates Import Loader Format | 381 |
| Identifying Search Key information | 382 |
| Preparing Currency rates data files | 383 |
| Loading Currency rates data | 383 |
| Importing Currency rates data | 384 |
| **Importing General Ledger journal entries** | **384** |
| Creating the GL journal Import Loader Format | 384 |
| Preparing GL journal data files | 386 |
| Loading GL journal data | 386 |
| Importing GL journal data | 387 |
| **Import Orders** | **387** |
| Creating the Order Import Loader Format | 388 |
| Preparing the Purchase Order data files | 389 |
| Loading the purchase order data | 389 |
| Importing Purchase Order data | 389 |
| Sales Order data import sample | 390 |

| | |
|---|---|
| **Importing Invoices** | **391** |
| Creating the Invoices Import Loader Format | 391 |
| Preparing Invoice Vendor data files | 392 |
| Loading Invoice Vendor data | 392 |
| Importing Invoice Vendor data | 393 |
| Invoice Customer data import sample | 393 |
| **Importing Inventory** | **394** |
| Creating the Inventory Import Loader Format | 394 |
| Preparing Inventory data files | 395 |
| Loading Inventory data | 395 |
| Importing Inventory data | 395 |
| **Importing a Bank Statement** | **396** |
| Creating the Bank Statement Import Loader Format | 396 |
| Preparing Bank Statement data files | 397 |
| Loading Bank Statement data | 398 |
| Importing Bank Statement data | 398 |
| **Summary** | **399** |
| **Chapter 12: Implementing Security** | **401** |
| **Managing ADempiere user IDs** | **401** |
| Creating a user ID in the system | 402 |
| **Managing user ID access control** | **403** |
| Introduction to ADempiere roles | 403 |
| Creating a new ADempiere role | 403 |
| Attaching a user ID to a specific role | 405 |
| Assigning organization access to a user ID | 405 |
| Working with the Access all Orgs option | 406 |
| Working with the Maintain Change Log option | 406 |
| Working with the Show accounting option | 407 |
| Working with the Can Report option | 408 |
| Working with the Can Export option | 409 |
| Accessing Info Window | 409 |
| Assigning Window Access | 410 |
| Identifying Process Access | 411 |
| Registering Process Access | 412 |
| Introduction to Document Action Access | 413 |
| Registering Document Action Access | 414 |
| Managing Form Access | 415 |
| **Recording access security rules** | **416** |
| Enabling Personal Lock | 416 |
| Blocking access to certain records | 417 |
| Restoring access to certain blocked records | 418 |
| Using Dependent Entities | 418 |

## Working with Role Data Access in detail — 419
### Restricting Table access — 419
### Restricting Report access — 419
### Restricting Export access — 420
### Restricting Column Access — 421
## Obscuring information — 422
### Enabling the encrypted feature — 422
### Working with the Obscure feature — 424
## Summary — 425
# Index — 427

# Preface

In the past seven years, as the author was starting his journey with the manufacturing and the services industries, he found that many tasks in these industries involved back offices using manual efforts. These industries made use of spreadsheet applications or implemented their own specific solution. Each of the departments such as Production, Purchasing, Accounting, and so on created their own data and often had a different figure on the same subject when preparing business reports. This led to extra efforts required when creating an analysis report.

**Enterprise Resource Planning (ERP)** is a system that integrates all of the functions, in each of the departments, into a single system that is designed to encapsulate all of business processes getting involved. With the existence of an open source ERP package, there is an option for an organization to manage their data in a centralized way, working with the same data and get the benefit with data integrity and can create business reports more accurately and faster.

ERP systems are essential in today's business market. There are many options for ERP systems; however, ADempiere offers a solid foundation for developing a powerful ERP system that helps your business to manage data efficiently, streamline different processes, at affordable costs, and improve the efficiency levels without too much complexity.

The ADempiere project was established and created on September 2006. ADempiere is a friendly fork of the Compiere ERP. The ADempiere community expected to use a proven platform, taking care of and listening to the customers' needs and feedback, and create a project that was community-driven and used **General Public License (GPL)** as its license; thus providing the freedom to extend its feature and capabilities.

From its inception, ADempiere attracted great attention from all over the world. According to the SourceForge.net download statistics for the year of 2009, there have been more than ten thousand downloads, as evident from `sourceforge.net`.

*Preface*

# About this book

This practical book offers a comprehensive understanding of ADempiere, and takes a look at the main features by way of developing and enhancing a sample case study from concept to deployment. This book will help you model complex business processes with ease.

You will learn to install ADempiere, followed by configuring the company structure and the initial client setup. You can start working with ADempiere immediately because this book will get you up and running quickly, and assumes no prior knowledge or experience of working with ADempiere. ADempiere 3.4 ERP Solutions enables you to: set up the accounting parts, define the prerequisite data, learn about product and price management, and perform procurement and sales activities. When you read the book, you'll understand the concept behind the ADempiere workflow and the important function of managing inventory. Activities such as making user-defined financial reports, procedures for importing data, and security considerations will be covered in detail, and you will also partly learn about the application dictionary configuration.

ADempiere generates accounting facts or journals automatically. In this book, you will understand the impact of these accounting facts. This book will provide you with a comprehensive study of how to easily implement ADempiere and make the best use of this open source ERP system.

To understand the content of this book thoroughly, it is suggested that readers learn and practice the topics sequentially from Chapter 1 through Chapter 10. The remaining chapters can be read and implemented as references.

# What this book covers

In Chapter 1: *ADempiere Installation*, you will be introduced to the hardware requirements, obtaining ADempiere and prerequisite applications, installing and setting up PostgreSQL databases, applying patches, and verifying the ADempiere server and client. Throughout the book, we will use Microsoft Windows as the operating system.

In Chapter 2: *Exploring the ADempiere Client and Performing Tasks*, you will learn the connection aspect of ADempiere, how to identify the ADempiere version, predefined user IDs, standard format of the ADempiere client user interface, and standard command and functions to perform tasks (including Record Info and the field context menu).

In Chapter 3: *Exploring Company Structures and the Initial Client Setup*, you will create and map a fictitious apparel company structure. In this chapter, you will be introduced to standard ADempiere company structures, preparing chart of accounts which are required during the initial client creation, creating a new client (company), and finally, you will set up and review organizations, warehouses, and locators. You will also be introduced to Accounting Schema, Calendar Year and Period, and the Accounting Processor features of ADempiere.

In Chapter 4: *Setting up Master Data and Knowing its Accounting Configuration*, before you start working with ADempiere, you need to set up some master or reference data in the system. For all of the basic or data references, it has a standard accounting configuration. This chapter shows you how the accounting related configuration takes part. With this information, we can configure and alter the default account for an account related with master or references data. With this basic accounting configuration, you will be introduced to managing the customer and the vendor (business partner), managing company financial management including the company bank and cash books. We conclude this chapter with managing currencies, price management, and product management.

In Chapter 5: *Procurement Activities* with the prerequisites and preconfigured data at hand, you will continue with the creation of a sample procurement flow. Before producing finished goods in the apparel company, we will define the raw materials required (to produce these finished goods). Then you will learn how to accomplish an order requisition, purchase order, material receipt, vendor invoice, vendor payment, and also how to reconcile a bank statement. To learn the General Ledger journal created, we will perform some tasks and generate the accounting facts.

In Chapter 6: *Landed Costs, Production, and Sales Activities*, you will be explained landed cost (for example, we show how to handle transportation charges), which is allocated and assigned to raw materials. You will configure the bill of material and learn how to manufacture finished goods. With the available finished goods, you will create quotations, sales orders, shipments, invoices, AR receipts, and also reconcile a bank statement. In this chapter, you will also learn how the General Ledger journal is automatically generated by the ADempiere system.

In Chapter 7: *Accounting Information and Configuration*, you will learn about the central accounting configuration in ADempiere. You will learn how to manage the Account Element (list of company accounts). You will also learn the Accounting Schema in more detail, and will have a hands-on experience of what the effects of modifying the configuration are. An example of how to avoid the Intercompany Due/To journal, avoid the product inventory clearing journal, commitment accounting, and configuring GL distribution will also be shown. At the end of this chapter, Product Cost will be explained.

*Preface*

In Chapter 8: *Managing Inventory*, you will learn about the various product attributes (for example, registering lot number, color, and so on) and how to work with these attributes. This chapter will guide you through the setup of attribute information, for both raw materials and finished goods. We will continue our discussion with managing internal use of the inventory, managing physical inventory that can be used to perform stock counting, and a way to migrate the existing material. We'll also discuss about how to perform inventory movement with or without creating a confirmation while receiving the material.

In Chapter 9: *ADempiere Workflow*, you will learn about how all the ADempiere documents, such as Purchase Requisition, Purchase Order, MM Receipt, and so on, implement the workflow by default. We'll discuss the workflow concept and give some examples on how to implement document process, document value, and general workflow. Through these examples, we'll guide you on how to perform the approval procedure with the help of the document process workflow. You can notify certain people through e-mail if needed. While running a document workflow, we can monitor the workflow progress or even cancel the workflow. You will be guided on how to perform these tasks.

In Chapter 10: *Reporting Management*, you will be introduced to the Reports and Print features. This chapter will explain what a print format is and how to set up a default print format for a document such as Purchase Order. You will also be informed about how the ADempiere window finds its print format template. You will learn how to customize standard reports by altering the logo, header layout, and detail layout. As an organization has its unique list of accounts, we will conclude this chapter by showing how to create and configure our own financial reports, which can be used to measure the organization's performance.

In Chapter 11: *Importing Data*, you will learn about the importing mechanism through ADempiere. This will involve activities, such as determining import loader format, preparing the data source, loading the data, and conclude with the importing activities. Based on the predefined loader format, you can practice preparing source files and importing business partners, products, currency rates, GL journals, Orders, Invoices, Inventories, and Bank Statements.

In Chapter 12: *Implementing Security*, you will finish this book by learning how ADempiere security works. You will be guided through managing user IDs and creating roles. While constructing a role, you will see the various attributes involved, such as access all orgs, maintain change log, and so on. Here, you will learn how to assign rights to access a window, identify a process, and give rights to it, how to register document access, and manage form access. Then, with an example, we will show you how to perform the access security rule for records, how to restrict access to tables, columns, reports, and export facilities. We will conclude this chapter by showing you the process of obscuring information in ADempiere.

# Getting involved with the ADempiere project

ADempiere is an open community. Wherever you are and whatever is your expertise, you can join us through our Internet Relay Chat (IRC) channel. You can access this website [1] to access our IRC channel. Enter your nickname and set #adempiere as the channel. You can meet many ADempiere developers, consultants, or end-users around the world and say hello to them.

Moreover, there is a forum [2] available, which can be used to find any information and to express your interest. There are some groups such as Functional-ERP, Functional-Financials, and Help that can be used to share and answer your ADempiere-related questions. When posting any issues through our ADempiere forum, make sure to check the aim of the group created. For example, Functional-Financials will be dedicated to discuss any issues related with Finance and the Accounting parts of ADempiere. When asking any issues through the ADempiere forum, it is wise to check out our friendly rules [3].

So, don't wait! Join us now.

1. http://webchat.freenode.net/
2. http://sourceforge.net/projects/adempiere/forums
3. http://www.adempiere.com/index.php/Etiquette

# Conventions

In this book, you will find a number of styles of text that distinguish between different kinds of information. Here are some examples of these styles, and an explanation of their meaning.

Any command-line input or output is written as follows:

```
c:\>java -version
java version "1.5.0_17"Java(TM) 2 Runtime Environment, Standard Edition
(build 1.5.0_17-b04)Java HotSpot(TM) Client VM (build 1.5.0_17-b04, mixed mode, sharing)
```

**New terms** and **important words** are shown in bold. Words that you see on the screen, in menus or dialog boxes for example, appear in the text like this: "Although this window has **Requisition** as its name, you need to ensure that you are using **Purchase Requisition** as the **Document Type** of the ADempiere document".

> Warnings or important notes appear in a box like this.

> Tips and tricks appear like this.

# Reader feedback

Feedback from our readers is always welcome. Let us know what you think about this book—what you liked or may have disliked. Reader feedback is important for us to develop titles that you really get the most out of.

To send us general feedback, simply send an email to feedback@packtpub.com, and mention the book title in the subject of your message.

If there is a book that you need and would like to see us publish, please send us a note in the **SUGGEST A TITLE** form on www.packtpub.com or email suggest@packtpub.com.

If there is a topic that you have expertise in and you are interested in either writing or contributing to a book on, see our author guide on www.packtpub.com/authors.

# Customer support

Now that you are the proud owner of a Packt book, we have a number of things to help you to get the most from your purchase.

> **Downloading the example code for the book**
> Visit http://www.packtpub.com/files/code/7269_Code.zip to directly download the example code.

## Errata

Although we have taken every care to ensure the accuracy of our content, mistakes do happen. If you find a mistake in one of our books—maybe a mistake in the text or the code—we would be grateful if you would report this to us. By doing so, you can save other readers from frustration, and help us to improve subsequent versions of this book. If you find any errata, please report them by visiting http://www.packtpub.com/support, selecting your book, clicking on the **let us know** link, and entering the details of your errata. Once your errata are verified, your submission will be accepted and the errata added to any list of existing errata. Any existing errata can be viewed by selecting your title from http://www.packtpub.com/support.

## Piracy

Piracy of copyright material on the Internet is an ongoing problem across all media. At Packt, we take the protection of our copyright and licenses very seriously. If you come across any illegal copies of our works, in any form, on the Internet, please provide us with the location address or web site name immediately so that we can pursue a remedy.

Please contact us at copyright@packtpub.com with a link to the suspected pirated material.

We appreciate your help in protecting our authors, and our ability to bring you valuable content.

## Questions

You can contact us at questions@packtpub.com if you are having a problem with any aspect of the book, and we will do our best to address it.

# ADempiere Installation

In order to establish a new company or monitor an existing company, we should take into consideration every aspect of the company. One aspect is to make the entire company operation run effectively.

If we are planning to implement **Enterprise Resource Planning (ERP)** systems (or any other Computer Automation System) for our company, then we will come across many solutions or options for commercial and open source ERP packages.

Moreover, for a small or medium-sized company, implementing a commercial or proprietary ERP system will be costly. A huge amount of money will be spent on both application and consultancy. So, the question is—"Is there an alternative to fulfill our company's needs and run the operations effectively at an affordable price?"

*ADempiere* (http://www.adempiere.com/wiki) *is an open source ERP application that is community driven, evolving, and that provides amazing features such as (but not limited to) purchasing, material receipts, sales, shipment, inventory, simple manufacturing, advanced accounting, and so on.*

These should be more than enough to cover a small or medium-sized company's needs.

In this chapter, you will be introduced to the following:

- Hardware and operating system requirements for ADempiere
- Obtaining ADempiere and the prerequisite applications
- Installing and setting up PostgreSQL database
- Installing and running ADempiere

We will start our activities after learning about the hardware and operating system requirements.

# ADempiere hardware and operating system requirements

Using Java (`http://en.wikipedia.org/wiki/Java_(programming_language)`) as its core programming language, ADempiere can run on a Java-supporting platform or machine and operating system. Examples of the Java-supporting platforms are Solaris and Intel, or any AMD-based architecture machine. Operating systems that can be used, based on the platform, are Solaris OS, Linux, BSD, Mac OS, and Microsoft Windows. Visit `http://java.sun.com/j2se/1.5.0/system-configurations.html` for further references.

ADempiere should be installed on both the server as well as client computers. The requirements for installation on both types will be different. On the client side, it can be run on a computer that has an old Pentium 4 processor or a higher specification with at least a GB of memory. For a server computer, we can use the Pentium Dual-Core processor with 2 GB of memory.

> This is just an example of hardware requirements in an Intel-based architecture machine. You can choose various brands of servers and desktops that are available in the market that suit your needs.

However, computer hardware requirements depend on the load and daily usage prediction level of the application. For internal testing and practice of the ADempiere features described in this book, both the ADempiere server and client system can be installed on a computer with low specifications, such as a PC-based computer, or even your modern-day notebook.

# Installing the Sun Java Development Kit (JDK)

All applications, that are written in Java programming language including ADempiere, require a **Java Virtual Machine (JVM)** for execution. The JVM is distributed along with a standard Java class library that implements the Java **Application Programming Interface (API)**. A complete implementation of JVM is included in the **Java Runtime Environment (JRE)**, which can be obtained during the installation of the **Java Development Kit (JDK)** or by installing Java Runtime Environment.

# Obtaining JDK/JRE

ADempiere can be installed on any operating system—Mac OS, Linux, BSD families, and so on, but in this book we will use **Microsoft Windows** as the operating system.

You can download the latest JDK/JRE available from the Sun Microsystems website at http://java.sun.com/. Throughout this book, JDK 5.0 will be used as a prerequisite for installing ADempiere. We can download JDK 5.0 from http://java.sun.com/javase/downloads/index_jdk5.jsp. At the time of writing this book, the latest version or release for JDK 5.0 is **JDK 5.0 Update 17**. Future versions or releases of JDK can also be used without any problems.

Click on the **JDK 5.0 Update 17 Download** button, and you will be directed to the download page. Set the platform as **Windows** and the language as **Multi-Language**. On the next page, choose **Windows Offline Installation**. The filename for this JDK is jdk-1_5_0_17-windows-i586-p.exe. It is about 52.15 MB in size. In order to manage the downloaded files, first create a C:\download\jdk folder, and then save the files to this folder.

JDK installation files are required for the ADempiere server installation, but they are not necessary for the ADempiere client installation. On the client side, only the JRE installation files are needed. To download these files, click on the **Java Runtime Environment (JRE) 5.0 Update 17 Download** button. Select the platform and language as mentioned previously, (including the **Windows Offline Installation** mode). Save the jre-1_5_0_17-windows-i586-p.exe file to the C:\download\jdk folder.

# Installing JDK/JRE

Due to the default installation behavior of Microsoft Windows, a new application installation will commonly be directed to the C:\Program Files folder. An important thing when installing JDK and/or JRE on Microsoft Windows is that we should avoid installing it to C:\Program Files directly. To avoid any problems during the ADempiere implementation, it is recommended that you install it to a folder that does not contain spaces in the directory or folder name, such as C:\Java.

*ADempiere Installation*

# JDK installation on the ADempiere server computer

Double-click on `jdk-1_5_0_17-windows-i586-p.exe` to start the Windows installer.

By default, the installer will install development tools, demo files, source code, and public JRE. For our reference, leave the **Development Tools** feature selected and deselect the other features by clicking on the buttons on the left-hand side of **Demos**, **Source Code**, and **Public JRE**, and then choosing **Don't install this feature now**. This is shown in the following screenshot:

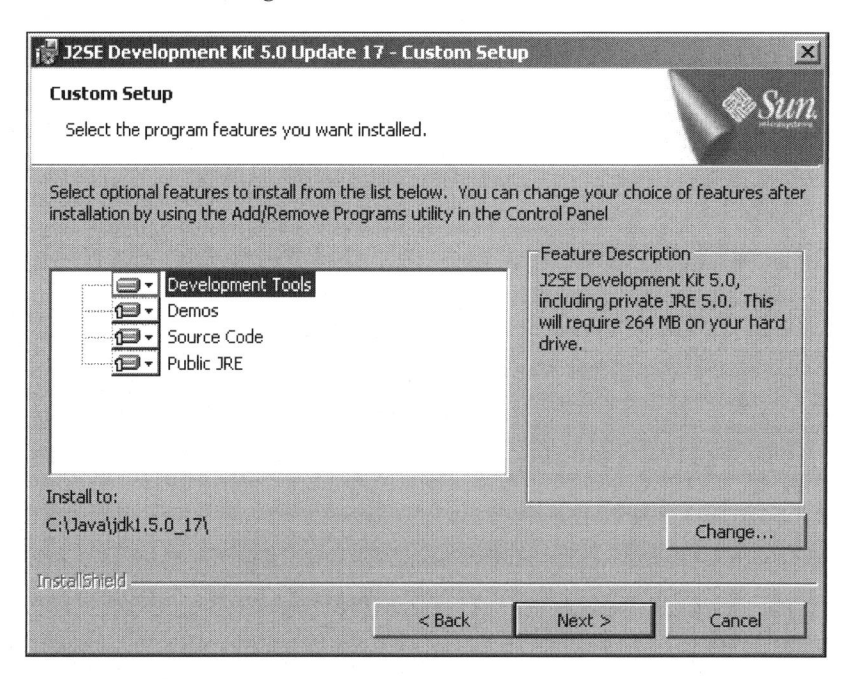

Select **Development Tools**, click on the **Change** button to alter the default or target directory to `C:\Java\jdk1.5.0_17`, and proceed to complete the JDK installation.

> During the Development Tools installation, a private JRE will automatically be installed. In our case, it will be installed at `C:\Java\jdk1.5.0_17\jre`.

# JRE installation on the ADempiere client computer

The ADempiere client installation requires installation of the **Java Runtime Environment** (**JRE**) only. Open the link http://java.sun.com/products/archive/j2se/5.0_17/ and double-click on jre-1_5_0_17-windows-i586-p.exe. At the license agreement, ensure that you choose the **Custom setup**, and click on the **Accept** button. Leave the **J2SE Runtime Environment** selected, and deselect the other features by clicking on the buttons to the left-hand side of **Support for Additional Languages** and **Additional Font and Media Support**. Choose **Don't install this feature now**. Select **J2SE Runtime Environment**, click on the **Change** button to alter the default or target directory to C:\Java\jre1.5.0_17, click on the **Next** button, and proceed to complete the JRE installation.

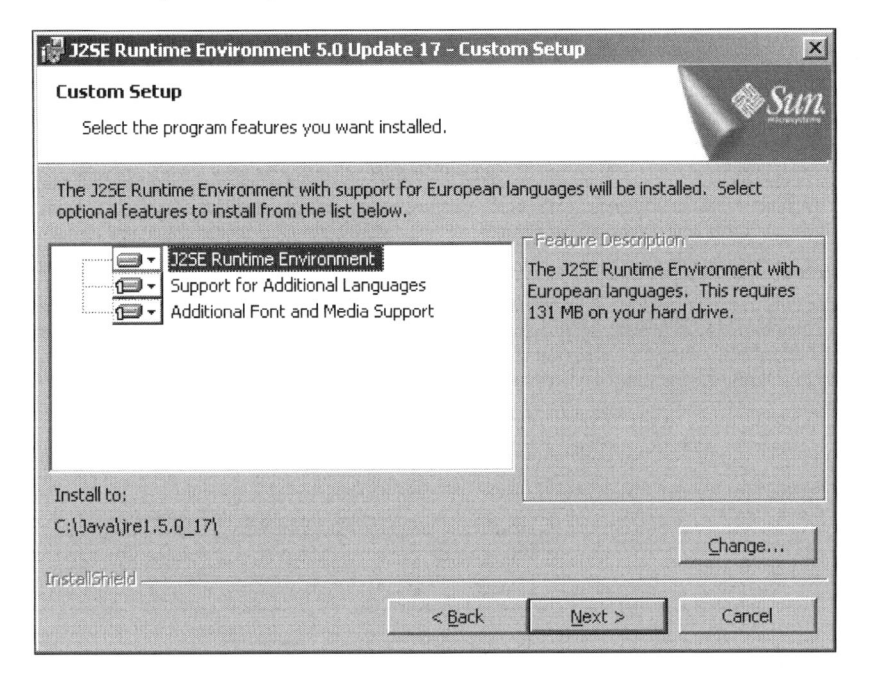

[ There is no need to install JRE if you are using the same computer for both the ADempiere Server and the Client. ]

# Configuring Java system variables and the Windows path

Now that we have installed JDK/JRE, we have to set up JAVA system variables and set Windows paths both for the ADempiere server and the client computer, as ADempiere runs on a Java platform.

We need to set these variables in the **System Properties** window. You can access this window through **Start | Control Panel | System** (or **Start | Settings | Control Panel | System** in the case of the Windows classic menu). Select the **Advanced system settings** tab, and click on the **Environment Variables** button.

The following table shows the value of a Java system variable and a Windows path for the ADempiere server installation to be set up in the **Environment Variables** window:

| No | Variable | Value |
| --- | --- | --- |
| 1 | JAVA_HOME | C:\Java\jdk1.5.0_17 |
| 2 | Path | %JAVA_HOME%\bin;%JAVA_HOME%\jre\bin\client |

For the ADempiere client installation, you may set the following Java system variable and Windows path in the **Environment Variables** window:

| No | Variable | Value |
| --- | --- | --- |
| 1 | JAVA_HOME | C:\Java\jre1.5.0_17 |
| 2 | Path | %JAVA_HOME%\bin;%JAVA_HOME%\bin\client |

The **Environment Variables** window is shown as follows:

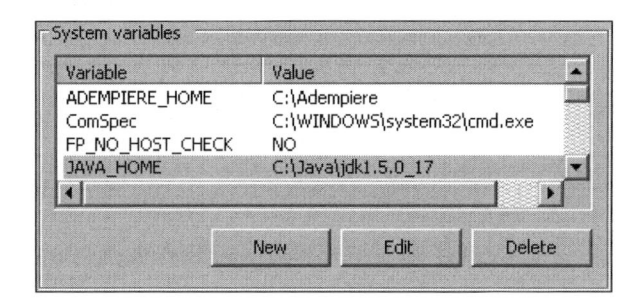

```
System variables
Variable            Value
ADEMPIERE_HOME      C:\Adempiere
ComSpec             C:\WINDOWS\system32\cmd.exe
FP_NO_HOST_CHECK    NO
JAVA_HOME           C:\Java\jdk1.5.0_17

           [ New ]  [ Edit ]  [ Delete ]
```

This is an example of **System variables** in the **Environment Variable** window from the author's computer. It might vary for your own computer's configuration.

You can set additional **JAVA_HOME** variables by clicking on the **New** button in **System variables**. To set your own **JAVA_HOME** variables, click on the **Edit** button by selecting an existing path variable entry and enter your additional path entries. In order to confirm the addition of system variables, click on **OK** in both the **Environment Variable** window and the **System Properties** window.

> While setting up the **Path** variable, any additional variable inclusion in these entries must be prefixed with a semicolon (;) character.

## Verifying system variables and the Windows path

Once we have finished adding the additional variables, we have to check whether the setup of the variables was configured properly. We shall check our variables' entries from the DOS prompt command line. We can access DOS prompt from **Start | Run**. Type cmd in the **Run** window, and click on the **OK** button. We will get the following command prompt:

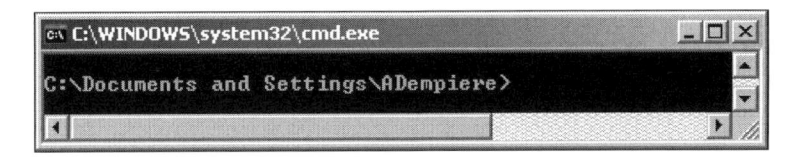

```
C:\WINDOWS\system32\cmd.exe
C:\Documents and Settings\ADempiere>
```

We can type the following in this command line, and *Enter*:

`C:\>SET`

Pay attention to the resulting information. On the author's ADempiere server computer, it displays the following statements:

`JAVA_HOME=C:\Java\jdk1.5.0_17`

and

`Path=C:\WINDOWS\system32;C:\WINDOWS;C:\WINDOWS\System32\Wbem;C:\Java\jdk1.5.0_17\bin;C:\Java\jdk1.5.0_17\jre\bin\client`

Whereas the ADempiere client computer will contain the following statements:

`JAVA_HOME=C:\Java\jre1.5.0_17`

and

`Path=C:\WINDOWS\system32;C:\WINDOWS;C:\WINDOWS\System32\Wbem;C:\Java\jre1.5.0_17\bin;C:\Java\jre1.5.0_17\bin\client`

The second procedure for checking the setup configuration is to use Java commands. For example, in order to find a command to know what the currently-installed Java version is, we can use the following command:

`C:\>java -version`

and press *Enter*. This showed the following statements on the author's computer:

```
java version "1.5.0_17"Java(TM) 2 Runtime Environment, Standard Edition
(build 1.5.0_17-b04)Java HotSpot(TM) Client VM (build 1.5.0_17-b04, mixed
mode, sharing)
```

# Installing databases

ADempiere requires a database to store its data. Currently, ADempiere officially supports both Oracle (XE) and PostgreSQL (EnterpriseDB) databases. The databases can be installed on the ADempiere server or onto a specific database computer server. In this book, we will set these databases up on an ADempiere server.

To support the open source movement, we will use PostgreSQL as our ADempiere database backend instead of Oracle. If you want to set up Oracle (XE) as your database backend, then visit `http://www.adempiere.com/index.php/ADempiere_Installing` for more information.

## Obtaining PostgreSQL databases

We can obtain PostgreSQL databases for Microsoft Windows from `http://www.postgresql.org/download/windows`. You will find an option to **Download the one click installer** or **pgInstaller**. Click on **Download the one click installer**, and you will be redirected to the Enterprise DB website: `http://www.enterprisedb.com/products/pgdownload.do#windows`. Download the installer for the Microsoft Windows operating system.

At the time of writing, the latest release of the PostgreSQL database for Windows is **PostgreSQL 8.3.5**. After we click on the **download** button on this site, we will be prompted to save the `postgresql-8.3.5-2-windows.exe` file (about 35.7 MB in size). Create a `C:\download\database` folder, and save this binary installation file to this location.

## Installing PostgreSQL databases

Double-click on the `postgresql-8.3.5-2-windows.exe` file to launch the Windows installer. During the installation, this installer will install additional required files for us automatically. It will install Microsoft Visual C++ 2005 Redistributable. When asked for the installation directory, point it to `C:\download\database\postgresql\8.3`, instead of the default installation directory, as shown in the following screenshot:

> We will refer to `C:\download\database\postgresql\8.3` as `%PostgreSQLHome%` throughout this book.

Click on **Next**, and you will be prompted with the data directory location confirmation. You can define your own data directory or location. On the author's computer, the data directory is left as it is—`C:\download\database\PostgreSQL\8.3\data`. Next, set a password for your Postgres account. In this installation, we use *postgres* as the default password for the Postgres account.

> Beware of your **Caps Lock** status. Ensure that you use lowercase while typing your password.

Leave the default **Port** used for this database as **5432**, set **Locale** to **English, United States**, and proceed to complete your database installation.

On the final installation screen, you need to deselect the **Launch Stack Builder at exit** option.

## Adding the PostgreSQL path

The PostgreSQL database server for ADempiere has been successfully installed. During ADempiere installation, there are many PostgreSQL application tools (`*.exe` files) that can help you to manage your database. Most of these tools can be found in the `%PostgreSQLHome%\bin` folder.

*ADempiere Installation*

Examples of these application tools are given in the following table:

| No | Tools name | Description |
|----|------------|-------------|
| 1 | `psql.exe` | Tools for executing interactive PostgreSQL commands |
| 2 | `createuser.exe` | Tools for creating PostgreSQL users |
| 3 | `createdb.exe` | Tools for creating PostgreSQL databases |

These tools will be used throughout this book. In order to add these folders to our **Path System variables**, do the following:

1. Access the **System Properties** window via **Start | Control Panel | System**.
2. Select the **Advanced** tab, and then click on the **Environment Variables** button.
3. Edit the **Path** system variable, and add the following entry:
   `;C:\download\database\PostgreSQL\8.3\bin`

> While editing the **Path** system variable, do not forget to add a semicolon (;) before the folder name!

## Verifying the additional PostgreSQL path

Just like we verified the Java system variables, we should verify our PostgreSQL path. Previously, we used the `SET` command to accomplish this task. We shall use the `path` command to verify the path.

Open the DOS prompt command-line window and type:

`C:\>path`

Press *Enter*, and the system will display the current computer PATH. Ensure that we have `C:\database\PostgreSQL\8.3\bin` in the contents of PATH. The following is the screenshot from the author's computer:

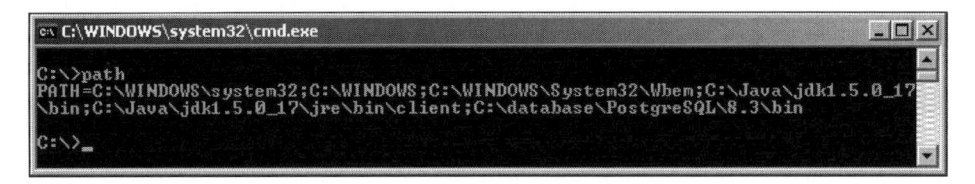

```
C:\>path
PATH=C:\WINDOWS\system32;C:\WINDOWS;C:\WINDOWS\System32\Wbem;C:\Java\jdk1.5.0_17\bin;C:\Java\jdk1.5.0_17\jre\bin\client;C:\database\PostgreSQL\8.3\bin
C:\>
```

[ 18 ]

The next procedure is to verify the additional PostgreSQL paths. Type the `psql` command on the command line, and press *Enter*. If we are prompted to enter a password, then our PostgreSQL path setting is working as expected. Press *Enter*, and the system will display the following information:

`psql: fe_sendauth: no password supplied`

> This message appears because `psql` cannot proceed, because no user password was supplied.

Thus, we have completed the database installation and verification.

## Configuring PostgreSQL

By default, the initial security configuration settings to access PostgreSQL databases are quite restrictive. This is a good practice as we can make sure that our databases can be accessed from trusted computers only. We can define an additional list of computers that can access our databases by altering some PostgreSQL configuration files.

### Modifying the client authentication configuration file

The name of the client authentication configuration file is `pg_hba.conf`. It can be found in the `%PostgreSQLHome%\data` folder. This file contains the information shown in the following screenshot:

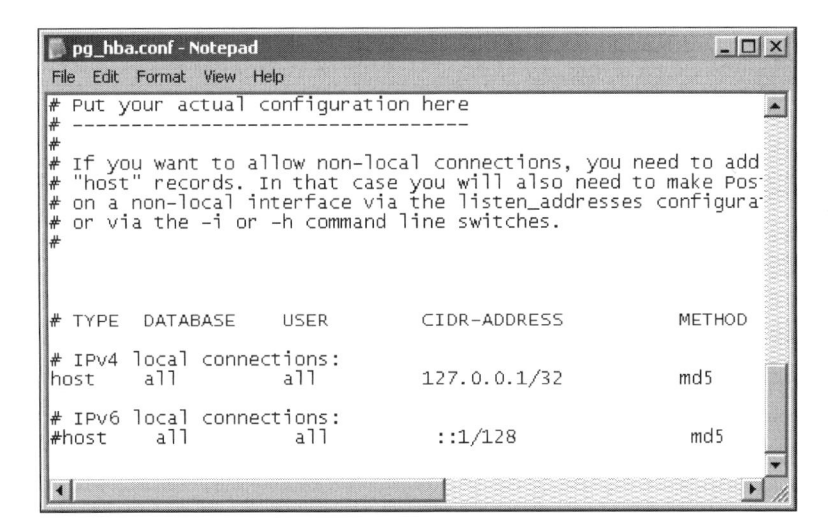

```
# pg_hba.conf - Notepad
File Edit Format View Help
# Put your actual configuration here
# ----------------------------------
#
# If you want to allow non-local connections, you need to add
# "host" records. In that case you will also need to make Pos
# on a non-local interface via the listen_addresses configura
# or via the -i or -h command line switches.
#


# TYPE   DATABASE   USER         CIDR-ADDRESS          METHOD

# IPv4 local connections:
host     all        all          127.0.0.1/32          md5

# IPv6 local connections:
#host    all        all          ::1/128               md5
```

*ADempiere Installation*

With this configuration, the database connection is accepted from a local computer only. If we wish to allow any computer within our local LAN, which is pre-installed with the ADempiere client—and let us assume that our computer server has a `10.10.101.107` IP address—then we should add the following two lines of configuration:

```
host    adempiere    adempiere    10.10.101.107/0    md5
host    template1    postgres     10.10.101.107/0    md5
```

to our `pg_hba.conf` file.

> The `10.10.101.107/0` defines the IP and subnet masks allowed. Visit `http://en.wikipedia.org/wiki/Subnetwork` for a further explanation.

## Verifying the PostgreSQL configuration file

The other client authentication file is `postgresql.conf`. It is present in the `%PostgreSQLHome%\data\` folder. If we go through this file, then we will find the following information:

```
listen_addresses = '*'
```

The above statement means that the PostgreSQL database for Windows is listening and is ready to make a connection with all of the available computer addresses. Leave this configuration unchanged, and our client will have a connection without any problems.

Refer to the PostgreSQL documentation for more detailed information. This document can be accessed from **Start | All Programs | PostgreSQL 8.3 | Documentation** (or **Start | Programs | PostgreSQL 8.3 | Documentation** on the Windows classic menu) for more detailed information.

## Configuring the firewall to allow database connections

For security reasons, the current Microsoft Windows installation's best practice is to block all incoming connections to unrecognized ports. We need to tell Microsoft Windows which port is being used by the PostgreSQL database by default.

During our PostgreSQL database installation, we used port **5432** as the standard database communication port on all of the connected computers within our network (including the host or database server itself). We will open this port from the Windows firewall, which can be accessed from **Start | Control Panel | Windows Firewall**.

Select the **Exception** tab, and click on the **Add port** button. Complete the PostgreSQL **Name** field, and enter **5432** as the **Port number**. Ensure that you select **TCP** instead of **UDP**. Click on the **OK** button.

# Installing ADempiere on the server side

All prerequisite applications for ADempiere are now configured properly. It is time to install the ADempiere application. A cup of coffee or tea would be refreshing before we begin.

## Downloading the ADempiere core installation files

Currently, all of the ADempiere binary files, source code, and any other files related to ADempiere are hosted at `http://sourceforge.net/`. Throughout this book, we will use **ADempiere 3.4.2s** (as the latest stable version for the 3.4 release series).

We can download this file from `http://downloads.sourceforge.net/adempiere/Adempiere_342s.zip`. The installation file is about 99.22 MB. Create the `C:\download\adempiere` folder, and save the file to this folder.

For checking the integrity of our ADempiere installer, we will download its MD5 signature. Download the MD5 signature for `ADempiere_342s.zip` from `http://sourceforge.net/projects/adempiere/files/Adempiere_342s.zip.MD5`.

## Downloading the latest ADempiere patch files

The ADempiere version 342s was released on December 21st, 2008. After the first release, there has always been an effort to fix bugs, and the ADempiere developer community has released regular application patch files. Along with these application patch files, sometimes the community provides files that need to be applied to the ADempiere database, too. We call these files, as migration script files which aim to alter the ADempiere database and make it comply with a newer database structure.

*ADempiere Installation*

## Obtaining the ADempiere application patch files

ADempiere developer community releases their patch files in the following format:

| No | Format name | Description |
|---|---|---|
| 1 | patches_xxxx_yyyymmdd.jar | ADempiere core patches for version xxxx and released on the year, month, and date mentioned in patch's filename |
| 2 | zkpatches_xxxx_yyyymmdd.jar | ADempiere ZK web user interface patches for version xxxx and released on the year, month, and date mentioned in patch's filename |

We can obtain a list of available ADempiere patch files from `http://sourceforge.net/project/showfiles.php?group_id=176962&package_id=230906&release_id=648627`. Here is an example of a list of ADempiere patch files that are currently available:

| File/Folder Name | Platform | Size | Date ↓ |
|---|---|---|---|
| **Subdirectory (view all files)** | | | |
| ADempiere Patches | | 149.6 MB | 2009-11-11 04:10:08 WIT |
| Patch 3.4.2 | | 149.6 MB | 2009-11-11 04:10:08 WIT |
| zkpatches_342s_20091110.jar.MD5 | | 62 Bytes | 2009-11-11 04:10:08 WIT |
| zkpatches_342s_20091110.jar | | 566.8 KB | 2009-11-11 04:10:07 WIT |
| patches_342s_20091110.jar.MD5 | | 60 Bytes | 2009-11-11 04:09:55 WIT |
| patches_342s_20091110.jar | | 1.1 MB | 2009-11-11 04:09:55 WIT |
| zkpatches_342s_20090916.jar.MD5 | | 62 Bytes | 2009-09-16 22:18:34 WIT |
| zkpatches_342s_20090916.jar | | 554.3 KB | 2009-09-16 22:18:33 WIT |
| patches_342s_20090916.jar.MD5 | | 60 Bytes | 2009-09-16 22:18:22 WIT |
| patches_342s_20090916.jar | | 1.1 MB | 2009-09-16 22:18:21 WIT |
| zkpatches_342s_20090901.jar.MD5 | | 62 Bytes | 2009-09-02 06:46:40 WIT |
| zkpatches_342s_20090901.jar | | 554.1 KB | 2009-09-02 06:46:39 WIT |

> For patch files, we need the latest files for both ADempiere core and the ADempiere ZK web user interface.

With this information, we shall download `patches_342s_20091110.jar` and `zkpatches_342s_20091110.jar`. For verification purposes, we shall download `patches_342s_20091110.jar.MD5` and `zkpatches_342s_20091110.jar.MD5` also. Put all of the downloaded files in the `C:\download\adempiere` folder.

## Obtaining the ADempiere database migration script

To make sure that we are working with the latest ADempiere database structure, we need to download the migration script files. These files are standard **SQL** (**Structured Query Language**) files with .sql as the file extension. The migration script provided for PostgreSQL databases is different from the Oracle database one. For PostgreSQL databases, you can obtain it from http://adempiere.svn.sourceforge.net/viewvc/adempiere/branches/adempiere343/migration/342s-trunk/postgresql/ whereas for Oracle, it's available at http://adempiere.svn.sourceforge.net/viewvc/adempiere/branches/adempiere343/migration/342s-trunk/.

As this book uses a PostgreSQL database, at the time of writing this book, the following list of files were available for download:

- 372_round.sql
- 379_FR1883270_NextIdByYear.sql
- 391_C_Currency_Rate.sql
- 398_currencyround.sql
- 413_BF2567104.sql
- 417_FR2582181.sql
- 436_MissingSysConfigKeys.sql
- 441_BF2710889_Add_Months.sql
- 442_BF2710889_PaymentTermDueDate.sql
- 443_BF2714803_InvoicepaidToDate.sql
- 444_BF2714831_InvoiceopenToDate.sql
- 566_FR1756793_RMA_JUST_FOR_343.sql

Put all of the downloaded files in the C:\download\adempiere\sql folder. We will apply these script files later.

## Verifying the ADempiere binary files

While downloading, due to the uncertainty of Internet connections, sometimes our download files remain in an incomplete state. On the other hand, if we download the binary file from an unknown site, there is a possibility that it might be modified by somebody out there who wants to introduce security holes! This can lead to an unrecognized behavior when trying to proceed further with this file.

To avoid any unnecessary headaches in the near future, we strongly recommend that you perform an integrity check and validate your ADempiere binary installation files.

## ADempiere Installation

ADempiere provides us with MD5 signature files on the SourceForge sites. MD5 is one of cryptographic methods that can be used for verifying the integrity of files.

For a complete explanation of MD5, you can read `http://en.wikipedia.org/wiki/MD5`.

Fortunately, there are a lot of free tools that can be used to help us check the validity of files. One of them is Mat-MD5 (`http://www.matsoftware.it/software/mat-md5`). Create the `C:\download\tools` folder, and then download this tool into this folder.

We will now proceed to check the integrity of all of our ADempiere binary files, including core files and patch files. As an example, we will try to verify our `ADempiere_342s.zip` files, by performing the following steps:

1. Extract the contents of the `matmd5_en_10.zip` file.
2. Double-click on `matmd5.exe`.
3. Click on the **Browse** button, and point to the `C:\download\adempiere\ADempiere_342s.zip` file.
4. Click on the **Open MD5 file** button, and open the `C:\download\adempiere\ADempiere_342s.zip.MD5` file. It will contain a value such as `0ddb4da70fdf3ee5af227083c6f7fe10 *Adempiere_342s.zip`.
5. Copy `0ddb4da70fdf3ee5af227083c6f7fe10` into the field **Add MD5 sums for each file added**, and click on the **Add** button.

If everything goes well, the system will indicate a successful integrity check, as shown in the following screenshot:

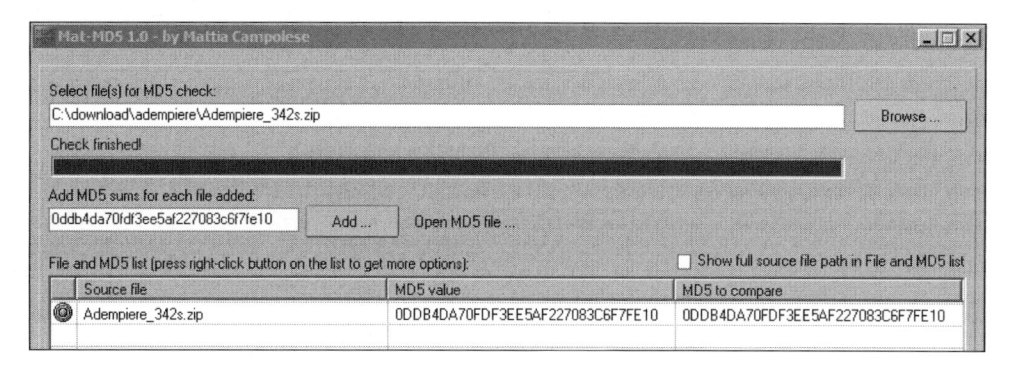

Otherwise, we need to download the ADempiere binary files again from `http://sourceforge.net/` and perform another integrity check until the files are successfully verified.

## Extracting the ADempiere core installation files

The ADempiere core installation file is `Adempiere_342s.zip`. This is only a ZIP file and not a windows installer. We need to extract the content of the ZIP file to the `C:\` drive. Navigate to the `C:\download\adempiere` folder, right-click on this file, and click on **Extract All**. When the system asks about the target directory, point it to the `C:\` drive. Click on the **Next** button to extract the files. Your ADempiere files should be found in the `C:\Adempiere` folder. The standard ADempiere folder structure is shown in the following screenshot:

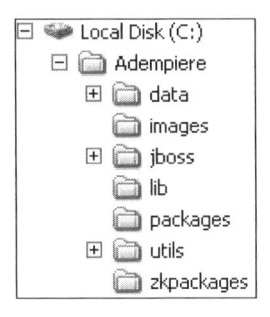

```
Local Disk (C:)
  Adempiere
    data
    images
    jboss
    lib
    packages
    utils
    zkpackages
```

## Applying the ADempiere application patch files

Applying patch files is an easy task. First, ensure that you back up your `patches_342s_20091110.jar` and `zkpatches_342s_20091110.jar` files by copying them to the `C:\download\adempiere\backup` folder. Rename the original files in the downloaded folder from `patches_342s_20091110.jar` to `patches.jar` and from `zkpatches_342s_20091110.jar` to `zkpatches.jar`.

Before copying the patch files to another folder, it's a good practice to keep a backup of the original `C:\adempiere\lib\patches.jar` and `C:\adempiere\lib\zkpatches.jar` files. We shall put these backup files into the `C:\download\adempiere\backup` folder as well. The last thing to do is to copy our downloaded `patches.jar` and `zkpatches.jar` files, which can be found at `C:\download\adempiere`, into the `C:\adempiere\lib` folder.

During the copying procedure, when the system prompts us with a **Confirm File Replace** question, just click on **Yes to All**, and we will have finished our tasks.

## Creating an ADempiere PostgreSQL database

ADempiere provides us with an initialized database dump. This file contains a list of SQL commands that can be used to create the ADempiere database structure and predefined data. The physical name of this file is Adempiere_pg.dmp. We will find this file in the C:\Adempiere\data folder.

> The C:\Adempiere\data folder will contain two DMP files. These are Adempiere.dmp and Adempiere_pg.dmp. The Adempiere.dmp file will be used for the Oracle installation, and the Adempiere_pg.dmp file will be used for PostgreSQL installation.

## Creating a PostgreSQL new login role

While configuring the ADempiere server, a special login role is required, which is used internally by ADempiere. We can define additional login roles by using the pgAdmin III tools. We can access these tools through **Start | All Programs | PostgreSQL 8.3 | pgAdmin III**.

Double-click on **PostgreSQL 8.3 (localhost:5432)** in **Object browser** to connect to the PostgreSQL database server. When the system prompts us with the **Connect to Server** window, we will supply our postgres account password and click on **OK**.

> During the PostgreSQL databases installation, we provided *postgres* as our postgres account password.

After successfully logging in by using this tool, the system will show a screen similar to the following screenshot:

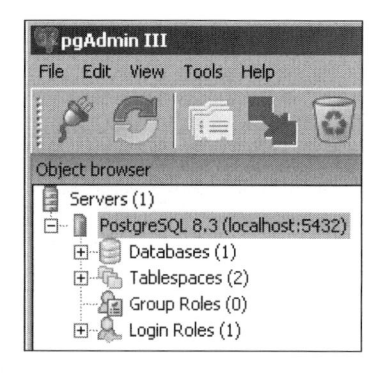

In order to add a new login role, right-click on the **Login Roles** node, and click on **New Login Role**. Create the role name *adempiere* with the password *adempiere*, and ensure that the following **Role Privileges** are selected:

- **Superuser**
- **Can create database objects**
- **Can create roles**
- **Can modify catalog directly**

> This role name is the user who was previously configured in the *Modify client authentication configuration file* section.

## Creating an ADempiere database

Using the pgAdmin III tools, we will create our new ADempiere database. Right-click on the **Databases** node, and then click on **New database** in the **Object browser**. Complete the information fields within the **Properties** tab, as shown in the following table:

| No | Field | Value |
|---|---|---|
| 1 | Name | adempiere |
| 2 | Owner | adempiere |
| 3 | Encoding | UTF8 |

Leave the other information as it is. Click on **OK** to proceed to the database creation procedure.

> By default, we will initially have an initial or blank ADempiere database due to the previous activities. We need to import the ADempiere database structure such as table, view, function, and initial data, from the existing database dump file later.

## Configuring the ADempiere server

ADempiere needs to be configured on the server side. This task is intended to notify ADempiere about predefined variables or information. This information is needed by ADempiere to integrate the database, to bind official ADempiere core patches and ZK web user interface patches to the ADempiere core application, and to host these core packages on their default embedded application server (JBoss).

## ADempiere Installation

Double-click on the `run_setup.bat` file, which can be found in the `C:\Adempiere` folder. We need to complete the fields using the information given in the following table:

| No | Field | Default value | Set value to |
|----|-------|---------------|--------------|
| 1 | Application server | *your computer name* | *your server ip address* |
| 2 | Database server | *your computer name* | *your server ip address* |
| 3 | Database type | oracleXE | postgresql |
| 4 | Database name | xe | adempiere |
| 5 | System password | *blank* | postgres |
| 6 | Mail server | *your computer name* | *your server ip address* |

Leave the other fields unchanged. Click on the **Test** button in the **Adempiere Server Setup** window. When the system prompts you with the **Key Store Dialog** window, complete the fields with your information, and ensure that the setup window displays an **Ok** message on the bottom-left info bar, as shown in the following screenshot:

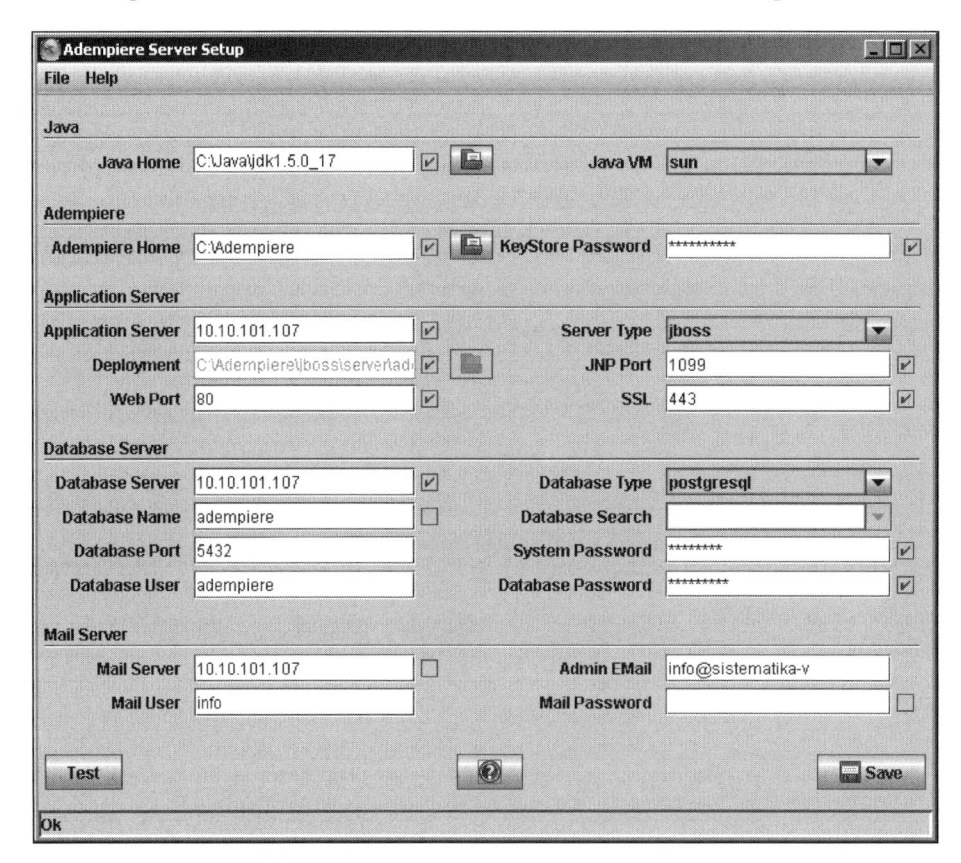

Click on **Save** to proceed with our ADempiere server installation configuration. Carefully read through the ADempiere license agreement window. Accept the terms of the agreement, and click on **OK** once again to start the ADempiere deployment. Wait for a moment as the ADempiere system performs its internal tasks to configure and build our ADempiere server.

At the end of these tasks, we will get the information shown in the next screenshot, which indicates successful packaging and deployment of the application to the embedded JBoss application server.

```
Install Adempiere Server
setupJBoss:
     [copy] Copying 1 file to C:\Adempiere\jboss\server\adempiere\conf
     [copy] Copying 1 file to C:\Adempiere\jboss\server\adempiere\conf
     [copy] Copying 1 file to C:\Adempiere\jboss\server\adempiere\deploy\http-in
voker.sar\META-INF
     [copy] Copying 1 file to C:\Adempiere\jboss\server\adempiere\deploy\jbosswe
b-tomcat55.sar
     [echo] AppsDeployment= C:\Adempiere\jboss\server\adempiere\deploy
     [unjar] Expanding: C:\Adempiere\lib\adempiere.ear into C:\Adempiere\jboss\se
rver\adempiere\deploy\adempiere.ear

setupTomcat:

setupDeploy:
     [echo] AppsDeployment= C:\Adempiere\jboss\server\adempiere\deploy

setup:
BUILD SUCCESSFUL
Total time: 3 minutes 24 seconds

*** 2009-01-14 14:39:35.677 Adempiere Log (CLogConsole) ***
ErrorLevel = 0
```

> During the **Test** procedure on the **Adempiere Server Setup** window, we might get a server setup error message — **Error JDBC Connection**. (**Error connecting: jdbc:postgresql://your_pc_name:5432/template1 – postgres/postgres**). Just make sure that you have defined the **Application Server**, **Database Server**, **Database Type**, **Database Name**, and **System Password**, as mentioned earlier, and set up the PostgreSQL client authentication properly, as mentioned in the section *Modifying client authentication configuration file*.

As mentioned earlier, the ADempiere developer community will release their patches regularly. If there are newer patches available, you can download those patch files, perform MD5 verification, copy them to the C:\Adempiere\lib folder, and then run run_setup.bat again.

*ADempiere Installation*

## Importing the initial ADempiere database

We need to import the structures such as tables, functions, initial data, and another prerequisite metadata into our blank ADempiere database previously created. ADempiere provides us with a script or batch file to load `Adempiere_pg.dmp` into our blank ADempiere database.

Find and execute `RUN_ImportAdempiere.bat`, which can be found in the `C:\Adempiere\utils` folder. During execution, this script will show you a message, as shown in the next screenshot:

Press *Enter*, and the import activity will run immediately.

> If you encounter a:
>
> `psql: FATAL database "adempiere" does not exist`
>
> error message, then you can rectify this problem by accessing http://adempiere.svn.sourceforge.net/viewvc/adempiere/branches/adempiere343/utils/postgresql/ImportAdempiere.bat.
>
> From this preview file, we can copy the content and save it as `ImportADempiere.bat`.
>
> Next, access the link http://adempiere.svn.sourceforge.net/viewvc/adempiere/branches/adempiere343/utils/postgresql/DBRestore.bat.
>
> Save it as `DBRestore.bat`.
>
> Put these files in `C:\Adempiere\utils\postgresql` as a replacement for the initial files. This should fix your problem.

Although it lists the `Adempiere.dmp` file with our configuration value while executing `run_setup.bat`, this batch file should load and import the `Adempiere_pg.dmp` file.

## Applying the database migration script

After importing the initial database structure, we need to apply all of the migration scripts available. The important thing, when applying the migration scripts, is that you have to process the files in a sequential order! You can check the number given in the file name of each of the available SQL files (based on sequential process). With our available migration script, the execution process would be in the following order:

1. `372_round.sql`
2. `379_FR1883270_NextIdByYear.sql`
3. `391_C_Currency_Rate.sql`

And so on.

To apply these SQL files, you need to open your DOS prompt. Change the active directory to `C:\download\adempiere\sql`. Then execute the following commands, one-by-one (and only execute each once):

```
psql -U adempiere -f 372_round.sql -o 372.txt
psql -U adempiere -f 379_FR1883270_NextIdByYear.sql -o 379.txt
psql -U adempiere -f 391_C_Currency_Rate.sql -o 391.txt
psql -U adempiere -f 398_currencyround.sql -o 398.txt
psql -U adempiere -f 413_BF2567104.sql -o 413.txt
psql -U adempiere -f 417_FR2582181.sql -o 417.txt
psql -U adempiere -f 436_MissingSysConfigKeys.sql -o 436.txt
psql -U adempiere -f 441_BF2710889_Add_Months.sql -o 441.txt
psql -U adempiere -f 442_BF2710889_PaymentTermDueDate.sql -o 442.txt
psql -U adempiere -f 443_BF2714803_InvoicepaidToDate.sql -o 443.txt
psql -U adempiere -f 444_BF2714831_InvoiceopenToDate.sql -o 444.txt
psql -U adempiere -f 566_FR1756793_RMA_JUST_FOR_343.sql -o 566.txt
```

You can supply the default password as *adempiere* (when system prompts with the **Password for user adempiere** message). After performing this activity, your database complies with the newer or latest ADempiere database structures.

For more information on migration scripts, you can access http://www.adempiere.com/index.php/Migration.

## ADempiere server memory management

We can check the physical memory available by opening **Windows Task Manager**. Use the shortcut keys *Ctrl + Shift + Esc*. Click on the **Performance** tab and you will see the **Physical Memory (K)** information, as shown in the following screenshot:

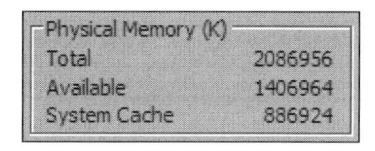

| Physical Memory (K) | |
|---|---|
| Total | 2086956 |
| Available | 1406964 |
| System Cache | 886924 |

This shows that the author's computer has 2086956 kilobytes (almost 2 GB) of physical memory.

During the initial loading of the ADempiere application server, the system will allocate a minimum memory for its operations, and if necessary, it will allocate more memory resources until it reaches the maximum value specified by the configuration. We can access this configuration from the `myEnvironment.bat` file in the `C:\Adempiere\utils` folder.

If you go through this file, then you will find the following information:

```
@SET ADEMPIERE_JAVA_OPTIONS=-Xms64M -Xmx512M -DADEMPIERE_HOME=C:\
Adempiere
```

With this default configuration, ADempiere will consume 64 MB of available memory (`-Xms64M`) during the initial loading. If required, the maximum memory could be allocated, that is, 512 MB (`-Xmx512M`).

We are not discussing how to perform efficient memory allocation. We are just ensuring that we have allocated the maximum memory, that is, 75 percent of our memory available.

With this requirement, we can set this configuration as follows:

```
@SET ADEMPIERE_JAVA_OPTIONS=-Xms256M -Xmx512M -DADEMPIERE_HOME=C:\
Adempiere
```

This means that we will allocate a maximum of 512 MB of memory from the available memory of 1406 MB on the author's computer.

## Starting up the ADempiere application server

On the server side, we need to start our application server. To start the application server, double-click on `Run_Server2.bat` in the `C:\Adempiere\utils` folder.

Check the DOS Prompt, and wait for a while, until you see a notification such as the following:

```
12:31:52,564 INFO [Server] JBoss (MX MicroKernel) [4.0.2 (build:
CVSTag=JBoss_4_0_2 date=200505022023)] Started in 1m:48s:637ms
```

Now our application server is ready.

Starting the application server will start ADempiere's accounting processors, internal schedulers, ADempiere's web user interface, ADempiere's web admin tools (that can be used to install ADempiere client), ADempiere's client Web Start feature, and all of the activities related to the ADempiere server.

After we finish our work with the ADempiere server, we have to shut down the application server. We can shut it down by double-clicking on `Run_Server2Stop.bat` in the `C:\Adempiere\utils` folder.

## Installing ADempiere on the client side

With the application server started, we can access its 'service' from our client computer. Open your browser (Firefox Mozilla, Google Chrome, Internet Explorer, or your own favorite browser), and type `http://your_ipaddress/admin/` in the browser's address bar.

We will have a screen similar to the one shown in the next screenshot:

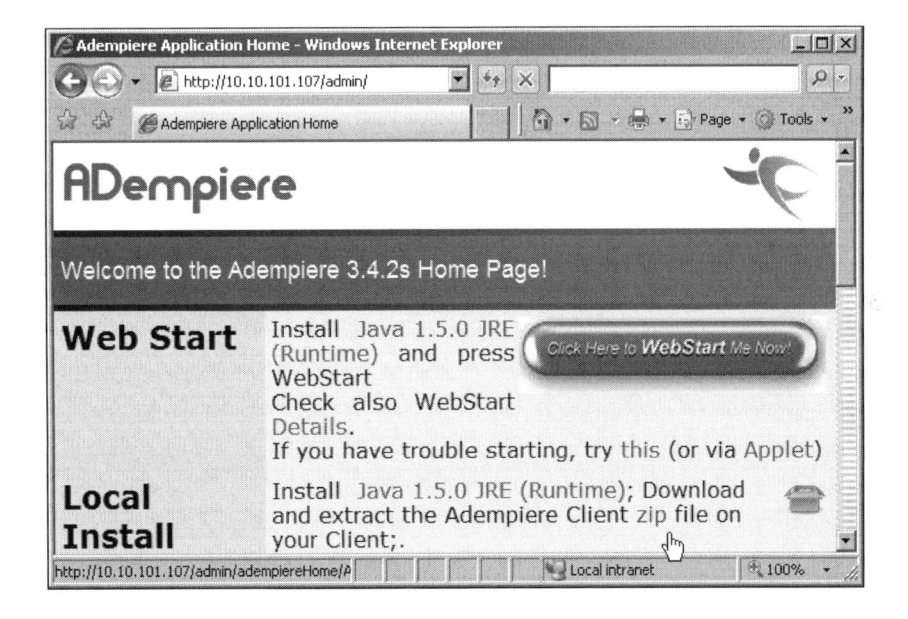

*ADempiere Installation*

ADempiere provides two types of ADempiere client installation: **Web Start** and **Local Install**. For easy administration, we recommend you to set up the ADempiere client installation using the **Web Start** feature.

## Web Start client installation

This is the easiest way to install the ADempiere client on a client computer. Click on **Click Here to WebStart Me Now!**, and the installation process starts automatically.

While accessing **Web Start** for the first time, the system will download the application from the ADempiere server, perform verification of the application, and launch the ADempiere client application itself.

The system will check the latest client application configuration on the server side, before launching ADempiere client application the next time. If there are updates available, then the system will download the application again and launch the latest client application. With these features, all clients connected to the server will always use the updated ADempiere client application.

> You can create a shortcut pointing to `http://your_server_ip_address/admin/adempiereHome/adempiereDirect.jnlp` to access this ADempiere client Web Start feature.

## Verifying the ADempiere client installation

Before using the ADempiere client application, we need to verify the ADempiere client connection through the ADempiere application server. Launch the **Web Start** application by double-clicking on the previously-created shortcut. The system will prompt us with the **Adempiere – License Agreement** window. Read it carefully, and accept the license.

This opens the **Adempiere Connection** window. Here, you need to change the following information:

| No | Field | Default value | Set value to |
|----|-------|---------------|--------------|
| 1 | **Application Host** | MyAppServer | *your server ip address* |

Leave the other fields unchanged. For example, on the author's computer, the application host is 10.10.101.107.

Click on the **Test Application Server** button, followed by a click on **Test Database**. Ensure that both buttons result in a green check mark, as shown in the following screenshot:

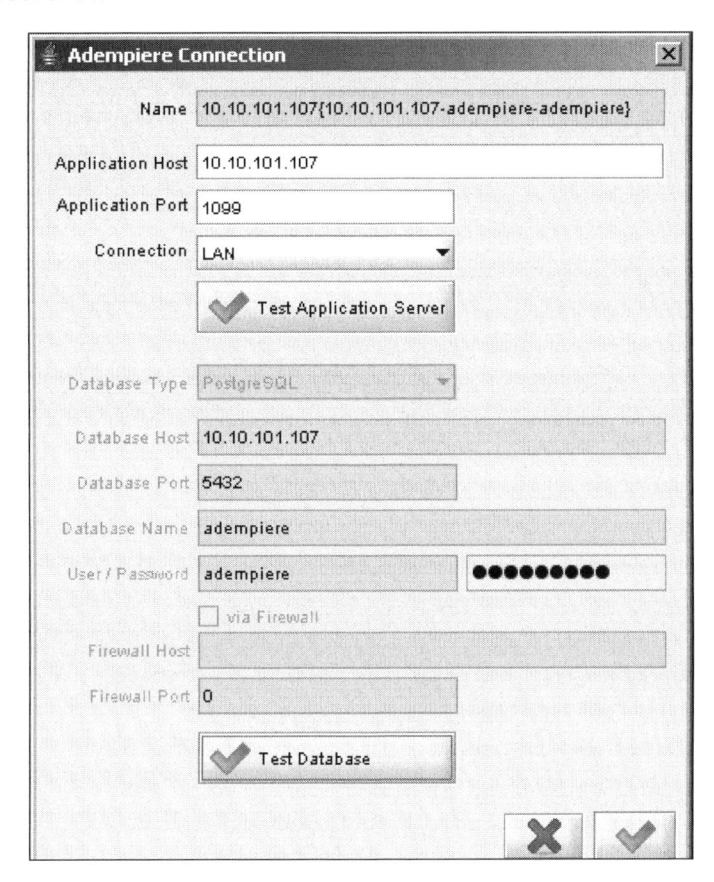

If you click on the **Ok** button (green check mark) on the bottom right-hand side of the window, then you will be directed to the ADempiere login window. For now, click on the **Cancel** button, and we are done.

# Reading the ADempiere 3.4.2s release notes

The ADempiere community has made some notes related to this ADempiere release. You can read these release notes carefully at `http://www.adempiere.com/index.php/Release_342`. You can follow the instructions that might be available there to make sure that you get the latest or updated instructions related to this ADempiere release.

## Summary

In this chapter, we have learned what is the minimum hardware specification for both the server and client computer, how to obtain the JDK, JRE, PostgreSQL databases, and the ADempiere application, and how to install JDK for the server and JRE for the client computer, set up the Java system variables and Windows path, and verify the settings with those of the computer. We also learned how to install the PostgreSQL database server, add and verify the PostgreSQL path, and configure the PostgreSQL client authentication properly, and how to configure the Windows Firewall to accept a database connection from the client computer.

We saw how to verify the ADempiere binary files, and how to set up the ADempiere server application and apply its patches. We were able to create a prerequisite login/role and an ADempiere database and to import a predefined database structure. We learned about the ADempiere application server memory usage allocation, starting and stopping an ADempiere application server, installing an ADempiere client application and verifying an established connection to the server.

In the next chapter, you will be introduced to performing certain tasks with ADempiere and you will be playing with a predefined GardenWorld sample company.

# 2
# Exploring the ADempiere Client and Performing Tasks

At the start of a training session, a student from the class asks the following question:

> *I have just installed ADempiere on my computer and launched the ADempiere Web Start client to log in to the application. However, I do not understand what to do with the application's screens. Even though I am already familiar with Microsoft Windows, the structure of these screens is quite new for me. Could you please explain these screens to me?*

This is not a naïve question. Like all new users who do not have experience in operating ERP software applications, this student needs to know the purpose of the screen along with information on the buttons, tabs, and so on inside each screen. Once the users know the main function of a certain screen, they will use and operate the software more effectively.

In this chapter, we will learn:

- How to establish a connection to a specific ADempiere server
- The standard format of an ADempiere screen
- Application preferences
- How to perform tasks

We will start our discussion by introducing you to the connection aspect of ADempiere.

# The Connection aspect of ADempiere

Our pre-installed ADempiere application will contain a sample company data called GardenWorld company. To make ourselves familiar with ADempiere, we will access this company data, using a predefined user ID and password. Launch your ADempiere application server, and then launch the ADempiere Web Start client.

## Checking the ADempiere client version

With ADempiere patches being frequently available, we need to know the version of ADempiere client that we are working on.

In the ADempiere Web Start client/fat client (not web-based version), through the **ADempiere Login** window, you can find the information that indicates the version of ADempiere in use. In this window, you can find the ADempiere client version by examining the information in the format **3.4.2s+P20091109**. With this information, the system tells you that you are using:

- The ADempiere 3.4.2s (stable) version
- The latest patches installed on the system released on November, 09 2009

## The predefined user ID and password

*Coming to the ADempiere Login window, the system supplies us with a GardenAdmin User ID and an obscured Password. The question is: What exactly is the GardenAdmin password?*

Within your current connection window, the system will serve us with the **GardenAdmin** user ID. However, this is not the only user ID that is available. Our ADempiere installation has a common list of user IDs and passwords, as mentioned in the following table:

| No | User ID | Password |
|---|---|---|
| 1 | System | System |
| 2 | SuperUser | System |
| 3 | GardenAdmin | GardenAdmin |
| 4 | GardenUser | GardenUser |

We can try all of these user IDs in the **Adempiere Login** window. When typing these user IDs and passwords, check the *Caps Lock* status. The system will check the capitalization of the characters being typed. When supplied with a wrong password, you will get a **User does not match password** error message.

After typing your **GardenAdmin** password, you will be directed to the **Defaults** tab of the **Adempiere Login** window. Here, you have an option to set the **Role**, **Client**, **Organization**, **Warehouse**, **Date**, and **Printer** values. Leave the information as it is, and click on the **Ok** button. You are now playing with a preconfigured **GardenWorld** sample client.

## Understanding the Client and System users

With the default ADempiere installation, we can group users into the following types:

- Client users
- System users

The type of user is determined by the kind of **Role** being used when connecting to the ADempiere system. A Client user is a type of user who has the rights to access Client information (for example, **GardenWorld** Client), whereas a System user is a type of user who has the rights to perform system-related tasks, such as accessing and configuring the **Application Dictionary** through the **System** Client.

> With the **Application Dictionary**, you can perform low-level configuration, such as:
> - Configure the Table and Column definitions to save your data
> - Construct a Window, Tab, and fields to build your ADempiere window
> - Set up a Report and Process to generate your reports
>
> Most of these parts can be done without altering the ADempiere source code. Any information in the **Application Dictionary** is user-extensible and can include user-specific configuration

The **GardenAdmin** user ID is an example of a Client user. This user ID should be able to connect to the ADempiere server with the **GardenWorld Admin** or the **GardenWorld User** role. The **System** and **SuperUser** user IDs are examples of System users. When logging in to the ADempiere system, these IDs can connect with the **System Administrator** role.

> **SuperUser** can be used to access both System and Client information.

## Changing our ADempiere server connection

During our testing phase, it's quite common to have multiple ADempiere servers. At least, we will have both a demo and a production ADempiere application server environment.

You can choose your target ADempiere server by clicking on the **Server** field on the **Adempiere Login** window, as shown in the following screenshot:

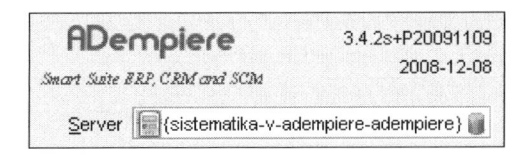

As mentioned in Chapter 1, *ADempiere Installation*, you will see an **ADempiere Connection** window. Complete the **Application Host** field with the target IP address (or computer name) of the ADempiere server, and leave the other fields with their default values. Ensure the connection between the client and the server computer by clicking on the **Test Application Server** button. If this button displays a green check mark, then the system will automatically put the information in the database connection information into this window. You can verify the database connection by clicking on the **Test Database** button.

When both of these buttons display a green check mark, this means that we have successfully connected to both, the ADempiere server and the database server. Finalize this task by clicking on the **OK** button.

## Which ADempiere server are we working on?

> *After logging onto the ADempiere web start client, information such as GardenAdmin@GardenWorld.HQ [sistematika-v{sistematika-v-adempiere-adempiere}] is displayed at the top of our main program. Could you explain what it means?*

Sometimes, after changing your ADempiere server connection, you need to check which ADempiere server you are working on. To do so, after logging into ADempiere, you can check the value displayed at the top of the main form, as shown in the following screenshot:

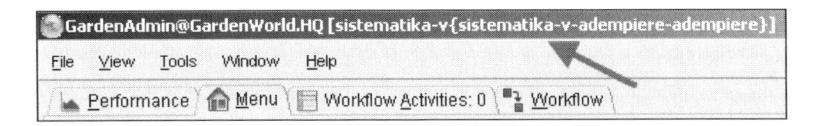

The format for the connection information is as follows:

> *user@client.warehouse [adempiere_server_computer_id {database_server_computer_id-database_name-database_user-id}]*

Refer to following table for an explanation of the information shown:

| No | Parts of information | Description |
|---|---|---|
| 1 | **GardenAdmin** | The user ID of the person using the ADempiere application |
| 2 | **GardenWorld** | The user is accessing the GardenWorld Company (client) |
| 3 | **HQ** | The user is using HQ as the default warehouse |
| 4 | **sistematika-v** (first) | The target ADempiere server ID—in this example, the user is working on the **sistematika-v** ADempiere application server |
| 5 | **sistematika-v** (second) | The target database server ID—the user is connected to the database on the **sistematika-v** server |
| 6 | **adempiere** (first) | The database name—the user is connected to the **adempiere** (name of database) database |
| 7 | **adempiere** (second) | The database user ID—the user is connected to the database with user ID **adempiere** |

# Managing ADempiere client

After successfully logging on to your ADempiere client using the **GardenAdmin** user ID, you will first be directed to the **Performance** tab. This tab contains a list of performance goal charts and bar charts. These charts are just an example of the default predefined charts. Navigate to the **Menu** tab to access the list of menus available, as shown in the following screenshot:

In general, there are four main tabs available on the screen: **Performance**, **Menu**, **Workflow Activities**, and **Workflow**.

- The **Performance** tab is used for measuring the performance of the company. This type of information is configurable and could be attached to a certain **Role**, in case we need to limit the user rights while accessing this information.
- The **Menu** tab allows you to access all of the menus within ADempiere. It can be used to access Windows, Forms, Reports, Processes, and General Workflows. Examples of menus are **Purchase Order**, **Sales Order**, **Product**, and so on. The availability of these menus is configurable and depends upon the access rights given to the **Role**.
- The **Workflow Activities** tab is used to display the active running document workflow that needs your confirmation.
- The last tab is the **Workflow** tab. This is used for General Workflow purpose. For example, while registering a product there is a step-by-step action to perform the product setup. First, we will define the **Warehouse & Locators**, followed by **Unit of Measure**, **Product Category**, **Tax Category**, and finally the **Product**. We shall discuss the workflow topics in more detail, later.

# Working with the Menu

Pressing *Alt + M* will direct you to the **Menu** tab. There are two main sections to this screen. The first (left-hand side) section is the Navigation Bar, which contains shortcuts to access the **Business Partner**, **Sales Order**, and **Product** (for now). The second (right-hand side) section contains the ADempiere menus that are available for the user's **Role**. Select the **Expand Tree** option and you will get a list of the granted ADempiere menus.

> Sometimes, there will be an underlined character in the menu name (for example, **M**enu, **F**ile, and so on). With this underlined character, you can access the menu by pressing *Alt + the underlined character*.

## Menu Icon

While we are taking a look at the menus available, there are currently four different icons present. The meaning of each icon is as follows:

| Icon | Description |
| --- | --- |
| | **Normal ADempiere Window or Form**: This window is used for managing records, entering records, or viewing our transactions (for example, **Purchase Order**, **Sales Order**, and **Accounting Fact Balances**). Moreover, this icon is used to perform an activity that utilizes the ADempiere form (for example, **Matching PO-Receipt-Invoice**, **Import File Loader,** and so on). |
| | **Process**: This performs tasks or jobs that could be done in the database (for example, **Generate Shipments** and **Update Accounting Balance**). |
| | **Reports**: Generates reports, which can be modified, exported, and printed easily (for example, **Trial Balance** and **Statement of Accounts**). |
| | **General Workflow**: Continuous step-by-step activities to achieve a goal (for example, **Accounting Setup** and **Tax Setup**). |

## Accessing menus

Throughout this book, you will be guided through the process of opening some menu or executing some processes. For example, "open the **Menu | System Admin | Client Rules | Client** window". With this guidance, in the ADempiere main menu, you can open the **Client** window by:

1. Clicking on **Menu**.
2. Clicking on **System Admin**.
3. Clicking on **Client Rules**.
4. Finally, clicking on the **Client** window.

as shown in the following screenshot:

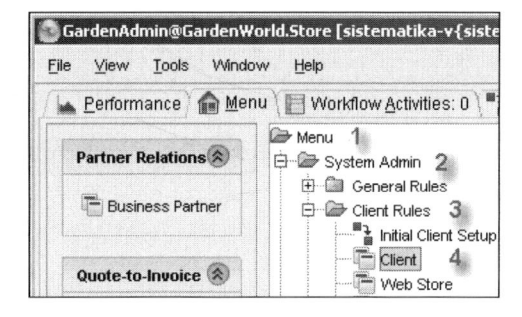

You can follow this approach later, when opening another window.

# Menu Lookup and creating shortcuts

*Well, as I start exploring ADempiere and select the Expand Tree option, it gives me tons of menus. While I try to access, let's say, the Request window, I have to scroll down the menu screen to accomplish this task. It is absolutely unmanageable! Is there a way to speed up the search process?*

- **First method:** In the **Menu** tab, you can access the **Lookup** feature. You can find this feature in the bottom right-hand side of the **Menu** tab. Press *Alt + L*, type any text contained in the menu you want to locate, and press *Enter*. You will be directed to the first menu that contains the requested word. Press *Enter* again, and you will be directed to the next menu containing the requested word. You can press *Enter* as many times required, until you reach your target menu. After reaching your target menu, press *Ctrl + Enter* to open or execute the menu.

- **Second method:** There are many windows that are used by our users while operating ADempiere everyday. Our accounting person will frequently access the **GL Journal** window, **Trial Balance** report, and other menus related to accounting. Fortunately, we can add our favorite windows, reports, and process menus to the Navigation Bar. Just find your menu (which you can do with our first method), then right-click on the menu, and it will show the **Add to Bar** popup menu, as seen in the following screenshot:

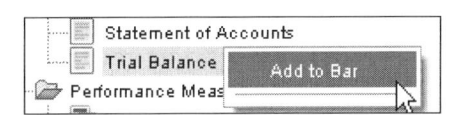

Click on **Add to Bar**, and your favorite menu will be added to the Navigation Bar. Next time, we may just go to the Navigation Bar and click on the appropriate menu to speed up our operation.

> A menu added onto the Navigation Bar is saved into the user's **Role**. All of the users connected to this **Role** can access the predefined menu listed in the Navigation Bar.

# User preferences

Occasionally, we may check our preference while working with the ADempiere client. We could access this window by selecting **Tools | Preference** on our main window or on each ADempiere window. Here, we will have five tabs of information, as shown in the following screenshot:

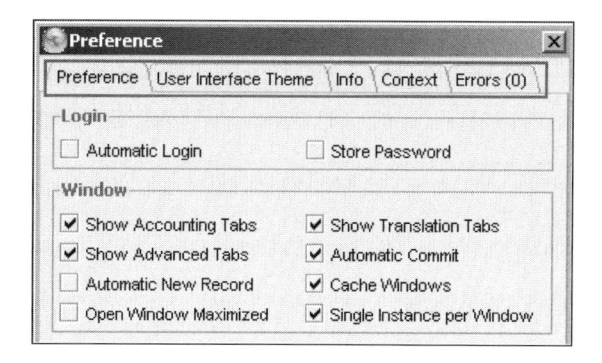

The explanation of each of the tabs is as follows:

- **Preference:** This contains a list of options that can be used to define the default ADempiere client behavior for the ADempiere user. This configuration is saved on the local computer and will work only on this computer. For example, when we select the **Automatic Login** and **Store Password** options, every time that the user runs the ADempiere client on the computer, the system will use the latest user ID and password. It will bypass the login window and go directly to the main ADempiere client window. Although this is useful when working with the ADempiere demo environment, it could be dangerous when working on a production or live ADempiere environment.

    A list of recommended values for the most important fields is as follows:

| Group | Field | Value | Description |
| --- | --- | --- | --- |
| Login | Automatic Login | Deselected | No need to enter login information. This will work if the **Store Password** option is selected. |
|  | Store Password | Deselected | Saves the password on the local computer. |

| Group | Field | Value | Description |
|---|---|---|---|
| Window | **Show Accounting Tabs** | Selected (if applicable) | This will show accounting information, such as setting up the default account and accounting facts/GL journal generated. This field is enabled when the user's **Role** has accounting access rights. You could grant a right by selecting **Show Accounting** fields in the **Role** window. |
| | **Automatic Commit** | Selected | After saving a document, the system automatically commits information into the database. |
| | **Cache Windows** | Selected | Every ADempiere window that has previously been called will be cached. With the cache enabled, this window will be available very quickly if it is called again, as there is no need to re-create this window. |
| | **Single Instance per Window** | Selected | If deselected, we can get more than one instance of a window. For example, when opening the **Product** window, click on the **Product** menu again. Now, there will be two instances of the **Product** window. To avoid any confusion when working with multiple **Product** windows, it is suggested to have a single instance of the window. |
| Connection | **Connection Profile** | LAN | Currently, the most implemented feature will use the **LAN** Connection Profile. |
| Trace Information | **Trace Level** | WARNING | If necessary, we can grab information about what is happening behind the scenes. Most of the information provided is for technical auditing purposes. If we set it to a deeper level (**FINE, FINER, FINEST, ALL**), then the performance of the application will dramatically degrade, as it will write or log all of the information. |
| | **Trace File** | Deselected | If selected, then all of the trace information will be saved in the file. |
| Printing | **Printer** | | If we have many printers connected to the computer, then we can choose the default printer for printing purposes. |
| | **Always Preview Print** | Deselected | When we click on the **Print** button, with this option deselected, the result will directly go to the printer. |

*Exploring the ADempiere Client and Performing Tasks*

- **User Interface Theme**: Change to the theme which best suits your needs.
- **Info**: Contains information about the ADempiere system itself. The most important information contained is: In which **Role** are we connected, and where is the `Adempiere.properties` file saved.
- **Context**: This is a list of internal ADempiere variables. These variables will be used intensively when applying the configuration in **Application Dictionary**.
- **Errors**: This contains information about the error from the application (if any).

> The **Info**, **Context**, and **Errors** tabs are mostly used by Technical Support if you encounter a problem with your ADempiere environment.

## More on the Cache Window option

ADempiere will build all of the ADempiere windows based on the configuration in the **Application Dictionary**. If you do not select the **Cache Window** option in **Tools | Preference**, then upon opening a window, ADempiere will read the configuration again and re-create the window. This will take time!

Although it is suitable for testing purposes, ensure that you select the **Cache Window** option in the ADempiere Production or Live environment.

## Parts of the ADempiere window

Open the **Menu | Requisition-to-Invoice | Purchase Order** window. All ADempiere windows will consist of six standard parts, as highlighted in the following screenshot:

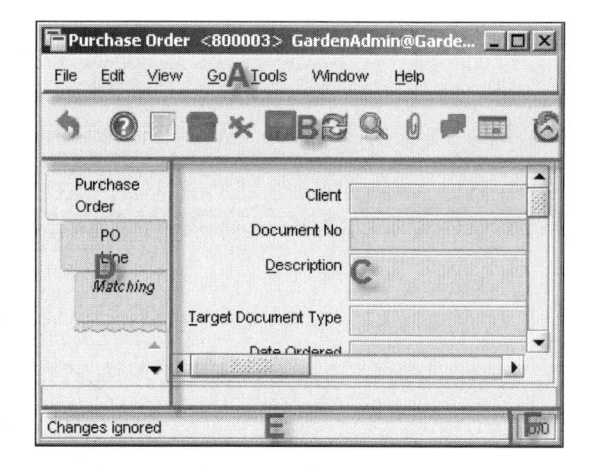

*Chapter 2*

The description of these parts is as follows:

| Part | Description |
|---|---|
| A | Main menu for this window. |
| B | Toolbar shortcut to access menus that are available on the main menu. |
| C | Area for entering or viewing information. |
| D | List of tabs of information. This will mostly be used for splitting master detail information. For the **Purchase Order** window, the first tab consists of **Purchase Order** header information, and the second tab consists of the **PO Line**. This contains items or products that we need to buy. |
| E | A status bar showing system information such as **Record saved**, **Navigate or Update record**, **Total value**, and so on. |
| F | Record information (Record Info) showing the database table name and internal record identity for information in the active tab. This can be used to track any changes, if necessary. |

## More on Record Info

To get a better understanding of **Record Info**, open the **Menu | Requisition-to-Invoice | Purchase Order** window. In the active **Purchase Order** tab you must double-click on part **F** of a window. The information we will get is similar to the following screenshot:

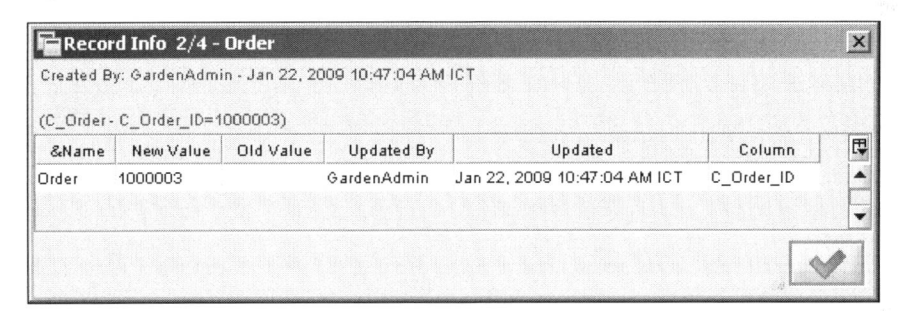

In the previous screenshot, we can see the following information:

- All information related to the Purchase Order header will be saved in the database to the table with the name **C_Order**.
- The Primary Key (internal unique record identity) for the **C_Order** table is **C_Order_ID**, and has the value **1000003**.
- If the auditing feature is enabled, you will have information about field value changes. In this screen, the column or field **C_Order_ID** has been updated with the value **1000003**, by **GardenAdmin**, at the time specified in the **Updated** column.

> When we have information such as **0/0** in the **F** window area, it means that there are no records available for this window. When it shows **2/5**, This means you are accessing the second record of a total of five available records. Please note that the system will show **Record Info** only if there are records available in a window.

## OK or Cancel button in the window

Throughout this book, there will be tasks that require you to click on either the **Cancel** or **OK** button in a certain window. Take a look at the following screenshot:

The **Cancel** button is the button indicated by a red cross, whereas the **OK** button is the button indicated by a green tick.

## Maintaining a log of data changes

The system will show the history of our data changes only if we have already activated the **Maintain Change Log** feature. There are two ways of activating this feature:

- **Role-based**: This feature can be set up in the **Role**, which is associated with the user, upon login to the ADempiere client. To activate this auditing feature, navigate to the **Menu | System Admin | General Rules | Security | Role** window. Set the active tab to **Role**, and select your targeted role. Find and select the **Maintain Change Log** checkbox, as shown in the following screenshot:

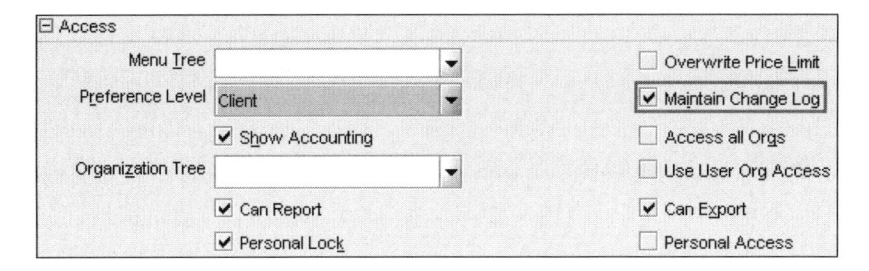

- **Table based**: You can activate this feature based on the Table. The Table is a place where you save information in your databases. Activate this feature by logging in with the **System** user ID and **System Administrator** as the role. Open the **Menu | Application Dictionary | Table and Column** window. Find your table, and select the **Maintain Change Log** checkbox.

## Standard window fields

When you enter or view information in part **C** of the ADempiere window, there will be a couple of standard fields available.

## Client and Organization fields

ADempiere has a feature to set up both multi-client and multi-organizational transactions. You can set up as many clients and organizations as you need. We will discuss how to set up clients and organizations later.

To segregate information, the **Client** and **Organization** fields are used to save both the client (or company) and the organization (or division) information in each ADempiere information or data.

The following screenshot shows us an example of the client and organization fields in the **Business Partner** window:

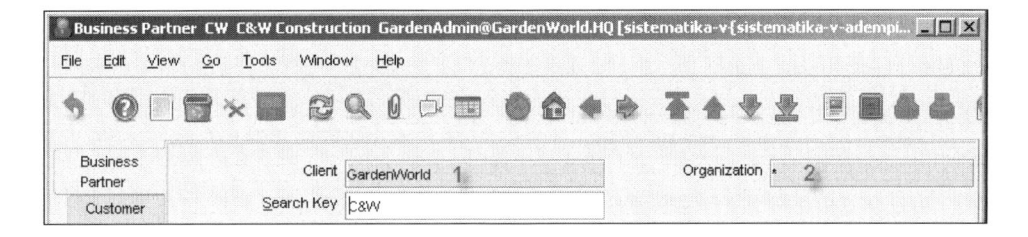

## Active checkbox fields

Within certain windows, there is another standard field available. This is known as the **Active** checkbox. Generally, this checkbox should be available in a window that is used to enter some data that is being repeatedly used within applications as references (something similar to master data).

Some examples of windows that contain **Active** checkboxes are **Warehouse**, **Business Partner**, **Price List**, and so on. Although this master data will not to be used in your further transactions, you are advised to not remove or delete this information for data integrity purposes. Instead, mark these information records as inactive by deselecting the **Active** checkbox.

## Performing tasks

The ADempiere window has editing features, similar to other applications that run on operating systems such as Linux and Microsoft Windows. However, it has several additional features that are unique to ADempiere itself.

## Data management

Take a look at the main menu (part **A**) and toolbar (part **B**) area of your window. A list of icons related to data and record management is as follows:

| Icon | Description | Shortcut |
|---|---|---|
| | **New**: Click on this button when you want to add some information or data. | F2 |
| | **Save**: After you finish entering or updating your data, click on this button to save the information to the database. | F4 |
| | **Cancel**: Use this button to cancel or ignore your changes. | Esc |
| | **Copy Record**: Duplicate the value of existing records to new records. | Shift + F2 |
| | **Delete**: Delete active records. For some data, you cannot delete the records. This is intended for auditing purposes. Instead, you can set their status to inactive. | F3 |
| | **Delete multiple**: Delete selected records or items. You will be prompted with a **Delete Selected Items** window, which contains a list of record IDs and document numbers, before proceeding with the deletion. | Ctrl + D |
| | **ReQuery**: Get the latest data, for the active records, from the databases. | F5 |
| | **Grid Toggle**: Show detailed information of one record only. This is suitable for adding (entering) or editing data. | F8 |
| | **Grid Toggle**: Shows the list of data or records in a grid mode. | F8 |

# Data navigation

While working with the ADempiere client, you need to navigate to and take a detailed look at your records. You can use the following list of icons in the toolbar (part **B**) section of your window. A description of this list of icons is as follows:

| Icon | Description | Shortcut |
|---|---|---|
| | **First record**: Go to the first record in a document. | *Alt + Page Up* |
| | **Previous record**: Go to the previous record in a document. | *Alt + Up* |
| | **Next record**: Go to the next record in a document. | *Alt + Down* |
| | **Last record**: Go to the last record in a document. | *Alt + Page Down* |
| | **Detail record**: While working with a master detail document, clicking on this button will move your pointer (active record) to the detail records of the document. | *Alt + Right* |
| | **Parent record**: While you are in the detail document (within a master detail document), clicking on this button will move your pointer (active records) to the master records of the document. | *Alt + Left* |
| | **History record**: When opening a transactional window, such as **Purchase Order**, for the first time in the login session, just click on this button to show partial data (for a day, week, or year) or all of the records. | *F9* |
| | **Lookup Record**: Intended to search your records by criteria. There are two tab options available for the purpose of searching. The first tab is for standard searching, and the second tab is for advanced searching. With advanced searching, you are able to search records by column name and can specify the data range. | *F6* |

## Other tasks

Other than the standard tasks that are available in the ADempiere window, a list of other tasks that can be performed in the ADempiere window is as follows:

| Icon | Description | Shortcut |
|---|---|---|
| | **Report in columnar format**: With a master detail data, we shall print the header information only with this printing feature. | F11 |
| | **Print Preview**: This will preview a document. It is suitable for the purpose of checking. | Alt + Shift + P |
| | **Print**: Printing the final document to the printer. With the **User Preference | Always Preview Print** configuration, we are able to preview the document before taking a final print. | F12 |
| | **Chat**: This is used for communicating with other ADempiere users. For example, you could make a clarification or confirmation related to an active document. This chat conversation will be recorded in the internal database. | |
| | **Menu**: Go back to the ADempiere client main menu. | |
| | **Attachment**: Add or attach a soft copy of a supporting document, or add some information related to the document, if necessary. | F7 |
| | **Archive**: When making a **Report** or **Print**, we can save an archive of our report or print for documentation purposes. We can access our archive's reports with this menu or access it via the **Archive Viewer** window. | |
| | **Zoom across**: This is used to see the list of documents created, using a reference to a particular selected data. For example, open your **Menu | Partner Relations Business Partner Rules | Business Partner** window, and find the **C&W Construction** record. When we click on **Zoom across** for this business partner, it will show a list of documents (**Sales Order**, **Shipment (Customer)**, and so on) or records (**User**) that use this business partner's information. | |
| | **Help**: Information about the purpose of the window and the meaning of each field. | |
| | **Exit window**: Close the window, and go to the main menu. | Alt + X |

# More on Lookup records

You could find lookup records in each of the ADempiere windows. For your reference, take a look at the **Purchase Order** lookup records. Open your **Menu | Requisition-to-Invoice | Purchase Order** window, and click on the **Lookup Record** button.

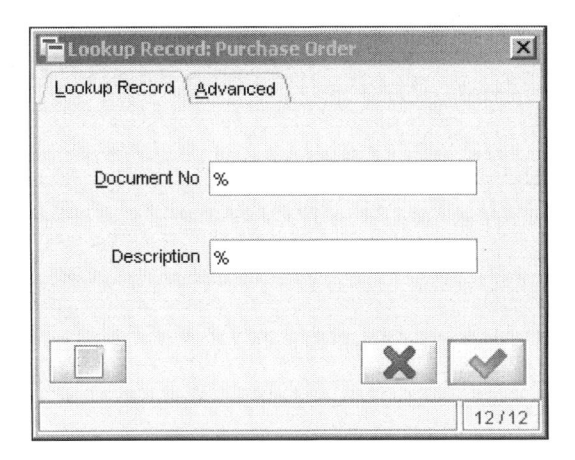

With this window, we are able to perform a search for records by only using the **Document No** and **Description** fields. However, you could perform a search for another information using the **Advanced** tab of lookup records. With this feature, you can perform a search by choosing any available column or field, setting the operator, and entering your selection criteria in the **Query Value** column, as shown in the following screenshot:

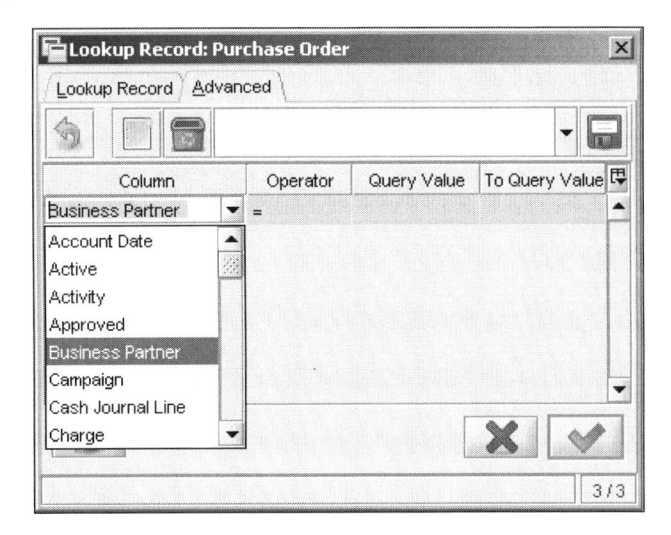

# Setting additional search criteria

*Is it possible to add an additional column or field to the standard Lookup Record search?*

With this procedure, we can add the **Order Reference** of a **Purchase Order** as a standard **Lookup Record**.

Log in as the user **System** and with the password **System**. Set the role to **System Administrator**, client to **System**, organization to **\***, and keep the warehouse value blank.

> Next time, if we need to "log in to **System**", then we will follow this procedure.

You will be directed to the Navigation Bar, which contains parts of the **Application Dictionary**, as shown in the following screenshot:

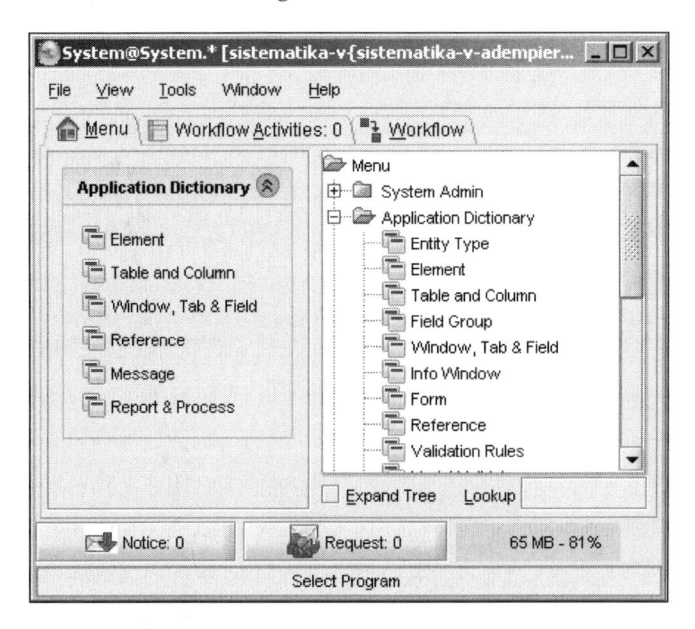

Click on the **Table and Column** menu. When the system displays a **Lookup Record** window, type **C_Order** in the field **DB Table Name**, and press *Enter*. Now we are in the **Table and Column Order** window, with **C_Order** as our value on the **DB Table Name** field. In this window, you can perform the following tasks:

1. Go to the **Column** tab, and find **Order Reference** in the **Name** field.
2. If we are in the **Grid Mode**, click on the **Grid Toggle** button to show detailed information.
3. Find and select the **Selection Column** checkbox, as shown in the following screenshot:

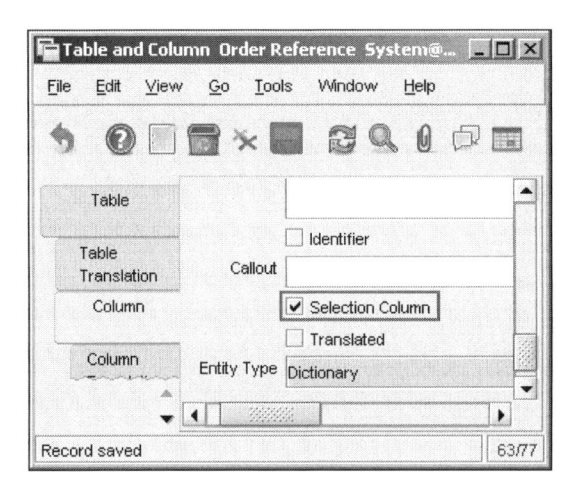

4. Save your changes.

Next time, when you are in the **Purchase Order** window, you will be able to look up the records based on the **Order Reference** field.

# More examples on the use of Zoom Across

> *My Manager told Rossy "Hi Rossy, could you help me check the status of our order to Patio Fun, Inc.. Has it already been delivered or not?"*

Rossy is your Warehouse Manager, isn't she? To answer the Manager's question, using the existing **GardenWorld** sample company data, she can perform the following tasks:

1. Log in with the **GardenAdmin** user ID, set the role to **GardenWorld Admin**, client to **GardenWorld**, organization to **HQ**, and warehouse to **HQ Warehouse**.

2. Open the **Menu | Partner Relations | Business Partner Rules | Business Partner** window. Navigate to the **Patio Fun, Inc**. records. Here, she can click on the **Zoom Across** button, which will result in the context menu shown in the following screenshot:

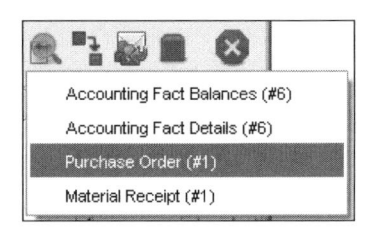

Well, we have one purchase order for this business partner.

3. Then, she can click on **Purchase Order (#1)**. The ADempiere system will prompt her with the **Purchase Order** window. She can then check and note down the document number (**800002**) and **PO Line** information. Now, if she wants to know the status of the material receipt of this purchase order, she can click on the **Zoom Across** button in this **Purchase Order** window. She will then notice that there is a **Material Receipt (#1)**, as shown in the following screenshot:

4. We have one document for this business partner. Rossy can click on **Material Receipt (#1)**, and the **Material Receipt** window will open. She can examine this document, check the **Receipt Line** information, and find out whether we have received our order.

Based on these tasks, Rossy should be able to answer the Manager's question.

## Field context menu

When working with the ADempiere window, there will be a menu, which will help us while we are working in each field. There will be three options: **Zoom**, **ReQuery**, and **Value Preference**. For our example, after opening the **Purchase Order** window, point your mouse at the **Warehouse** field, and right-click in the field. The system will show a menu similar to the one shown in the following screenshot:

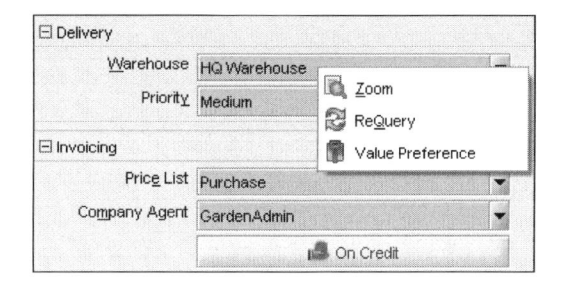

## Zoom

Data that is repeatedly used in an ADempiere window (such as, Customer, Vendor, Currency information, and so on) will be registered as master data. Some examples of master data that can be set up are: **Warehouse**, **Business Partner**, **Product**, **Bank**, **Cash book**, and so on. With this best practice, we just set the information once and you can re-use the existing data as references.

This menu will be active or available only if the field has a link to the master or reference data. The purpose of this feature is to show you the detailed information of the selected information in the field.

In the previous screenshot, **Warehouse** is an example of the field where you can browse for detailed information on **HQ Warehouse**. Click on **Zoom** in this information. The system will open the **Warehouse** window, which contains the detailed information of the **HQ Warehouse**.

Although this feature works for the **Warehouse** field, it is also applicable to all fields that have links to the master data. Try it out yourself to see how it works for the **Business Partner**, **Organization**, and **Price List** fields in the **Purchase Order** window.

## ReQuery

Similar to **Zoom**, this menu will be active or available only if the fields have a link to master data. The purpose of this menu is to get the latest information from databases for the field on which we open the context menu.

Previously, the **Warehouse** option listed only the **HQ Warehouse**. In case, at the same time, there was additional HQ warehouse information being entered by another user, this new information is not available as an option. To get the latest warehouse information, just click on the **ReQuery** menu.

## Value preference

This menu is available for all kinds of fields. The purpose of this menu is to set up a default value when working with an ADempiere document. We can set a value and make it a default value that can be configured to *all or a specific organization*, *all or a specific user* and/or *all or a specific window*.

For example, open a **Purchase Order** window and point your mouse to the **Price List** field, and then pick **Purchase** from the list. We can make **Purchase** values a default value by right-clicking and selecting the **Value Preference** menu, and then selecting the **Organization** checkbox, **User/Contact** checkbox, and **Window** checkbox, as shown in the following screenshot:

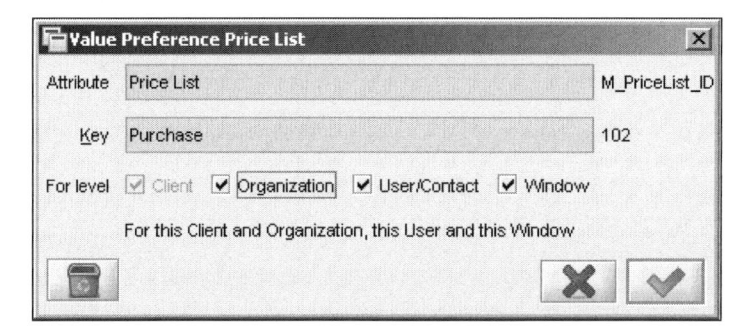

With this set up, the next time this specific user opens the **Purchase Order** window and uses the **HQ** as its organization, the default value for the **Price List** field would be **Purchase**.

If you deselect the **Organization** and **User/Contact** checkbox as your value preference, then when all of the users connected to the ADempiere client, using any Organization, open this **Purchase Order** window, the default value for the **Price List** field will be **Purchase**.

# Summary

In this chapter, you have learnt the basics of the ADempiere Web Start client, and have learnt how to perform common tasks.

Working with the default ADempiere installation, you were provided with a predefined user ID and password. There were two types of users that could be used (Client and System). During your testing phase, you might have more than one ADempiere server running. You can access your specific ADempiere server by changing your server connection.

Next, you saw the basics of the ADempiere client. There is a list of menus available, and you have learnt the meaning of each menu icon. You can easily search your menu using the Menu Lookup feature. You learnt that you could create a shortcut for the menus that you use and how to access this menu. We saw the standard layout of the ADempiere window, and explained the six parts that the window is comprised of. In each ADempiere window, we saw the standard fields such as the **Client**, **Organization**, and **Active** checkboxes.

We looked at how to perform some common tasks. These tasks included data management, data navigation, printing, and the lookup of records. Finally, we introduced the field context menu feature, including **Zoom**, **ReQuery**, and **Value Preference**.

Continuing our discussion, you will explore company and client structures and the initial client setup in our next chapter. You will also learn how to create a apparel company sample structure.

# 3
# Exploring Company Structures and the Initial Client Setup

While preparing for an ADempiere implementation, we have to know exactly how to map our company structures into ADempiere. Consider the next example from the fashion industry. An apparel company will have at least one or more **Facility** (plant) at which to manufacture clothes. It will also have one or more **Warehouses** in which to put the **Raw Materials** and **Finished Goods**.

There is no strict guidance on how to map your company structure into ADempiere. It is an art. In ADempiere, company structures will involve configuration of at least the Client, Organization, and Warehouse.

Based on our final company structure configuration, our upcoming document transaction will generate **General Ledger (GL) journal entries** in ADempiere accounting parts, which will also contain Client, Organization, and if applicable, Warehouse information.

By using these GL journal entries, you can create financial reports. GL journal entries aid in better analysis to achieve the company goals.

In this chapter, we will learn about and explain:

- A sample of a fictitious apparel company structure
- ADempiere company structures
- Preparing a chart of accounts
- Creating a new ADempiere client
- Setting up the organization, warehouses, and locations

# Sample apparel company structure

**Sistematika Fashion Ltd** is an apparel company that manufactures a variety of clothes. It produces mainly dresses, shirts, and jackets. The complexity to produce such types of clothes is different. It requires a different set of skills to manage and make these products. Hence, it has a different plant for each of these types of product.

Currently, Sistematika has three plants and each plant has one or two warehouses. In each warehouse, there is at least one location in which to put the raw materials and/or finished goods.

Based on the *physical location* approach, the following is a complete representation of the company's structure:

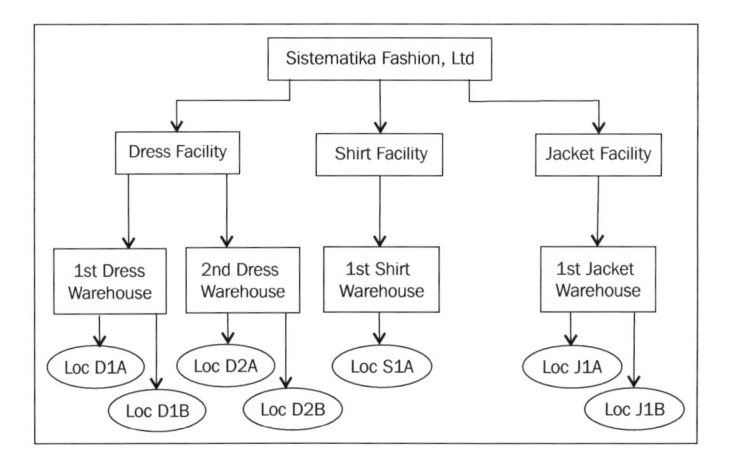

This figure tells us that the company has three facilities—**Dress Facility**, **Shirt Facility**, and **Jacket Facility**. The **Dress Facility** has two warehouses—**1st Dress Warehouse** and **2nd Dress Warehouse**. The first warehouse internally contains two locations to put your stuff—**Loc D1A**, which means *Dress facility, first warehouse and location A*, and **Loc D1B** means *Dress facility, first warehouse and location B*.

With the above explanation, it is easy to read the figure.

# ADempiere company structures

*How do we map company structures into ADempiere?*

ADempiere generally sets up a company hierarchy and we can map it with Sistematika Fashion, Ltd., as shown in the following screenshot:

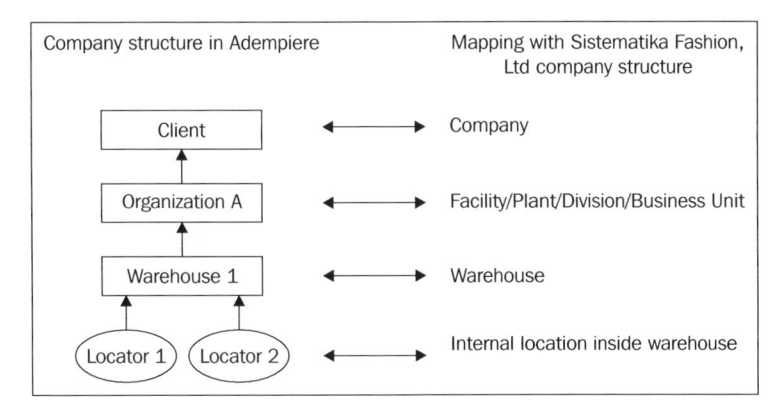

| Company structure in Adempiere | Mapping with Sistematika Fashion, Ltd company structure |
|---|---|
| Client | Company |
| Organization A | Facility/Plant/Division/Business Unit |
| Warehouse 1 | Warehouse |
| Locator 1, Locator 2 | Internal location inside warehouse |

In short, it means that one or more **Locators** will be connected to only one **Warehouse**, one or more **Warehouses** will be connected to only one **Organization**, and one or more organization will be connected to only one **Client**.

Refer to the table below for a detailed description of terms:

| Terms | Description |
|---|---|
| **Client** | The highest entity in ADempiere that can be set up as our company's legal entity. All of the data that is set up in this level can be read by all organizations belonging to this company. ADempiere allows us to have one or more clients in the system. If we enter any information for a specific client (and not System client), no other client will be granted access to, or be allowed to share that data. When we enter information through the System client, all other clients will be granted access to this information. We can map Sistematika Fashion Ltd. here. |
| **Organization** | An entity that can be set up as a subunit entity, company division, or business/production unit. We can set this organization up as a sub-unit of product division (in our case, it could be Dress, Shirt, or Jacket), accounting division, and so on. One or more organizations can be linked to a specific or parent organization, which normally has a division organization type. |
| **Warehouse** | A place where we can put, get, or save the raw materials or finished goods. A warehouse will contain one or more physical locations. An organization can contain one or more warehouses. |

Now, we can further segregate our preliminary Sistematika Fashion Ltd. company structures, as shown in the next figure:

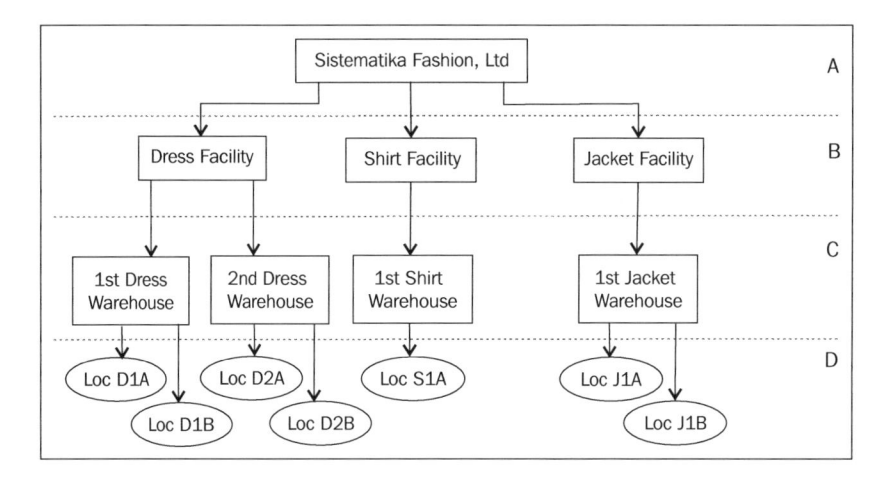

Even though mapping a company structure is an art, throughout this book, we will map structures as shown in the previous figure, which means that **A** will be the area for the Client, **B** for Organizations, **C** for Warehouses, and **D** for the internal locations within a warehouse.

# Managing the Chart of accounts template

While creating a client in ADempiere, we will require an initial chart of accounts to make the ADempiere accounting engine run properly. As you are no doubt aware of what a chart of accounts means by now, we will not get into the details of it. If you still need to know what chart of accounts exactly is, refer to `http://www.accountingcoach.com/online-accounting-course/15Xpg01.html`.

ADempiere has a feature to import an initial chart of accounts. This needs to be written in a specific format. For clarity, we can learn a lot about chart of accounts format from a predefined example of chart of accounts. In a standard installation, there will be a default list of charts of accounts examples that can be used for your reference. You can access this file from the `C:\ADempiere\data\import` folder. This folder contains several examples of charts of accounts in **Excel** format (**xls**) files and **Comma Separated Values** (**csv**) files.

It will be feasible to use the more familiar **xls** format file, and after you are ready with your chart of accounts format, you can save this file in **csv** format. ADempiere will use the **csv** file format for importing purposes.

… Chapter 3

# Exploring the accounting format template files

One example of files for our study is `AccountingUS.xls`. Although this file comes in a default Microsoft Excel format, you can use the OpenOffice Calc to work on this file. Open this file with any of your favorite spreadsheet applications. The following screenshot shows an example of the standard contents of the `AccountingUS.xls` file:

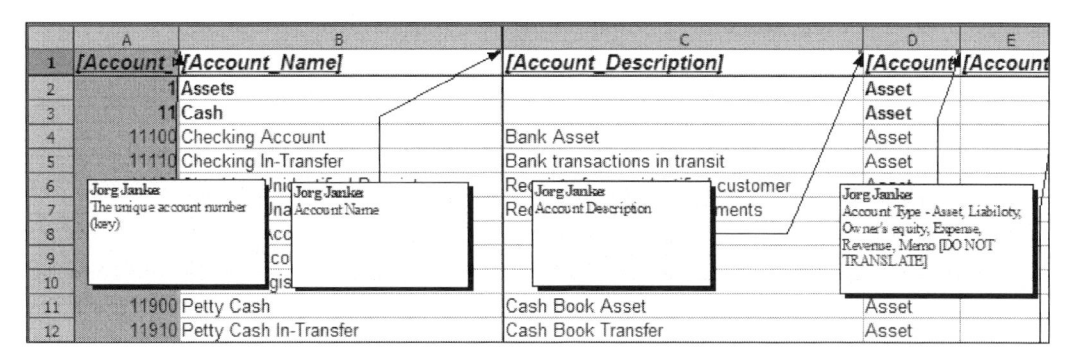

|   | A | B | C | D | E |
|---|---|---|---|---|---|
| 1 | [Account_V | [Account_Name] | [Account_Description] | [Account_ | [Account |
| 2 | 1 | Assets |   | Asset |   |
| 3 | 11 | Cash |   | Asset |   |
| 4 | 11100 | Checking Account | Bank Asset | Asset |   |
| 5 | 11110 | Checking In-Transfer | Bank transactions in transit | Asset |   |
| 6 | … | … | … | … |   |
| 11 | 11900 | Petty Cash | Cash Book Asset | Asset |   |
| 12 | 11910 | Petty Cash In-Transfer | Cash Book Transfer | Asset |   |

Comment annotations (Jorg Janke):
- Column A: "The unique account number (key)"
- Column B: "Account Name"
- Column C: "Account Description"
- Column D: "Account Type - Asset, Liability, Owner's equity, Expense, Revenue, Memo [DO NOT TRANSLATE]"

As we can see in the above screenshot, this file contains several columns, and there are simple descriptions about what each column is intended for. The following table provides the descriptions of the values from columns **A** to **I** on this sheet:

| Column | Value | Description |
|---|---|---|
| A | Account_Value | This column contains a list of account numbers in the General Ledger. The account format uses a numerical format, and the column cannot contain a duplicate number. This field is mandatory. |
| B | Account_Name | This contains short meaningful names of the accounts. These names will appear on financial reports. This field is mandatory. |
| C | Account_Description | This provides a clear description of the account name. |
| D | Account_Type | In standard accounting principles, there are standard accounting types. ADempiere uses six standard account types, namely, **Asset**, **Liability**, **Owner's Equity**, **Revenue**, **Expense**, and **Memo**. This field is mandatory. |
| E | Account_Sign | This indicates if the expected balance of an account should be **Debit** or **Credit**. If set to **Natural**, then the account sign will follow the default behavior of that account's type. For example, **Asset** and **Expense** will use the **Debit** account sign. If you do not supply any value in this field, it will use **Natural** as the default account sign value. |

| Column | Value | Description |
|---|---|---|
| F | Account_Document | Indicates whether this account is document controlled. Examples of document are MM Receipt and AR Receipt. If **Yes**, then you cannot use this account manually within the GL Journal transaction. If you try to complete a GL Journal transaction using this document controlled account, then you will get this message **Account used is document controlled - Do not use for manual journals**. |
| G | Account_Summary | A summary account is an account whose balance represents the total balance of other account balances. If we set an account up as an account summary, we cannot create a transaction using this account. |
| H | Default_Account | While posting ADempiere documents (for example, MM Receipt), the system should use the default account to determine where to post both the **Asset** and **Not Invoiced Receipt** account. Examples of default accounts involved in this document are **B_ASSET_ACCT** and **NOTINVOICEDRECEIPTS_ACCT**. Defining **B_ASSET_ACCT** in this column means that the account value in this line is to be used for this purpose. There are 71 types of default accounts, which need to be bound to **Account Value**. |
| I | Account_Parent | This defines the parent of an account value. Mostly, the account parent is **Summary Account (Account_Summary)**. |

This file is only a sample format of how to arrange and construct the ADempiere chart of accounts. Once you are familiar with this format, you can define your own chart of accounts. Throughout this book, we will use the chart of accounts taken from the `C:\Adempiere\data\import\AccountingUS.xls` file.

## Account editor tools

> *Altering and inserting new accounts in the AccountingUS.xls file is an exhausting task and error prone. Is there any better way to make sure that our initial chart of accounts format files was configured properly?*

ADempiere has been powered by its community. The community listens to user expectations in order to minimize or reduce problems when working with the initial chart of accounts. To make our life easier when managing the pre-import chart of accounts, there are tools available for free to fulfill our needs. For example, the Account Editor 1.2 tool written by Daniel Tamm.

*Chapter 3*

Download the tool from `http://downloads.sourceforge.net/adempiere/adempiereAcctEdit_v1.2.zip` and put the file into the `C:\download\tools` folder. This ZIP file contains two files: `adempiereAcctEdit.bat` and `adempiereAcctEdit.jar`.

Extract the contents of this file to the `C:\Adempiere` folder. This tool will read and save your work in the **Comma Separated Values (csv)** file format. Double-click on the `adempiereAcctEdit.bat` file, and then on the main menu, click on **File | Open Schema File**. When prompted, pick the `AccountingUS.csv` file from the `C:\Adempiere\data\import` folder. Check out the following screenshot for reference:

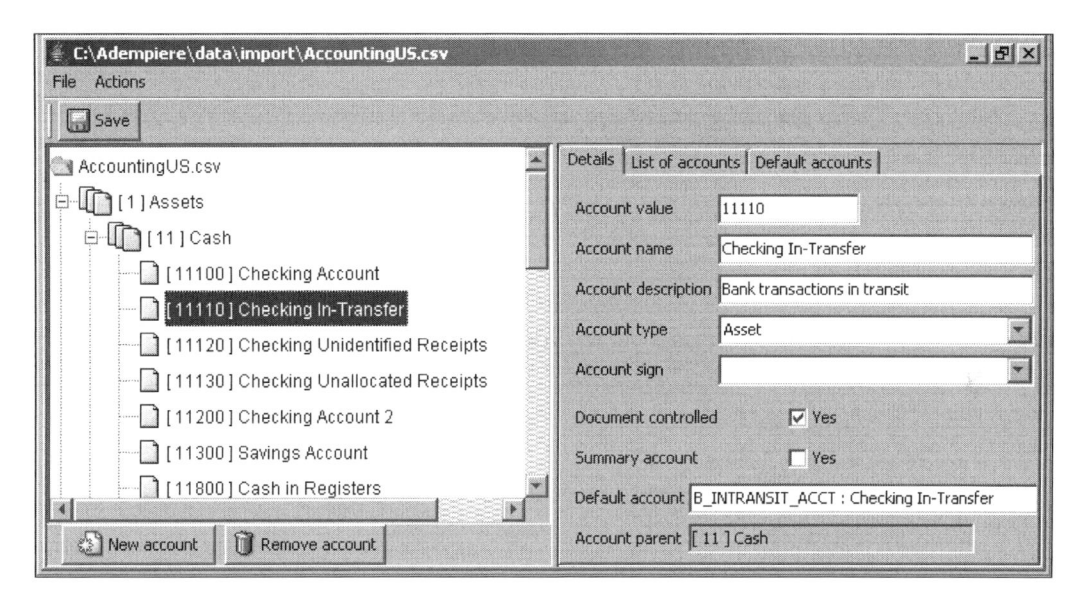

[screenshot of adempiereAcctEdit tool showing AccountingUS.csv opened, with account tree on the left showing [1] Assets > [11] Cash containing accounts [11100] Checking Account, [11110] Checking In-Transfer (selected), [11120] Checking Unidentified Receipts, [11130] Checking Unallocated Receipts, [11200] Checking Account 2, [11300] Savings Account, [11800] Cash in Registers; Details tab on the right showing Account value: 11110, Account name: Checking In-Transfer, Account description: Bank transactions in transit, Account type: Asset, Document controlled: Yes, Summary account: No, Default account: B_INTRANSIT_ACCT : Checking In-Transfer, Account parent: [11] Cash]

This screen has two sides. The left-hand side is for account tree visualization, and the right-hand side contains **Details**, **List of accounts**, and **Default accounts** tabs.

- The **Details** tab contains detailed information about the selected account, as previously described in the table listing the A to I column information.
- **List of accounts** is a complete list of our accounts.
- **Default Accounts** contains all 71 default accounts that need to be linked to your account value definition.

Along with entering or altering the data in the **Details** section, you also need to select **Document controlled** or **Summary account**, or choose an option: **Account type**, **Account sign**, or **Default account**, to avoid any error.

This is shown in the following screenshot:

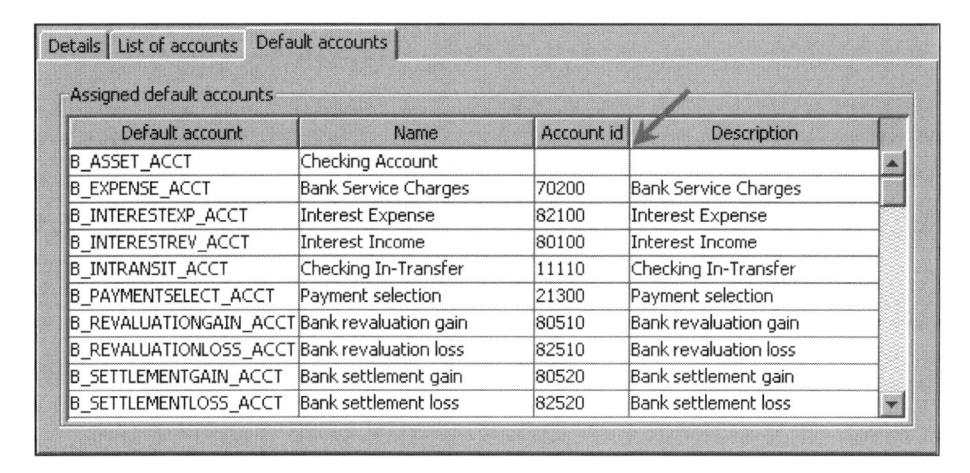

| Default account | Name | Account id | Description |
|---|---|---|---|
| B_ASSET_ACCT | Checking Account | | |
| B_EXPENSE_ACCT | Bank Service Charges | 70200 | Bank Service Charges |
| B_INTERESTEXP_ACCT | Interest Expense | 82100 | Interest Expense |
| B_INTERESTREV_ACCT | Interest Income | 80100 | Interest Income |
| B_INTRANSIT_ACCT | Checking In-Transfer | 11110 | Checking In-Transfer |
| B_PAYMENTSELECT_ACCT | Payment selection | 21300 | Payment selection |
| B_REVALUATIONGAIN_ACCT | Bank revaluation gain | 80510 | Bank revaluation gain |
| B_REVALUATIONLOSS_ACCT | Bank revaluation loss | 82510 | Bank revaluation loss |
| B_SETTLEMENTGAIN_ACCT | Bank settlement gain | 80520 | Bank settlement gain |
| B_SETTLEMENTLOSS_ACCT | Bank settlement loss | 82520 | Bank settlement loss |

You will notice that **B_ASSET_ACCT** default account is still not associated or linked with an account value yet. We know this from the blank value in the **Account id** field.

To link this default account to account **11100**, just scroll to the left-hand side of this tool, find the **11100** account, and click on it. After pointing to this account, click on the **Details** tab, set the mouse pointer to the **Default Account** field information, choose the **B_ASSET_ACCT: Checking Account** from the drop-down list, and click on the **Save** button. That is all.

Ensure that all of the ADempiere default accounts are linked to one and only one account value. Although there are no validation procedures to check the validity of your work, this tool will save you a lot of time.

Finally, when you are comfortable with the new chart of accounts configuration, the `AccountingUS.csv` file is ready to be imported into ADempiere.

# Creating a new ADempiere client

Let's start by creating a fictitious client. Log in to the system by using the user ID **System** and using **System Administrator** as the role, and then open the **Menu | System Admin | Client Rules | Initial Client Setup** window. You will see the screen shown in the following screenshot:

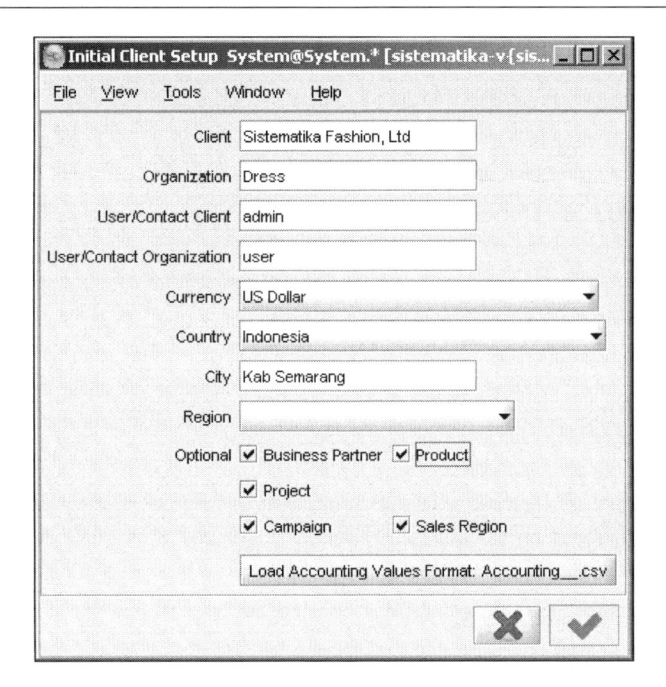

As you can see from the above screenshot, you have to enter the information shown in the following table:

| Field | Description |
| --- | --- |
| Client | Enter your company name. As per our sample apparel company structure, enter **Sistematika Fashion, Ltd** here. |
| Organization | We have three organizations. In this part, we will enter the first organization, **Dress**. We will enter other organizations later, after we have successfully created this client. |
| User/Contact Client | Here you can enter your user ID that has administrator rights. For simplicity, we put the default user ID **admin** here. Although we are not provided with a password for this user, ADempiere will provide a default password for this user, which is the same as the user ID name. You should change this default password immediately. It will also create template administrator roles based on these values. |
| User/Contact Organization | Set a regular user ID that holds restricted rights. Enter the user ID name **user** here. ADempiere will provide a default password for this user ID. The password is the same as the username. |
| Currency | This is the default currency for this company. This currency will be used as the standard currency in the ADempiere accounting schema. Set the currency you wish. In this book, we will choose **US Dollar** as our company currency. |

*Exploring Company Structures and the Initial Client Setup*

| Field | Description |
|---|---|
| **Country** | Set your country for the company. |
| **City** | Set the city of your company. |
| **Region** | Set the region for your company. |
| **Optional** | This is used to define information about the accounting schema element as a part of our accounting dimension. For now, select **Business Partner, Product, Project, Campaign,** and **Sales Region**. |

Click on the **Load Accounting Values Format: Accounting__.csv** button. Select `AccountingUS.csv` from the `C:\Adempiere\data\import` folder, and click on **OK** to proceed with our initial client creation. Wait for a moment, and ensure that you get a successful client creation window, as shown in the following screenshot:

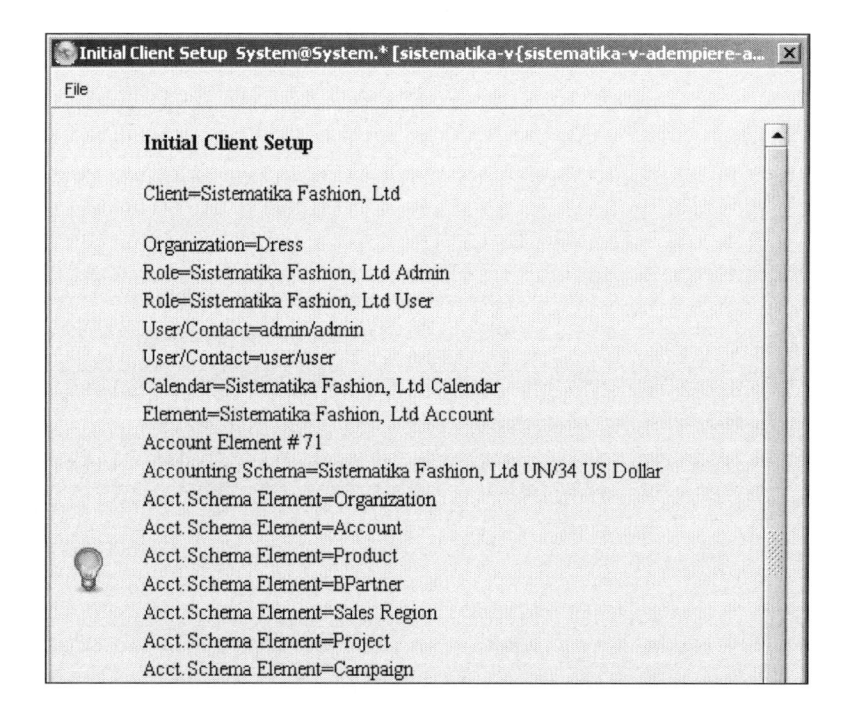

```
Initial Client Setup  System@System.* [sistematika-v{sistematika-v-adempiere-a...]
File

    Initial Client Setup

    Client=Sistematika Fashion, Ltd

    Organization=Dress
    Role=Sistematika Fashion, Ltd Admin
    Role=Sistematika Fashion, Ltd User
    User/Contact=admin/admin
    User/Contact=user/user
    Calendar=Sistematika Fashion, Ltd Calendar
    Element=Sistematika Fashion, Ltd Account
    Account Element # 71
    Accounting Schema=Sistematika Fashion, Ltd UN/34 US Dollar
    Acct.Schema Element=Organization
    Acct.Schema Element=Account
    Acct.Schema Element=Product
    Acct.Schema Element=BPartner
    Acct.Schema Element=Sales Region
    Acct.Schema Element=Project
    Acct.Schema Element=Campaign
```

If you are facing an error message such as **Error while creating the Accounting Setup,** you will have to re-check your `AccountingUS.csv` chart of accounts files. Make the appropriate changes, and then perform the initial client creation again.

> For our test, it is recommended to not alter the original `AccountingUS.csv` file. While using the original file, the initial client creation procedure can be done without any problems.

# Reviewing your new ADempiere client creation

With the successful creation of the Sistematika Fashion, Ltd. client, we can access this client as soon as possible.

> For our reference, when asked to *log in with user ID admin*, it means that you need to log in with your **admin** user ID, with the default password **admin**, click on the **Ok** button, set the role to **Sistematika Fashion, Ltd Admin**, client **Sistematika Fashion, Ltd**, and organization to **\***, and click on **Ok** once again.

*Log in with user ID admin*—The new client will show only three active tabs—**Menu**, **Workflow Activities**, and **Workflow**. The difference between GardenWorld and this one is that this client does not have a **Performance** tab. The newly-created Sistematika Fashion, Ltd. client by itself does not have any shortcut menu.

Open another ADempiere client instance, *log in to GardenWorld*, and perform a side-by-side comparison of the main tab and menu appearance.

For verification purposes, you can find the procedure in the **Menu | System Admin | Client Rules | Initial Client Setup Review** general workflow.

We can perform a client review by accessing the following list in the window:

- **Client**
- **Organization**
- **Role**
- **User**
- **Import File Loader**
- **Import Account**
- **Calendar Year and Period**

This is a standard workflow that comes with a default ADempiere installation. This is an example of what is referred to as a **general workflow**. Click on **Client** in this workflow, and you will be directed to the client window. We do not need to alter any information in this window.

# Setting additional organizations

We have one organization (**Dress**), one warehouse (**Standard**), and one locator (**Standard**) in the Sistematika Fashion, Ltd client at the moment. We need to add more organizations, warehouses, and locators to comply with our initial company structures. To proceed with this activity, you need to *log in with user ID admin* (remember to set **Organization** to *).

## Creating the organization type

We will set up a **Division** and **Sub Unit** organization type. Open the **Menu | System Admin | Organization Rules | Organization Type** window. Click on the **New** button, and complete the fields with the following information:

| Field | 1st record | 2nd record |
| --- | --- | --- |
| Client | Sistematika Fashion, Ltd | Sistematika Fashion, Ltd |
| Organization | * | * |
| Name | Division | Sub Unit |
| Active | select (default) | select (default) |
| Print Color | Black | Black |

Leave the other fields unchanged. Click on the **Save** button, perform the same tasks for the 2nd record, and finally we will have two records of organization type.

## Creating an additional organization

We are now at the stage where we can enter a new organization. Open the **Menu | System Admin | Organization Rules | Organization** window. This window contains three tabs—**Organization**, **Organization Info**, and **Org Assignment**.

Click on the **Organization** tab and then click on the **New** button. Set the value to **Shirt** in both the **Search Key** and **Name** fields. Ensure that the **Active** checkbox is selected, and then click on the **Save** button. When the system displays the **Do you want to save changes?** confirmation window, just click on the **OK** button.

Click on **New** once again, set the value to **Jacket** in both **Search Key** and **Name** fields, and click on the **Save** button to complete your additional organization.

## Updating organization information

In this subsection, we will update the existing organization info (**Dress**, **Shirt**, and **Jacket**), set the organization type to **Sub Unit**, and set your address to *organization name* **Facility Address**.

Ensure that you are on the **Organization** tab, and set the active records in **Dress** organization by clicking on **Dress** record, as shown in the following screenshot:

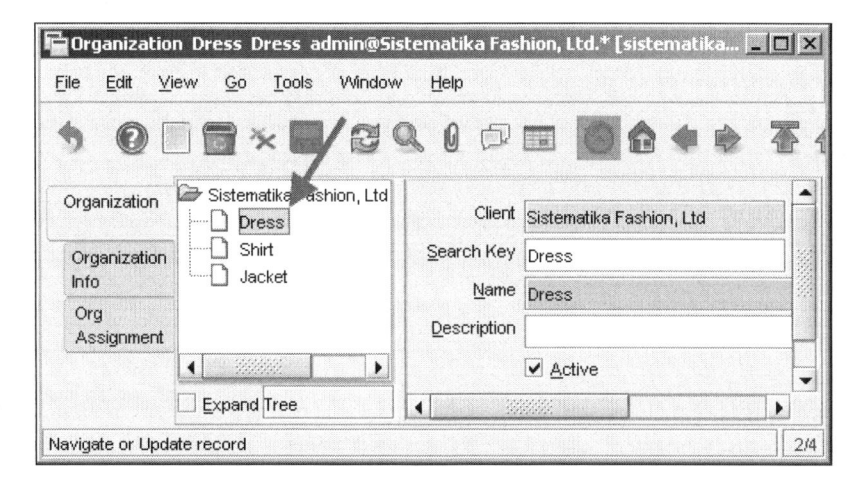

Click on the **Organization Info** tab and set **Organization Type** field to **Sub Unit**. Click on the **Address** field, complete the field with **Dress Facility Address**, click on the **OK** button to confirm your address information, and then click on the **Save** button. When the system shows the **Do you want to save changes?** confirmation window, just click on the **OK** button.

Set the **Organization Type** field to **Sub Unit** in both **Shirt** and **Jacket**. Set the address to **Shirt Facility Address** for the **Shirt** organization and **Jacket Facility Address** for the **Jacket** organization.

> In the **Do you want to save changes?** confirmation window, you will also be prompted to *re-login and restart your application server* for most changes made here to be effective. This is a normal confirmation and you can follow this suggestion after completing or altering all of your organization records.

# Setting up an additional warehouse

During client creation, the system provides us with one warehouse, named **Standard**, that contains one **locator** also named **Standard**.

> **Locator** is a place or a location to put our stuff such as raw materials and finished goods.

In your company structure illustration, there will be a total of four warehouses and seven locators.

## Altering the existing default warehouse and locators

Open the **Menu | Material Management | Material Management Rules | Warehouse & Locators** window. This window contains five tabs—**Warehouse**, **Locator**, **Storage**, **Replenish**, and **Accounting**. We will only be working with the **Warehouse** and **Locator** tabs at the moment. When you open this window, you will be redirected to the **Warehouse** tab with the **Standard** warehouse records. Perform the following steps:

1. Change the values of **Search Key** and **Name** fields from **Standard** to **1st Dress W/h**.
2. Click on the small button inside your **Address** field.
3. Set your address to **1st Dress W/h Address**.
4. Click on the **OK** button, and then click on the **Save** button.

Update **Standard** locator records, which are already linked with **1st Dress W/h** as follows:

1. Click on your **Locator** tab.
2. In the existing **Standard** locator record, change the value of the **Search Key** field from **Standard** to **Loc D1A**.
3. Click on the **Save** button.

One remaining activity is to add the locator **Loc D1B** to this warehouse. This is done as follows:

1. Click on the **New** button in the **Locator** tab.

   The default value for **Organization** field is **Dress** and **1st Dress W/h** for the **Warehouse** field. These values are automatically inserted and cannot be changed.

2. Set the **Search Key** field to **Loc D1B**, enter **1** in the **Aisle** field, and **0** in the **Bin** and **Level** fields.

3. Finalize your settings by clicking on the **Save** button.

> **Aisle**, **Bin**, and **Level** are more specific or detailed places inside a warehouse. We cannot set the same combination of value for aisle, bin, and level inside one warehouse. The system will automatically reject duplicate combination values of aisle, bin, and level inside a warehouse.

Thus, we now have a complete location for the **1st Dress** warehouse. Using this data, we can visualize our company structure, as shown in the next figure:

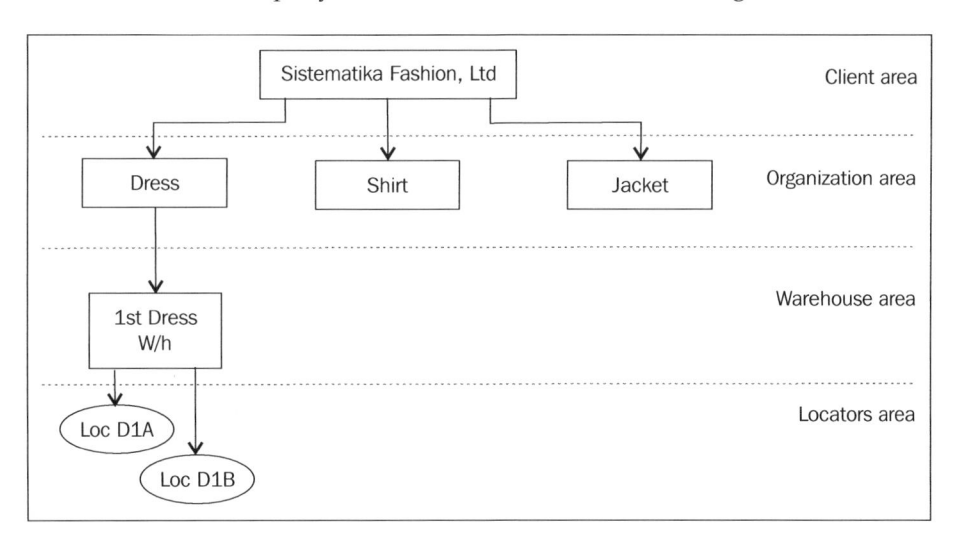

[ 77 ]

## Adding extra warehouses and locators

Adding an extra warehouse and locators is an easy task.

First, we need to define the additional warehouses. In the **Warehouse & Locators** window, ensure that we are on the **Warehouse** tab. The following information needs to be entered in the Warehouse tab fields:

| Field | 2nd record | 3rd record | 4th record |
|---|---|---|---|
| Organization (pick one from the list) | Dress | Shirt | Jacket |
| Search Key | 2nd Dress W/h | 1st Shirt W/h | 1st Jacket W/h |
| Name | 2nd Dress W/h | 1st Shirt W/h | 1st Jacket W/h |
| Address | 2nd Dress W/h Address, Country Indonesia | 1st Shirt W/h Address, Country Indonesia | 1st Jacket W/h Address, Country Indonesia |

Click on **New**, enter information for the 2nd record, and then click on the **Save** button. Perform the same steps for the 3rd and 4th records.

After adding additional warehouses, we need to supply their locators. We will add a locator for the **2nd Dress** warehouse. On the **Warehouse** tab, when you are not in grid mode, click on the **Grid Toggle** button. Ensure that your active record is in **2nd Dress W/h**. Click on the **Locator** tab, and enter the information as follows:

| Field | 1st record | 2nd record |
|---|---|---|
| Organization (automatically) | Dress | Dress |
| Warehouse (automatically) | 2nd Dress W/h | 2nd Dress W/h |
| Search Key | Loc D2A | Loc D2B |
| Default | *select* | *deselect* |
| Aisle | 0 | 1 |
| Bin | 0 | 0 |
| Level | 0 | 0 |

Leave the other fields unchanged. Click on the **New** button, complete the information fields for the 1st record, and then click on the **Save** button. Perform the same tasks for the 2nd record.

Next, we will add a locator for **1st Shirt** warehouse. On the **Warehouse** tab, ensure that your active record is in **1st Shirt W/h**. Click on **Locator** tab, click on **New**, and then enter the information for the 1st record, as shown in the table below:

| Field | 1st record |
| --- | --- |
| Organization (automatically) | Shirt |
| Warehouse (automatically) | 1st Shirt W/h |
| Search Key | Loc S1A |
| Default | select |
| Aisle | 0 |
| Bin | 0 |
| Level | 0 |

Leave the other fields unchanged. Click on **Save**.

And finally, we will add a locator for the **1st Jacket** warehouse. On **Warehouse** tab, ensure that your active record is in the **1st Jacket W/h**. Click on the **Locator** tab, click on **New**, and complete the information fields for the 1st record, as shown in the following table:

| Field | 1st record | 2nd record |
| --- | --- | --- |
| Organization (automatically) | Jacket | Jacket |
| Warehouse (automatically) | 1st Jacket W/h | 1st Jacket W/h |
| Search Key | Loc J1A | Loc J1B |
| Default | select | deselect |
| Aisle | 0 | 1 |
| Bin | 0 | 0 |
| Level | 0 | 0 |

Leave the other fields unchanged. Click on **Save**. Perform the same tasks for the 2nd record.

With all of the additional organizations, warehouses, and locators, we now have a complete company structure, as shown in the figure below:

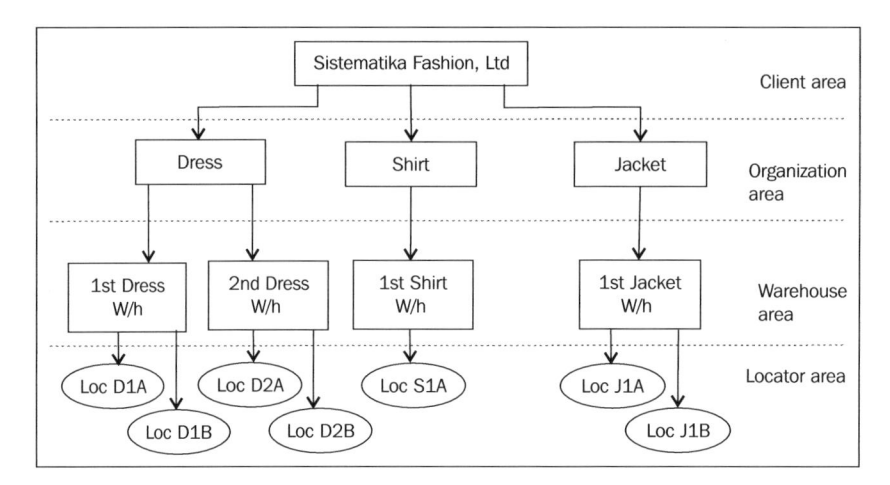

## Re-importing the chart of accounts

Now, the next important thing that needs to be done is **re-importing the chart of accounts**, along with **Import File Loader** and **Import Account**! During the *Initial Client Setup*, the system imported only 71 default accounts. Complete list of accounts from predefined chart of accounts will be imported along with the File Loader and Account, and will be internally restructured and reconfigured by ADempiere.

Open the **Menu | Performance Analysis | Accounting Rules | Account Element** window. This window contains three tabs—**Element**, **Element Value**, and **Sub Account**, as shown in the following screenshot:

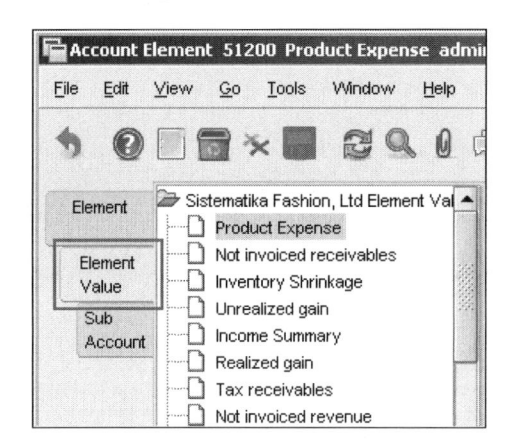

The previous screenshot shows the initial records, that is, the records before performing the re-importing activity.

## Import File Loader

As the `AccountingUS.csv` file is on the server computer, ensure that you perform this task on the server computer. Open the **Menu | System Admin | Data | Data Import | Import File Loader** window, and perform the following steps:

1. Click on the **Select File to Load** button.
2. Select the `C:\Adempiere\data\import\AccountingUS.csv` file.
3. Set **UTF-8** in the charset (located on the right-hand side of **Select File to Load** button). In the **Import Format** field, select **Accounting – Accounts** from the list.
4. Click on the **OK** button to proceed with re-importing task.
5. Wait for some time, and you will be prompted with the **Rows in file | loaded and ready to import** message.

Thus, the chart of accounts information will be now saved in the internal ADempiere temporary table that needs to be further processed, that is, by running Import Account.

## Import Account

Open the **Menu | System Admin | Data | Data Import | Import Account** window. As mentioned in the Record Info, it shows **1/362**, which means this window contains 362 records that need to be processed.

The first record is blank. There is no information in the **Search Key**, **Name**, and **Account Type**. These values come from the header information of your `AccountingUS.csv` file. Delete the blank record by clicking on the *F3* button. Finally, we will have only 361 records that need to be processed.

In the active records, the pointer should now be in account **1** (in the **Search Key** field) and have **Assets** value in its **Name** field, as shown in the following screenshot:

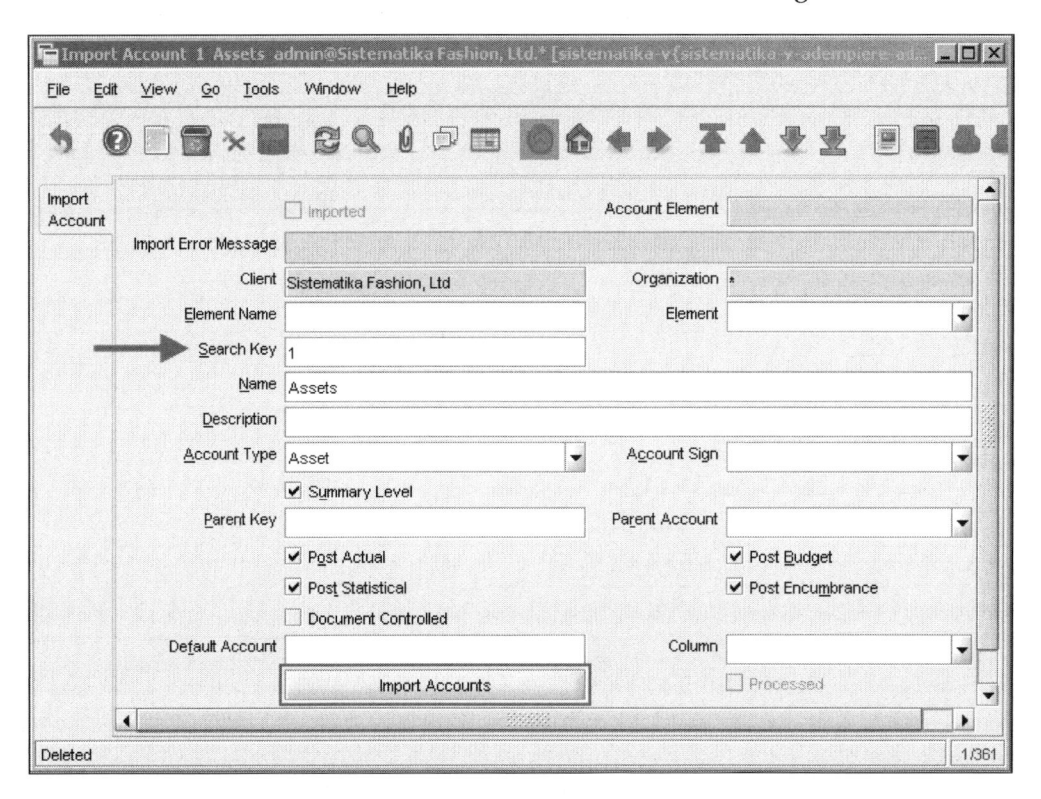

Click on the **Import Accounts** button. This will bring up an accounts confirmation window. Perform the following tasks:

- Enter **Sistematika Fashion, Ltd** in the **Client** field
- Enter **Sistematika Fashion, Ltd Account** in the **Element** field
- Select all of the **Update Default Accounts**, **Create New Combination**, and **Delete old imported records** options, and then click on the **OK** button

> Although we processed the first records, ADempiere automatically processes all of the unprocessed account records in this **Import Accounts** window.

Wait for some time, and it will bring up the screen shown in the following screenshot:

```
Import Accounts

0 Errors

290 Account Element: Inserted
71 Account Element: Updated
350 Parent Account: Updated
0 AcctSchema[1000000-Sistematika Fashion, Ltd UN/34 US Dollar]: Errors
0 AcctSchema[1000000-Sistematika Fashion, Ltd UN/34 US Dollar]: Updated
70 AcctSchema[1000000-Sistematika Fashion, Ltd UN/34 US Dollar]: OK
1 Acct.Schema Element: Updated
```

Ensure that we have **0 Errors** in this message.

> If you get an error message stating **1 Errors**, in the **Import Accounts** confirmation results window, it means that you might not have deleted the first blank account, as mentioned previously. Find the first record in this window. You will see an **ERR=No Name, ERR=No Key** message in the **Import Error Message** field. You are free to delete this record.

Now, open the **Account Element** window. Click on the **Element Value** tab, select the **Expand Tree** checkbox, and you will have a complete list of accounts that has been properly configured.

# Taking a look at the other configuration parts

There is so much stuff that is involved during the initial creation process. These can be either accounting configuration related, or entities such as calendar and periods, the standard user ID, default role and user ID rights, the standard ADempiere documents, and so on.

In this section, you will be introduced to the most important things to know.

# Accounting schema

Accounting schema is a standard for ADempiere, and is also the mother of all accounting configurations. This window will show a predefined **International GAAP** accounting **Generally Accepted Accounting Principles (GAAP)**, **Accrual** or cash-based accounting, **Standard Costing** for costing methods, **USD** as its base currency, **History** and **Future Days** for allowing document completions, and will define the standard accounts that can be used as default accounts (such as Product Asset, Product Revenue, and so on). This can be found on the **Defaults** tab.

The standard account values come from the predefined `AccountingUS.csv` chart of accounts mentioned earlier.

Open the **Menu | Performance Analysis | Accounting Rules | Accounting Schema** window. This window is shown in the following screenshot:

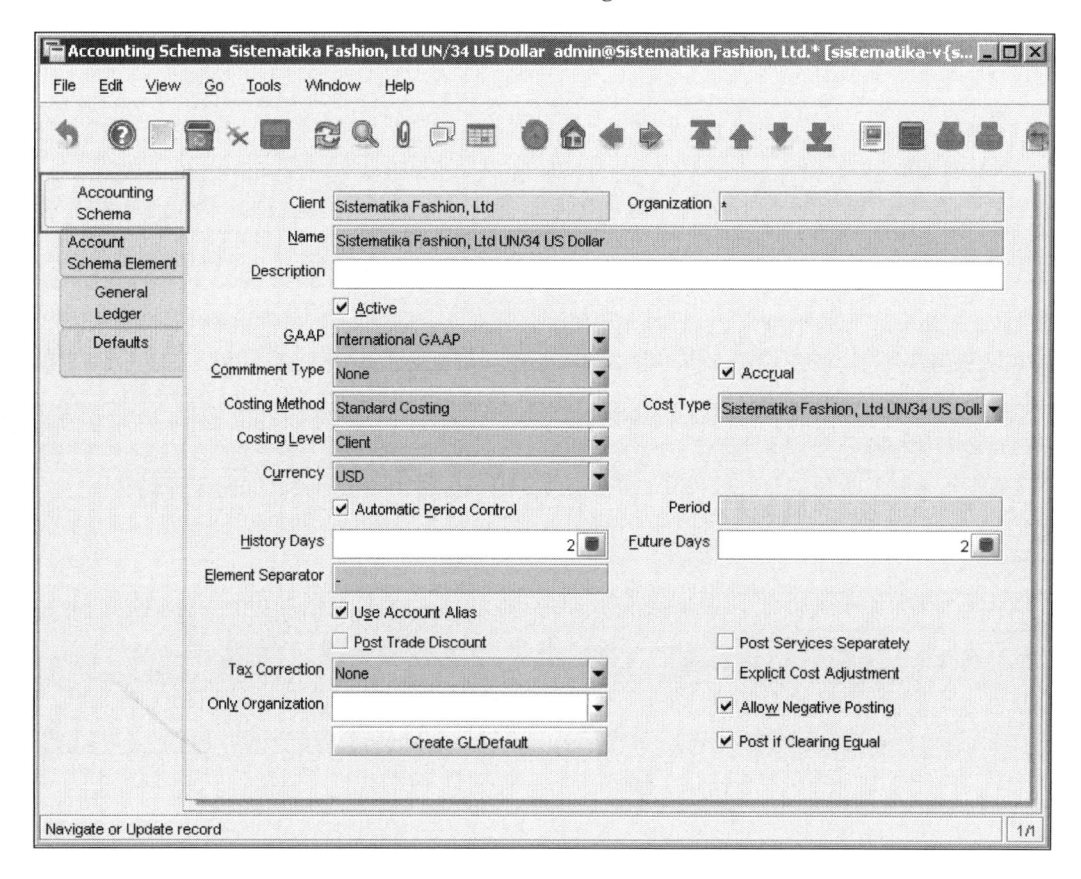

Once the accounting schema is configured, it is better if we do not change our configuration during the implementation of ADempiere ERP; especially for accrual or cash-based accounting, costing method, costing level, and currency info.

Although we can create or register more accounting schemas, throughout this book, we will use only the standard predefined accounting schema. We will discuss this accounting schema in more detail in Chapter 7, *Accounting Information and Configuration*.

# Calendar Year and Period

When creating a new client, ADempiere will create years and periods for you. When creating a client in the year 2009, internally ADempiere will create year 2009 and a list of periods from January to December. Open the **Menu | Performance Analysis | Accounting Rules | Calendar Year and Period** window. It will contain five tabs: **Calendar**, **Year**, **Period**, **Period Control**, and **Non Business Day**. You can check the generated calendar and periods data here.

## Creating a new year and periods

If you need to create a year and periods for the year 2010 (or another year), perform the following tasks:

1. Go to the **Year** tab.
2. Click on the **New** button, enter 2010 in the **Year** field, and save your work.
3. Click on the **Create Periods** button, and then click on the **OK** button in the confirmation window.

Examine the **Period** tab, and all of your defined periods should be present there.

## Opening document types

To open all of the document types for January 2009, click on the **Calendar** tab first, ensure that you have a record active at **Sistematika Fashion, Ltd Calendar** (this tab contains one record only), click on the **Year** tab, and lastly, click on year **2009**. Click on the **Period** tab, and select the **Jan-09** records. While you are in grid view mode, click on **Grid Toggle** button to switch to show the detailed information of any one record. You will find the **Open/Close All** button. Click on it, and enter **Open Period** in the list of the **Period Action** field, and click on the **OK** button.

Examine your period control by clicking on the **Period Control** tab, and you will get all of the document types that were set up to **Open** in the **Period Status** field.

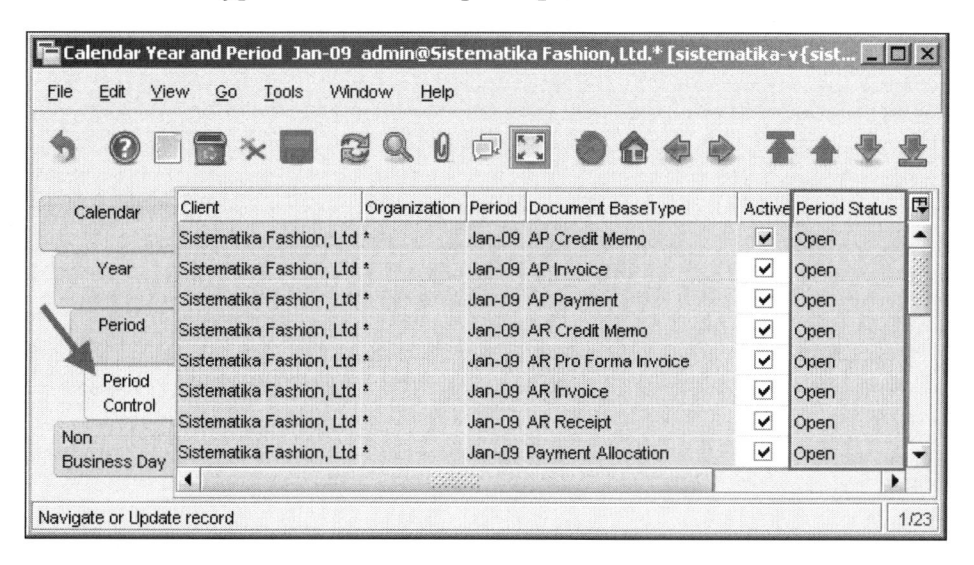

## Period Closed error message

*Guys, while playing with GardenWorld and creating a Sales Order, entering the data for both Order and Order Line went fine. The problem was, while attempting to 'Complete' this document, I got a Period Closed error message on the bottom left-hand side of the window. Can you help me with this issue?*

This is a general symptom when trying to complete a document. With a **Period Closed** message and accounting schema's **Automatic Period Control** checkbox selected, it could mean one of the following:

- You have not opened (or closed) the periods for such a document type — in this case, it is the **Standard Order** document type
- You have not created a year calendar and the periods yet
- You are setting up your transactional date outside the **History Days** and **Future Days** field in the accounting schema.

If we are working on the first day of a New Year, it is a quite possible that our ADempiere administrator has not created the New Year's record in the **Calendar Year and Period** window yet. Any action attempting to complete a document will fail.

> When we create a New Year and a Period, although it mentions that the period has a **Never Opened** status on the **Period Control** tab, we can continue to complete a document. It is better if we mark all periods to **Close Period** by clicking on the **Open/Close All** button (in the **Period** tab), select **Close Period** from the **Period Action** field, and click on the **OK** button in the confirmation window. You can open the periods later when needed.

## Accounting processor

*After creating and completing a document, such as Purchase Order and MM Receipt, when we select Show Accounting Tabs in Tools | Preferences, we will find a Not Posted (not processed yet) button. If we click on this button, ADempiere will post this document. Do we need to click on this button in each of our document transactions?*

> **Posting document** is an ADempiere task to perform accounting activities such as creating the necessary accounting facts or General Ledger journals.

## Automatically posting documents

ADempiere has some features to automatically process and post documents that have an unposted status, without user intervention. Open the **Menu | System Admin | General Rules | Server | Accounting Processor** window. As a default, there will be one record with active status, blank **Accounting Schema**, blank **Table**, **Frequency Type** as **Hour**, and **Frequency** having value **1**, as shown in the next screenshot:

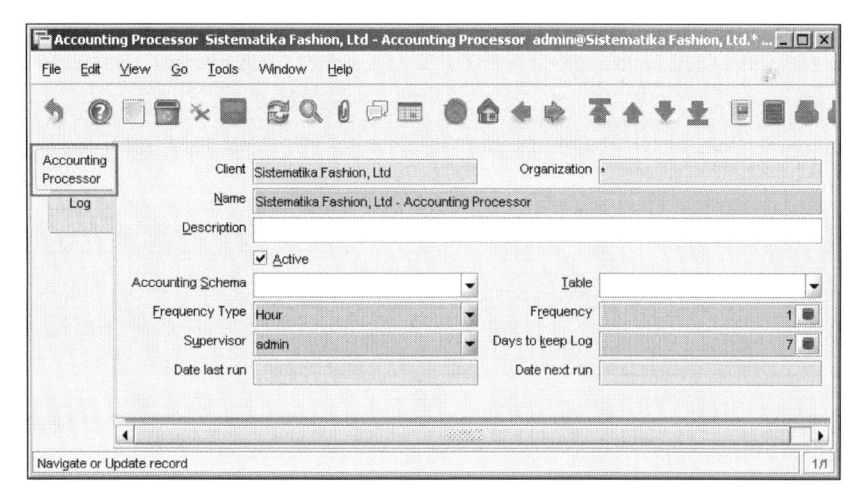

This information tells us that in every one hour, ADempiere server has a 'to do list' to post all of the un-posted documents that reside in all of the tables and all of the accounting schemas registered. Just ensure that you have already started your ADempiere server application, as mentioned in Chapter 1, *ADempiere Installation*. Then the accounting processor will work periodically for you behind the scene.

> Although we let the ADempiere system post our document automatically, until we reach Chapter 5, *Procurement Activities*, of this book, and for testing purposes, we need to know on what basis are the accounting facts (General Ledger journal) generated within the related document. To reach this goal, we need to set the accounting processor to an *inactive* status and post the document manually. Deselect the **Active** checkbox, and click on the **Save** button. Restart your ADempiere server to ensure that the server reads the latest accounting processor configuration.

## Common errors during manual posting

When practicing the posting of your document, sometimes you may get the message shown in the next screenshot:

This will be followed by a **Posting Error NoAppsServer** confirmation message. This means that you have not started your ADempiere server yet. Do not forget to start your ADempiere server. Wait until the application is ready, then log out and log back in to your ADempiere client, and finally you will be able to post your document.

# Summary

In this chapter, we saw the example of an apparel company structure. Before setting up our company structure, we discussed the concept of ADempiere company structures. Based on this information, we mapped the sample company structure within ADempiere.

While creating our own client, we needed to import a pre-configured chart of accounts. Before this activity, we learnt how to set up a chart of accounts in a standard ADempiere format by using the Account Editor tool, followed by the creation of our own client, and reviewing the new ADempiere client.

With the help of a sample company structure, we set up additional Organizations, Warehouses, and Locators. As ADempiere imported only the default accounts when creating a new client, we continued our activities by re-importing the chart of accounts.

We took a look at the preliminary information of Accounting Schema, Accounting Processors, and how to manage a calendar year and periods.

With this successful new client set up, we are ready to use our own client. In the next chapter, we will discuss how to set up the prerequisite data and its accounting configuration.

# 4
# Setting up Master Data and Knowing its Accounting Configuration

As we have a preconfigured company structure, ADempiere is ready for your test transaction. However, as we are using our own new ADempiere client—Sistematika Fashion, Ltd.—and are working with ADempiere windows such as Purchase Order, Sales Order, and so on, we will need to set up some master data. The examples of master data needed could be a list of products, a customer, a vendor, currency, bank account, cash book, and so on. We could also identify this master data as reference data.

In this chapter, you will be escorted through and learn how to set up, configure, and observe any existing accounting related information that is related to master or reference data. This chapter will introduce you to:

- Master or reference data accounting configuration parts
- Business Partners
- Bank and Cash books
- Multi-currency
- Price management
- Products

# Introduction to master data accounting configuration

When working with master or reference data, there is an **Accounting** tab within a window, which contains accounting configuration information. In order to become familiar with it, let us play with our Garden World client. *Log in to GardenWorld* with the user ID **GardenAdmin** and using **GardenWorld Admin** as the role. Make sure that you select the **Show Accounting Tabs** option in **Tools | Preference**.

# Example of a Product's accounting configuration

Open the **Menu | Material Management | Material Management Rules | Product** window. This window is the place to register your product. In this window, you can choose one of the available products to play with. Select **Azalea Bush** as your sample product.

For this product, navigate to its accounting configuration parts by clicking on the **Accounting** tab. This contains many default account configurations, which are used by the **Azalea Bush** product. The list of information in this tab is as follows:

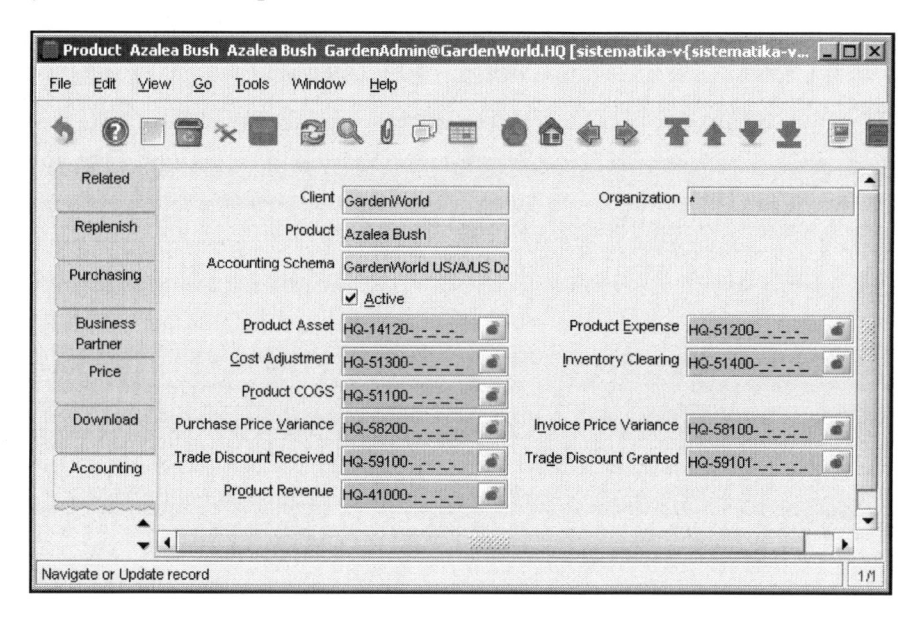

*Chapter 4*

In the previous screenshot, the Product Asset's default account uses the HQ-14120-_-_-_-_ account combination. Observe the other products and examine their **Accounting** tab. Although the tab has the same information (for now), each product actually has its own accounting configuration parts, as shown in the following figure:

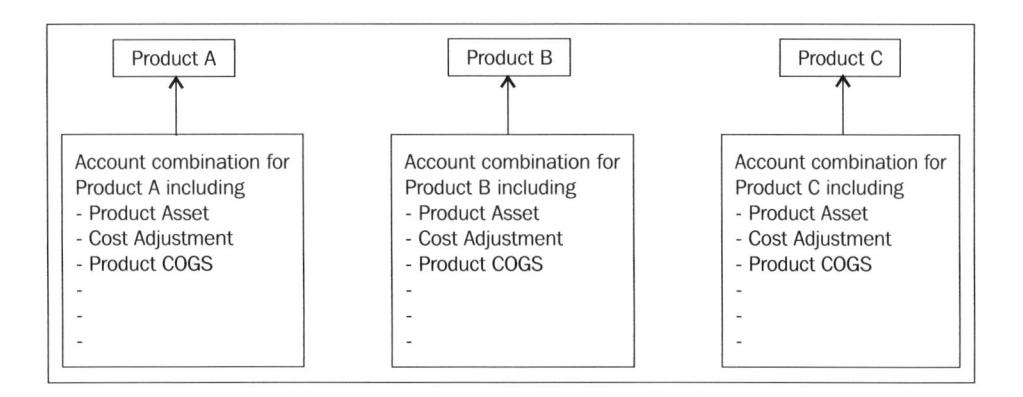

With this feature, you can configure your accounting configuration parts on a per-product basis!

## The meaning of HQ-14120-_-_-_-_

*Yes, I am familiar with Product Asset, Product COGS, and so on. I just want to know more about the Account format in this tab. Previously, we had a list of accounts, which contained numbers such as 14120, 51300, 51100, and so on. Could you give me a better explanation of what HQ-14120-_-_-_-_ for a Product Asset means?*

You may have experience with other ERP or accounting packages. When entering a General Ledger journal transaction, generally, you have to enter the data for each of the account dimensions. Let's say, dimension 1 for account, dimension 2 for profit centre, dimension 3 for cost centre, dimension 4 for product, and so on. Refer to the encircled area in the following screenshot for a clearer picture:

With ADempiere, all of the dimension information is combined into a single data. The **HQ-14120-_-_-_-_** is an **account combination** of six dimensions, such as *organization*, *account*, *product*, *business partner*, *project*, and *campaign*. In this account combination example, it means the organization is **HQ**, account is **14120**, product is blank, business partner is blank, project is blank, and campaign is blank.

Do not worry about the blank information for now. If we have a transaction with a document such as **MM Receipt** (receiving material from vendor) for our products; information about the product, business partner, project, and campaign data will be provided automatically by the system, based on the information available in the **MM Receipt** document. This information will be reflected in the General Ledger journal generated upon posting the **MM Receipt** document.

This is just one example of accounting configuration for the **Product** window. In general, this concept will be applied to most of the ADempiere master or reference data. For another example, take a look at the **Menu | System Admin | Organization Rules | Bank** window. Select the **MoneyBank** record in the **Bank** tab. Then select a particular account from the **Account** tab, and navigate to the **Accounting** tab. Observe the predefined account combination for **Bank Asset**, **Bank In Transit**, **Payment Selection**, or other default accounts. As with Product, the **Accounting** tab information is unique for each bank **Account** record.

> With the GardenWorld client, the account combination (such as the previous example for Product Asset's default account) will have the format **HQ-14120-_-_-_-_** format. But with our new **Sistematika Fashion, Ltd** client, it will have a different format, such as **\*-14120-_-_-_-_**. The \* represents the Organization information. The real organization information will be entered based on the document transaction.

# Account combination

*We have already talked about the account combination. How do we configure or add the account combination itself?*

Before we set up an additional account combination, we have to think about the purpose of the newly-created account combination. Generally, all registered account combinations will be used for:

- Entering manual GL Journal transactions
- Replacing the default account's account combination (such as the Product Asset default account)

## Common rules when creating an account combination

When creating a new account combination to be used for manual GL Journal transactions, it is important that all of the accounts that are used with your newly created account combination, satisfy the following criteria:

- The account is not set to Summary Level
- The account is not set to Document Controlled

> For a list of accounts that do not have Summary Level and Document Controlled in their attributes, just re-observe your `AccountingUS.xls` file, or open your `AccountingUS.csv` chart of accounts file with your Account Editor tools. You can obtain this file from the `C:\Adempiere\data\import` folder.

When creating the new account combination that will be used to replace the default account's account combination, the account involved should have the following criteria:

- The account is not set to Summary Level
- The account is set to Document Controlled

We will practice creating our own new account combination in the subsequent sections.

## Creating a new account combination

There are two ways to create a new account combination:

- Through the Account Combination window
- Through the Account Dialog window

Let us practice using the **Account Combination** window. Open the **Menu | Performance Analysis | Accounting Rules | Account Combination** window. With this window, the default standard ADempiere installation does not give us the right to create a new account combination—you may have observed that the **New** button is disabled!

*Setting up Master Data and Knowing its Accounting Configuration*

*So, how can we add our new account combination when the system does not provide us with such a facility? Is there anything we need to know to perform this task?*

ADempiere contains many windows, which are already configured, in its application dictionary. The ADempiere window can be set up using an option from the list of available **Window Type** options:

- **Maintain**: This window allows the user to add or modify data. Most of the master or reference data will be maintained with a window that has this Window Type option. The examples of ADempiere windows that have this Window Type are: **Product**, **Bank**, and **Cashbook**.

- **Query Only**: This window just displays information. Any action to update or add data is prohibited. For example, the **Accounting Facts** and **Access Audit** windows.

- **Transaction**: This window is used for transactional purposes. For example, the **GL Journal**, **Purchase Order**, and **Material Receipt** windows.

The **Account Combination** window has a **Query Only** window type. To examine, *log in to System*, and using the **System Administrator** role, we will access our ADempiere **Application Dictionary** configuration for the **Account Combination** window.

Open the **Menu | Application Dictionary | Window, Tab & Field** window, or just click on the **Window, Tab & Field** shortcut menu. In the **Lookup Record** (search dialog) window, fill the **Name** field with the value **Account Combination%**, and click on either **OK** or the **Query Enter** button. While you are in the grid mode, click on the **Grid Toggle** button to show the detailed records, as shown in the following screenshot:

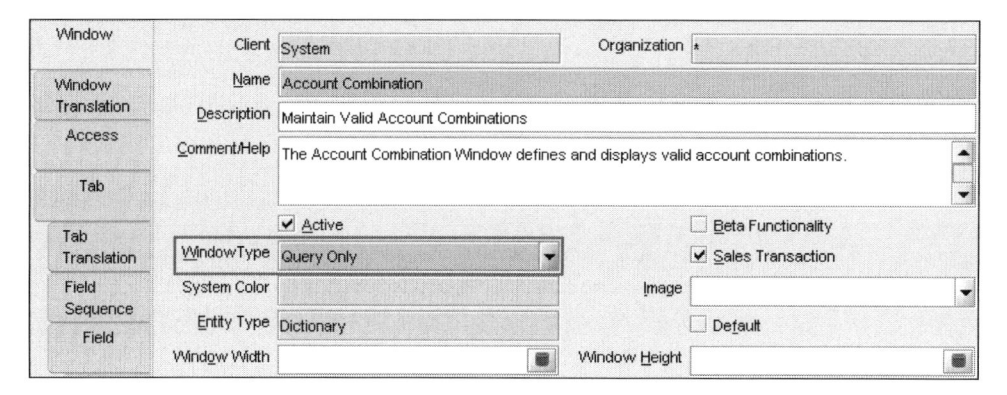

With this information, just place the cursor in the **Window Type** field, and select **Maintain** as the new Window Type. Save the information, and close this window. With this new configuration, the **Account Combination** window will be able to create new data. Now, log out from the application.

*As explained, with this small ADempiere application dictionary change, we will be able to create a new account combination. Could you please help me in the creation of an account combination?*

*Log in to GardenWorld*, using user ID **GardenAdmin**, and **GardenWorld Admin** as the role. Open the **Menu | Performance Analysis | Accounting Rules | Account Combination** window. We will practice making a combination for the **64500 - Other Consulting Fees** account. Click on the **New Record** button, and enter the following information:

| Field | Information |
| --- | --- |
| Alias | 64500 |
| Organization | HQ (in the option it is HQ-HQ) |
| Account | 64500 |

When entering the **Account** information, just type **64500**, and press the *Tab* key. The system will show an **Info Account Element** window. In this window, we can search for our target account by just typing the account number in the **Key** field. Make sure that you have **Other Consulting Fees** in the **Name** field and then just click on the **OK** button. Leave the **Product**, **Business Partner**, **Project**, and **Campaign** fields blank, and save the information.

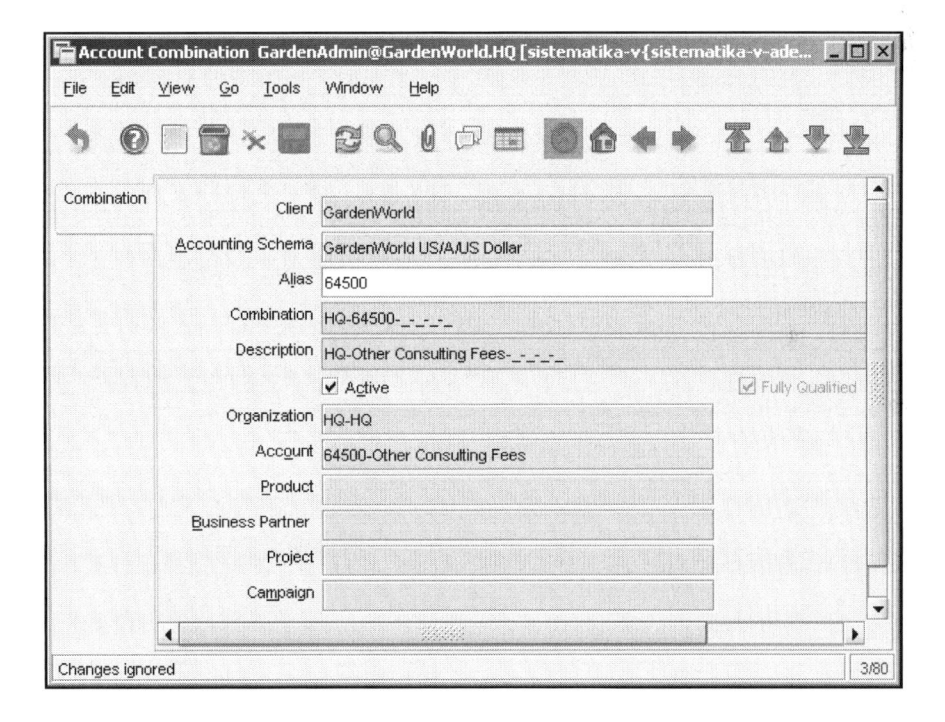

By performing this activity, we have created a new **HQ-64500-_-_-_-_** account combination with the alias **64500**. You can now use this account combination for your transactions. You could similarly create another account combination as per your requirements.

> Beware! Although we have already created a **HQ-64500-_-_-_-_** account combination, we could still create the same account combination again. To avoid any confusion, just ensure that you are not creating a duplicate account combination. Once a duplicate account combination has been created, you cannot delete this information. Instead, you need to set it to inactive by deselecting the **Active** checkbox, in the account combination is no longer used.

# Changing the account combination of the ADempiere default account

Changing an account combination for the ADempiere default account, such as the **Product Asset (B_ASSET_ACCT)**, **Not-invoiced Receipts (NOTINVOICEDRECEIPTS_ACCT)**, and other default accounts, is a simple task. For our simulation, we will change the **Product Asset** default account set up for one of our products from **HQ-14120-_-_-_-_** to **HQ-17710-_-_-_-_**.

## Account alias

*I examined all of the data inside the Account Combination window. Except for the newly created account combination, the account combination does not contain alias information. What is the exact purpose of alias information?*

Alias information is used for faster searching of an account combination. Therefore, it can speed up our data entry. For your reference, find **HQ-17710-_-_-_-_** in an **Account Combination** window (you can utilize **Lookup Record**, and enter **HQ-Project%** in the **Description** field). In the information within this window, set the **Alias** to **17710**, and save your changes. We will call this account combination using its alias in the subsequent section.

## Altering the Product Asset default account

Open the **Menu | Material Management | Material Management Rules | Product** window.

In order to have a sample product to work with, pick **Azalea Bush** as your target product, and perform the following tasks:

- From the tabs available in the **Product** window, click on the **Accounting** tab. On the right-hand side of the **Product Asset** field, click on the small red button. The system will show you an account combination's **Product Asset** window (we could also call this window as the **Account Dialog** window).

- In this window, find out and click on the **Undo changes** button (number **2** in the following screenshot). Now move your pointer to the **Alias** field, and type **17710**, and then click on the **ReQuery** button (number **1** in the following screenshot) to show a valid combination for the HQ organization and the 17710 account.

We will now have an active window, as shown in the following screenshot:

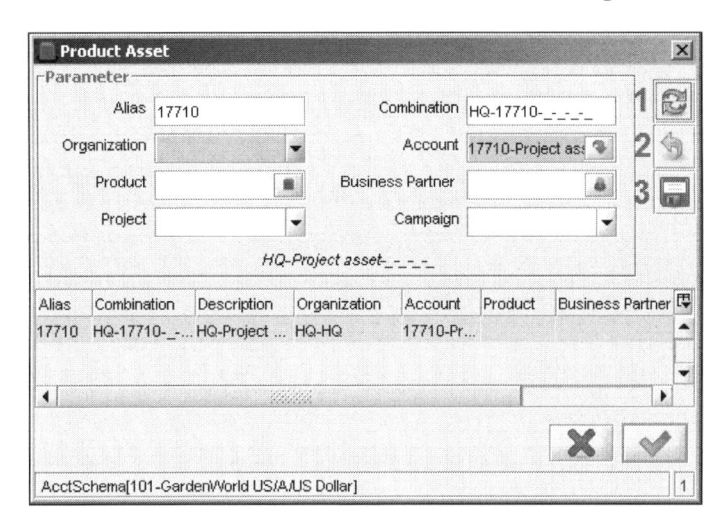

Within this **Account Dialog** window, click on the **OK** button, and (right now) your **Product Asset** field has already been set to the **HQ-17710-_-_-_-_** account combination. In order to finalize your changes, click on the **Save** button in the **Accounting** tab.

> In the **Account Dialog** window, you can also create your new account combination. Click on the **Undo changes** button, search for your target account, set your account **Alias** and **Organization**, and then click on the **Save** button (number **3** in the previous screenshot). Your new account combination can now also be accessed in the **Account Combination** window.

## Managing a Business Partner

With other proprietary ERP systems, if a third party such as a customer, vendor, or employee has a relationship with the company, then information related to the third party will be set up in a certain window. It is up to the ERP system to handle this data and manage the third-party data effectively.

ADempiere has a different approach to managing its customer, vendor, and employee information. In general, they all have the same data characteristics or attributes such as name, addresses, tax identity, and so on. If there is any specific information required, then ADempiere will have a special tab to set this information. With this flexibility, we can enter our customer, vendor, and employee information into just one centralized window called **Business Partner**.

In this window, we can set a third party to become:

- Either a customer or a vendor
- Both a customer and a vendor
- A customer, a vendor, and also an employee

Thus, we can eliminate third-party data duplication.

## Business Partner Group

During the creation of a business partner, we can group several business partners into one business partner group. *Log in with user ID admin*, open the **Menu | Partner Relations | Business Partner Rules | Business Partner Group** window. This window contains three tabs: **Business Partner Group**, **Accounting**, and **Assigned Partners**.

## Grouping criteria

You can define a type of business partner group by yourself. For example, it can be divided into Retail Customers, Wholesale Customers, VIP Customers, and so on. Using this scenario, we can set up a business partner relationship, as shown in the following diagram:

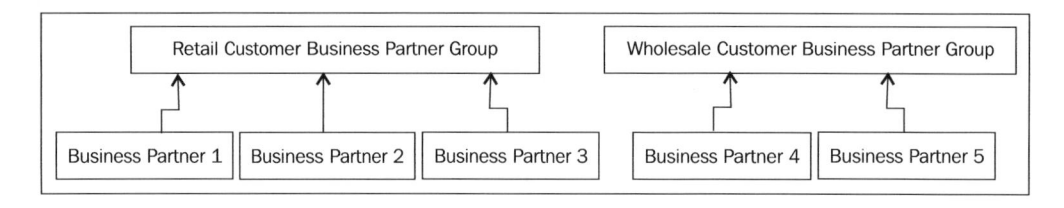

In this diagram, business partners **1**, **2**, and **3** will be grouped into the **Retail Customer Business Partner Group**, whereas business partners **4** and **5** will be grouped into the **Wholesale Customer Business Partner Group**.

> You can specify a unique business partner group to achieve your specific goal.

## Accounting configuration

With the availability of the **Accounting** tab, we can define accounting configuration in the business partner group. The accounting can be categorized into two parts for the default account as follows:

- Shared default account
- Private default account

*Shared default account* means that the default account value will be used, and it will become the reference account combination for all of the business partners connected to this business partner group. You can set up and change this default account's account combination value only in the **Accounting** tab of the **Business Partner Group** window.

*Private default account* means that the default account value will be used, and it will become the reference account combination to specific business partners.

> Although you can set up and change the private default account's account combination value (both on the **Business Partner Group** and the **Business Partner** window), it is advisable that you set your changes only in the **Accounting** tab of the **Business Partner** window.

The list of shared default accounts can be found in the sections highlighted in the following screenshot:

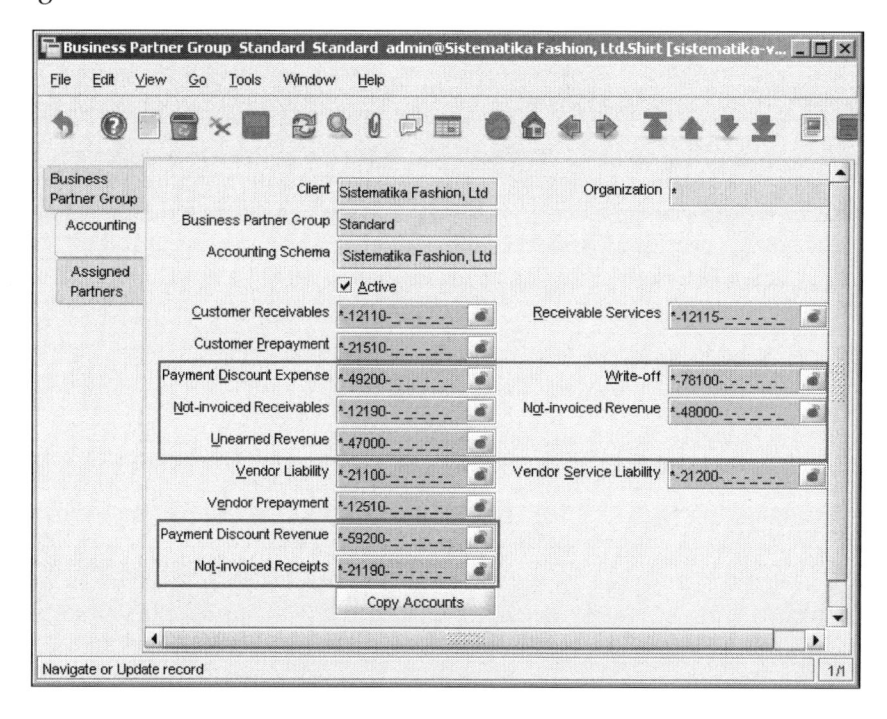

**Customer Receivables**, **Receivable Services**, **Customer Prepayment**, **Vendor Liability**, **Vendor Service Liability**, and **Vendor Prepayment** are categorized as private default accounts.

## Creating a new business partner group

With our newly-created client, ADempiere provides us with one business partner group named **Standard**, and three business partner data named **Standard** (as our business partner template data), **admin**, and **user**. The last two business partners are our predefined ADempiere user IDs, which act as an "employee" type of business partner.

You can create many business partner groups. For our reference transaction, in this book, we will create two types of business partner groups, namely, **Import** and **Local**. All of our business partners residing outside our country will be grouped into the **Import** business partner group. All of our business partners residing in our country will be grouped into the **Local** business partner group.

In the existing **Business Partner Group** window, on the **Business Partner Group** tab, we need to enter the following information:

| Field | 1st records | 2nd records |
|---|---|---|
| Search Key | Import | Local |
| Name | Import | Local |

> When entering the information into all of the master data, in this chapter, you should set the **Client** to **Sistematika Fashion, Ltd** and **Organization** to *.

Actually, there are many fields available in this tab. For our convenience, we will enter the information for the two fields mentioned, and leave the rest as it is.

> When setting up or entering information into all of the ADempiere windows, there will be many fields that can be filled or set up. There are some color indicators, which will help us when entering information into these fields. All fields that are red, are mandatory fields and yet do not have a value entered. The fields that are blue are mandatory fields, which already have a value assigned. Fields which do not have a blue or red color assigned, can be filled with a value specified by you, or can be left blank.

# Business Partner

Manufacturing garments such as shirts will require several raw materials. The types of materials include fabrics, buttons, threads, labels, and so on. Sistematika Fashion, Ltd. has to buy materials from several vendors. When the finished goods are ready, the company will ship these goods to the customers. We need to set these vendors and customers up using the **Business Partner** window.

Open the **Menu | Partner Relations | Business Partner Rules | Business Partner** window. We will learn how to set up both the vendor and the customer information in the following sections.

## Registering a new Vendor

We will set up the following information in the **Business Partner** tab:

| Field | Description |
|---|---|
| Search Key | Hempel China Limited |
| Name | Hempel China Limited |
| Description | Fabric Supplier |
| Business Partner Group | Import |

## Setting up Master Data and Knowing its Accounting Configuration

After saving this information, perform the following tasks:

- Navigate to the **Vendor** tab, and select the **Vendor** checkbox; leave the rest as it is, and save this information. Here, we are setting this business partner as a vendor.

- Navigate to the **Location** tab. Here, we need to set up the vendor's address. Click on the **New** button, and then click on the button inside the **Address** field. Enter the value **Sample of street** in the **Address 1** field, **Ningjin** in the **City** field, and set the **Country** field to **China**. Click on the **OK** button, and then click on the **Save** button.

- Navigate to the **Contact (User)** tab. Here, you can specify your vendor's marketing people. Click on the **New** button, enter the value **Gong Li** in the **Name** field, and save this information.

Perform the same set of tasks for the following list of vendors. Ensure that you select the **Vendor** checkbox in the **Vendor** tab:

| Field | 2nd record | 3rd record | 4th record |
|---|---|---|---|
| Search Key | Ching Fung Apparel Accessories Co, Ltd | Coats and Clarks | Wilson Garment Accessories, Ltd |
| Name | Ching Fung Apparel Accessories Co, Ltd | Coats and Clarks | Wilson Garment Accessories, Ltd |
| Description | Buttons Supplier | Threads Supplier | Labels Supplier |
| Business Partner Group | Import | Import | Import |
| Address 1 | Street in Kowloon | Street in California | Street in Kowloon |
| City | Kowloon | California | Kowloon |
| Country | Hong Kong | United States | Hong Kong |
| Contact (Users) | Susan | Hillary | Andrew |

> You can enter more than one address to register the shipping address, invoice address, pay from address, and remit to address, of these vendors in the **Location** tab. Select the appropriate checkboxes to fulfill your needs.

Now, we should check the accounting configuration applicable for the Vendor type of business partner.

## Vendor accounting configuration

You can select the **Vendor Accounting** tab, and examine the account combination sets in its default account. Here, you will find the default account applicable (as a part of our private business partner default accounts) for the Vendor type of business partner, as highlighted in the following screenshot:

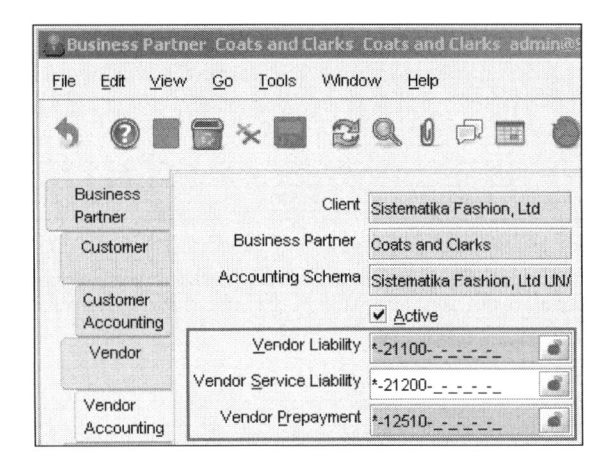

Now, all of the information required for the vendors has been set up. We will now continue with our activity by setting up a Customer type of business partner.

## Registering a new Customer

We will set up the following information in the **Business Partner** tab:

| Field | Description |
|---|---|
| Search Key | Liz Claiborne Inc |
| Name | Liz Claiborne Inc |
| Business Partner Group | Standard |

Save the information, and continue with the following tasks:

1. Navigate to the **Customer** tab, and select the **Customer** checkbox; leave the remaining fields as they are, and then click on the **Save** button. With this activity, we have set this business partner as a customer.

2. We need to set the customer address. Navigate to the **Location** tab, click on the **New** button, and then click on the button inside the **Address** field. Enter **Sample of street** in the **Address 1** field, **New York** in the **City** field, and set the **Country** field to **United States**. Click on the **OK** button, and then click on the **Save** button.

3. Navigate to the **Contact (User)** tab. You can set your customer's representative here. Click on the **New** button, enter the value **Paul** in the **Name** field, and save this information.

We will now check the Customer accounting parts.

## Customer accounting configuration

Observe the **Customer Accounting** tab. There is a list of private default accounts, that will be used for this Customer type of business partner, as shown and highlighted in the following screenshot:

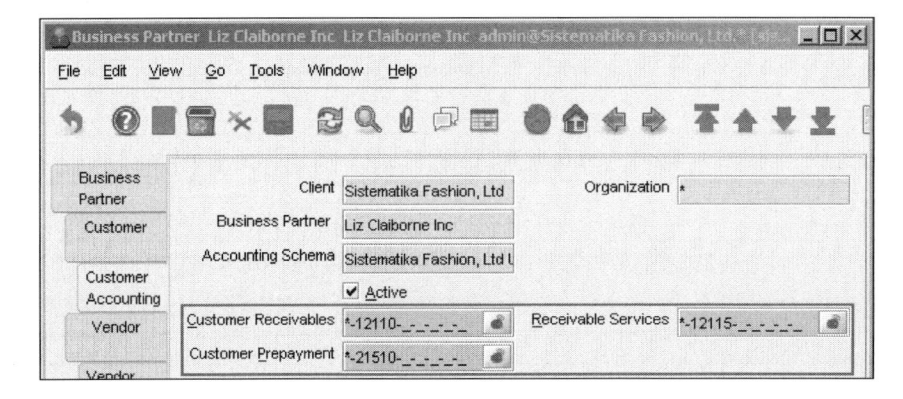

![Customer Accounting tab screenshot]

# Company financial management

> *Most companies have at least one bank account and one petty cash fund to record and support their business activities. It seems that we need to register our bank account and petty cash master data in the system. Could you show me the ADempiere feature to manage both, the bank account and petty cash transactions?*

To handle your needs, ADempiere can definitely help you manage your bank account and its activities. It also provides support to record your petty cash transactions. Here, we need to set up both, a bank account and the petty cash master data. There is no limitation in terms of how many bank accounts and petty cash accounts can be set up in the system.

In this section, you can play with and examine the accounting configuration for both the bank account and petty cash accounts.

# Managing your bank information

You can set up your bank account by navigating to the **Menu | System Admin | Organization Rules | Bank** window. This window contains six tabs: **Bank, Account, Bank Account Document, Payment Processor, Statement Loader**, and **Accounting**.

Use the following procedure to enter your bank information:

- Enter the bank name into the **Bank** tab. Feel free to set up multiple bank name records here.
- Enter your bank account into the **Account** tab. Here, you can save more than one bank account.
- Set your bank account document. In this record, we will define the standard printing document for *cash*, a *bank check*, and other payment document rules. You could also set up many bank account documents.
- With the selected bank account, you can open the **Accounting** tab to check your accounting configuration.

## Registering your bank information

Enter the bank information in the **Bank** tab as follows:

| Field | Value |
|---|---|
| Name | Citibank |
| Own bank | *deselect* |
| Routing No | 000001 |

*With this bank, we have two accounts, one in USD currency and the second one in IDR currency. Both of these accounts are checking accounts. Could you help me configure these accounts?*

With the current active Citibank record, go to the **Account** tab, and enter the following information:

| Field | 1st records | 2nd records |
|---|---|---|
| Organization | Shirt | Shirt |
| Account no | USD-1-001-888888 | IDR-2-001-999999 |
| Currency | USD | IDR |
| Bank Account Type | Checking | Checking |

> There is no * option in the organization list. Here, we set **Shirt** as our organization.

## Registering a bank account document

Now, we will continue to enter our bank account document.

In the **Account** tab, select the **USD-1-001-888888** account number, and navigate to the **Bank Account Document** tab. With this example, we are just trying to utilize a bank check document. We will set up following information:

| Field | Value | Description |
|---|---|---|
| Name | Check document | |
| Payment Rule | Check | Pick from the available options |
| Check Print Format | PaySelection_Check ** Template ** | Pick from the available options |

Save this information. Perform the same tasks for the **IDR-2-001-999999** account number. We now have a bank account in this system.

> This record is mandatory and should be used when printing a bank account document.

## Bank account configuration

With your **USD-1-001-888888** bank account number, you can examine its accounting configuration in the **Accounting** tab. There is a list of default accounts that will be used for this bank account, as highlighted in the following screenshot:

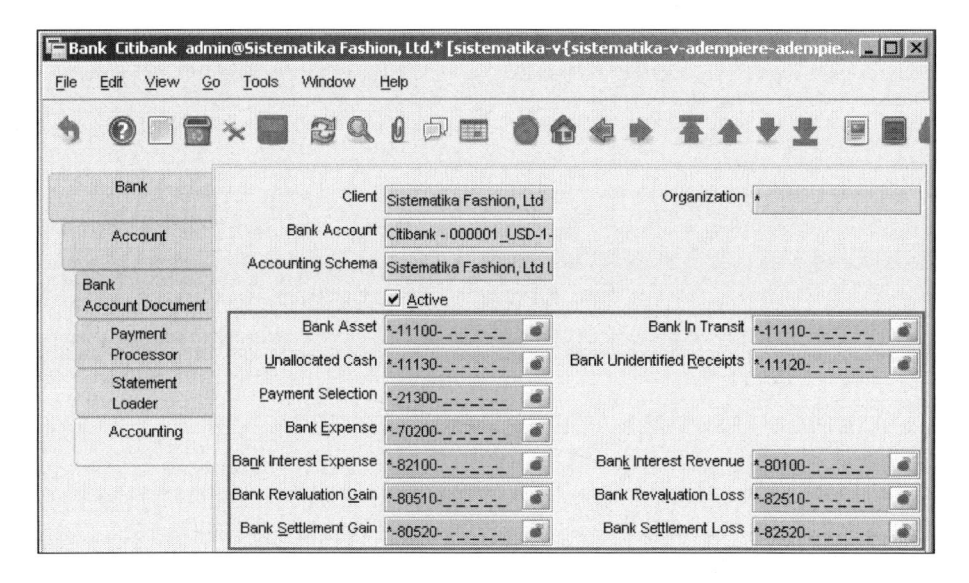

We have completed the configuration of our bank accounts and will now continue with the set up and configuration of petty cash accounts in the system.

## Managing a Cash Book

To book a transaction related to direct cash owned by the company, such as buying sugar for employees' coffee or tea, lunch for company guests, or any other type of expenses, we shall record this kind of a transaction in the Cash Book feature provided by ADempiere.

## Configuring your own cash book

Prior to utilizing this feature, you have to know how to set up your cash book in the system. Open the **Menu | System Admin | Organization Rules | Cashbook** window. With your new client installation, ADempiere comes with a default cash book set up named **Standard**.

The default cash book configuration uses **USD** as a default currency. The **USD** comes from our default currency, which was configured previously during the ADempiere client creation. Rename your cash book name from **Standard** to **USD Cash Book**.

To register another transaction in the IDR currency (in case we use currencies other than USD), we need to create another type of cash book. You can set the following information:

| Field | Value |
|---|---|
| Organization | Dress |
| Name | IDR Cash Book |
| Currency | IDR (pick from an available option) |

Save this information. Now, you have two cash books to work with.

## Cash book accounting configuration

Take a look at the list of default accounts listed in the **Accounting** tab for the **USD Cash Book**, as shown in the following screenshot:

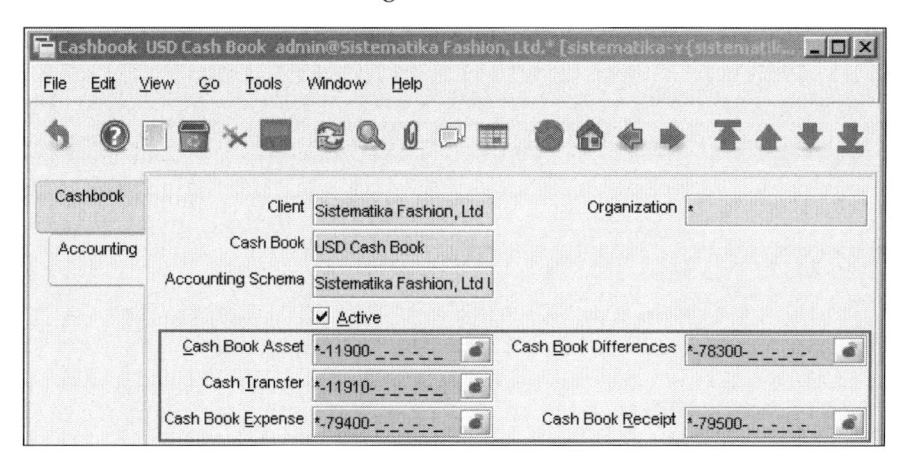

When utilizing this Cash Book feature, we can divide our transaction into two transaction types:

- General expenses
- General receipts

When working with these types of transactions in the **Cash Journal** window, posting this document will generate the accounting facts/GL journal format, as shown in the following table:

| No | Description | Db | Cr |
| --- | --- | --- | --- |
| 1 | General Expenses | Cash Book Expense (*-79400-_-_-_-_-) | Cash Book Asset (*-11900-_-_-_-_-) |
| 2 | General Receipts | Cash Book Asset (*-11900-_-_-_-_-) | Cash Book Receipt (*-79500-_-_-_-_-) |

# Introduction to Charge

*Currently, we have a specific account to determine the type of expenses. For example, we have an account for Postage, Newspaper, Bank Charges, Vendor Charges, Handling Charges, and so on. We are using these samples of accounts when entering petty cash transactions. With the prior information provided, the standard cash book General Expense transaction will be directed to the 79400 account. How can we allocate such transactions to the proper account?*

Yes, you can still create that type of transaction using the ADempiere cash book. When you have a specific cash book requirement, instead of using **General Expense**, there is an option to use **Charge** while working with the **Cash Journal** window.

> We can use **Charge** as an alternative that can be used to map an expense or even receipt allocation.

## Preparing new account combinations for Charge

You need to prepare an account and create a new account combination prior to creating your Charge. With the standard ADempiere chart of accounts available (taken from AccountingUS.csv), we can choose the following accounts when creating the upcoming account combination:

- 73100 as Postage Expense account
- 71200 as Subscription Fees account

Open **Account Combination** or your **Account Dialog** window, and create an account combination for both, the 73100 and 71200 accounts. Ensure that you set 73100 as an alias for the 73100 account combination, and 71200 as the alias for the 71200 account combination, as shown in the following table:

| Alias | Organization | Account |
|---|---|---|
| 73100 | Dress | 73100-Postage Expense |
| 71200 | Dress | 71200-Subscription Fees |

Next, we need to bind this account combination to the correct Charge's default account.

## Creating a new type of Charge

ADempiere provides the **Charge** window to define your own Charge. Here, you can create a list of charges that suit your needs. You can access this window from **Menu | Performance Analysis | Accounting Rules | Charge**.

I will now introduce you to the process of creating a sample of an ADempiere **Charge** for both **Postage** and **Newspaper**, using the following procedure:

1. Open the **Charge** window, click on the **New** button, and set the **Organization** field to **\***, the **Name** field to **Postage**, leave the rest as it is, and save this data.
2. Click on the **Accounting** tab. By default, the **Charge Expense** and **Charge Revenue** default accounts will be filled up with the 79600 and 79700 account combination. Click on the small button in the **Charge Expense** field. Within the upcoming **Account Dialog** window, create your new **73100** account combination. Click on the **OK** button in the **Account Dialog** window to set this new account combination to the **Charge Expense** default account. Set your **Charge Revenue** field to the **73100** account combination.
3. Go back to your **Charge** tab, click on the **New** button, and set the **Organization** field to **\***, the **Name** field to **Newspaper**, and then save.
4. Click on the **Accounting** tab. Create a new **71200** account combination, and set this new account combination to its **Charge Expense** and **Charge Revenue** default account.

With our newly-created **Charge** set up, our upcoming cash journal transaction involving the Postage and Newspaper types of charge will generate the accounting facts/GL journal, as shown in the following table:

| No | Description | Db | Cr |
| --- | --- | --- | --- |
| 1 | Postage | Postage Charge (*-73100-_-_-_-_-_) | Cash Book Asset (*-11900-_-_-_-_-_) |
| 2 | Newspaper | Newspaper Charge (*-71200-_-_-_-_-_) | Cash Book Asset (*-11900-_-_-_-_-_) |

# Using multiple currencies

> As seen previously, the ADempiere cash book can be set up not only for one currency, but also for more. It seems that ADempiere has a multi-currency feature. What is the most important point that we need to know when implementing a multi-currency transaction?

Like many standard ERP systems, ADempiere has an ability to handle multi-currency transactions. For the prerequisites, you have to know and configure the:

- Currencies that will be used
- Currency conversion type, such as Spot, Average, and so on
- Currency conversion rates

We will learn how to manage currencies in the following sections.

## Currency

Currently, you have two ADempiere clients in your system: Sistematika Fashion, Ltd and Garden World. While working with multiple clients, there is a standard feature to share information among the ADempiere clients. An example of shared information is Currency.

To access master data like currencies, ADempiere provides a pre-configured System client. There is an option to set up master or reference data in the System client. When setting up master data in the System client, this data should be available to all of your clients.

*Log in to System*, and set the role to **System Administrator**. In the main menu window, select the **Expand Tree** option. Open the **Menu | Performance Analysis | Accounting Rules | Currency** window. This window contains three tabs: **Currency**, **Accounting**, and **Conversion Rates**. With the **Currency** tab, you will be prompted with all of the registered standard currency information (in all, it's about 174 records!)

> For Currency code standardization, refer to http://www.iso.org/iso/support/currency_codes_list-1.htm.

### Deactivating unneeded currencies

> *I am logged in to GardenWorld. While working with a sample window, such as Menu | Open Items | Payment, it requires a Currency for the Payment transaction document. I clicked an option in the Currency field, and it shows us tons of currency options. Well, within our daily transactions, we utilize just four currencies: IDR, USD, EUR, and HKD. Can we restrict the options to just four currency codes?*

We can set a minimum list of currencies available for all of your transactions. If you are working with those four currencies only, you can inactivate all of the unneeded currencies. *Log in to System*, navigate to the **Currency** window, and deselect the **Active** checkbox for all of the unneeded currencies.

> Beware! These inactive currencies will not be available to any of your clients. Another way to restrict the list of currencies is by implementing the record access security rule. We will discuss this topic in Chapter 12, *Implementing Security*.

You can test the impact of inactivating currencies. *Log in with user ID admin*, open the **Payment** window, select the **Currency** field, and examine the result. The options will contain currency data, as shown in the following screenshot:

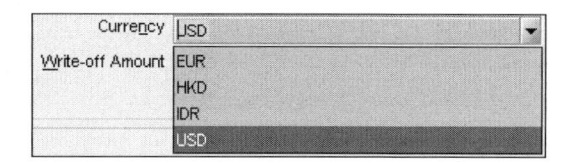

## Currency conversion rate types

When working with multi-currencies, we are faced with a lot of methods of conversion. For example, *Log in to System*, and open the **Menu | Performance Analysis | Accounting Rules | Currency Type** window. The predefined currency conversion types are **Average**, **Company**, **Period End**, and **Spot**.

These are just the predefined names of the available currency conversion types. You are free to add more conversion rate types to fulfill your needs. For common manufacturing companies in Indonesia, we are familiar with two such conversion types: **Daily** and **Weekly** rate. The Indonesian **Daily** rate type is similar to the **Average** type, while the **Weekly** rate type is an average of rates over a week. We will set up two of these rate types for our currency conversion rate type.

### Creating a new currency type

In the **Currency Type** window, enter the following information:

| Field | 1st data | 2nd data |
| --- | --- | --- |
| Search Key | D | W |
| Name | Daily | Weekly |
| Description | Average Daily rates | Weekly rates |
| Default | *select* | *deselect* |

For our upcoming test transaction, set the **Average**, **Company**, and **Period End** currency conversion rate type to inactive. Pay attention to the **Spot** currency type. Deselect the **Default** checkbox for this record.

With all of this activity, when working with a sample transaction such as Payment, the **Currency Type** options are similar to the options shown in the following screenshot:

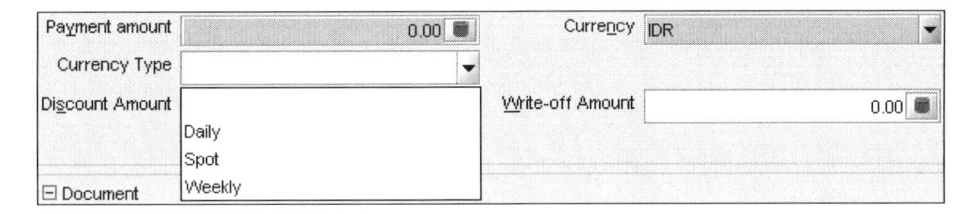

> With the current standard ADempiere configuration, the **Currency Type** field is available only if we use a document currency other than the accounting schema currency. In the previous example, we are using **IDR** currency in the document, while the default accounting schema currency is **USD**.

## Currency rates

After defining the currency conversion rate type, we need to enter the currency rates. Although we can set the rates in the System Client, we would prefer to set up the rates information in the target client.

### Entering new currency rates

*Log in with user ID admin*, and open the **Menu | Performance Analysis | Accounting Rules | Currency Rate** window. For simplicity, we will set up IDR rates against US$ 1, as shown in the following table:

| Date | Rate Type | IDR value |
|---|---|---|
| March 16, 2009 | Daily | IDR 10000 |

We enter the rate shown in the table by using the following procedure:

1. Click on the **New** button. Enter **IDR** in the **Currency** field, and **USD** in the **Currency to** field.

2. Select the **Active** checkbox, set the **Currency Type** to **Daily** and the **Valid from** field to **03/16/2009**.

3. Enter the value **10000** in the **Divide Rate** field, and press the *Tab* key. When you press the *Tab* key, the system will automatically fill in the value for the **Multiply Rate** field with **0.0001**. Save this information.

## Entering reciprocal rates

Although we have already entered the **IDR** to **USD** conversion rate, we also have to enter a *reciprocal rate* as a means of entering **USD** to **IDR** conversion rates. Enter the following information:

1. Click on the **New** button. Enter **USD** in the **Currency** field and **IDR** in the **Currency to** field.
2. Select the **Active** checkbox, set the **Currency Type** to **Daily** and the **Valid from** field to **03/16/2009**.
3. Enter the value **10000** in the **Multiply Rate** field, and press the *Tab* key. When you press the *Tab* key, the system will automatically fill the value for the **Divide Rate** field with **0.0001**. Save this information.

After completing these activities, we can use this currency information for future transactions. Next, we will learn about how to manage product prices.

# Price management

> *Generally, while talking about the product price, we could categorize or divide it into two parts: purchasing and sales price. This is just an example. We can add an additional type of price. I am wondering how I can manage the purchase and sales prices with ADempiere.*

During the creation of both the **Purchase Order** and **Standard Order** documents, ADempiere requires a price list. With this requirement, logically, we have to set up a price list.

ADempiere products require a **List Price**, **Standard Price**, and **Limit Price** as part of their price list's information. The following is the meaning of the price list's parts associated with sales price:

- **List Price**—is the recommended retail price.
- **Standard Price**—is the standard price we sell at.
- **Limit Price**—is a price limit that we will sell our products at. We cannot sell our products below this price.

Using the sales price list, the value taken from the **List Price** will be used when creating a Standard Order document. With this document, we can offer a discount price with the value taken from the **Standard Price**. For our loyal customers, we can offer a very competitive price, which is taken from the **Limit Price**.

There are three ADempiere windows in relation to the price list. They are **Price List Schema**, **Discount Schema**, and **Price List**.

When configuring our product prices, we need to:

- Create one or more **Price List Schema**. In the schema line, we configure the **List Price**, **Standard Price**, and **Limit Price**.
- Create one or more **Price List** instances. Each **Price List** can contain one or more **Price List Version** instances.
- Define and configure the **Price List Version**. You need to set up the **Price List Schema** as part of its information.

Continuing our configuration, we will follow the previous procedure and create a sample **Price List Schema** in the subsequent section.

## Managing Price List Schema

*Log in with user ID admin*, and open the **Menu | Material Management | Material Management Rules | Price List Schema** window. This window contains two tabs: **Price List Schema** and **Schema Line**. ADempiere has a default **Price List Schema** named **Standard**. At the moment, this price list schema data does not have **Schema Line** information.

> We can utilize **Schema Line** to set up and manage an intermediate price list configuration. With **Schema Line**, we can automatically calculate the product's **Standard Price** and **Limit Price** value, based on the product's **List Price** information. An example of a **Schema Line** implementation is covered in the *The Price tab* section of this chapter.

### Registering a new price list schema

In the **Price List Schema** tab, enter the following information:

| Field | 1st data | 2nd data |
|---|---|---|
| Name | Purchase Schema | Sales Schema |
| Valid from | 03/01/2009 | 03/01/2009 |
| Discount Type | Pricelist | Pricelist |

Save the information shown in the table.

# Creating a Price List

Open the **Menu | Material Management | Material Management Rules | Price List** window. This window contains three tabs: **Price List**, **Version**, and **Product Price**. As we are not yet configuring the **Product**, we will only work with the first two tabs.

## Registering a new Price List

In the **Price List** tab, enter the following information:

| Field | 1st data | 2nd data |
| --- | --- | --- |
| Name | Purchase PL | Sales PL |
| Default | *deselect* | *deselect* |
| Currency | USD | USD |
| Sales Price list | *deselect* | *select* |

Save this information.

> By deselecting the **Sales Price list** checkbox, this price list is acting as a purchase price list.

This tab will now contain three kinds of data: **Standard** comes with the default client installation and two of our newly created price lists, **Purchase PL** and **Sales PL**. In the **Standard** price list, you need to deselect the **Default** checkbox.

## Creating a Price List version

Following the previous activity, we will create the price list version for both of our newly-created price lists.

*What is the aim of the price list version creation? I still have no idea about it!*

The price list version will be useful if you want to manage the history of the price list. Assume that the price list for the period of February is different from the price list for the period of January. With the price list version, we will create the price list for both January and February. This is just one of the possibilities of the price list version implementation.

For our reference, we will set up both, the purchase and sales price list versions for March.

In the **Price List** tab, ensure that your active record is **Purchase PL**. Click on the **Version** tab, and follow this procedure:

1. Click on the **New** button, and change the **Name** field to the value **Purchase PL March version**.
2. Set the **Price List Schema** field to **Purchase Schema**.
3. Set the date in the **Valid from** field to **03/01/2009**.
4. Save this information.

Next, click on the **Price List** tab again, and then find and set your active record to **Sales PL**. Click on the **Version** tab, and follow this procedure:

1. Click on the **New** button, and change the **Name** field to the value **Sales PL March version**.
2. Set the **Price List Schema** field to **Sales Schema**.
3. Set the date in **Valid from** field to **03/01/2009**.
4. Save this information.

The last task is to set up the product's **List Price**, **Standard Price**, and **Limit Price** values. As we do not yet have our own product, we will set up these prices later.

# Product management

In ADempiere, Products is a term used for something that you buy or sell. These products include products sold to customers, products used in the manufacturing of products that are sold to customers, and products that are purchased by an organization. When you buy or sell a Product, it will require a price as one of the Product's attributes.

## Product Type

Another important Product attribute is **Product Type**. The list of ADempiere Product Types and their meanings are listed as follows:

| No | Product Type | Description |
|----|--------------|-------------|
| 1  | Item         | Physical goods that you buy or sell: The system will set an inventory for these goods. For example, Shirts and Dress cloth. |
| 2  | Expense Type | Physical or non physical goods that you buy or sell: The system will not set an inventory for these goods. For example, stationery expenses. |

| No | Product Type | Description |
|---|---|---|
| 3 | Service | No physical goods are received or sent when we buy or sell this product type: It is just a service. For example, consulting fees. |
| 4 | Resource | This is like Service, but it is restricted in terms of availability. For example, hiring a consultant who will be available for a limited period only. |

The following are the effects that the **Product Type** has on the General Ledger postings made:

| No | Product Type | Db | Cr |
|---|---|---|---|
| 1 | Item | Asset (Product Asset) | Not Invoiced Receipt |
| 2 | Expense Type, Service, Resource | Expenses (Product Expenses) | Not Invoiced Receipt |

> These General Ledger postings are referred to as "Accounting Facts" in ADempiere.

## Product configuration

*Activities such as Purchase Order, Sales Order, Material Receipt, Invoicing, and so on, require Products for their data. Could you give us an example on how to configure a Product?*

Configuring products involves at least two ADempiere windows: the **Product Category** and **Product** window. As a hierarchy, the following is the relation between a **Product Category** and a **Product** window:

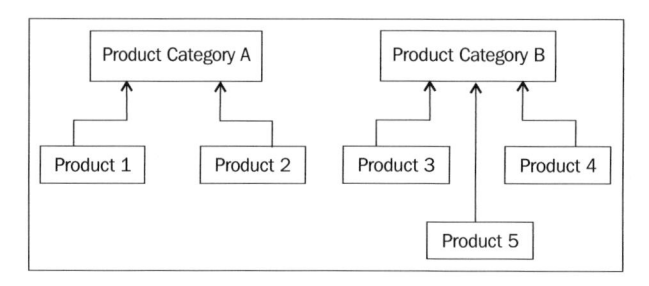

```
        Product Category A              Product Category B
              ↑      ↑                    ↑           ↑
              |      |                    |           |
          Product 1  Product 2      Product 3      Product 4
                                          ↑
                                       Product 5
```

As seen in the previous diagram, one or more products are connected to only one product category. You can specify the product categories based on your own grouping criteria. We will be grouping our products based on inventory types: Finished Goods or Raw Material.

## Creating a Product Category

Open the **Menu | Material Management | Material Management Rules | Product Category** window. This window contains three tabs: **Product Category**, **Accounting**, and **Assigned Product**. Previously, when setting up the Sistematika Fashion, Ltd. client, ADempiere automatically created a default product category named **Standard**. For this data, navigate to the **Product Category** tab, deselect the **Default** checkbox, and save the information.

We will set up two product categories: **Finished Goods** and **Raw Material**. Set the following information in the **Product Category** tab:

| Field | 1st data | 2nd data |
|---|---|---|
| Search Key | FG | RM |
| Name | Finished Goods | Raw Material |
| Material Policy | FIFO | FIFO |
| Print Color | Black | Black |

## Product Category accounting configuration

In the **Accounting** part, there are about ten default accounts involved. Here, you can set up both the **Costing Method** and the **Costing Level**.

> ADempiere has a *multi costing* feature. To show you this feature, we can set up different costing methods and costing clients based on the product category.

In our two new product categories, we will set up a specific costing method only for the **Raw Material** product category. Follow these instructions:

1. Ensure that you have **Raw Material** as the active record in the **Product Category** tab. Navigate to the **Accounting** tab.

2. Set the **Costing Method** to **Average PO**, **Costing Level** to **Client**, and save this information.

> Check the **Costing Method** and **Costing Level** configuration for the **Finished Goods** product category. There are no changes required for this product category, and most fields can be left as blank values. When there is no information (left blank) in the **Costing Method** and **Costing Level** fields, the system uses the default **Costing Method** and **Costing Level** values in the **Menu | Performance Analysis | Accounting Rules | Accounting Schema** window, which is the *Standard Costing* for the costing method and the *Client* for costing level.

For your reference, examine the following screenshot for the **Raw Materials** product category accounting configuration in the **Accounting** tab:

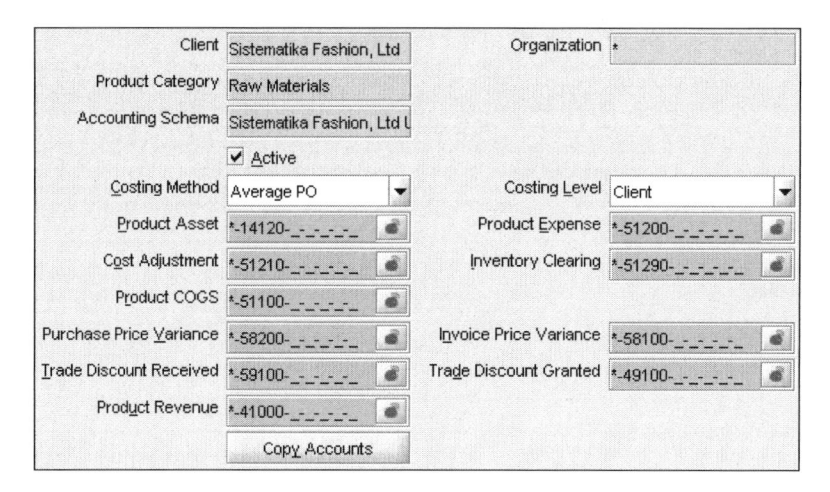

|  |  |  |  |
|---|---|---|---|
| Client | Sistematika Fashion, Ltd | Organization | * |
| Product Category | Raw Materials | | |
| Accounting Schema | Sistematika Fashion, Ltd | | |
| Active | ✓ | | |
| Costing Method | Average PO | Costing Level | Client |
| Product Asset | *-14120- | Product Expense | *-51200- |
| Cost Adjustment | *-51210- | Inventory Clearing | *-51290- |
| Product COGS | *-51100- | | |
| Purchase Price Variance | *-58200- | Invoice Price Variance | *-58100- |
| Trade Discount Received | *-59100- | Trade Discount Granted | *-49100- |
| Product Revenue | *-41000- | | |

Keep in mind the **Costing Method** and **Costing Level** fields for now. We will discuss more details in our upcoming chapters.

# Creating a new Product

The Sistematika Fashion, Ltd. production plant produces shirts, dresses, and jackets as products. Shirt products generally require at least fabric, thread, buttons, and a label as raw materials. With this requirement, we can set up about five ADempiere product data records. The first record is for the Shirt product's finished goods and the other four are for raw materials.

## Preparing a new unit of measurement

Prior to entering our products, we need to set up the additional units of measurement. Open the **Menu | Material Management | Material Management Rules | Unit of Measure** window. Enter the following information in the **Unit of Measure** tabs:

| Field | 1st data | 2nd data | 3rd data | 4th data |
|---|---|---|---|---|
| UOM Code | m | pc | cone | yd |
| Symbol | m | pc | cone | yd |
| Name | Meter | Piece | Cone | Yard |
| Standard Precision | 2 | 0 | 2 | 2 |
| Costing Precision | 4 | 4 | 4 | 4 |

Save this information.

> In each of the unit of measurement records, there is a **Conversion** tab, in which you can define conversion rates between product's unit of measurement. For example, if you have both the Meter and Yard unit of measurement, according to http://www.conversion-metric.org, 1 yard is equal to 0.9144 meters. You can define this information in the conversion tab.
>
> Conversion should be recorded based on products. With this feature, you can define different conversion rates between yards and meters for different products.

We are ready to enter our own products. Open the **Menu | Material Management | Material Management Rules | Product** window. It will contain about 11 tabs. For our practice, we shall concentrate on only three tabs: **Product**, **Purchasing**, and **Price**.

## The Product tab

Select your **Product** tab, and enter and save the following information:

| Field | 1st data | 2nd data | 3rd data | 4th data | 5th data |
|---|---|---|---|---|---|
| Search Key | Shirt | S Fabric | S Thread | S Button | S Label |
| Name | Shirt Finished Goods | S Fabric | S Thread | S Button | S Label |
| Product Category | Finished Goods | Raw Material | Raw Material | Raw Material | Raw Material |
| Tax Category | Standard | Standard | Standard | Standard | Standard |
| UOM | Piece | Meter | Cone | Piece | Piece |
| Product Type | Item | Item | Item | Item | Item |
| Locator | Loc S1A | Loc S1A | Loc S1A | Loc S1A | Loc S1A |
| Purchased | *deselect* | *select* | *select* | *select* | *select* |
| Sold | *select* | *deselect* | *deselect* | *deselect* | *deselect* |

## The Purchasing tab

Here, you can define list price information for all of your products. We shall set up price information for each of our products in the **Purchasing** tab as follows:

| Field \ Product | Shirt Finished Goods | S Fabric | S Thread | S Button | S Label |
|---|---|---|---|---|---|
| Business Partner | Lis Claiborne Inc | Hempel China Limited | Coats and Clarks | Ching Fung Apparel Accessories, Ltd | Wilson Garment Accessories, Ltd |
| Currency | USD | USD | USD | USD | USD |
| List Price | 20 | 4 | 2 | 0.1 | 0.1 |
| UOM | Piece | Meter | Cone | Piece | Piece |

Follow these tasks when entering the purchasing information:

1. In the **Product** tabs, ensure that **S Fabric** is an active record.
2. Select the **Purchasing** tab, click on the **New** button, set the information for **S Fabric** as mentioned in the previous table, and save the information.
3. Perform the same tasks for **S Thread**, **S Button**, **S Label**, and **Shirt Finished Goods**.

> Related to our raw material products, this information should be a pre-requisite for executing Replenish reports. We will discuss Replenish reports later.

## The Price tab

We will now set up our product price (including **List Price**, **Standard Price**, and **Limit Price**) in the **Price** tab. There are two methods of entering price information into this tab, **manually** or **automatically**. To give you an idea of how to set up product prices through ADempiere, we will guide you through setting up a purchase price list.

**Manual processes**: For an example of the manual method, follow these instructions:

1. Set the **S Button** as an active record in the **Product** tab, and navigate to the **Price** tab.
2. Click on the **New** button, and set the **Price List Version** field to **Purchase PL March version**.

Chapter 4

3. You can enter your products' prices (**List Price**, **Standard Price**, and **Limit Price**) save this information, and you are done.

**Automatic processes**: Next, we'll try to automatically insert or update the product's price information. We need to set up a **Schema Line** in the **Price List Schema** window to help us accomplish this task. Open the **Menu | Material Management | Material Management Rules | Price List Schema** window. Choose the **Purchase Schema** records in the **Price List Schema** tab, and navigate to the **Schema Line** tab.

Click on the **New** button, and enter the information listed in the following table:

| Field | Data |
|---|---|
| Sequence | 10 |
| Currency Type | Weekly |
| Product Category | Raw Material |
| List price Base | List Price |
| Standard price Base | List Price |
| Standard price Discount % | 20 |
| Limit price Base | Fixed Price |
| Fixed Limit Price | 0.00 |

Now, proceed to the automatic price list setup of our **Raw Material** product category, and open the **Menu | Material Management | Material Management Rules | Price List** window. Select the **Purchase PL** record in the **Price List** tab, and then click on the **Version** tab. Ensure that you are now on the **Purchase PL March version** record, as shown in the following screenshot:

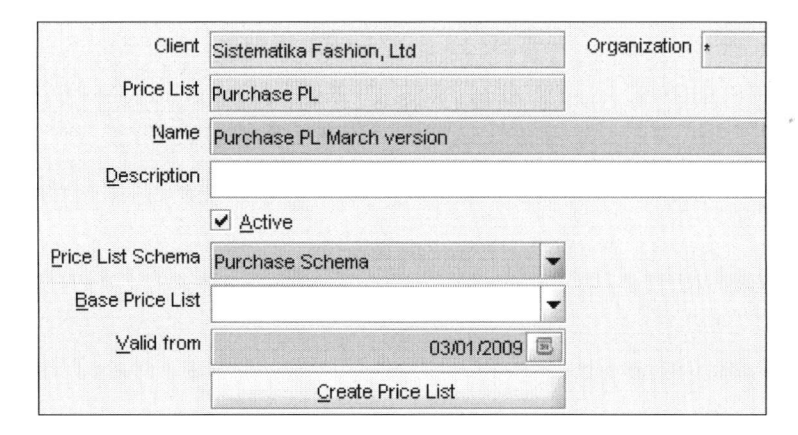

| | |
|---|---|
| Client | Sistematika Fashion, Ltd |
| Price List | Purchase PL |
| Name | Purchase PL March version |
| Description | |
| | ✔ Active |
| Price List Schema | Purchase Schema |
| Base Price List | |
| Valid from | 03/01/2009 |
| | Create Price List |

Organization *

## Setting up Master Data and Knowing its Accounting Configuration

Click on the **Create Price List** button. In the **Create Price List** confirmation window, just click on the **OK** button. You will get a **Create Price List** confirmation result window, which contains messages such as **Selected=4**, **Deleted=3**, **Inserted=4**, **Updated=4**, or something similar.

Take a look at the **Price** tab for four of our products. It will contain the price information listed in the following table:

| Field \ Product | S Fabric | S Thread | S Button | S Label |
| --- | --- | --- | --- | --- |
| Price List Version | Purchase PL March version | Purchase PL March version | Purchase PL March version | Purchase PL March version |
| List Price | 4 | 2 | 0.10 | 0.10 |
| Standard Price | 3.2 | 1.6 | 0.08 | 0.08 |
| Limit Price | 0.00 | 0.00 | 0.00 | 0.00 |

*Could you explain how ADempiere calculated this price? I want to know the concept behind these generated values.*

Examine your **Purchase Schema** records in your **Price List Schema** window. Go through your **Schema Line** tab. As per our confguration, ADempiere will set the **List Price** information in the **Price** tab of the **Product** window from the **List Price** field in the **Purchasing** tab of the **Product** window. Take an example of the **List Price** for **S Fabric**, as shown in the following screenshot:

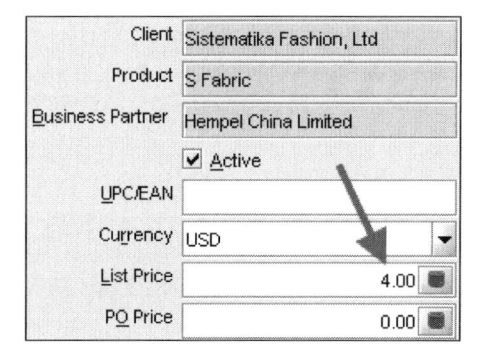

ADempiere says that you have already told me that the value for the **Standard Price** field should be taken from **List Price**, but at a **20%** discount from the **List Price** value. So, I have given you **4 – (4 * 20%)** equals to **3.2**. While determining the **Limit Price** value, you have told me to set a **Fixed Price** and to take a value from the **Fixed Limit Price** field, which therefore configures as **0.00**.

[ 126 ]

> *Interesting! It seems that the Schema Line configuration will apply to our entire Raw Material product category, which has information in the Purchasing tab. How do we set a specific discount for, let's say, the S Fabric raw material?*

We can set an additional **Schema Line** data for **Purchase Schema** records in the **Price List Schema** window. Just insert your second **Schema Line** record that contains:

1. The **Sequence** field with the value **20**, the **Currency Type** field with the value **Weekly**, the **Product Category** field with the value **Raw Material**, and the **Product** field with value **S Fabric**.
2. Set the **List Price** option for both the **List price Base** and the **Standard price Base** fields. Fill the **Standard price Discount %** field with the value **5**.
3. Set the **Limit price Base** field to **Fixed Price**, and enter **0** in the **Fixed Limit Price** field.

Click on the **Create Price List** button, as described previously, and examine your **S Fabric** pricing results in your **Product** window's **Purchasing** tab.

> The rule for **Schema Line** configuration is: set the first record for generic rules. In our case, this will apply to the specific **Product Category** with all of the existing Business Partners and Products. The second record will be more specific than the first record. In our example, we just set it only for **S Fabric**. The third record should be more specific when comparing it with the second one, and is set for the **S Fabric** for a specific **Business Partner**.

Well, this is just an example to define the product price list for the **Raw Material** product category. You can also perform a similar process for your **Finished Goods** product category.

# Summary

In this chapter, we saw the basic connection between master data and its accounting parts (if applicable). With these accounting parts, you were introduced to ADempiere account combinations and how to create your own account combination. With this account combination, you can set up or alter a predefined ADempiere default account for your new account combination.

You created a Business Partner with which you have a relationship when operating the company. We also know how the accounting configuration works. Also, we introduced a topic on how to manage our company's financial activity, including bank accounts and cash books.

While we were working with multiple currencies, instead of using all of the registered currency, we activated only a small number of currencies. This was followed by the creation of the currency rate type and the currency rate for our currency. With this currency configuration, we can now use this data for our transactions.

In the next part, we showed you how to configure a price list for our products, and how to configure the price list schema and its impact on the Product's price list. Prior to this discussion, we saw how to setup both a Product Category and a Product. The ADempiere Product can contain both physical goods and non physical goods, such as services.

In the next chapter we will show you how to perform procurement activities using the master data in our sample transaction, and also show you how our accounting configuration takes place during the generation of accounting facts/GL journal entries.

# 5
# Procurement Activities

As a company, Sistematika Fashion, Ltd., produces its finished goods using two methods: *make to order* and *make to stock*. With make to stock, the company will produce the goods and keep the finished goods in their warehouse prior to the sales activity.

We will practice a *make to stock* activity and learn how to perform tasks related to this activity (especially the procurement parts) step-by-step, and will see the result in our accounting fact/General Ledger journal entry generation. In short, we will practice the following activites:

- Purchase Requisition
- Purchase Order
- Receiving material
- Managing Vendor Invoice
- Performing a Vendor Payment
- Reconciling a Vendor Payment

Before we start working on these activities, we will begin by introducing you to the ADempiere Document.

## Introduction to the ADempiere Document

Sistematika Fashion, Ltd. has many activities that need to be done when running their business. Examples of these activities are:

- The Purchasing staff making a Purchase Order document
- The Warehouse staff receiving material from the Vendor
- The Accounting staff registering the incoming Vendor Invoices and making a payment

*Procurement Activities*

- The Production staff creating finished goods from the available material
- The Shipping staff performing the shipment of finished goods to the Customer
- The Accounting staff creating an invoice document for the Customer

On the other hand, the Accounting department has some additional responsibilities, such as:

- Entering manual general ledger journal entries for all of the documents
- Recording account payables for existing vendor invoices
- Recording account receivables for existing customer invoices

We can interpret these activities as a list of standard business processes in the company.

Fortunately, ADempiere can help us simplify these activities through the use of the existing ADempiere Document. The ADempiere Document encapsulates the complexity of each of the business processes (such as Purchase Order, Receiving Material, Invoicing, and so on) and provides a window or form to enter data related to the business process (such as Sales Order, Material Receipt, Invoice (Vendor), and so on).

With the ADempiere Document, posting the document generates the necessary general ledger journal entries, and you can create some reports based on the general ledger entries.

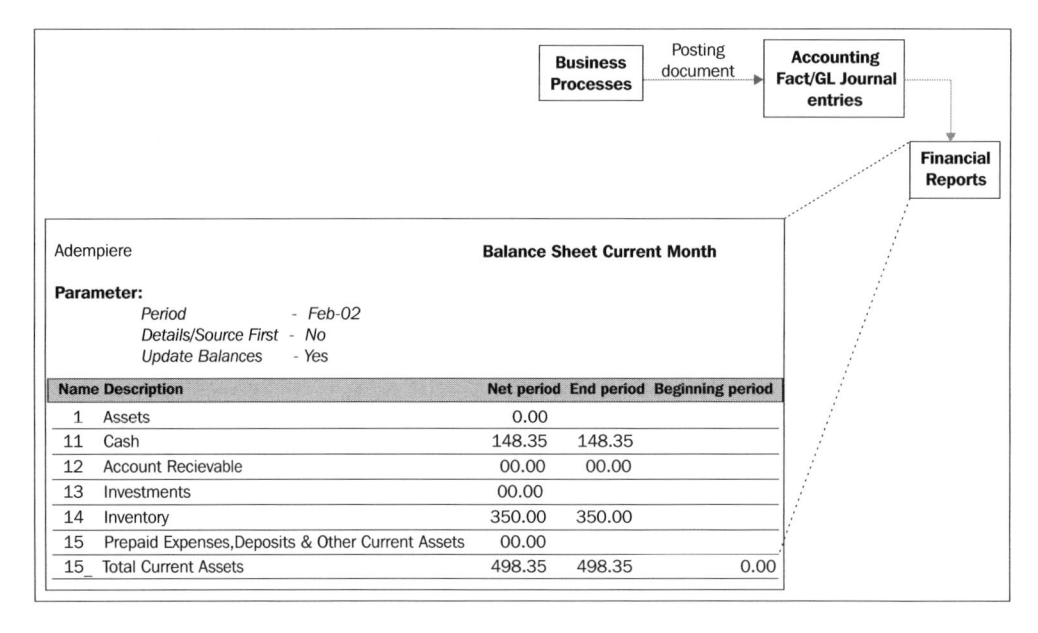

Adempiere — **Balance Sheet Current Month**

**Parameter:**
- Period — Feb-02
- Details/Source First — No
- Update Balances — Yes

| Name | Description | Net period | End period | Beginning period |
|---|---|---|---|---|
| 1 | Assets | 0.00 | | |
| 11 | Cash | 148.35 | 148.35 | |
| 12 | Account Recievable | 00.00 | 00.00 | |
| 13 | Investments | 00.00 | | |
| 14 | Inventory | 350.00 | 350.00 | |
| 15 | Prepaid Expenses,Deposits & Other Current Assets | 00.00 | | |
| 15 | Total Current Assets | 498.35 | 498.35 | 0.00 |

Flow: Business Processes → Posting document → Accounting Fact/GL Journal entries → Financial Reports

# Working on a Purchase Requisition

As a part of the organization's internal financial controls, the organization may use a purchase requisition to help manage requests for purchases. With this activity, the request for the purchase of goods is documented and can be monitored.

There are two ways of creating an ADempiere requisition document:

- Manual entries
- Performing a replenish report

## Creating a Purchase Requisition manually

With manual entries, you could *log in with user ID admin*, using **Shirt** as the **Organization** and **1st Shirt W/h** as your **Warehouse**. Open the **Menu | Requisition-To-Invoice | Requisition** window, enter the data in the **Requisition** and **Requisition Line** tabs, fill all of the mandatory fields, complete the document, and you are done. Although this window has **Requisition** as its name, you need to ensure that you are using **Purchase Requisition** as the **Document Type** of the ADempiere document.

The following is an example of the data entered in the **Requisition** tab in the **Requisition** window:

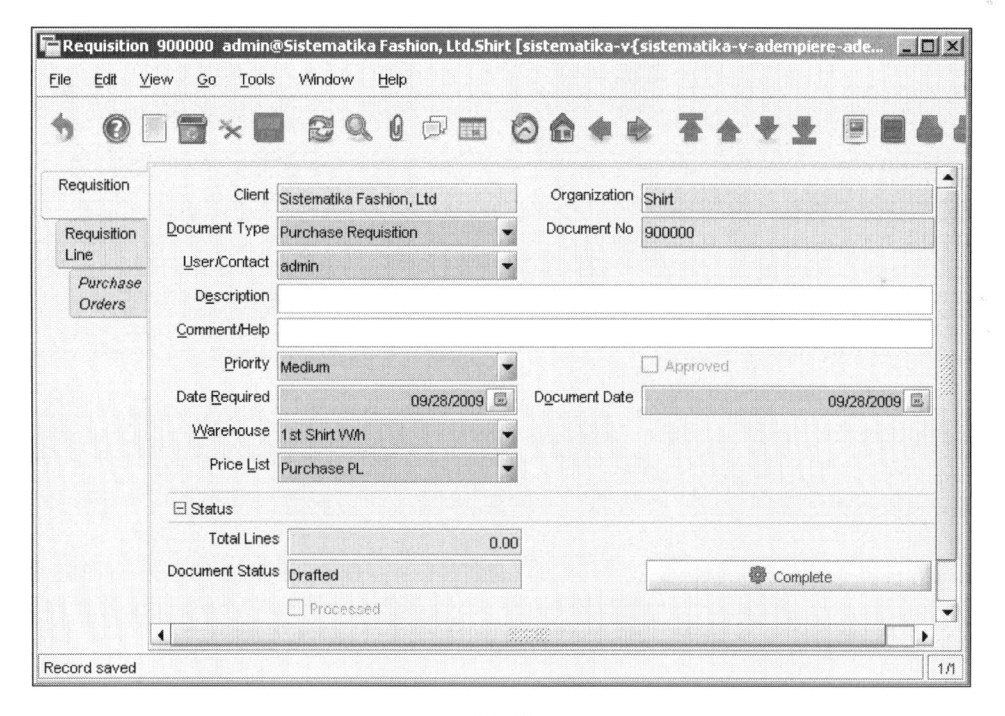

*Procurement Activities*

We will create a purchase requisition that uses the replenish report method in the following sections.

# Working with Replenish Reports

We can create a purchase requisition document using the Replenish Reports feature. There is some configuration that needs to be done prior to executing Replenish Reports.

The following is just an example of running Replenish Reports without the correct configuration. Open the **Menu | Material Management | Replenish Report** process window. In the upcoming confirmation window, enter the following values:

| Field | Value |
| --- | --- |
| Warehouse | Shirt W/h (select from the options) |
| Create | Requisition (select from the options) |
| Document Type | Purchase Requisition (select from the options) |

Click on the **Start** button to proceed with the generation of the Replenish Reports. Wait for a while, and you will then be prompted with blank Replenish Report results. Blank reports!

# Setting up replenish information

> *Is this feature not working, or is there any condition or configuration that needs to be set up to successfully create a Replenish Report?*

Behind the scenes, ADempiere will read a replenish configuration within the **Replenish** tab of a **Product** window. Through this tab, there are several replenish types that we can use to achieve our target. For example, we can set up a reorder below a minimum level.

Open the **Menu | Material Management | Material Management Rules | Product** window. Select your **S Button** raw material. Using this record, click on the **Replenish** tab, and perform the following tasks:

1. Click on the **New** button, and enter the value **1st Shirt W/h** in the **Warehouse** field.
2. Set the **Replenish Type** field to **Reorder below Minimum Level**.
3. Set the **Minimum Level** field to **200**, and then click on the **Save** button.

## Setting up the default Price List

*Ok, after setting up this record, I ran the Replenish Report again. But, it still shows me nothing! Is there any error information in ADempiere that you could share with me?*

Unfortunately, ADempiere does not prompt us with any information to find out what the problem may be. However, even though there seems to be no error information available, you can still find out what has happened within the ADempiere system. You can access any error information from the **Tools | Preference** main menu. In this window, you will find the **Errors** tab, as shown in the following screenshot:

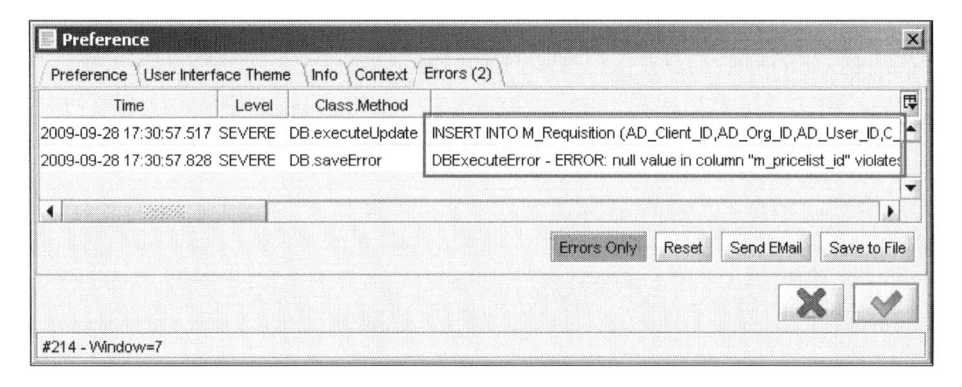

Here, ADempiere shares with us the information that an error occurred while entering the purchase requisition information in the **M_Requisition** database table (the first error information displayed).

> **M_Requisition** is a table used by the **Requisition** window. Check your Record Info in the **Requisition** window. While inserting information, ADempiere says, **ERROR: null value in column "m_pricelist_id"** (second error information). This means ADempiere requires information in the **m_pricelist_id** field. And yes, for most ADempiere users, this is not a user-friendly error message format.

Delving into the ADempiere internal procedure, this message occurs while we *have no default price list within our price list records*. To rectify this problem, we need to set **Purchase PL** as our default price list. Open the **Menu | Material Management | Material Management Rules | Price List** window. Select **Purchase PL** as your active record. Edit this record, select the **Default** checkbox, and then save this record.

*Procurement Activities*

Now, you can run your **Replenish Report** again, and it will show you a purchase requisition successfully created, as shown in the following screenshot:

| ADempiere | | Replenish Report | | Page 1(1,1) of 3(1,3) |
|---|---|---|---|---|
| **Parameter:** | | | | |
| | Warehouse = 1st Shirt W/h | | | |
| | Create = Requisition | | | |
| | Document Type = Purchase Requisition | | | |
| **Create** | **Process Instance** | **Business Partner** | **Doc Type** | **Maximum Level** |
| Requisition | 1000024 - RV_T_Replenish - Replenish Report | Ching Fung Apparel Accessories, Ltd | Purchase Requisition | 200 |

## Completing the replenish information

Although this Replenish Report works only for the S Button material, we need to ensure that the Replenish Reports are created for all of our raw material. Open the **Menu | Requisition-to-Invoice | Requisition** window to access our newly-created requisition. For now, press the *F3* key to delete this requisition data.

You can enter the following data for the other raw materials' replenish configuration:

| Field\Raw Material | S Fabric | S Thread | S Label |
|---|---|---|---|
| Warehouse | 1st Shirt W/h | 1st Shirt W/h | 1st Shirt W/h |
| Replenish Type | Reorder below Minimum Level | Reorder below Minimum Level | Reorder below Minimum Level |
| Minimum Level | 100 | 50 | 1000 |

Upon completion, execute the **Replenish Reports** once again, and examine the results in the **Requisition** window. You will see you one requisition document containing four requisition lines. Complete this requisition document by clicking on the **Complete** button.

> The **Replenish Report** is not a full **Material Requirements Planning** (**MRP**) implementation.

## Accounting facts

While you are logged in to ADempiere using the **admin** user ID and **Sistematika Fashion, Ltd Admin** as the role, you have the rights to access all of the accounting configuration and information. With this role, after completing a document, you will be shown a **Not Posted** button in the window:

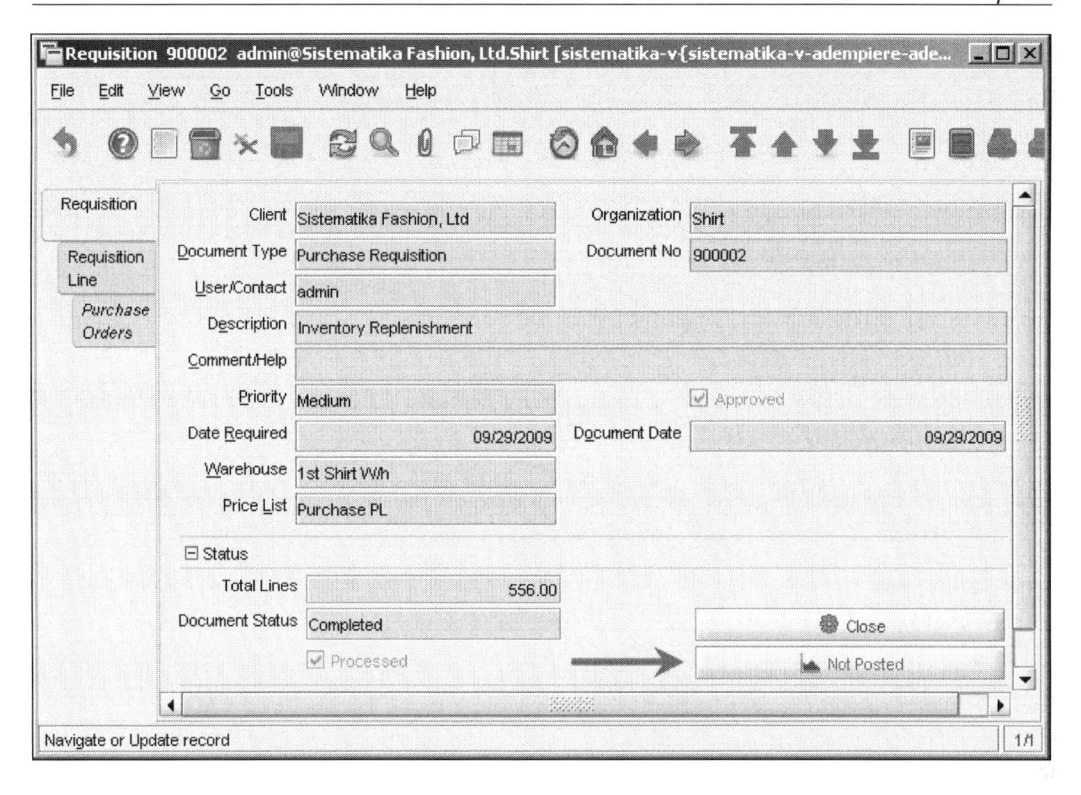

[Screenshot of Requisition window showing document 900002 with Document Status "Completed", Total Lines 556.00, and a "Not Posted" button highlighted by an arrow.]

In your current record in the **Requisition** window, click on the **Not Posted** button. You will get a **Post now and create Accounting entries?** confirmation window. Once you click on the **OK** button, the **Not Posted** button becomes a **Posted** button.

As expected, **Requisition** does not generate accounting facts. To check this, click on the **Posted** button. You will be prompted with the **Account Viewer** window. This window contains two tabs: **Enter Query** and **View Results**. The **View Results** tab will contain nothing.

> For other window processes, if you need to check the accounting facts/GL journal entries generated, you can click on the **Posted** button, and the system will show the **Account Viewer** window that contains the accounting facts information (if any).

# Working with Purchase Orders

According to Wikipedia (`http://en.wikipedia.org/wiki/Purchase_order`):

> *A purchase order is a commercial document issued by a buyer to a seller, indicating types, quantities, and agreed prices for products or services the seller will provide to the buyer. Sending a purchase order to a supplier constitutes a legal offer to buy products or services.*

Creation of a purchase order document can be done in two ways:

- Manual entries
- Transfer data from purchase requisition document

Open the **Menu | Requisition-to-Invoice | Purchase Order** window. There will be five tabs: **Purchase Order**, **PO Line**, **Matching**, **Requisition Lines**, and **Order Tax**. If the **Show Advanced Tabs** checkbox is in a *deselected* state in **Tools | Preference**, then this **Purchase Order** window will only show three tabs: **Purchase Order**, **PO Line**, and **Order Tax**. We will work with the first two tabs.

On entering information in the **Purchase Order** window, you need to set a document type, which should be used in this window. There are two document types available in this window:

- Purchase Order
- Vendor Return Material

> The **Vendor Return Material** document type should be used if you need to create a delivery note document when returning a material to your vendor.

## Creating a Purchase Order manually

With manual entries, you need to set the information in the **Purchase Order** tab as follows:

1. Set the **Target Document Type** to **Purchase Order**.
2. Set your **Date Ordered**, target **Warehouse** for material received, **Business Partner**, and **Price List** to be used, as necessary.
3. In the **PO Line** tab, you may set the following information:
    - **Date Promised** is a required/expected date to receive the material ordered.
    - **Product**, **Quantity**, and **Price**.

We believe that manually entering a purchase order would be an easy task for you to perform. Just enter the information in both, the **Purchase Order** and **PO Line.** Save and complete this information, and you are done.

# Creating a Purchase Order from a Purchase Requisition

We are now trying to convert our purchase requisition document to a purchase order. All you need to do is to execute the **Menu | Requisition-to-Invoice | Create PO from Requisition** process. In the displayed confirmation window, enter the following information:

- Complete the **Organization** field with the value **Shirt**
- Complete the **Warehouse** field with the value **1st Shirt W/h**

Leave the other fields unchanged. Click on the **Start** button. Wait for a moment, and the system will automatically create the Purchase Order document for you. Upon completion, you will get the confirmation window, as shown in the following screenshot:

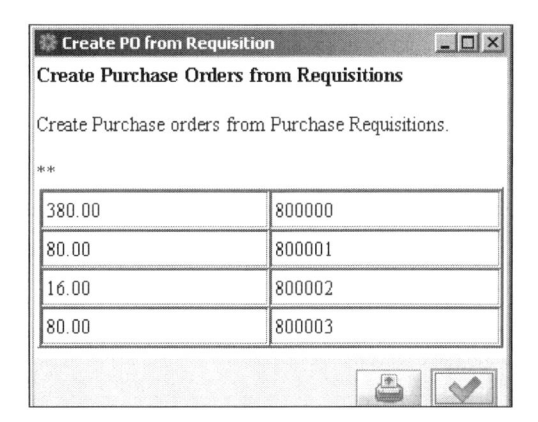

**Create PO from Requisition**

**Create Purchase Orders from Requisitions**

Create Purchase orders from Purchase Requisitions.

\*\*

| | |
|---|---|
| 380.00 | 800000 |
| 80.00 | 800001 |
| 16.00 | 800002 |
| 80.00 | 800003 |

Now, open the **Menu | Requisition-to-Invoice | Purchase Order** window. Congratulations! You will get your four purchase order documents that have a **Drafted document** status. Examine your purchase order and the purchase order lines. There is no need to alter any information for now.

In these purchase order documents, click on the **Prepare** button. You will be prompted with a **Document Action** confirmation window. Select **Complete** from the document action option list, and click on the **OK** button. The **Prepare** button will now change its status from **Prepare** to **Close**. Perform the same tasks for the rest of the purchase order documents (three documents in all).

## Accounting facts

If the purchase order document has a **Completed** status, then there will be a **Not Posted** button available. Click on the **Not Posted** button to post all four of our purchase order documents.

With the default ADempiere configuration, the system does not generate the accounting fact/GL journal entries for all of these purchase order documents.

## Receiving material

> *In other proprietary ERP systems, we can perform a material receipt if we have a reference to the Purchase Order document. In such cases, if we are receiving goods without the Purchase Order mentioned in the delivery notes, we have to contact our purchasing department to clarify the Purchase Order this material belongs to. In ADempiere, will it take time to complete this activity?*

Fortunately, ADempiere has the capability to perform the material receipt activity with or without prior knowledge of the Purchase Order document. While we can process without the knowledge of the Purchase Order document, at the time of receiving the materials or goods, we can put this transaction in the system immediately, without any delay.

To work with activities related to receiving materials, ADempiere provides the **Menu | Requisition-to-Invoice | Material Receipt** window. This window contains five tabs: **Material Receipt**, **Receipt Line**, **Confirmations**, **Matched POs**, and **Matched Invoices**.

In this window, there are two document types available:

- MM Receipt
- MM Returns

For performing activities related to receiving materials, we will use the MM Receipt document type.

> The MM Returns document can be used for returning raw material from our warehouse to the vendor.

To understand the basic material receipt activities, we will perform a material receipt with a purchase order reference, in the following section.

# Receiving materials with a Purchase Order reference

We will practice on our **S Button** and **S Label** purchase order. In your **Material Receipt** window, set the following information one-by-one in the **Material Receipt** tab:

| Field\Data | 1st Data | 2nd Data |
|---|---|---|
| Organization | Shirt | Shirt |
| Document Type | MM Receipt | MM Receipt |
| Business Partner | Ching Fung Apparel Accessories, Ltd | Wilson Garment Accessories, Ltd |
| Warehouse | 1st Shirt W/h | 1st Shirt W/h |

Leave the other fields unchanged. After saving this information, ensure that the active material receipt record is **Ching Fung Apparel Accessories, Ltd**.

Because we have a Purchase Order reference, we can click on the **Create lines from** button, as shown in the following screenshot:

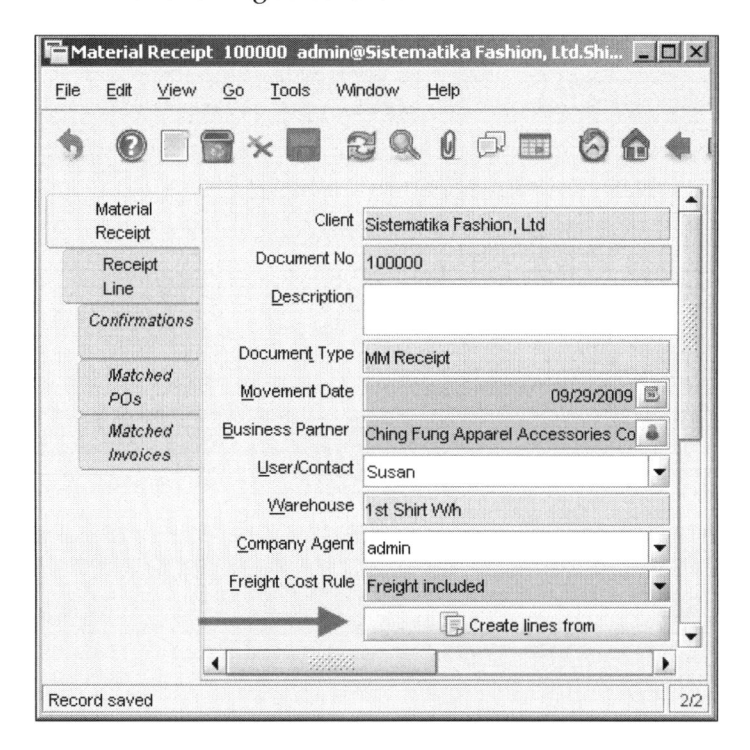

## Procurement Activities

In the upcoming window, you have to:

1. Select a Purchase Order from the option list related to this material receipt.
2. Select the checkbox in the **Select** field for our target Purchase Order line (PO Line).
3. Complete the activity by clicking on the **OK** button.

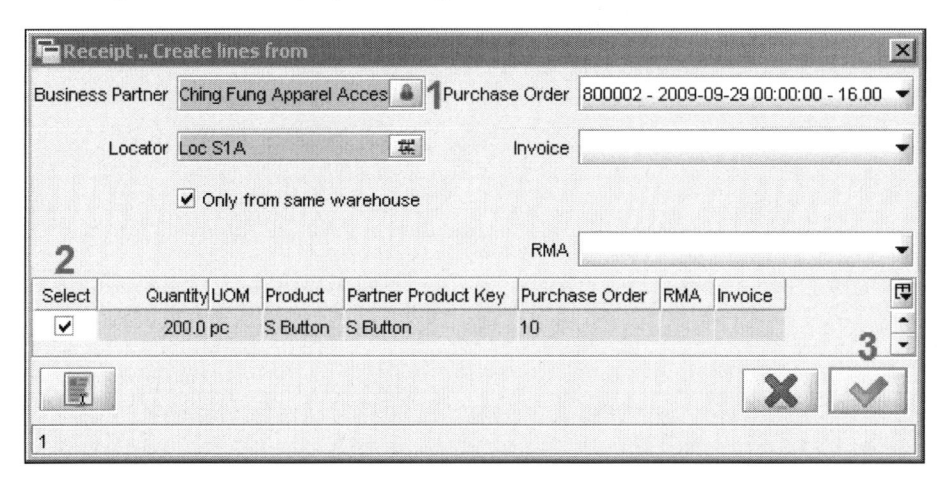

With this activity, ADempiere will:

- Copy the **PO Line** source data, and put it in your material receipt's **Receipt Line** record.
- Set a flag to indicate that this material receipt is already associated with a Purchase Order line. Take a look at the **Purchase Order** field within the **Material Receipt** tab.

> When performing a partial receipt of your purchase order quantity, you are free to alter or update the **Receipt Line** quantity field. In our case, we are receiving the full quantity.

After examining your **Receipt Line** data, go back to the **Material Receipt** tab, and click on the **Complete** button to finalize our activity.

You can proceed with the same procedure while processing the material receipt from **Wilson Garment Accessories, Ltd**.

## Accounting facts

Click on the **Not Posted** button for both of our **MM Receipt** documents. The material receipt accounting fact general journal entry format would be:

| Window | Document | Sign | Description | Posting Type |
|---|---|---|---|---|
| Material Receipt | MM Receipt | Db | Product asset | Actual |
|  |  | Cr | Not invoiced receipts | Actual |

After clicking on the **Posted** button, an example of the accounting fact/GL journal entry generated when receiving the **S Button** raw material is displayed, as shown in the following screenshot:

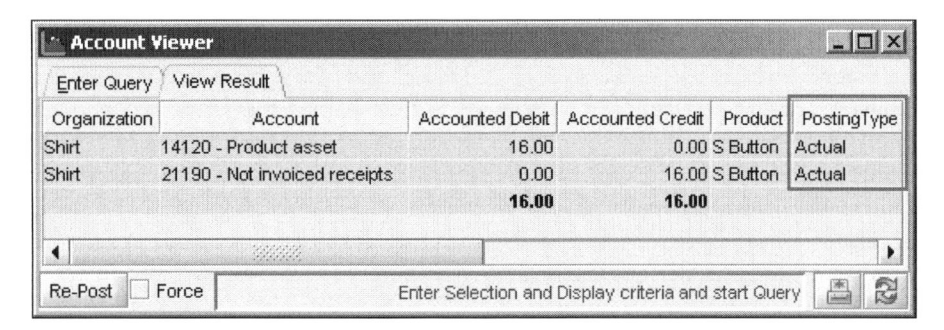

| Organization | Account | Accounted Debit | Accounted Credit | Product | PostingType |
|---|---|---|---|---|---|
| Shirt | 14120 - Product asset | 16.00 | 0.00 | S Button | Actual |
| Shirt | 21190 - Not invoiced receipts | 0.00 | 16.00 | S Button | Actual |
|  |  | **16.00** | **16.00** |  |  |

# Receiving material without a Purchase Order reference

We will practice with two of our purchased materials, namely **S Fabric** and **S Thread**. Here, we will perform manual material receipt activities. Open the **Material Receipt** window. In the **Material Receipt** tab, you will enter and set the following information, one-by-one:

| Field\Data | 3rd Data | 4th Data |
|---|---|---|
| Organization | Shirt | Shirt |
| Document Type | MM Receipt | MM Receipt |
| Business Partner | Hempel China Limited | Coats and Clarks |
| Warehouse | 1st Shirt W/h | 1st Shirt W/h |

We can alter the **Movement Date** and **Account Date** fields if necessary. For now, just accept the default date for both the fields, leave the other fields unchanged, and then save your data.

*Procurement Activities*

Next, we need to manually enter our material receipt line. Ensure that your material receipt active record is for the **Hempel China Limited** business partner, and click on the **Receipt Line** tab. Enter the following information for the received material:

1. Set the **Product** field to **S Fabric**.
2. Set the **Locator** field to **Loc S1A**.
3. Set the **Quantity** field to **100**.
4. Set the **UOM** field to **Meter**.
5. Click on the **Save** button.

> You can set the order reference field with the transaction reference number, taken from the vendor delivery notes document.

Go back to the **Material Receipt** tab. Set your material receipt active record to the **Coats and Clarks** business partner, and then click on the **Receipt Line** tab. Enter the following information:

1. Set the **Product** field with **S Thread**.
2. Set the **Locator** field with **Loc S1A**.
3. Set the **Quantity** field with **50**.
4. Set the **UOM** field to **Cone**.
5. Click on the **Save** button.

Along with the previous two activities, you now have two MM Receipt documents that have one receipt line each. Complete both of these documents by clicking on the **Complete** button.

## Posting error

> *When I try posting this document by clicking on the Not Posted button, I get the message shown in the following screenshot. In addition to this error message, the button flag now changes from Not Posted to Posting Error. Is there something wrong with our procedure?*

> **Posting Error**
>
> Resubmit - No Costs for S Fabric

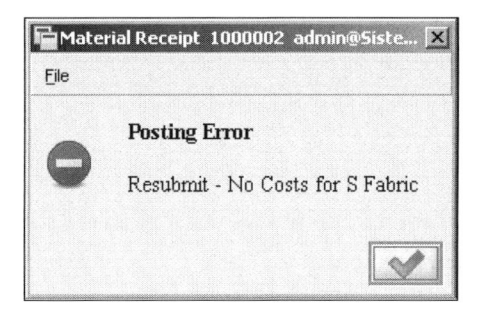

You may have also seen a similar posting error when trying to post the MM Receipt documents for **S Thread**. This is a normal warning given by ADempiere.

Previously, we set up an **Average PO** costing method for all of our raw materials (refer to the *Product Category accounting configuration* section in Chapter 4, *Setting up Master Data and Knowing its Accounting Configuration*). For this costing method, upon posting the procedure, ADempiere requires a cost value for our received material. As we have no reference to a Purchase Order document, ADempiere failed to find the proper cost, and raised an error message.

# Matching a Purchase Order to a Receipt

*So, what should I do to rectify this problem?*

This is a trivial task. The problem has been correctly mentioned—the MM Receipt document does not have a link or a reference to the Purchase Order document. You need to create a link between the MM Receipt document (information in the material receipt line, to be precise) and the Purchase Order document (information in the purchase order line, to be precise).

Open the **Menu | Requisition-to-Invoice | Matching PO-Receipt-Invoice** form, and enter the following information:

1. Set the **Match From** field to **Purchase Order**.
2. Set the **Match To** field to **Receipt**.
3. Set the **Search Mode** field to **Not Matched**.
4. Set the **Business Partner** field to **Hempel China Limited**.

*Procurement Activities*

Click on the **Search records** button, and ADempiere will give you a list of data (available in the **Purchase Order** grid), which needs to be linked, as shown in the following screenshot:

Within this example form, I have clicked on **800000** in the **Document No** column (this may vary depending on your data) in the **Purchase Order** data grid. By clicking on this record, ADempiere will show an eligible record that is available for manual matching, in the **Receipt** data grid, as shown in the following screenshot:

Select the record (by selecting the checkbox on the left-hand side of the **Document No** field), and proceed by clicking on the **Process** button. By performing this activity, you have set up a manual matching for the **S Fabric** material receipt.

Perform the same tasks for the **S Thread** material receipt. You can set the same form information for **Match From**, **Match To**, and **Search Mode**. Set the **Business Partner** field to **Coats and Clarks**, and continue.

## Accounting facts

Now, our Material Receipt has a relation with the Purchase Order. We shall proceed to post our material receipt document. Re-open your **Menu | Requisition-to-Invoice | Material Receipt** window, and post both of the documents by clicking on the **Posting Error** or **Not Posted** button.

The following screenshot shows the accounting facts/GL journal entries when posting the MM Receipt document with **Hempel China Limited** as the business partner.

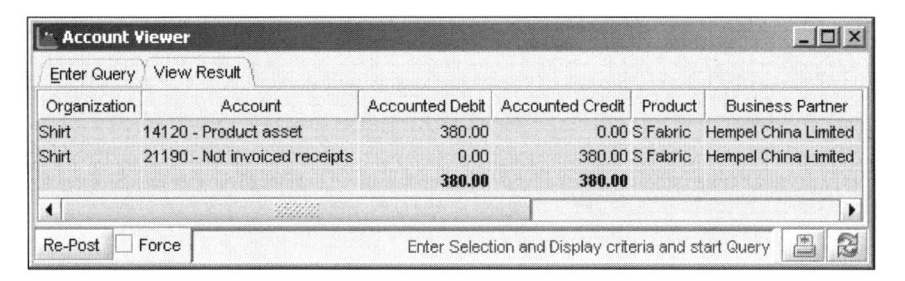

| Organization | Account | Accounted Debit | Accounted Credit | Product | Business Partner |
|---|---|---|---|---|---|
| Shirt | 14120 - Product asset | 380.00 | 0.00 | S Fabric | Hempel China Limited |
| Shirt | 21190 - Not invoiced receipts | 0.00 | 380.00 | S Fabric | Hempel China Limited |
| | | 380.00 | 380.00 | | |

> The **380** values come from multiplying the **Purchase Order price** with the **Material Receipt quantity**.

You can examine the material receipt accounting fact results for the **Coats and Clarks** business partner.

## Matched Purchase Orders

Behind the scenes, ADempiere created matched Purchase Order records, while having the Material Receipt connected to the Purchase Order. Open the **Menu | Requisition-To-Invoice | Matched Purchase Orders** window.

*Procurement Activities*

This will contain four records that represent the interconnection or relationship among four purchase order lines with the material receipt lines document. The following is an example of the matched records for our **S Fabric** product:

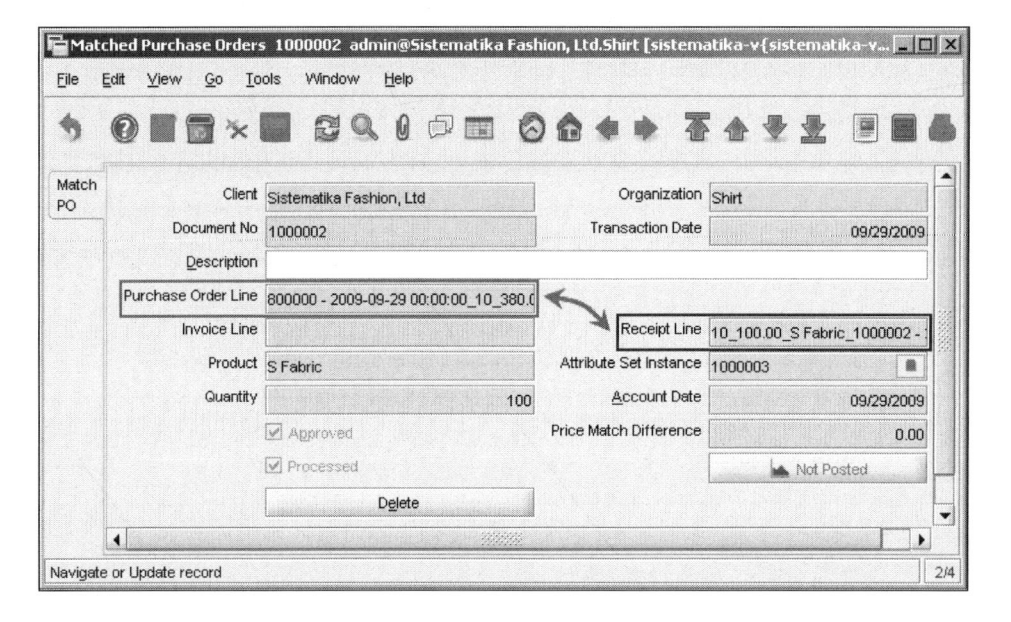

The aim of using this document is as follows:

- It shows the relationship between the Purchase Order line and the Material Receipt line information. You can evaluate the matching document information in this window.
- On posting the Matched Purchase Order document, the system will check the costing methods of the Product mentioned in this document. When using Standard Costing as the product's costing method, if there is any variance between the product's Standard Cost and the product's Purchase Order price, the system will book a price variance.

> Performing a manual **Matching Purchase Order - Receipt** can incidentally set an incorrectly-matching document. You can identify them within this window and take action to remove these records by clicking on the **Delete** button (in this window, you cannot remove records by pressing the *F3* key). Then you can set a correct relationship with the **Matching PO-Receipt-Invoice** form again.

## Accounting facts

In our case, we are using the **Average PO** as our raw material **costing method**. Try to post all four of our **Matched Purchase Orders** documents. And yes, it shows you nothing for the accounting fact.

If we have Standard Costing as the product's costing method, there may be a price variance if we have a difference between the Purchase Order price and product Standard Cost.

If the product's Standard Cost is *less than* the Purchase Order price, the general journal entry format for Matched Purchase Orders document will be:

| Sign | Description | Posting Type |
|---|---|---|
| Db | Purchase price variance | Actual |
| Cr | Purchase price variance offset | Actual |

In this example, a Purchase price variance is set as the Debit (Db) position. If the product Standard Cost is *more than* the Purchase Order price, the journal entry format will be:

| Sign | Description | Posting Type |
|---|---|---|
| Db | Purchase price variance offset | Actual |
| Cr | Purchase price variance | Actual |

## Managing vendor invoices

On sending an ordered raw material, usually our vendor sends us a document called an Invoice. An Invoice is a commercial document issued by a seller to the buyer, indicating the products, quantities, and agreed prices for products or services that the seller has provided to the buyer. An invoice indicates that the buyer must pay the seller, according to the payment terms.

When working with an invoice from your vendor, sometimes the invoice document will not be available at the time of receiving raw material. This invoice will be available to you later or it will be presented prior to receiving the raw material.

Like the material receipt activity, ADempiere has flexibility when entering an invoice from a vendor or supplier. You can create an invoice document with or without knowing the MM Receipt document reference.

*Procurement Activities*

We shall practice entering the invoice issued by our vendor, with and without the Material Receipt document reference. Here, we will be working with the **Menu | Requisition-to-Invoice | Invoice (Vendor)** window. By default, this window will contain eight tabs: **Invoice**, **Invoice Line**, **Landed Cost**, **Landed Cost Allocation**, **Matched POs**, **Matched Receipts**, **Invoice Tax**, and **Allocation**.

> If the **Show Advanced Tabs** checkbox in **Tools | Preference** has been *deselected*, the **Invoice (Vendor)** window will only show three tabs: **Invoice**, **Invoice Line**, and **Invoice Tax**.

There are two document types available in the **Target Document Type** field in this window:

- AP Invoice
- AP Credit Memo

In our case, we will use the AP Invoice document type.

> AP Credit Memo can be used to create a commercial document issued by a seller to a buyer. It will list the products, quantities, and agreed prices for the products or services that the seller has provided to the buyer, but that the buyer did not receive or return the products.

## Invoicing with a Material Receipt reference

We shall practice invoicing with a Material Receipt reference using **S Button** and **S Label** as references. In your **Invoice (Vendor)** window, you should enter and set the following information, one-by-one, in the **Invoice** tab:

| Field\Data | 1st Data | 2nd Data |
| --- | --- | --- |
| Organization | Shirt | Shirt |
| Target Document Type | AP Invoice | AP Invoice |
| Business Partner | Ching Fung Apparel Accessories, Ltd | Wilson Garment Accessories, Ltd |
| Price List | Purchase PL | Purchase PL |

Leave the other fields unchanged. After saving this information, ensure that you are now working with the invoice that has **Ching Fung Apparel Accessories, Ltd.** as the business partner (in this example, this is the first data), and set this invoice as your active record. With the material receipt reference, you can just click on the **Create lines from** button, as shown in the following screenshot:

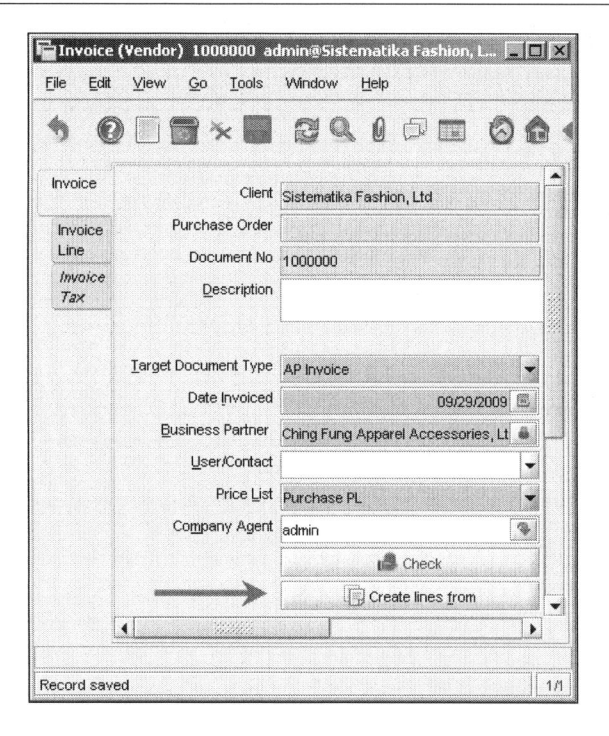

ADempiere will show an **Invoice Create lines from** window confirmation. Proceed with the following procedure:

1. In the **Receipt** field, just select an option from the list.
2. Select your targeted Material Receipt line records in the **Select** checkbox.
3. Finalize the process by clicking on the **OK** button.

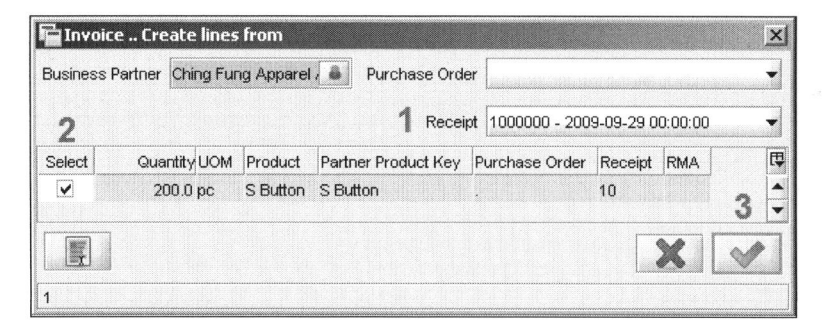

> In our simulation, the **Receipt** option contains only one list. In a real life scenario, it might contain more than one receipt list and more than one material receipt lines.

*Procurement Activities*

In the **Create lines from** activity, ADempiere copies the **Material Line** source data and puts it in your **Invoice (Vendor)**, **Invoice Line** record internally. It will take the price from the product price list. Of course, with your **Invoice Line** data, you will still be able to alter all of the necessary information when needed. Again, for our simplicity, we are keeping the original information.

Complete the **Ching Fung** and **Wilson Garment** invoices.

## Accounting facts

On posting your **Ching Fung** and **Wilson Garment** invoices, the **Invoice (Vendor)** will have a general journal entry format as follows:

| Window | Document | Sign | Description | Posting Type |
|---|---|---|---|---|
| Invoice (Vendor) | AP Invoice | Db | Product Inventory Clearing | Actual |
| | | Cr | Account Payable Trade | Actual |

The following screenshot shows the accounting facts/GL journal entries generated for the **Ching Fung** sample invoice:

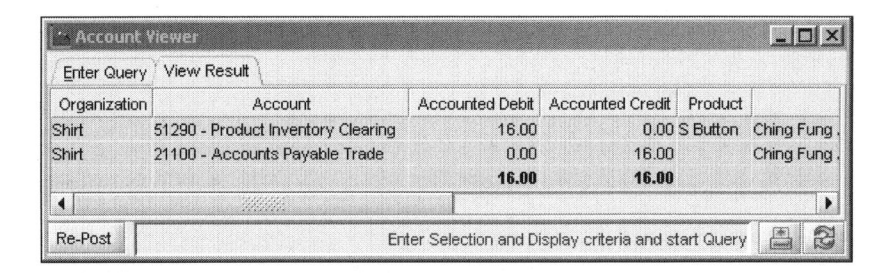

| Organization | Account | Accounted Debit | Accounted Credit | Product | |
|---|---|---|---|---|---|
| Shirt | 51290 - Product Inventory Clearing | 16.00 | 0.00 | S Button | Ching Fung |
| Shirt | 21100 - Accounts Payable Trade | 0.00 | 16.00 | | Ching Fung |
| | | **16.00** | **16.00** | | |

## Invoicing without a Material Receipt reference

For our next transaction, we will enter the invoice information for both **S Fabric** and **S Thread**. You need to enter the following information, one-by-one, in the **Invoice** tab:

| Field\Data | 3rd Data | 4th Data |
|---|---|---|
| Organization | Shirt | Shirt |
| Target Document Type | AP Invoice | AP Invoice |
| Business Partner | Hempel China Limited | Coats and Clarks |
| Price List | Purchase PL | Purchase PL |

You can set the **Date Invoiced** and **Account Date** field information. However, just leave the default date information as it is for now, and leave the other fields unchanged.

Like other manual entries transactions, we need to enter the detailed invoice information. In the **Invoice** tab, ensure that your active invoice record has **Hempel China Limited** as a business partner. Click on the **Invoice Line** tab, and enter the following information:

1. Set the **Product** field to **S Fabric**.
2. Set the **Quantity** field to **100**.
3. Set the **UOM** field to **Meter**.
4. Set the **Price** field to **3.80**.
5. Click on the **Save** button.

Here, you can set a payment method used for this invoice. The default setting is to use check as the payment rule. There is a **Check** button on the **Invoice** tab, which can be clicked on to change your payment rule.

Now, go back to the **Invoice** tab, and choose your second invoice (the one that has **Coats and Clarks** as a business partner). Enter the following information in the **Invoice Line** tab:

1. Set the **Product** field to **S Thread**.
2. Set the **Quantity** field to **50**.
3. Set the **UOM** field to **Cone**.
4. Set the **Price** field to **1.60**.
5. Click on the **Save** button.

> Prior to entering the information, ensure that you enter the **Quantity**, **UOM**, and **Price** information, as explicitly mentioned in the invoice document that comes from the Vendor.

In our simulation, all of the information in our **Purchase Order** document is the same, and it contains only one invoice line. In your real life situation, the **Quantity**, **UOM**, and **Price** might differ from the **Purchase Order** and may contain more than one invoice line.

Set the active tab to **Invoice**, and complete both of the **Invoice (Vendor)** documents by clicking on the **Complete** button.

## Accounting facts

After completing this document, as usual, there will be a **Not Posted** button that appears on your window. Click the **Not Posted** button to post both of your **Invoice (Vendor)** documents.

> *In the Material Receipt activity that we previously saw, we cannot post our Material Receipt document if there is no reference to a Purchase Order document and we are using Average PO as the product's costing method. Is it also applicable for Invoice (Vendor)?*

The answer is no. Although we do not have a reference to the Purchase Order or MM Receipt document, we will still be able to post the invoice document.

We can practice by posting the AP Invoice document, which has **Hempel China Limited** as a business partner. The accounting fact/GL journal entries generated results should be as shown in the following screenshot:

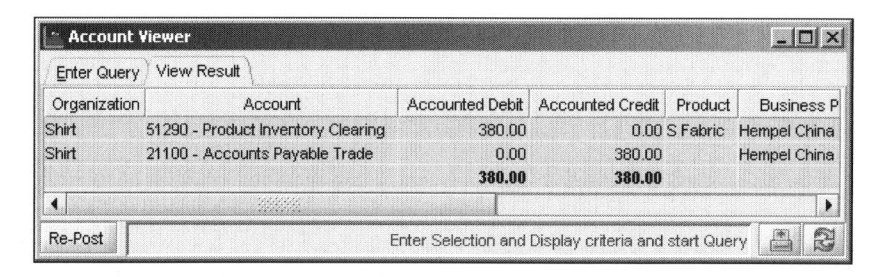

| Organization | Account | Accounted Debit | Accounted Credit | Product | Business P |
|---|---|---|---|---|---|
| Shirt | 51290 - Product Inventory Clearing | 380.00 | 0.00 | S Fabric | Hempel China |
| Shirt | 21100 - Accounts Payable Trade | 0.00 | 380.00 | | Hempel China |
| | | 380.00 | 380.00 | | |

Next, you need to post the **Coats and Clarks** invoice, and examine the accounting facts/GL journal entries generated for this AP Invoice document.

## Matching an Invoice to Material Receipt documents

By invoicing without the material receipt reference, we have to create a manual link from the vendor invoice to its material receipt. You will perform this task in the **Menu | Requisition-to-Invoice | Matching PO-Receipt-Invoice** form.

To match our invoice to its material receipt, set the following information:

1. Set the **Match From** field to **Invoice**.
2. Set the **Match To** field to **Receipt**.
3. Set the **Search Mode** field to **Not Matched**.
4. Set the **Business Partner** field to **Hempel China Limited**.

Click on the **Search records** button in the form, and ADempiere will show you a list of invoices that matched the criteria specified and that need to be processed further. Click on an available invoice line data (in the **Invoice** grid), and ADempiere will show you the eligible material receipt line records that you can proceed with (in the **Receipt** grid). Select the material receipt record, and click on the **Process** button to finalize our matching procedure.

> The steps to proceed with this task are almost the same as matching a material receipt to a purchase order using the **Matched Purchase Orders** window, as mentioned in the *Matching a Purchase Order to a Receipt* section.

You should process the invoice that belongs to the **Coats and Clarks** business partner by using the same procedure.

## Evaluating Matched Invoices

When performing an activity such as:

- Manually matching an AP Invoice to an MM Receipt document using the **Matching PO-Receipt-Invoice** form
- Entering invoice line information by clicking on the **Create lines from** button in the **Invoice (Vendor)** window

behind the scenes, ADempiere creates a matched invoice record. The record serves the following purposes:

- It shows the relationship between the **Invoice Line** and **Material Receipt Line** information. You can evaluate the matching document information in this window.
- The system will book a price variance (if any) between the Invoice Line product price and Purchase Order Line product price.

You can access these records in the **Menu | Requisition-to-Invoice | Matched Invoices** window.

With the prior invoice entry activities, this will result in four **Matched Invoices** records: two from manually matching invoice—material receipt (the **S Fabric** and **S Thread** invoices, which were taken from the **Hempel China Limited** and **Coats and Clarks** business partners) and two from creating vendor invoices with material receipt reference by clicking on the **Create lines from** button in the **Invoice (Vendor)** window (the **S Button** and **S Label** invoices, which were taken from the **Ching Fung** and **Wilson Garment** business partners).

The following screenshot shows an example of our **Matched Invoices** records:

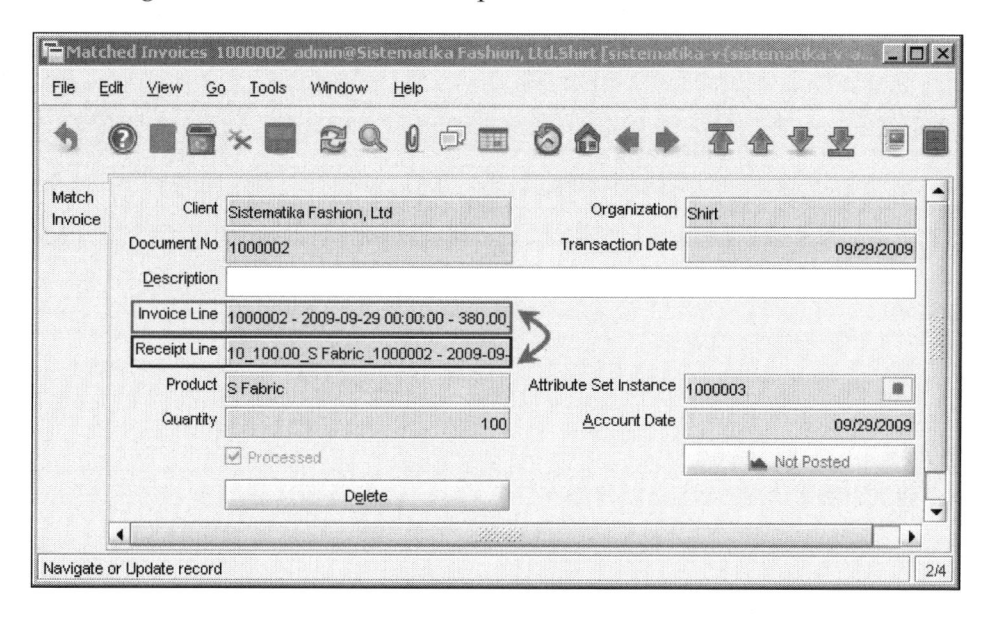

Performing manual **Matching Invoice – Receipt** activities may lead to incorrectly setting a document relationship. You can identify this within the window and take action to remove the records by clicking on the **Delete** button (in this window, you cannot remove the records by pressing the *F3* key). Then you can set a correct relationship using the **Matching PO-Receipt-Invoice** form again.

## Accounting facts

We will now learn about the accounting facts/GL journal entries generated in this window. The accounting facts general entry journal format in the **Matched Invoices** window should be:

| Sign | | Description | Posting Type |
|------|------|-------------|--------------|
| Db | | Not invoiced receipts | Actual |
| | Cr | Product Inventory Clearing | Actual |
| Dr | Cr | Invoiced Price Variance | Actual |

For example, select the records that have **S Fabric** as a product from the list of available **Matched Invoices** records, and post this document. The accounting facts/GL journal entries generated is shown in the following screenshot:

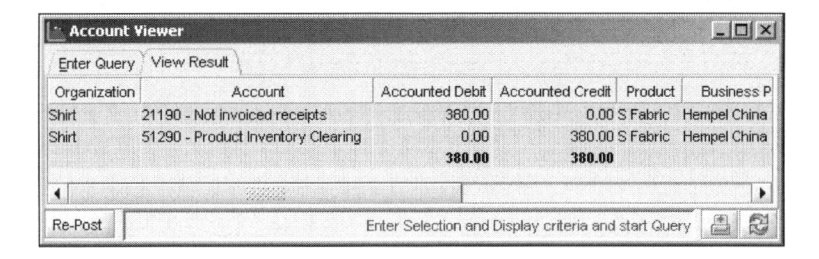

| Organization | Account | Accounted Debit | Accounted Credit | Product | Business P |
|---|---|---|---|---|---|
| Shirt | 21190 - Not invoiced receipts | 380.00 | 0.00 | S Fabric | Hempel China |
| Shirt | 51290 - Product Inventory Clearing | 0.00 | 380.00 | S Fabric | Hempel China |
| | | **380.00** | **380.00** | | |

If we do not have a product price variance, as is the case in our **S Fabric** example, ADempiere only generates a debit **Not invoiced receipt** and a credit **Product Inventory Clearing**. Now you are free to post the rest of the **Matched Invoices** documents.

> The debit or credit **Invoiced Price Variance** will be present if there is any product price variance between our **AP Invoice** document and **Purchase Order** document. The debit or credit position of the **Invoiced Price Variance** depends on whether the invoice price is *less than* or *more than* the purchase order price.

# Summary of Material Receipt and Invoice (Vendor) accounting facts

Now that we have seen all of the activities involved when processing our vendor invoices, we will summarize our accounting facts/GL journal entries generated with the **Material Receipt, Invoice (Vendor)**, and **Matched Invoices** as follows:

| Window | Document | Dr/Cr | Description | Value | |
|---|---|---|---|---|---|
| Material Receipt | MM Receipt | Dr | Product Asset | 380 | |
| | | Cr | Not invoiced receipts | | 380 |
| Matched Invoices | | Dr | Not invoiced receipts | 380 | |
| | | Cr | Product Inventory Clearing | | 380 |
| Invoice (Vendor) | AP Invoice | Dr | Product Inventory Clearing | 380 | |
| | | Cr | Account Payable Trade | | 380 |

With this journal, you know that the final result of the accounting facts is **debit Product Asset** *against* **credit Account Payable Trade**.

*Procurement Activities*

# Making a payment to the vendor

After booking our **AP Invoice** document in the **Invoice (Vendor)** window, we admit that we have some liabilities to four of our vendors. As a company common behavior, the payment method could be set to use the company bank account, or to make payment by cash. It is up to the company to choose the desired payment method.

In our example, we have four invoices that we need to pay. Of course, for a real company, there will be hundreds or even thousands of invoices. ADempiere can accommodate both bank account and cash transaction payment methods. In the following sections, we will practice both of these payment methods.

## Outstanding liabilities

The easiest way to check Sistematika Fashion, Ltd.'s liabilities is by accessing your Business Partner window. Open your **Menu | Partner Relations | Business Partner Rules | Business Partner** window, and point your record to **Hempel China Limited** in the **Business Partner** tab, as shown in the following screenshot:

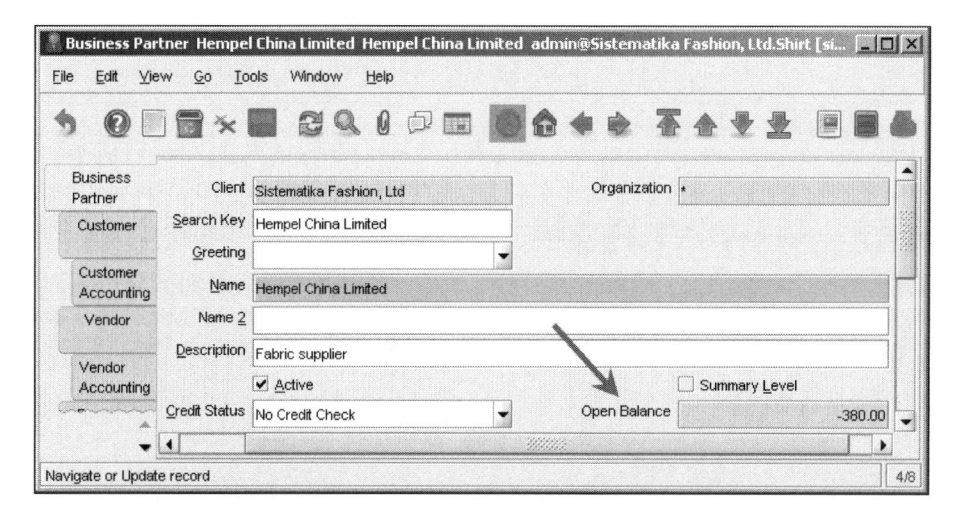

With this information, ADempiere tells us the value of the total liabilities that we have in the **Open Balance** field. The value is **-380**. If we have more than one invoice that belongs to this vendor, the **Open Balance** will sum up all of the liabilities to this vendor. In this case, we have one unpaid AP Invoice document for **Hempel China Limited**, which has 380 as the invoice value.

[ If we have liabilities, the **Open Balance** will show a negative value. ]

# Payment Selection

Imagine that we have several outstanding invoices for **Hempel China Limited**, and we need to schedule how much money to spend for such payments.

## Creating a list of unpaid invoices

ADempiere provides us with a report to show a list of unpaid invoices. You can display this list by using **Menu | Open Items | Open Items** reports. Click on this report, *deselect* the **Sales Transaction** checkbox, and then click on the **OK** button. As a result, the system will show you reports. Click the **Next Page** button to go to page two, as shown in the following screenshot:

| Business Partner | Due Date | Grand Total | Invoice | Invoice Pay Schedule | Net Days |
|---|---|---|---|---|---|
| Ching Fung Apparel Accessories, Ltd | 09/29/2009 | 16.00 | 1000000 - 2009-09-29 00:00:00 - 16.00 | | 0 |
| Wilson Garment Accessories, Ltd | 09/29/2009 | 80.00 | 1000001 - 2009-09-29 00:00:00 - 80.00 | | 0 |
| Hempel China Limited | 09/29/2009 | 380.00 | 1000002 - 2009-09-29 00:00:00 - 380.00 | | 0 |
| Coats and Clarks | 09/29/2009 | 80.00 | 1000003 - 2009-09-29 00:00:00 - 80.00 | | 0 |

We can choose one-by-one from a list of our outstanding unpaid invoices that need to be set for a payment. The task of manually selecting the records could be exhausting when we have hundreds of invoices. Fortunately, instead of preparing a manual payment by yourself, ADempiere has a feature to automatically create a list of payment drafts or payment proposals for you.

## Creating a payment proposal

> *If I want to see all of the outstanding invoices that need to be set for payment, ADempiere gives me a list of outstanding invoices. From the upcoming list of outstanding invoices, ADempiere still needs my decision to approve the payment. Here, could I set a full or partial payment, or even not process the payment by removing invoices from the list of payment proposal?*

You use the **Menu | Open Items | Payment Selection** window to perform this activity. Using this window, we can proceed with the payment proposal for **Hempel China Limited** for our example.

You can now open this window. This window will contain three tabs: **Payment Selection**, **Payment Selection Line**, and **Prepared Payment**.

*Procurement Activities*

> Opening this window will automatically set the status record to the **Inserted** state. With this state, there is no need to click on the **New** button to enter our data. However, you can click on the **New** button just in case you are not in the **Inserted** state.

In the **Payment Selection** tab, set the **Name** field to **PS Hempel 093009** and the **Bank Account** field to **USD-1-001-888888**, as shown in the following screenshot:

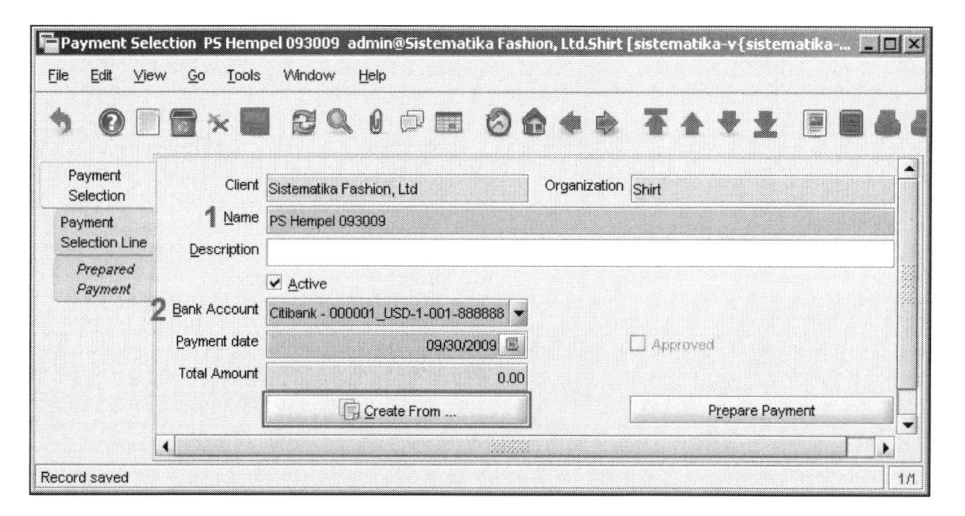

Click on the **Save** button. We need to enter a list of invoices that need to be paid, in the payment selection line. For our practice, we can create a list of invoices by clicking on the **Create From** button. ADempiere will show us a confirmation window. In this window, set the following information:

1. Set the **Business Partner** field to **Hempel China Limited**.
2. Deselect the **Only Discount** checkbox.
3. Select the **Only Due** checkbox.
4. Set the **Payment Rule** to the blank option.
5. Click on the **OK** button to proceed with a **Payment Selection**.

With our sample data (which has four outstanding invoices), the **Payment Selection Line** tab will contain one outstanding invoices record (it might vary with your installation) for **Hempel China Limited**.

As previously explained, in the available **Payment Selection Line** data, we are free to do one of the following:

- Set a full amount payment
- Enter a certain amount in the **Payment amount** field for partial payment
- Remove this record from the **Payment Selection Line**

However, we do not touch the result of the **Create From** process. This means that we will set a full payment for one invoice of **Hempel China Limited**.

There is one last thing we need to do before we proceed to our **Payment Selection**. In the **Payment Selection** tab, we can click on the **Prepare Payment** button to finalize the tasks. In the upcoming **Create Prepared Payments to be paid** confirmation window, to support further processing, you need set the **Overwrite Payment Rule** to **Check**, and click on the **OK** button.

## Payment Print/Export

In the previous **Payment Selection** activity, because we are using **Check** as our payment rule, we need to print our **Check**. Open the **Menu | Open Items | Payment Print/Export** window.

Ensure that you select **PS Hempel 093009 - 380.00** as your **Payment Selection**, as shown in the following screenshot

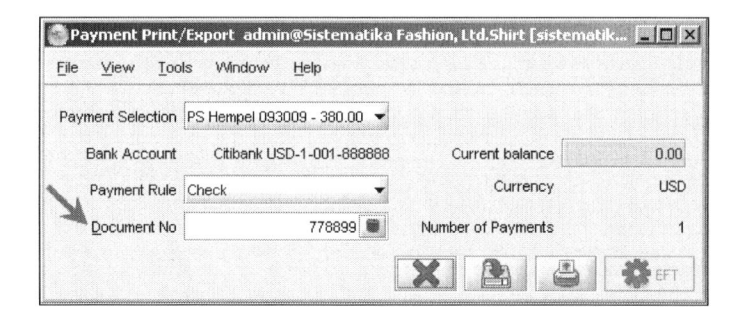

Here, you can set your bank check number in the **Document No** field. For our example, you should supply **778899** as your bank check number, and click on the **Print** button. Examine your bank check print document format. During the confirmation to print a remittance advice, you can click on the **Cancel** button.

## Account Payable payments

After printing the bank check document, ADempiere internally creates an **AP Payment** document with a **Completed** status. You can access this document in the **Menu | Open Items | Payment** window. This **Payment** window contains three tabs: **Payment**, **Allocate**, and **Allocations**.

There are two types of document type here:

- AP Payment
- AR Receipt

In this discussion, ADempiere automatically uses AP Payment as its document type. We will discuss and set an AR Receipt document implementation later.

> If you need to create a manual **Payment** document, you can directly enter your data in this window. Just ensure that you use the AP Payment document type with your new records.

## Accounting facts

Posting an **AP Payment** document will give you a general journal entry format as follows:

| Window | Document | Sign | Description | Posting Type |
|---|---|---|---|---|
| Payment | AP Payment | Db | Payment Selection | Actual |
| | | Cr | Checking In-Transfer | Actual |

In our **Hempel China Limited** example, the following is the real accounting fact/GL journal entries created after posting the **AP Invoice** document:

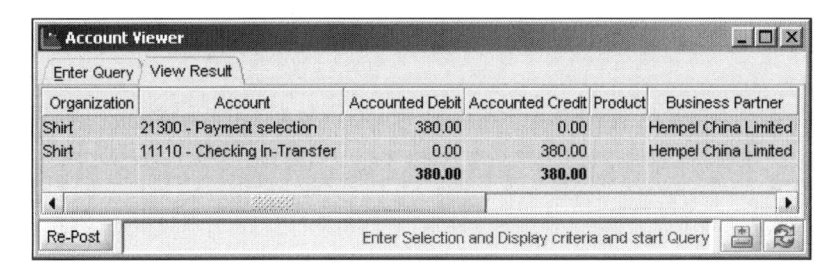

| Organization | Account | Accounted Debit | Accounted Credit | Product | Business Partner |
|---|---|---|---|---|---|
| Shirt | 21300 - Payment selection | 380.00 | 0.00 | | Hempel China Limited |
| Shirt | 11110 - Checking In-Transfer | 0.00 | 380.00 | | Hempel China Limited |
| | | 380.00 | 380.00 | | |

## Viewing payment allocation

In the previous payment activity, the accounting facts or journal entry was generated by using **21300 – Payment selection** in the journal debit position. We have not yet touched the **Account Payable** account.

> *Logically, with such an AP Payment transaction, our vendor liabilities should be deducted. Why is it not going to the Account Payable account directly?*

ADempiere has its own workflow for working with **AP Payment** documents. After completing an AP Payment document, the system automatically generates the Payment Allocation document. As indicated by the document name, the aim of this document is to show us the AP Invoice in which the payment has been allocated.

You can access this Payment Allocation document in the **Menu | Open Items | View Allocation** window. In the **Allocation** tab, find the document that has **Payment: 778899 [n]** as its description (it could vary with your results). Go to the **Allocation Line** tab to see the list of AP Invoice documents applicable to this payment allocation.

## Accounting facts

Post this document, and it will generate a general accounting fact/GL journal entry format as follows:

| Sign | Description | Posting Type |
|------|-------------|--------------|
| Db | Account Payable Trade | Actual |
| Cr | Payment Selection | Actual |

The following is a real journal created based on our **Hempel China Limited** payment allocation document example:

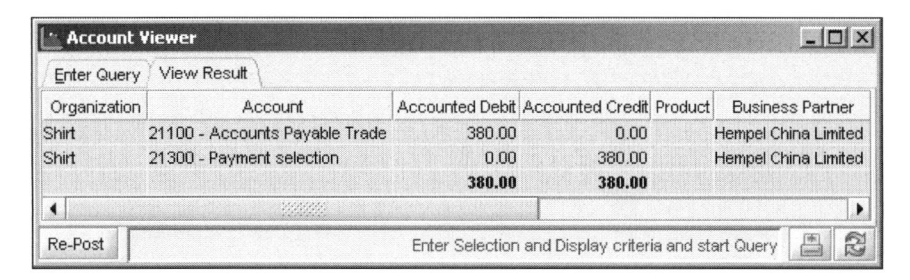

| Organization | Account | Accounted Debit | Accounted Credit | Product | Business Partner |
|---|---|---|---|---|---|
| Shirt | 21100 - Accounts Payable Trade | 380.00 | 0.00 | | Hempel China Limited |
| Shirt | 21300 - Payment selection | 0.00 | 380.00 | | Hempel China Limited |
| | | 380.00 | 380.00 | | |

These transactions affect your vendor liabilities and are deducted from your **Accounts Payable Trade** account.

# Bank Statement

*In the previous AP Payment document, the credit accounting facts generated was Checking In-Transfer. In-Transfer? As far as I know, performing a payment should be deducted from our asset (bank account in this case). It seems this is not a real Asset type of account. Is this a mediator or a clearing account?*

Yes, you are correct. This is a clearing account. The real Checking account journal entries (member of the Asset type of account) will be generated when we print an ADempiere Bank Statement document.

> The aim of the ADempiere Bank Statement document is to reconcile your ADempiere bank account transaction against your banking statement.

On request, the company can print their bank statement. They can go to the bank customer service and take this bank statement document. Furthermore, if you have online banking access, you can get your bank statement through your banking website.

On receiving your bank statement document, you can start a reconciliation activity by entering this information into the ADempiere **Bank Statement** window. You can access the ADempiere **Bank Statement** window at **Menu | Open Items | Bank Statement**.

## Entering Bank Statement information

Now, open the **Bank Statement** window. This will contain two tabs: **Bank Statement** and **Statement Line**. To set our bank statement information, enter the following information:

1. Set the **Organization** field to the value **Shirt**.
2. Set your Bank Account reconciliation target. In our example, set the **Bank Account** field to **USD-1-001-888888**.
3. Set the **Name** field to **First Bank Statement**. For our example, set your bank account **Beginning Balance** to **1000**.
5. Click on the **Save** button.

# Entering a Bank Statement Line

Navigate to the **Statement Line** tab. In this tab, normally we will enter all of our bank statements, which were previously taken from our bank customer service or online banking access. This bank statement might contain transactions such as:

- Payment to our vendor
- Receipts from our customer
- Cash transfer to or from a bank account
- Bank charges
- Bank interest

These five types of transactions can be managed by ADempiere out of the box.

For our **Hempel China Limited** payment, within the **Bank Statement Line** tab, you should enter your bank statement information as follows:

1. Set the **Statement Line date**, **Account Date**, and **Effective Date** fields to **09/30/2009**.
2. Set the **Statement Amount** to **-380**. This information represents the amount in the bank account.
3. Next, we need to reconcile the **Statement Amount** value with our ADempiere bank account transaction. Select your payment data by clicking on the **Payment** field. In the upcoming **Payment Info** confirmation window, you have to *deselect* the **Receipt** checkbox, which indicates that we will be choosing our payment transaction to the vendor. Within the available payment list, select an appropriate record, and click on the **OK** button.
4. Enter your necessary **Reference No** or **Memo**.

Save your information.

In this activity, we actually entered data from the bank statement, and set the reconciliation with our ADempiere bank account transaction (Payment field). Now, you need to finalize this document by clicking on the **Complete** button in the **Bank Statement** tab.

With your real company bank statement data, you will enter all of the bank statements and perform the necessary reconciliation.

> To speed up your bank statement entry, you can use the **Create lines from** button in the **Bank Statement** tab. You can make a selection of *in transit* transactions against the bank account selected in the header, from here. For this task, you need to enter a transaction that is not yet available in the bank account transactions.

## Accounting facts

Based on the previous bank statement entries, you can now post your **First Bank Statement** record. The general journal entry format generated for previous activities are:

| Sign | Description | Posting Type |
|------|-------------|--------------|
| Db   | Checking In-Transfer | Actual |
| Cr   | Checking Account | Actual |

The following is our sample accounting facts/GL journal entries for the ADempiere bank statement transaction:

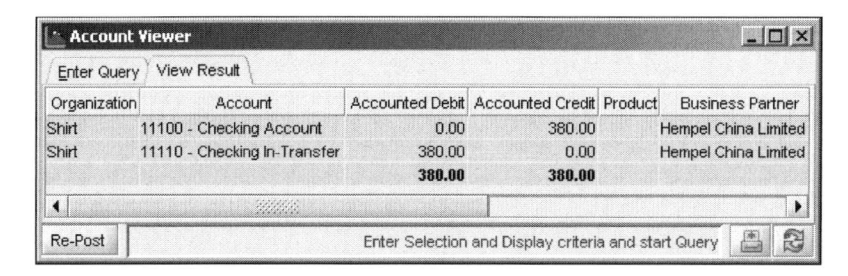

| Organization | Account | Accounted Debit | Accounted Credit | Product | Business Partner |
|--------------|---------|-----------------|------------------|---------|------------------|
| Shirt | 11100 - Checking Account | 0.00 | 380.00 | | Hempel China Limited |
| Shirt | 11110 - Checking In-Transfer | 380.00 | 0.00 | | Hempel China Limited |
|       |                              | **380.00** | **380.00** | | |

# Summary of Payment, Allocation, and Bank Statement accounting facts

> *In our understanding, while we have a payment, the accounting facts/journal finally has a debit Account Payable Trade against the credit Checking Account. Is this applicable in our ADempiere?*

Yes, it is applicable in our ADempiere. Refer to the following table for our accounting facts/GL journal entry summarized for **View Allocation**, **Payment**, and **Bank Statement**:

| Window | Document | Dr/Cr | Description | Value | |
|--------|----------|-------|-------------|-------|---|
| View Allocation | | Dr | Account Payable Trade | 380 | |
|  | | Cr | Payment Selection | | 380 |
| Payment | AP Payment | Dr | Payment Selection | 380 | |
|  | | Cr | Checking In-Transfer | | 380 |
| Bank Statement | | Dr | Checking In-Transfer | 380 | |
|  | | Cr | Checking Account | | 380 |

As you can see here, the **Payment Selection** and **Checking In-Transfer** are in transit or clearing account that could be swept out for the final journal entry format.

For your practice, you will perform a **Payment Selection**, **View Allocation**, and **Bank Statement** transaction for **S Thread**, with **Coats and Clarks** as a business partner.

# Cash payment

We have two purchase orders left for payment, **Ching Fung Apparel Accessories** for **S Button**, and **Wilson Garment Accessories** for **S Label**. With these purchase orders, we will proceed to the payment using the available cash in Sistematika Fashion, Ltd. Open the **Menu | Open Items | Cash Journal** window. This window contains two tabs: **Cash Journal** and **Cash Line**.

# Cash Type

> *In our old application, while we were working with a cash transaction (for example, money spent on food expenses), our transaction used to consist of entering an account for food expenses against an account for cash/petty cash. How do I perform such a transaction?*

With ADempiere, all of the transactions related to cash will be booked with the help of the cash type. There is no need to book these like the traditional general ledger transaction mentioned previously. In general, there are six cash types available:

- **Bank Account Transfer**: Used for activities related to transfers to and from a bank account.
- **Charge**: Used to book specific charges, such as Newspaper and Postage expenses. You can set up a many types of charges as you like.
- **Difference**: Used to book any cash variances.
- **General Expenses**: Used to book general expenses. These expenses shall affect only one account and are not as flexible as the Charge cash type.
- **General Receipts**: Used to book general receipts, and affect to one account only.
- **Invoice**: Used to book any cash transaction related to an invoice.

> Beware that **Cash Journal** transactions could be entering a positive or negative amount value. This is unusual when compared to other common types of old or other proprietary systems. Fortunately, both positive and negative amount values are legal with ADempiere.

*Procurement Activities*

The meaning of the positive and negative amount values in the **Cash Journal** are explained as follows:

| Amount value sign | Description |
|---|---|
| + (positive) | All of + (positive) amount values shall **increment** our cash |
| - (negative) | All of – (negative) amount values shall **decrement** our cash |

# Invoice cash payment

We will practice setting the cash payment for **Ching Fung Apparel Accessories**. In your **Cash Journal** window, enter the following information in the **Cash Journal** tab:

1. Set the **Cash Book** field to **USD Cash Book**.
2. Set the **Name** field to **Payment for Ching Fung** (you can enter anything here).
3. Set the **Statement Date** and **Account Date** field to **09/30/2009** (you can enter any date here).
4. Set your **Beginning Balance**. For our example, we have set it as **1000**.
5. Then click on the **Save** button.

After setting the **Cash Journal** tab information, we need to enter our detailed transaction. Navigate to the **Cash Line** tab, and enter the following information:

1. Set the **Cash Type** field to **Invoice** (pick from the list).
2. Set the **Amount** field to **-16**.
3. Click in the **Invoice** field, and the system will show the **Invoice Info** confirmation window. *Deselect* the **Sales Transaction** checkbox, select the **Ching Fung** invoice, and then click on the **OK** button.
4. Then click on the **Save** button to persist your **Cash Line** document. You are done!

Go back to your **Cash Journal** tab, and finalize this activity by clicking on the **Complete** button.

## Accounting facts

The general journal format for the cash journal with cash type invoice is:

| Sign | | Description | Posting Type |
|---|---|---|---|
| Db | | Petty Cash In-Transfer | Actual |
| | Cr | Petty Cash | Actual |

The following is an example of the accounting facts/GL journal generated for our cash payment to **Ching Fung**:

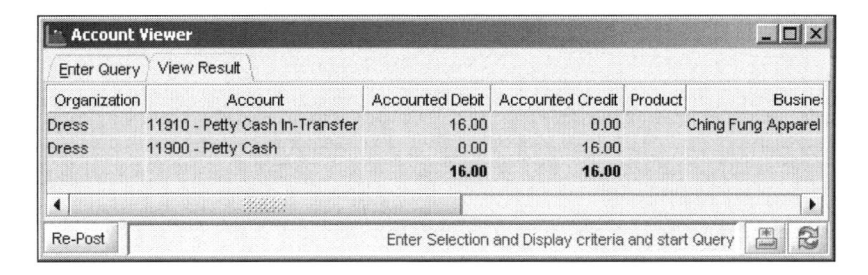

| Organization | Account | Accounted Debit | Accounted Credit | Product | Busine: |
|---|---|---|---|---|---|
| Dress | 11910 - Petty Cash In-Transfer | 16.00 | 0.00 | | Ching Fung Apparel |
| Dress | 11900 - Petty Cash | 0.00 | 16.00 | | |
| | | 16.00 | 16.00 | | |

## Cash Payment Allocation

*With the cash type invoice, the debit account is Petty Cash In-Transfer. We have not yet touched the Invoice (Vendor). It seems that we need to allocate a payment to the correct Invoice.*

Yes, you are absolutely correct. Internally, ADempiere will automatically create an **Allocation** document. This document has a completed document status. We will access the cash payment allocation in the **Menu | Open Items | View Allocation** window. In the author's system, the allocation document has **Cash Journal: Payment for Ching Fung – Line No 10** as its description.

## Accounting facts

You need to post this document. The general journal format for the cash invoice payment allocation is:

| Sign | | Description | Posting Type |
|---|---|---|---|
| Db | | Accounts Payable Trade | Actual |
| | Cr | Petty Cash In-Transfer | Actual |

The following is the accounting facts/GL journal entries for our **Ching Fung** cash payment example:

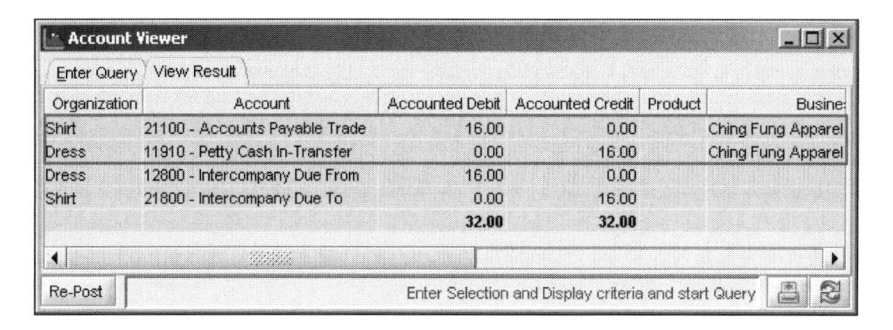

| Organization | Account | Accounted Debit | Accounted Credit | Product | Busine: |
|---|---|---|---|---|---|
| Shirt | 21100 - Accounts Payable Trade | 16.00 | 0.00 | | Ching Fung Apparel |
| Dress | 11910 - Petty Cash In-Transfer | 0.00 | 16.00 | | Ching Fung Apparel |
| Dress | 12800 - Intercompany Due From | 16.00 | 0.00 | | |
| Shirt | 21800 - Intercompany Due To | 0.00 | 16.00 | | |
| | | **32.00** | **32.00** | | |

> Do not worry about the additional **Intercompany Due From** and **Intercompany Due To** accounting facts/GL journal entries. This happens because we have a transaction in multiple organizations. For your reference, do you remember that our cash book has been set up in the **Dress** organization, while our transaction (Material Receipt, Invoice (Vendor), and so on) took place in the **Shirt** organization? Anyway, with some configuration, we could avoid the **Intercompany Due From** and **Intercompany Due To** journal entries. We will discuss this in the *Avoiding Intercompany Due From/To journal entries* section of Chapter 7, *Accounting Information and Configuration*.

# Summary of Cash Payment and Cash Allocation accounting facts

As you may have expected, our final accounting facts/GL journal is a debit **Accounts Payable Trade** against a credit to **Petty Cash**. Refer to the following table for a summary of accounting facts:

| Window | Dr/Cr | | Description | Value | |
|---|---|---|---|---|---|
| Cash Payment Invoice allocation | Dr | | Accounts Payable Trade | 16 | |
| | | Cr | Petty Cash In-Transfer | | 16 |
| Cash Journal | Dr | | Petty Cash In-Transfer | 16 | |
| | | Cr | Petty Cash | | 16 |

For your practice, you can perform a cash payment with the **Invoice** cash type for **S Label** with **Wilson Garment Accessories** as the business partner.

# Summary

In this chapter, we talked about how to perform procurement activities using ADempiere.

To know exactly what goes on behind the scenes related to the accounting facts/GL journal activities, we have performed manual document postings. Using this approach, in return, we have learned exactly what the accounting facts/GL journal entries generated are, and when these accounting facts are generated.

In our discussion in this chapter, prior to creating a Purchase Order document, we have seen that it's quite common to first create a Purchase Requisition document. There is an option provided to create the Purchase Requisition document automatically. We have seen that this task can be done by setting up a replenish configuration. We have also seen how to set up the replenish configuration.

We have learned that one of the replenish configuration's requirement is the availability to set a default price list. With all of this information, we have then created our first requisition document by running the replenish report. Based on the replenish document, we could then generate a Purchase Order document.

Next, we performed a material receipt, vendor invoicing, and payment to our vendor, and reconciled this payment with our bank statement. These activities generated an accounting fact, and with this, we learned about exactly how and when an accounting fact occurs.

With all of the available raw material, in the next chapter, we will see how to handle all of the charges related to material procurement, how to manufacture a shirt, and then perform a sales activity. With this sales activity, we shall receive a payment or receipt from your customer, and we will then introduce you to the process of how to reconcile this receipt's transaction.

# 6
# Landed Costs, Production, and Sales Activities

*Procurement activities* and *payment to vendor* topics have been covered in the previous chapter. We also already know about the accounting facts or GL journal entries generated related to those activities.

In this chapter, we will discuss how to handle all of the charges related to raw material procurement in the *Landed cost* section. With the availability of material in-house, we can manufacture our goods, and sell these finished goods to our customers.

In this chapter, we will discuss and practice the following:

- Landed cost
- Manufacturing finished goods—shirts
- Quotations
- Sales orders
- Dispatching finished goods to customers
- Receiving payment from customers
- Reconciling the bank statement with regard to customer payment
- Handling direct sales

We will activate the accounting processor, and explain the accounting facts/GL journal entries generated, wherever applicable.

## Activating the accounting processor

Previously, we worked with the accounting processor in a disabled state. In this condition, we had to post the documents one-by-one, manually. Ideally, the posting of documents should be done behind the scenes, and it is not a laborious task. From this chapter onwards, we will enable the accounting processor and watch the impact of the activated accounting processor.

To enable and activate accounting processors, use the following procedure:

1. *Log in with user ID admin*, using **Sistematika Fashion, Ltd Admin** as the role. and * as the **Organization**.
2. Open the **Menu | System Admin | General Rules | Server | Accounting Processor** window. By default, it will contain one record.
3. Click on the **Grid Toggle** button, to show detailed information.
4. Select the **Active** checkbox.
5. Set **Frequency Type** to **Minute**.
6. Set **Frequency** to **1**.

These conditions instruct the ADempiere server to process the unposted documents every minute.

> You can alter the **Frequency Type** and **Frequency** information according to the needs of your ADempiere implementation.

Log out from the ADempiere client, and then stop (by executing `C:\Adempiere\utils\RUN_Server2Stop.bat`) and restart (by executing `C:\Adempiere\utils\RUN_Server2.bat`) your ADempiere server.

## Landed costs

We have to import material, and it's quite common that we need some help from the transportation company to pick our material up from the airport or seaport and send this material to our company's warehouses. For this type of service, the transportation company will raise an invoice document to get the payment.

There are many types of expenses that are incurred when handling raw material procurement. For example:

- Transportation charges
- Clearance charges
- Custom duties
- Handling charges, and so on

It would be better if ADempiere was able to handle these types of charges and apply these costs or charges directly to the raw material. With all of charges assigned to the raw material, we will know exactly how much to spend to acquire this material.

In the procurement context, **landed cost** is the total cost of goods including purchase price and all types of charges that may be incurred in delivering the ordered material to the company's warehouses.

The question is: how to map and book these type of charges into ADempiere?

> *It will be amazing if we can extend these types of costs (transportation or any other type of cost related to material procurement) directly to our material. With our current system, we just need to allocate and set these costs to an expenses type of account.*

Yes, ADempiere has a mechanism to book these charges to the material. With this mechanism, we can and will distribute the total expenses raised during the procurement and/or receipt of materials directly to our material.

We will now practice how to implement the transportation charges and examine its impact on the valuation of our material. For this, we need to set up some additional information.

# Prerequisite configuration

We need to set up some additional information to prepare for the landed cost example transaction. *Log in with user ID admin*, using **Sistematika Fashion, Ltd Admin** as the role, and * as the organization.

## Entering an additional business partner

As we have not yet registered the transportation company as our business partner, we will enter the relevant information in the **Menu | Partner Relations | Business Partner Rules | Business Partner** window. Open this window, and then set and save the following information:

| Field | Description |
|---|---|
| Organization | * |
| Search Key | Maersk |
| Name | Maersk Logistic |
| Description | Transporter Company |
| Business Partner Group | Standard |

After completing the fields mentioned in the previous table, perform the following steps:

1. Go to the **Vendor** tab, and select the **Vendor** checkbox.
2. Go to the **Location** tab, click on the **New** button, and then click on the button inside the **Address** field. Enter **Semarang** in the **City** field, set the **Country** field to **Indonesia**, and then click on the **OK** button.
3. Go to the **Contact (User)** tab, and set **Andrea** in the **Name** field.

Next, we will need to prepare a new account combination.

## Creating a new account combination

When working on the transportation charges, we can utilize the **73300 – Shipping Expenses** account from the chart of accounts. Moreover, for future reference, we will create an account combination using the **14120 – Product Asset** account.

Open the **Menu | Performance Analysis | Accounting Rules | Account Combination** window, set and save the following information:

| Field | 1st data | 2nd data |
|---|---|---|
| Alias | 73300 | 14120 |
| Organization | Shirt | Shirt |
| Account | 73300 | 14120 |

## Setting transportation charges

We need a special **Charge** record to book our transportation charges. Open the **Menu | Performance Analysis | Accounting Rules | Charge** window, click on the **New** button in the **Charge** tab, and set the following information:

1. Enter * in the **Organization** field.
2. Enter **Transportation** in the **Name** field.
3. Click on the **Save** button. Go to the **Accounting** tab, and change the default **Charge Expense** and **Charge Revenue** to the **Shirt-73300** account combination, as shown in the following screenshot:

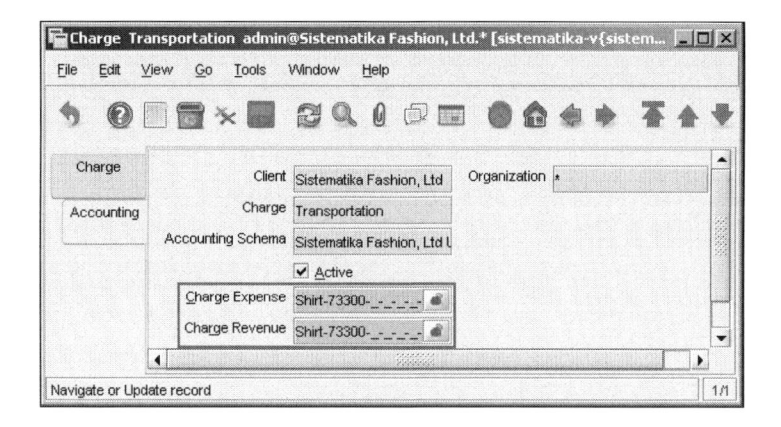

*Is there a way to create a Charge through a more compact solution?*

As an alternative, you can use the **Generate Charges** window to create a **Charge**. There is no need to create a new accounting combination and to manually set up both the charge expense and revenue in the **Charge** window.

To create new charges, open the **Menu | Performance Analysis | Accounting Rules | Generate Charges** window. This window contains a list of accounts that have revenue and expense account types, and that can be used to create a new **Charge**.

For example, you can create the **73300 – Shipping Expenses** charge as follows:

1. Select the **Select** checkbox in the **73300** account.
2. Click on the **Create From Account** button.

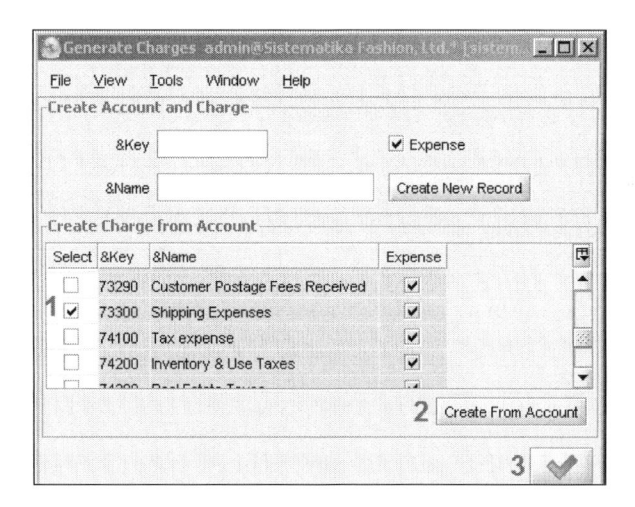

3. You will be prompted with the **Charge created** confirmation window that indicates a successful **Charge** creation.

Check your **Charge** window, and you will find that a new **Shipping Expenses** charge is now available.

## Setting a new cost element

The purpose of a cost element is to capture, retrieve, and display different categories of cost, such as material, overhead, burden, and freight cost types; in a single product costing model.

To distribute transportation costs (or other eligible costs) to the material, we will create a new cost element. Open the **Menu | Performance Analysis | Costing | Cost Element** window. Click on the **New** button, and complete the following information fields:

1. Set the **Organization** field to **\***.
2. Set the **Name** field to **Freight**.
3. Set the **Description** field to **Additional material cost element as an example of landed cost implementation**.
4. Set the **Cost Element Type** field to **Material** (select from the given options).
5. Set the **Costing Method** field blank, and then click on the **Save** button.

We will continue our configuration by altering the product's **cost adjustment** default account.

## Altering the product cost adjustment default account

If we post the future **Transaction Charge** transactions through the **Invoice (Vendor)** window by using the **AP Invoice** document type, it will generally produce accounting facts/GL journal entries in the format shown in the following table:

| Window | Document | Sign | Description | Posting Type |
|---|---|---|---|---|
| Invoice (Vendor) | AP Invoice | Db | Cost Adjustment | Actual |
| | | Cr | Account Payable Trade | Actual |

In the current configuration, the product **Cost Adjustment** default account is set to the **\*-51210-_-_-_-_-_** account combination. For your reference, open the **Menu | Material Management | Material Management Rules | Product** window. Navigate to the **S Fabric** records, click on the **Accounting** tab, and find the **Cost Adjustment** field information.

*Earlier, you told us that we can allocate our landed costs to raw materials directly. But depending on the accounting facts/GL journal entries generated when booking the transportation costs, it seems that we also need to alter our cost adjustment default account configuration from \*-51210-\_-\_-\_-\_ to the Product Asset account. Do I need to alter this configuration?*

You are definitely right. We will have to alter the **Cost Adjustment** default account to our newly-created **Shirt-14120-\_-\_-\_-\_** account combination. Apply this configuration to the **S Fabric**, **S Thread**, **S Button**, and **S Label** products. Refer to Chapter 4, *Setting up Master Data and Knowing its Accounting Configuration*, for the procedure to alter the account combination.

The following screenshot shows the new **Cost Adjustment** configuration for the **S Fabric** products, listed in the **Accounting** tab of the **Product** window:

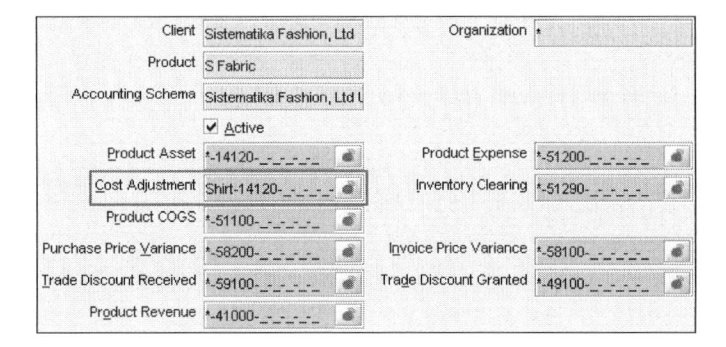

## Creating additional Price Lists

*As the Currency field has a read-only status, you will notice that you cannot create a new AP Invoice document in the Invoice (Vendor) window with other than in USD currency.*

The currency that is used when creating the AP Invoice document will be taken from the Price List configuration. Due to the unavailability of the IDR price list, we need to create a price list that uses IDR currency.

Log out from system and *login again using user ID admin*. Instead of using \* as organization, set **Shirt** as your organization and **1st Shirt W/h** as your warehouse. Open the **Menu | Material Management | Material Management Rules | Price List** window. In the **Price List** tab, set the following field information:

1. Set the **Organization** field to \*.
2. Set the **Name** field to **IDR Purchase PL**.
3. Set the **Currency** field to **IDR**.

After saving this information, go to the **Version** tab, and set the following field information:

1. Set the **Name** field to **IDR Purchase PL version**.
2. Set the **Price List Schema** field to **Standard**.

With this existing IDR price list, we can now enter our transportation charges.

# Registering for the transportation charges

For the services provided by the transportation company, they will supply us with invoice document. Based on this document, we can proceed with our payment. We will book this invoice through the **Invoice (Vendor)** window.

> Before we proceed with this invoice, we have to know exactly how to allocate this cost to the material. Imagine that we receive an invoice document consisting of bills for two or more deliveries. Examine what currency they used with this invoice. As the transportation will happen internally within your country, the local currency will be used when issuing the invoice. In our case, we can set it to the IDR currency (recall that our accounting schema used USD currency).

We will assume that we received an invoice from Maersk Logistic worth IDR 2,000,000 for their service to transport material to our company warehouses.

## Cost distribution type

This transportation cost will be distributed to our material. Maersk Logistic provided the following details of the goods:

| Raw Material | Qty | Value/Cost (US$) |
|---|---|---|
| S Fabric | 100 meters | 380 |
| S Thread | 50 Cone | 80 |
| S Button | 200 Pieces | 16 |
| S Label | 1000 Pieces | 80 |

With this data, we can distribute the cost based on **Qty** or **Cost**. The most applicable method for such data is distribution based on **Cost**.

The following is a complete list of the cost distribution types available:

- **Cost**: It is calculated on the invoice value of our material receipt. If you do not have an AP Invoice document for your material receipt then you can NOT proceed further.
- **Line**: It is calculated on the total number of lines.
- **Quantity**: It is calculated on the receipt quantity.
- **Volume**: It is calculated on the receipt quantity multiplied by its volume.
- **Weight**: It is based on receipt quantity multiplied by its weight.

> You can define a product's volume or weight in the **Menu | Material Management | Material Management Rules | Product** window. Go to the **Product** tab and find **Volume** and/or **Weight** fields there.

Choosing a distribution type from this list of cost distribution types is your decision. Thus, ADempiere provides us with this feature of defining the distribution type in a logical way.

## Expected distribution value

We will practice distributing our transportation cost based on the **Cost** distribution type. In the end, we will get the distribution values shown in the following table:

| Raw Material | Cost (US$) | Distribution variable | Distribution IDR value | Distribution US$ value |
|---|---|---|---|---|
| S Fabric | 380 | 380/556 = 0.68345 | 1,366,906.48 | 136.6906 |
| S Thread | 80 | 80/556 = 0.14388 | 287,769.78 | 28.7770 |
| S Button | 16 | 16/556 = 0.02877 | 57,553.96 | 5.7554 |
| S Label | 80 | 80/556 = 0.14388 | 287,769.78 | 28.7770 |
| Total | 556 | | 2,000,000.00 | |

We have assumed that our daily exchange rate is US$ 1 = IDR 10,000.

## Entering our transportation cost

The transportation costs are now booked to the accounting department. Open the **Menu | Requisition-to-Invoice | Invoice (Vendor)** window.

Ensure that you select the **Show Advanced Tabs** checkbox in the **Tools | Preference** window. We will use two of its advance tab features: **Landed Costs** and **Landed Cost Allocation**.

*Landed Costs, Production, and Sales Activities*

In the **Invoice** tab, complete the following information fields:

1. Set the **Organization** field to **Shirt**.
2. Set the **Target Document Type** field to **AP Invoice**.
3. Set the **Date Invoiced** and **Account Date** fields to their default values.
4. Set the **Business Partner** field to **Maersk Logistic**.
5. Set the **Price List** field to **IDR Purchase PL**.
6. Set the **Currency Type** field to **Daily**.

Next, set the following information in the **Invoice Line** tab fields:

1. Set the **Charge** field to **Transportation** (previously defined as **Charge type**).
2. Set the **Quantity** field to **1**.
3. Set the **Price** field to **2000000**.

Next, click on the **Landed Costs** tab, and set the following information, one set of data at a time:

| Field | 1st data | 2nd data | 3rd data | 4th data |
| --- | --- | --- | --- | --- |
| Cost Distribution | Costs | Costs | Costs | Costs |
| Cost Element | Freight | Freight | Freight | Freight |
| Receipt (document number) | 1000000 | 1000001 | 1000002 | 1000003 |

Note that the receipt (document number) is a MM Receipt document number and it depends on your own data. With the author's data, the material receipt document number is 1000000 for **S Button**, 1000001 for **S Label**, 1000002 for **S Fabric**, and 1000003 for **S Thread**. Set the **Receipt** field using the following procedure:

1. Click on the search button (the green arrow button) in the **Receipt** field.
2. Remove the information from the **Business Partner** field in the **Shipment Info** window, and press *Enter*.
3. In the **Business Partner Info** window, click on the **Cancel** button.
4. You will be directed back to the **Shipment Info** window. Press *F5* (or click on the **ReQuery** button) to show the available material receipt documents, and select one from the list.

> After clicking on the **Receipt** field in the search list, we will be prompted by the **Shipment Info** window. Note that the field is labeled **Receipt**, but the search window that it opens is titled **Shipment**. The reality is this is a material movement search window. The **Sales Transaction** flag indicates the difference between a **Shipment** (a sales related transaction) and a **Receipt** (a purchase related transaction).

After entering four of our landed costs data, you can choose one of these data, click on the **Grid Toggle** button to check out the detail view of records, and then click on the **Distribute Costs** button. With the completion of these tasks, ADempiere will calculate and distribute the costs to the registered material receipt document.

You can find the distribution values by accessing the **Landed Cost Allocation** tab. Refer to the following screenshot for the allocation values generated:

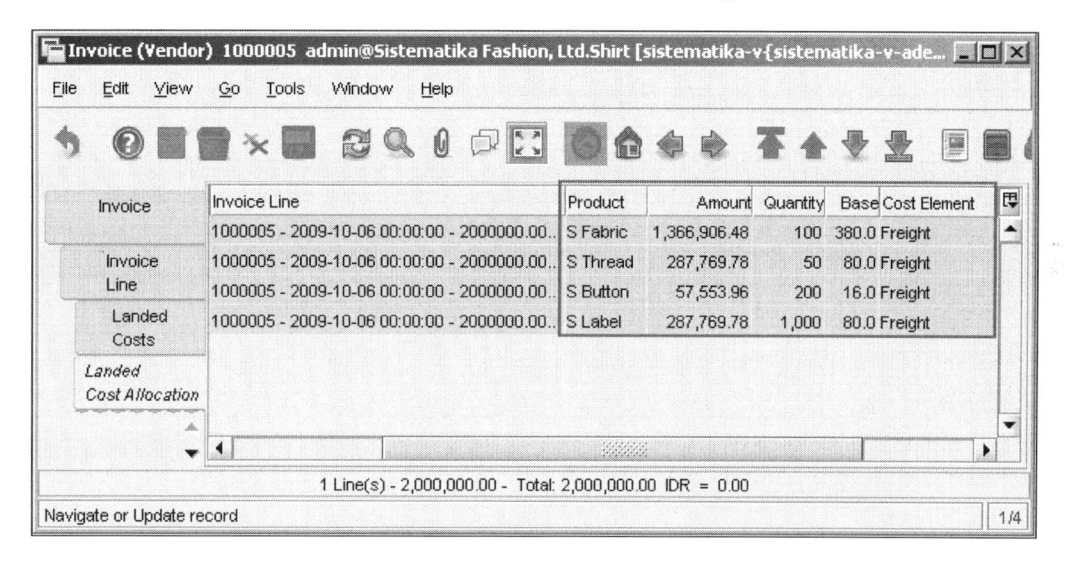

## Accounting facts

In the **Invoice** tab, there is no need to click on the **Not Posted** button right now. Wait for a moment, press *F5*, or click on the **ReQuery** button, repeatedly, until you get the **Posted** button status. This means that we are waiting for the accounting processor to post this document, and we can find out the latest status of this document by re-reading these records after pressing *F5*. Having a **Posted** status on this button means that the ADempiere accounting processor has posted this document automatically for you.

Now, click on this button to gain the accounting facts/GL journal entries generated in the **Account Viewer** window.

> *As far as I know, this is a multi-currency transaction. This means that we created an Invoice in the IDR currency, while our accounting schema currency is USD. How can we access the transaction currency (IDR) and its USD conversion value from this transportation charges transaction?*

Good question. Click on the **Enter Query** tab in the **Account Viewer** window. This tab contains two areas: **Selection** and **Display**. In the **Display** section, select the **Display Source Info** checkbox, and click on the **ReQuery** button (the button at the bottom right-hand side of the **Account Viewer** window), and you will see the information shown in the following screenshot:

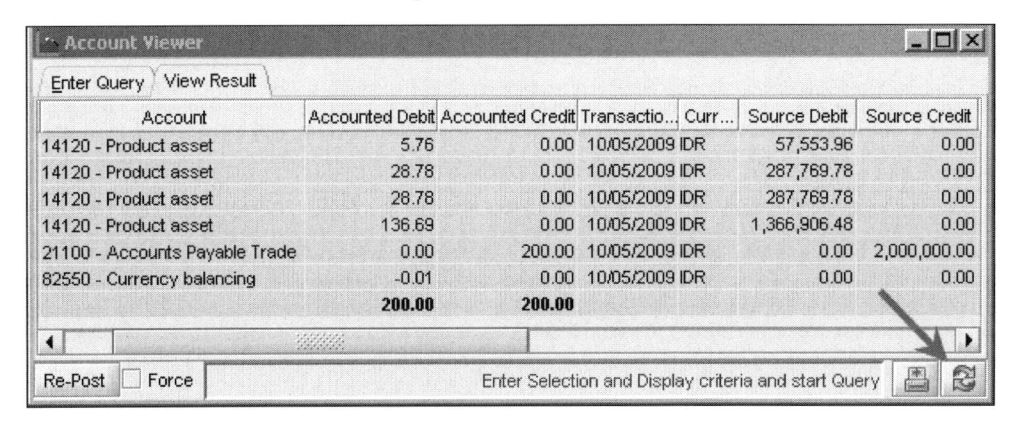

| Account | Accounted Debit | Accounted Credit | Transactio... | Curr... | Source Debit | Source Credit |
|---|---|---|---|---|---|---|
| 14120 - Product asset | 5.76 | 0.00 | 10/05/2009 | IDR | 57,553.96 | 0.00 |
| 14120 - Product asset | 28.78 | 0.00 | 10/05/2009 | IDR | 287,769.78 | 0.00 |
| 14120 - Product asset | 28.78 | 0.00 | 10/05/2009 | IDR | 287,769.78 | 0.00 |
| 14120 - Product asset | 136.69 | 0.00 | 10/05/2009 | IDR | 1,366,906.48 | 0.00 |
| 21100 - Accounts Payable Trade | 0.00 | 200.00 | 10/05/2009 | IDR | 0.00 | 2,000,000.00 |
| 82550 - Currency balancing | -0.01 | 0.00 | 10/05/2009 | IDR | 0.00 | 0.00 |
| | 200.00 | 200.00 | | | | |

As shown in the previous screenshot, the debit transaction is set up to use the **14120 – Product Asset** account instead of the standard **51210 – Product Cost Adjustment** account.

# Manufacturing finished goods—shirts

We are now ready to manufacture shirts. The prerequisites to manufacture shirts are:

- Setting up a **Bill of Material**. This is to define the raw material composition used to produce the final product.
- Creating a **Production**.

With this version of ADempiere, the manufacturing process will be a simple task. It requires the **Bill of Material** configuration only. We will practice manufacturing ten shirts.

# Bill of material (BOM)

Consider the real life situation where you need to buy a lot of food products to fulfill the necessities of life. This could include bread, milk, fruits, snacks, vegetables, and so on. Closely observe what's written the milk carton. The carton contains a list of its ingredients. Manufacturers share the information of the composition of milk with the customers.

In our discussion, **bill of material** is the term used to describe the specification of the raw materials and quantities needed to manufacture a product. In this case, the creation of shirts requires at least four common raw materials: fabric, thread, buttons, and labels.

The following is the required raw material composition to manufacture a shirt:

| Raw Material | Composition |
|---|---|
| S Fabric | 1.89 (meter) |
| S Thread | 0.4 (cone) |
| S Button | 6 (pieces) |
| S Label | 1 (pieces) |

## Entering the bill of material information

> *I was browsing for the Bill of Material window, and it seems that it does not exist. How do I configure the Bill of Material?*

ADempiere 3.4.2s version does not provide a **Bill of Material** window. You will find the bill of material in the **Product** window, on the **Bill of Materials** tab. We will set up the bill of material for the finished goods product—**Shirt Finished Goods**.

Open the **Menu | Material Management | Material Management Rules | Product** window. Look for the **Shirt Finished Goods** records. To set up a bill of material for this product, you have to do the following:

1. Select the **Bill of Materials** checkbox in the **Product** tab for your product (**Shirt Finished Goods**).

2. Enter the following bill of material information in the **Bill of Materials** tab:

| Field | 1st data | 2nd data | 3rd data | 4th data |
|---|---|---|---|---|
| Line No | 10 | 20 | 30 | 40 |
| Active | Select | Select | Select | Select |
| BOM Type | Standard Part | Standard Part | Standard Part | Standard Part |
| BOM Product | S Fabric | S Thread | S Button | S Label |
| BOM Qty | 1.89 (meter) | 0.4 (cone) | 6 (pieces) | 1 (pieces) |

3. Go back to the **Product** tab, and click on the **Verify BOM** button. This procedure will check that the BOM products entries do not have a circular reference to **Shirt Finished Goods** or to other BOM products. Ensure that you get the **OK** message in the status bar.

# Expense type of product as a part of bill of material

*In order to manufacture a product, besides the raw material, we also need to set a fixed value to represent how much overhead cost (including labor, electricity type of cost, and so on) is allocated to manufacture a single unit of the product. How do I manage this cost allocation for the products?*

In ADempiere, we need to define special products that are indicated as *overhead cost* products. As we need to set a fixed overhead cost, we can use the **Standard Costing** costing model for these types of products.

To fulfill this requirement, we need to perform the following tasks:

- Create a new product and product category
- Set a standard cost for the product
- Alter the new product's **Product Asset** default account

In the next section, we will learn how to set up a new product category.

## Creating an overhead product category

We need to create a new product category and set up Standard Costing as its costing method. Open the **Product Category** window, and then set and save the following information in the **Product Category** tab:

1. Set the **Organization** field to **\***.
2. Set the **Search Key** and **Name** fields to **Overhead**.

Navigate to the **Accounting** tab, and set the following information:

1. Set the **Costing Method** field to **Standard Costing**.
2. Set the **Costing Level** field to **Client**.

With this accounting configuration, the standard cost will now be applicable to the Sistematika Fashion, Ltd client (including all of the registered organizations in this client).

> You can define separate standard cost values for your products in each of the available organizations by defining **Costing Level** field to **Organization** in the **Accounting** tab

## Creating labor and electricity products

After defining a product category, we need to create the *labor and electricity* products, which have a standard or fixed cost when manufacturing the **Shirt Finished Goods**. Open the **Product** window, navigate to the **Product** tab, and then set and save the following information:

1. Set the **Organization** field to *.
2. Set the **Search Key** and **Name** fields to **Labor & Electricity**.
3. Set the **Product Category** field to **Overhead**.
4. Set the **UOM** field to **Piece**.
5. Set the **Product Type** field to **Expense type**.
6. Deselect the **Purchase** and **Sold** checkboxes.

Next, we need to alter the **Product Asset** and **Product Expense** default accounts.

## Altering the product's default account

When manufacturing the finished goods, we need to reserve this labor and electricity type of cost, but not book this cost into the expense type of account directly. In this approach, we need to book this overhead cost into a *balance account*. At the end of the accounting periods (monthly), the accounts department should take care of the reversal of an outstanding balance in the *balance account* and book the real labor and electricity costs to the correct expenses account type.

In the chart of accounts, we can use **15190 – Prepaid Others** account as our *balance account*. We will alter the **Product Asset** and **Product Expense** default accounts of the **Labor & Electricity** product to the **15190 – Prepaid Others** account by performing the following steps:

1. Create a new **Shirt-15190-_-_-_-_-_** account combination.
2. Change both the **Product Asset** and **Product Expense** default accounts to the **Shirt-15190-_-_-_-_-_** account combination.

The following screenshot shows the **Accounting** tab configuration after performing the previous steps:

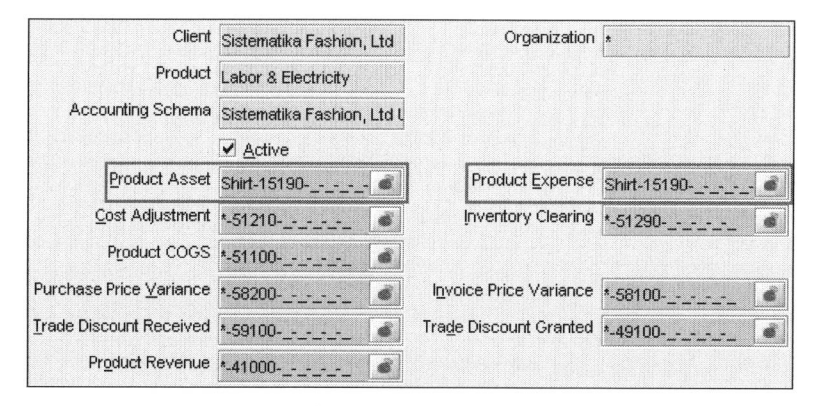

| | |
|---|---|
| Client: Sistematika Fashion, Ltd | Organization: * |
| Product: Labor & Electricity | |
| Accounting Schema: Sistematika Fashion, Ltd U | |
| ✓ Active | |
| Product Asset: Shirt-15190-_-_-_-_-_ | Product Expense: Shirt-15190-_-_-_-_-_ |
| Cost Adjustment: *-51210-_-_-_-_ | Inventory Clearing: *-51290-_-_-_-_ |
| Product COGS: *-51100-_-_-_-_ | |
| Purchase Price Variance: *-58200-_-_-_-_ | Invoice Price Variance: *-58100-_-_-_-_ |
| Trade Discount Received: *-59100-_-_-_-_ | Trade Discount Granted: *-49100-_-_-_-_ |
| Product Revenue: *-41000-_-_-_-_ | |

## Setting up the product's standard cost

As per the accounting department policy, only after analyzing the trend of labor and electricity costs in the past six months will they allocate US$ 1.25 to each of the finished shirt products.

With this information, we can set a standard cost for the product cost by performing the following steps:

1. Navigate to the **Menu | Performance Analysis | Costing | Product Costs** window.
2. On the **Select Product** tab, ensure that your active record is **Labor & Electricity** products.
3. Navigate to the **Product Costs** tab, and then set and save the following information:
   ○ Set the **Organization** field to *
   ○ Set the **Accounting Schema** field to **Sistematika Fashion, Ltd UN/34 US Dollar** (select the option from the list; it has only one option)

- Set the **Cost Type** field to **Sistematika Fashion, Ltd UN/34 US Dollar** (just select the option from the list)
- Set the **Cost Element** field to **Standard Costing**
- Set the **Current Cost Price** field to **1.25**

This is shown in the following screenshot:

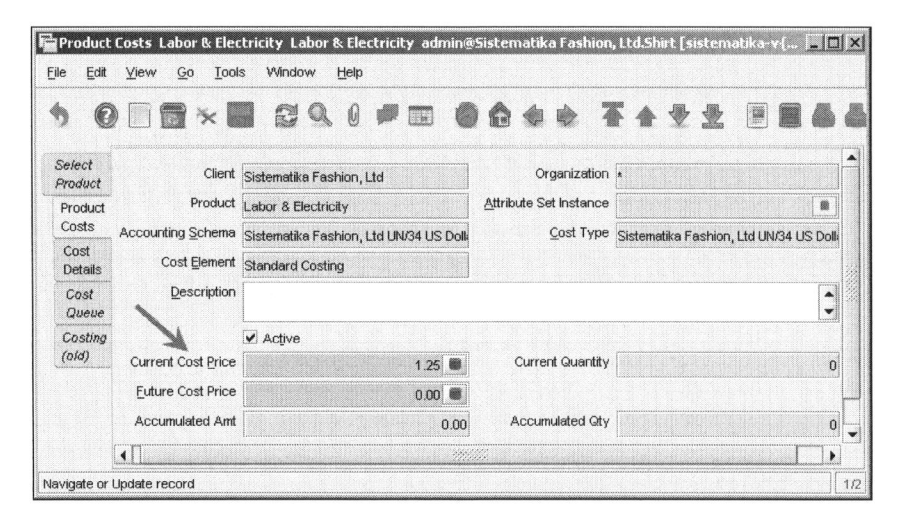

Note that we are not defining the currency information here. The currency information should be taken from the **Accounting Schema** currency.

> If you set the **Costing Level** to **Organization** in the **Accounting** tab of **Product Category** window, then you can define each of the organization standard costs in this **Product Costs** tab. Instead of using *, you can set it to an appropriate organization.

# Registering labor and electricity products into the Shirt's BOM

After creating and configuring the labor and electricity products, we need to register these products as a part of the bill of material for **Shirt Finished Goods**.

Open the **Product** window, and ensure that you are working with the **Shirt Finished Goods** product. Navigate to the **Bill of Materials** tab, and set and save the following information:

1. Set the **Line No** field to **50**.
2. Set the **Description** field to **Capturing labor and electricity costs**.

Landed Costs, Production, and Sales Activities

3. Set the **BOM Type** field to **Standard Part**.
4. Set the **BOM Product** field to **Labor & Electricity**.
5. Set the **BOM Quantity** field to **1**.

Navigate back to the **Product** tab, and click on the **Verify BOM** button again.

# Production

Now that we have configured the bill of material, we will be able to manufacture our product by using the production feature of ADempiere.

Navigate to the **Menu | Material Management | Production** window. This window contains three tabs: **Production Header**, **Production Plan**, and **Production Line**. On the **Production Header** tab, set the following information:

1. Set the **Organization** field to **Shirt**.
2. Set the **Name** field to **Manufacture Shirts FG**.
3. Set the **Movement Date** field to the default date.

After saving this information, click on the **Production Plan** tab, and complete the following information fields:

1. Set the **Product** field to **Shirt Finished Goods**.
2. Set the **Production Quantity** field to **10**.
3. Set the **Locator** field to **Loc S1A** (select from the available options).

Finally, click on the **Save** button. Navigate back to the **Production Header** tab. Examine the following screenshot:

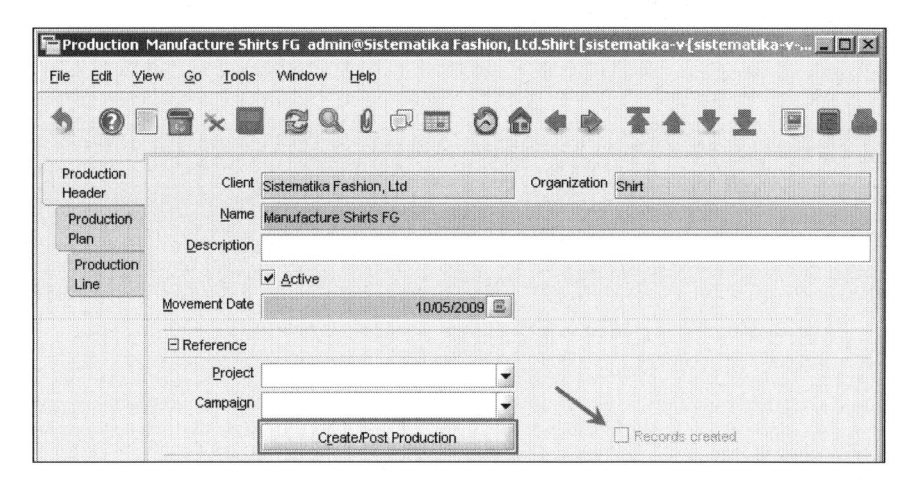

Initially, the **Records created** checkbox will be deselected. Now click on the **Create/Post Production** button. In the upcoming **Create/Post Production** confirmation window, click on the **OK** button.

Completion of the above activities will create a record on the **Production Line** tab. This tab will contain information on how much material is required to manufacture 10 qty of **Shirt Finished Goods**.

Due to the updated records in the **Production Line** tab, the **Records created** checkbox will now have a selected status. Click on the **Create/Post Production** button once again to complete the production activity. ADempiere will prompt us with a **Create/Post Production** confirmation window, and all you need to do is click on the **OK** button.

## Accounting facts

The general accounting facts/GL journal entry format in **Production** should be as shown in the following table:

| Window | Sign | Description | Posting Type |
|---|---|---|---|
| Production | Db | Product Asset (*final product*) | Actual |
| | Cr | Product Asset (*bill of material products*) | Actual |

Wait for a moment, and then press *F5*, or click on the **ReQuery** button, repeatedly, until you get a **Posted** status for this document. Click on the **Posted** button, and you will be prompted with an **Account Viewer** screen, as shown in the following screenshot:

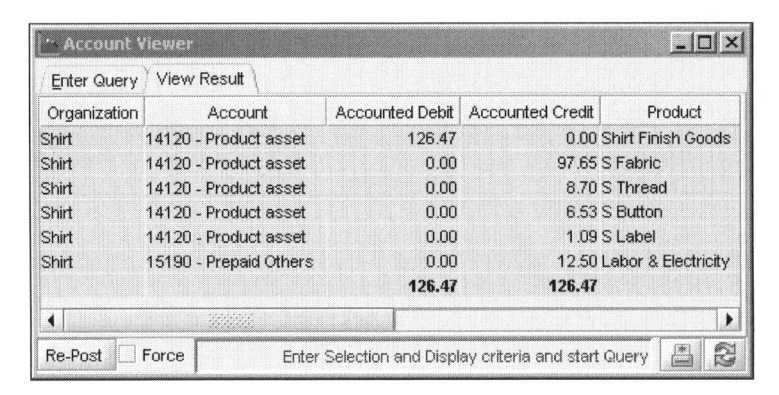

| Organization | Account | Accounted Debit | Accounted Credit | Product |
|---|---|---|---|---|
| Shirt | 14120 - Product asset | 126.47 | 0.00 | Shirt Finish Goods |
| Shirt | 14120 - Product asset | 0.00 | 97.65 | S Fabric |
| Shirt | 14120 - Product asset | 0.00 | 8.70 | S Thread |
| Shirt | 14120 - Product asset | 0.00 | 6.53 | S Button |
| Shirt | 14120 - Product asset | 0.00 | 1.09 | S Label |
| Shirt | 15190 - Prepaid Others | 0.00 | 12.50 | Labor & Electricity |
| | | 126.47 | 126.47 | |

*Landed Costs, Production, and Sales Activities*

*Good to know about the accounting facts. Could you explain more clearly about how the values appear?*

The material consumption value produced during the posting of documents as principal comes from *Qty * cost*. In this case, it will be:

Qty to produce

*

((Average cost price per UOM * Qty required to produce 1 final product)

+

(Landed costs per UOM * Qty required to produce 1 final product))

For a detailed breakdown, refer to the following table:

| Product | A | B | C<br>(A*B) | D | E | F<br>(D/E) | G<br>(B*F) | H<br>(C+G) | I<br>(H*10) |
|---|---|---|---|---|---|---|---|---|---|
| S Fabric | 3.80 | 1.89 | 7.182 | 136.6906 | 100 | 1.3669 | 2.5835 | 9.7655 | 97.65 |
| S Thread | 1.60 | 0.40 | 0.640 | 28.7770 | 50 | 0.5755 | 0.2302 | 0.8702 | 8.70 |
| S Button | 0.08 | 6.00 | 0.480 | 5.7554 | 200 | 0.0288 | 0.1727 | 0.6527 | 6.53 |
| S Label | 0.08 | 1.00 | 0.080 | 28.7770 | 1000 | 0.0288 | 0.0288 | 0.1088 | 1.09 |
| Labor & Electricity | 1.25 | 1.00 | 1.250 | 0.0000 | 0 | 0.0000 | 0.0000 | 1.2500 | 12.50 |

The following is an explanation of what each column in the above table contains:

| | | |
|---|---|---|
| A | = | Average cost for this material per Unit of Measurement (we use average costs because we have used the Average PO costing method previously; especially for Labor & Electricity products, it is using Standard Costing). |
| B | = | Bill of Material consumption |
| C | = | Material cost for producing 1 shirt |
| D | = | Landed costs for material |
| E | = | Quantity of material |
| F | = | Landed costs per Unit of Measurement |
| G | = | Landed costs value for producing 1 shirt |
| H | = | Cost to produce 1 shirt |
| I | = | Cost to produce 10 shirts |

*For a better understanding, can you explain the S Fabric list of cost in this table?*

Manufacturing one garment (or a shirt in our case) will require (B) **1.89** meters of **S Fabric**. When we set the **Average PO** for this material's costing method, the cost calculation will be taken from the average purchase price value of these goods. As we made only one purchase at the time, the cost for these goods will be same as the purchase price value, that is, US$ **3.80** (A). The value for **S Fabric** consumption is US$ **7.182** (C).

To acquire **S Fabric**, we are charged for the transportation costs of four raw materials. We distribute this cost based on the **Cost** distribution method. From IDR **2,000,000**, the distribution value pointed to **S Fabric** is IDR **1,366,906.4**. As our accounting schema uses USD as the main currency, we divide this distribution value by the currency rate which is currently effective, which means that US$ 1 equals IDR 10,000. Finally, the total distribution cost for **S Fabric** is USD **136.6906** (D).

The transportation cost is for the total quantity of **S Fabric**. We will distribute it to a per UOM cost basis. Divide it by **100** (E) and the result is US$ **1.3669** (F). As 1 shirt consumes **1.89** meter, the **S Fabric** transportation cost allocated is US$ **2.5835** (G).

We get US$ **9.7655** (H) as a combination cost for **S Fabric** in order to manufacture 1 shirt. If we manufacture 10 shirts, the total cost is US$ **97.65** (I)

# Proposal or Quotation document

With the completion of stock activities, we now have ten finished shirts and we are ready to create sales. In business, it is quiet common to create an offer letter for our customers. Through this offer letter, we inform our customers about our products, specifications (if applicable), and price information.

## Introduction to Proposal and Quotation

In general, we can prepare an offer letter and create this document as a **Proposal** or **Quotation** document. These types are described as follows:

- A **Proposal** aims to create an offer without binding the customer. It just provides information. Without binding the customer, the stock quantity of our products is not reserved, and we are free to offer our product to other customers.

- A **Quotation** aims to create an offer letter that binds the customer. In this type of document, our stock will be reserved for the customers who are offered the letter.

We have ten finished shirts and an offer letter offering, let's say, six pieces to a customer. Based on the Document Type, below is the free remaining quantity to offer available.

| Document Type | Offering Qty | Available Qty (in stock) | Reserved Qty | Free qty to offer to another customer |
|---|---|---|---|---|
| Proposal | 6 | 10 | 0 | 10 |
| Quotation | 6 | 10 | 6 | 4 |

Assume that we have four free products to offer after, the first quotation. When creating the next quotation document which requires five products, ADempiere will give us a warning, such as **Insufficient Inventory Available**.

> In the default ADempiere installation, the **Insufficient Inventory Available** warning is just a warning, and we can still proceed with this document.

## Setting up a product's sales price

In Chapter 4, *Setting up Master Data and Knowing its Accounting Configuration*, we saw that the price of raw material is given in the **Menu | Material Management | Material Management Rules | Product** window, and we can get the price information from the **Price** tab.

After determining the raw material costs, we need to set a price for our **Shirt Finished Goods** product.

Before creating a proposal or quotation document, follow this procedure to set up the price for our finished goods. Navigate to the **Product** tab, and ensure that your active record is **Shirt Finished Goods**. Then, navigate to the **Price** tab, and save the following information fields:

1. Set the **Price List Version** field to **Sales PL March Version**.
2. Set the **List Price**, **Standard Price**, and **Limit Price** fields to **20**.

> The **Sales PL March version** is a version instance of the **Sales PL** price list.

If you enter products that do not have price list information, or that use a price list other than the price list configured for these products, then you will get an error message, as shown in the following screenshot, when saving your Proposal or Quotation line document:

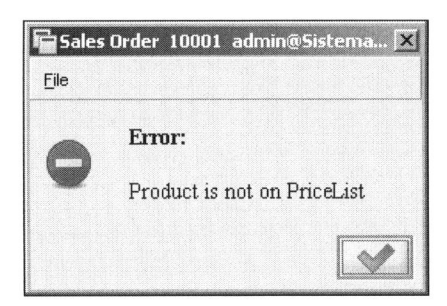

> **Sales Order 10001 admin@Sistema...**
> File
>
> **Error:**
> Product is not on PriceList

## Entering a Proposal or Quotation document

*I tried to find a Proposal or Quotation window, but had no luck. How do I proceed with the Proposal or Quotation documents?*

Unfortunately, there are no **Proposal** or **Quotation** windows available. But in ADempiere, we can create both of these documents by using *Binding offer* and *Non binding offer* document types from the **Menu | Quote-to-Invoice | Sales Orders | Sales Order** window.

This window will provide you with three tabs: **Order**, **Order Line**, and **Order Tax**. In the **Order** tab, you will find a **Target Document Type** field, which contains a list of document types applicable to the **Sales Order** window. The following is a complete list of document types that can be used in the **Sales Order** window:

- Binding offer
- Credit order
- Non-binding offer
- POS order
- Prepay order
- Return material
- Standard order
- Warehouse order

> In our discussion, the **Binding offer** is analogous to **Quotation** and the **Non-binding offer** is analogous to **Proposal**.

Navigate to the **Sales Order** window, and we will practice how to create a Proposal (**Non-binding offer**) document, by entering the following information in the **Order** tab:

| Field | Data |
| --- | --- |
| Organization | Shirt |
| Target Document Type | Non-binding offer |
| Business Partner | Liz Claiborne Inc |
| Warehouse | 1st Shirt W/h |
| Price List | Sales PL |

In the Invoicing parts of this tab, you can set up how your customer pays the subsequent invoices raised from this document. In the **Non-binding offer** document type, the default payment rule method is **On Credit**. You can change the payment rule method by clicking on the **On Credit** button, and there will be a small pop-up window mentioning the list of available payment rules. Select the payment rule method that suits your needs.

The payment rule methods available are:

- Check
- Direct Debit
- Credit Card
- On Credit
- Cash

Following the payment rule is the **Payment Term** option. This option should be enabled when using the **On Credit** and **Direct Debit** payment methods. You can configure the payment terms through the **Menu | Partner Relations | Business Partner Rules | Payment Term** window. For now, we are using the default—**Immediate**—payment term.

After saving this document, navigate to the **Order Line** tab, and complete the following information fields:

| Field | Data |
|---|---|
| Product | Shirt Finished Goods |
| Quantity | 15 |
| UOM | Piece |

After entering the quantity as fifteen, press the *Tab* key to move out of the **Quantity** field, you will get an **Insufficient Inventory Available** warning message, as shown in the following screenshot:

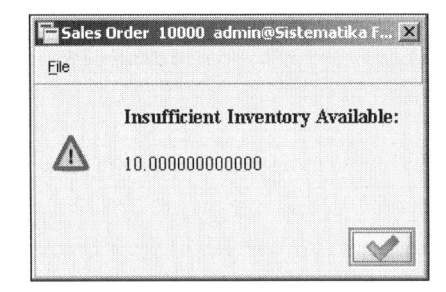

ADempiere will inform us that *we do not have enough stock – that is, we only have 10 shirts available*. For practice, we will set the **Quantity** field to **10**, and click on the **Save** button.

Navigate to the **Order** tab, and finalize this **Non-binding offer** document by clicking on the **Complete** button. In the upcoming **Document Action** window, set **Prepare** (as the next default document action) in the **Document Action** option list, and click on the **OK** button. Once you have done this, your document will have an **In Progress** status.

> With this **In Progress** document status, we will use this document for our example in the subsequent section

# Sales Order

We have created and sent an offer letter to our customers. We are now waiting for their response. If we get a positive response, then we can continue to convert the **Proposal** or **Non-binding offer** document to a **Standard Order** document type of **Sales Order**.

## Proposal conversion to a Standard Order

You can create a new **Sales Order** by using the **Standard Order** document type to fulfill customer orders. Set the **PO Line** information with the same information mentioned in the proposal document. To make it easy, ADempiere has a predefined feature to convert previous proposal documents into **Standard Order** document types.

> The Proposal, or **Non-binding offer**, document needs to be in the **In Progress** status in order to be converted.

You can convert your Proposal, or **Non-binding offer**, document as follows:

1. Navigate to the **Menu | Quote-to-Invoice | Sales Orders | Quote convert** process.
2. When you click on this ADempiere process, you will be prompted with a **Convert open Proposal or Quotation to Order** confirmation window.
3. In this window, you can set the following information:
    - Set the **Order** field to your proposal document number.
    - Set the **Document Type** field to the targeted document type. Here, we will use **Standard Order**.
    - Set the **Document Date** field to the desired date (if necessary).
    - Select the **Close Document** checkbox. If you select this checkbox, then all the documents mentioned in the **Order** field will be closed (in this case, the **Non-binding offer** document).
4. Finalize the order by clicking on the **Start** button.

ADempiere has now created a new **Sales Order** document that has **Standard Order** as the **Target Document Type**. It will copy the proposal information to the newly created document.

## Examining the resulting standard order document

Navigate to the **Menu | Quote-to-Invoice | Sales Orders | Sales Order** window to find your newly converted standard order document. This new document has **Drafted** as the **Document Status**. Go through both the **Order** and **Order Line** tabs, and examine the document itself. If required, you can make any changes at this document status level.

In addition to the document type, the following important information can also be set up:

- Delivery rule
- Invoice rule

The **Delivery Rule** indicates when an order should be delivered. For example, should the order be delivered when the entire order is complete, when a line is complete, or as the products become available? The options available for the delivery rule are:

- After Receipt (means after receiving a payment)
- Availability
- Complete Line
- Complete Order
- Force
- Manual

The **Invoice Rule** defines how our customer is invoiced and the frequency of invoicing. The options available for the invoice rule are:

- After Delivery.
- After Order is delivered.
- Customer Schedule after Delivery. You can define and set up the default customer invoice rule and invoice schedule through the **Customer** tab in the **Business Partner** window.
- Immediate.

In our sample Sales Order document, we used the default values for both Delivery and Invoice rules. Click on the **Complete** button to finalize this document.

# Accounting facts

Wait for a moment, press *F5*, or click on the **ReQuery** button, repeatedly, until you get a **Posted** status. Click on the **Posted** button to check for the accounting facts. With the default ADempiere configuration, no accounting facts or GL journal entries are generated here.

# Shipments

In the previous activities, we have reserved our finished goods, and now we need to prepare shipment documents based on the Sales Order document type that we created. There are a three ways to create this document. They are as follows:

- **Manual**: By entering the data yourself in the **Shipment (Customer)** window
- **Semi automatic**: By using the **Generate Shipments (manual)** window
- **Automatic**: Generated when executing the **Generate Shipments** process

## Generating Shipments

*What is the best way to generate and process the shipment documents?*

There are no strict rules for generating a shipment document. We can choose any one of the available options. Usually, it is a good idea to use the **Generate Shipments** process, as this is the most efficient of the options. The other two options can only be used if the volume of transactions is low. We can generate shipments as follows:

1. Navigate to the **Menu | Quote-to-Invoice | Shipments | Generate Shipments** process window.
2. We will process the shipments by setting the fields as follows:
    - Set the **Warehouse** field to **1st Shirt W/h**
    - Set the **Shipment Date** field to the required target date, or leave it blank for the current default date
    - Set the **Business Partner** field to **Liz Claiborne Inc**
    - Set the **Document Action** field to **Prepare**

> Do not select **Complete** at this stage, as we might need to alter some of the information in the generated shipment document, later.

You are free to select or deselect the **Consolidate to one Document** checkbox. Selecting this checkbox means that if there are several standard orders for a business partner that have the same location and same delivery rule, these orders will be consolidated to a single shipment.

Refer to the following screenshot:

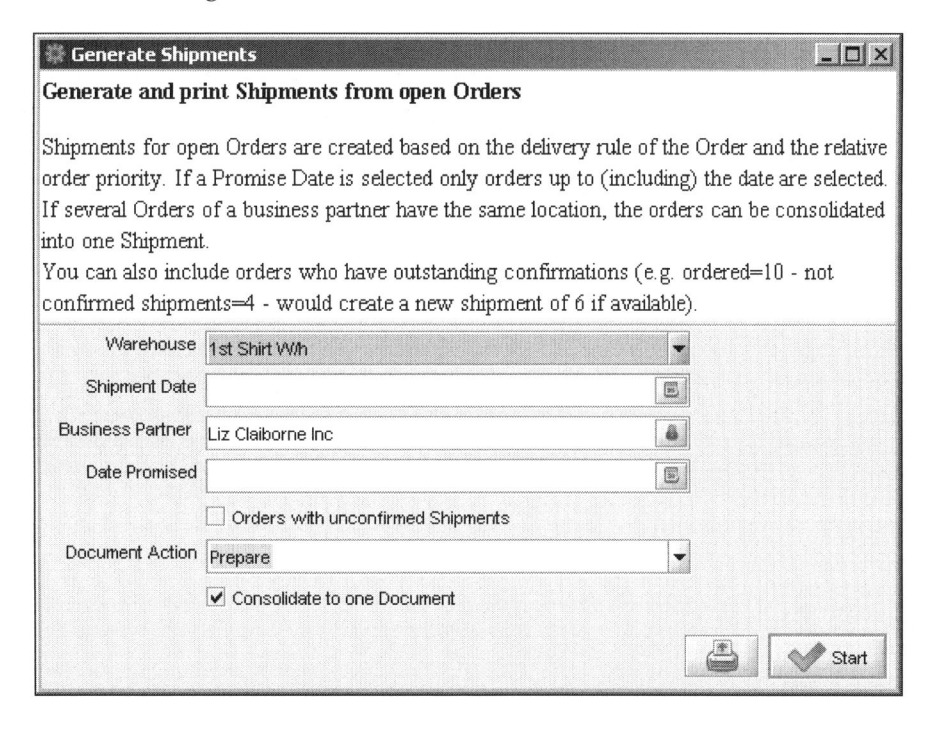

[Screenshot: Generate Shipments window showing "Generate and print Shipments from open Orders" with fields for Warehouse (1st Shirt W/h), Shipment Date, Business Partner (Liz Claiborne Inc), Date Promised, Orders with unconfirmed Shipments checkbox, Document Action (Prepare), Consolidate to one Document checkbox, and Start button.]

Click on the **Start** button, and in the upcoming **Print Shipments** confirmation window, click on the **OK** button. Examine the delivery report produced. Thus, you will get a successfully-generated shipment document, along with log information.

# Shipment (Customer)

You can access your generated shipment document now. Open the
**Menu | Quote-to-Invoice | Shipments | Shipment (Customer)** window.
You will notice that your shipment document has an **In Progress** status in the **Document Status** field.

As an ADempiere standard, when using the **Generate Shipments** process, the document created in the **Shipment (Customer)** window will use the **MM Shipment** as its document type. There are several document types that can be used in this window. They are as follows:

- MM Shipment
- MM Shipment Indirect
- MM Vendor Return

*Landed Costs, Production, and Sales Activities*

The **MM Shipment Indirect** is almost the same as **MM Shipment**. The difference between these two document types is that the **MM Shipment Indirect** will be used when using **POS Order** as its **Sales Order** document type. The **MM Vendor Return** document type will be used when a customer wants to return the materials.

## Shipment confirmation

*In our company, we have a different section to handle the shipment activities. The documentation tasks are handled by the Shipping personnel. They do not physically touch the goods that need to be shipped. The goods are handled by our Warehouse persons. In this case, the Shipping personnel need to be convinced that their document matches the finished goods that the company is sending out.*
*How do we do that?*

Communication between two departments can be done by using the confirmation feature of ADempiere.

Imagine that the Shipping personnel (Bob) and the Warehouse personnel (Steve) have the following conversation:

*Hi Steve, we have prepared the commercial document to deliver shirts to our customer Liz. Can you crosscheck this document with its shipping confirmation document?*

Prior to the conversation with Steve, Bob opens the **Menu | Quote-to-Invoice | Shipments | Shipment (Customer)** window, navigates to the **Shipment** tab, and finds out the records that have an **In Progress** status. He then clicks on the **Create Confirmation** button. In the **Create Confirmation** window, he sets **Ship/Receipt Confirm** as the **Confirmation Type**, as shown in the following screenshot:

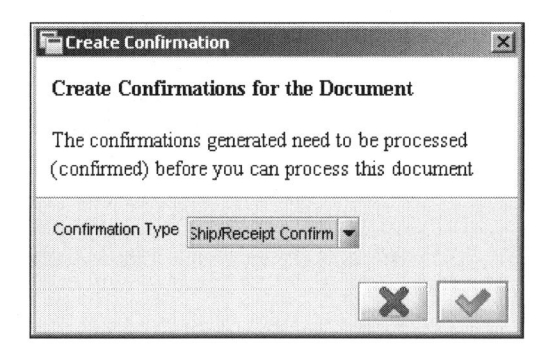

Click on the **OK** button. Upon successful creation confirmation, you will see a number in the status bar (on the bottom left-hand side of the **Shipment (Customer)** window). This number is the **Ship/Receipt Confirm** document number.

ADempiere will now generate a **Ship/Receipt Confirm** document, and Bob can see this information in the **Confirmations** tab of the **Shipment (Customer)** document. As this document needs a confirmation from the warehouse personnel, at this stage, Bob cannot complete the **MM Shipment** document. Trying to complete this document will generate a warning message such as **Open Ship/Receipt Confirmation: Ship/Receipt Confirm –** *document number* in the status bar.

Okay, now we will play the role of the warehouse person, Steve. He periodically checks the **Menu | Material Management | Ship/Receipt Confirm** window. This window contains two tabs: **Confirmation** and **Line** tabs. Steve examines the incoming information in this window, physically examines the finished goods, that is, shirts, and thus completes the document.

> *"Bob, we have confirmed the Ship/Receipt document. You can now check the document and continue with your tasks"*, says Steve.

Bob will now complete the **MM Shipment** document by clicking on the **Complete** button in the **Shipment (Customer)** window.

## Updating the Shirt Finished Goods standard cost

Do you remember what costing method we used for the Shirt Finished Goods product? Revisit the *Product Category accounting configuration* section from Chapter 4, *Setting up Master Data and Knowing its Accounting Configuration*, and you will find that our Shirt Finished Goods use the *Standard Costing* costing method.

In this costing method, we have to define a standard cost for these products. As usual, you can define a product's standard cost in the **Product Costs** window. We can define its standard cost by calculating the product's total cost incurred when manufacturing the product. This includes the cost of raw materials, freight, labor, and electricity in our case.

In addition to manually updating the standard cost information, we can transfer the total cost of the products into **Shirt Finished Goods** by performing the following activities:

- Create Costing Records
- Update Standard Cost

First execute the **Menu | Performance Analysis | Costing | Create Costing Records** process. In the upcoming confirmation window, set the **Product** field to **Shirt Finished Goods**, and then click on the **Start** button. After performing this activity, you can access these records from the **Product Costs** tab of the **Product Costs** window of the **Shirt Finished Goods** product, as shown in the following screenshot:

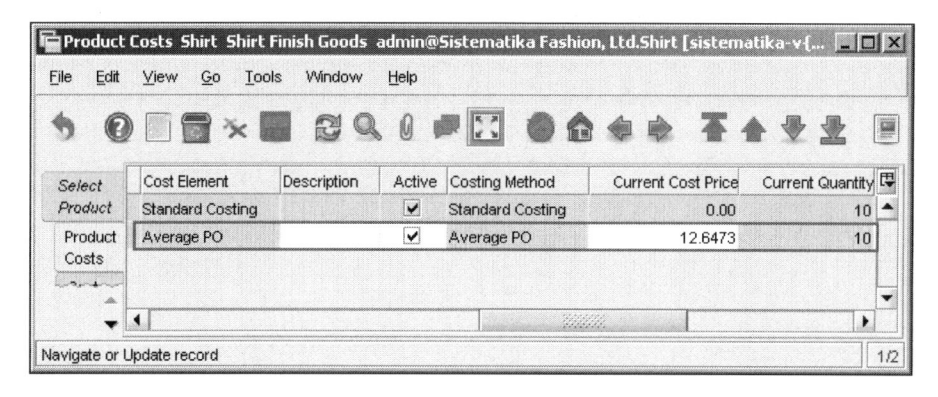

Next, execute the **Menu | Performance Analysis | Costing | Standard Cost Update** processes to update product's standard costs, and set the following information in the upcoming confirmation window:

1. Set the **Product Category** field to **Finished Goods**.
2. **Standard Cost** field to **Average PO**.

Click on the **Start** button. This will transfer the Average PO cost price into the Standard Costing cost price.

## Accounting facts

Wait for a moment, and then press *F5* repeatedly, until you get a **Posted** status for this document. Click in the **Posted** button on the **Shipment (Customer)** window, and you will get the general accounting fact/GL journal entry format shown in the following table:

| Window | Document | Sign | Description | Posting Type |
|---|---|---|---|---|
| Shipment (Customer) | MM Shipment | Db | Product CoGS | Actual |
| | | Cr | Product Asset | Actual |

*What is COGS?*

**COGS** stands for **Cost of Goods Sold**. In accounting, COGS is the total direct expense incurred during the production of a product. COGS includes the cost of materials used to make these goods or products and the cost of labor to manufacture them.

The following is an example of the accounting fact/GL journal entry generated by our previous transaction:

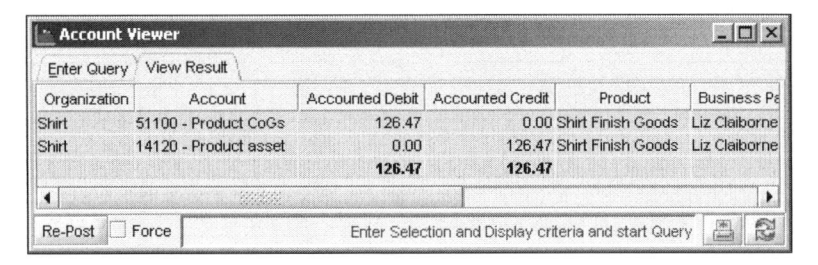

As expected, the **126.47** is calculated as: *product's standard costs* multiplied by *shipment quantity*.

# Generating customer invoices

During shipment, to obtain payment, we raise an invoice document to our customer. ADempiere provides us with the following three methods for raising an invoice:

- **Generate Invoices (manual)**: Although this is named as manual, it is actually semi-automatic invoice generation.
- **Generate Invoices**: We can issue an invoice with the **Prepare** status in **Document Action**.
- **Invoice (Customer)**: We can manually issue an invoice through this window.

# Generating invoices using Generate Invoices (manual)

This procedure is almost the same as the one for shipments. For the sake of variety, we will use **Generate Invoice (manual)** for practice. Navigate to the **Menu | Quote-to-Invoice | Sales Invoices | Generate Invoices (manual)** window. Set the following information fields:

1. Set the **Organization** field to **Shirt**.
2. Set the **Document Type** field to **Order**.

This will show a list of eligible order documents. Select the checkbox to the left of the **Organization** field, as shown in the following screenshot:

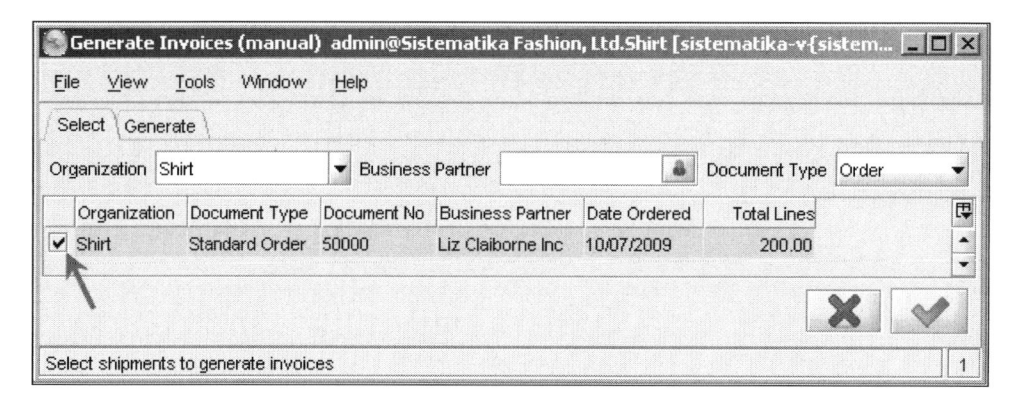

Click on **OK**, and in the next **Print Invoices** confirmation window, and then click on the **OK** button again. Finally, you will get a successfully-generated invoice document with log information. Thus, we will now have an invoice that has a **Complete** status as its **Document Status**.

> You can also use the **Generate Invoices** process. In this case, the resulting status of the invoice will be **In Progress**. This status means that you will be able to alter any information inside the invoice document.

## Examining the Invoice (Customer) window

Navigate to the **Menu | Quote-to-Invoice | Sales Invoices | Invoice (Customer)** window. You will find the generated invoice. After getting the **Complete** status for the document, take a print of the document.

Thus, we have generated an invoice using **AR Invoice** as its document type. The following are the document types that can be used in this window:

- AR Credit Memo
- AR Invoice
- AR Invoice Indirect

The **AR Invoice Indirect** is almost the same as the **AR Invoice**. The difference between these document types is that the **AR Invoice Indirect** will be used when **POS Order** is used as its **Sales Order** document type. We will create an invoice using the **AR Credit Memo** document type, only if our customer returns a product or material.

The other important aspects that need your attention are the **Payment Rule** and **Payment Term** used in the invoice. The generated invoice uses **On Credit** as its **Payment Rule**, and **Immediate** as its **Payment Term**. The information on both is taken from the **Sales Order** document.

> Although the status of the invoice is **Complete**, we can still alter the **Payment Rule** and **Payment Term** conditions.

For your reference, check out the **Payment Term** and the **Payment Rule** for the generated sample invoice, in the following screenshot:

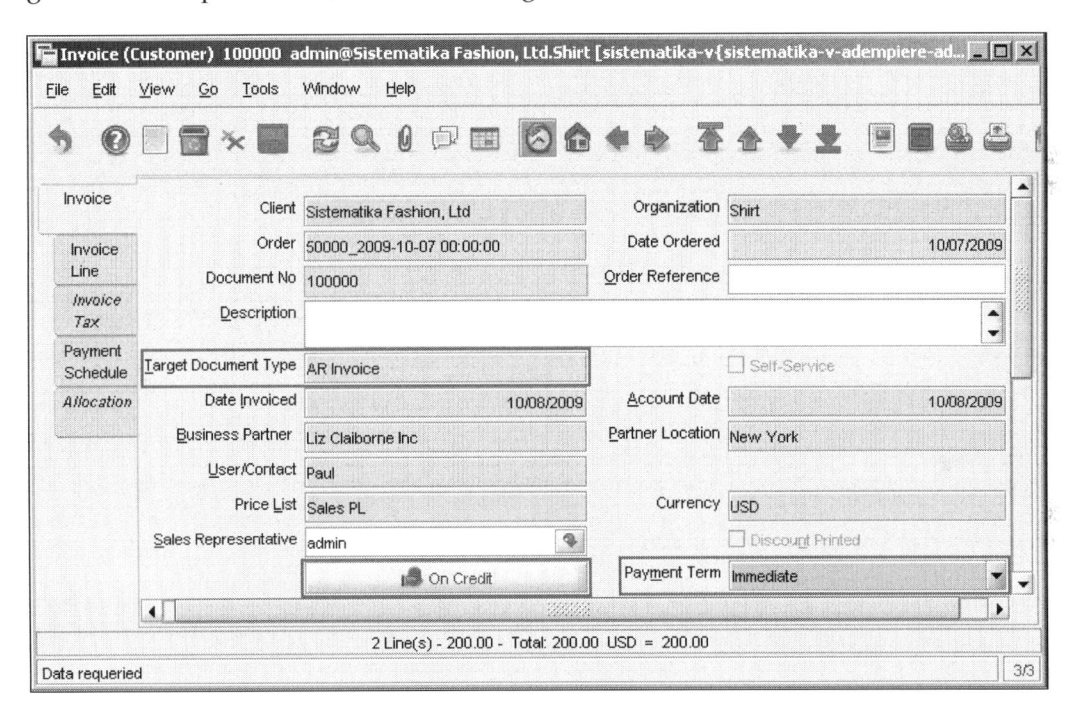

*Landed Costs, Production, and Sales Activities*

## Accounting facts

Wait for a moment, and then press *F5* repeatedly, until you get the **Posted** status for this document, and then click on the **Posted** button. The general accounting fact/GL journal entry generated format is shown as follows:

| Window | Document | Sign | Description | Posting Type |
|---|---|---|---|---|
| Invoice (Customer) | AR Invoice | Db | Account Receivable - Trade | Actual |
|  |  | Cr | Trade Revenue | Actual |

Refer to following screenshot for the accounting facts/GL journal entry that is generated:

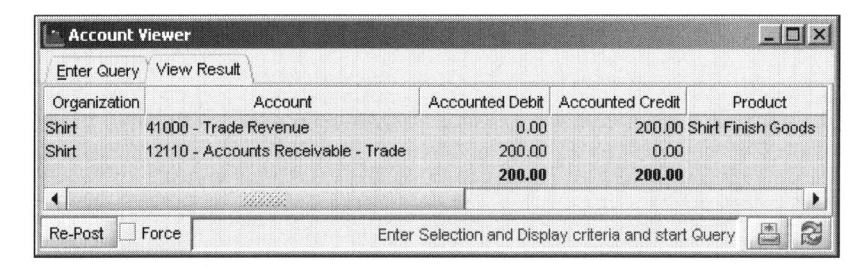

# Account receivable payment

Our accounting person receives the following email from a customer:

> Dear Supplier,
>
> Thank you for delivering the goods. The required amount will be transferred to your bank account today. Enclosed is a scanned copy of the **TT** (**Telegraphic Transfer**) document, for your reference.
>
> Thanks and regards,
> Liz Claiborne
> Accounting Department

Great! The company has finally received the payment from its customer.

[ 206 ]

# Customer payment

Based on the confirmation from the customer, the company can make an entry for the received payment in ADempiere, as follows:

1. Navigate to the **Menu | Open Items | Payment** window.

   > This window is the same window as the one that you encountered when making the payment to the vendor in the *Account Payable payment* section of Chapter 5, *Procurement Activities*. The difference between the vendor payment document and the customer payment document is the **Document Type**.

2. To book a customer payment, we will use **AR Receipt** (Account Receivable Payment) as the document type.

3. According to the **TT** document, you can complete the following information fields in the **Payment** tab:
   - Set the **Organization** field to **Shirt**
   - Set the **Bank Account** field to **USD 1-001-888888**. Set your targeted bank account here.
   - Set the **Document Type** field to **AR Receipt**
   - Set the **Business Partner** field to **Liz Claiborne Inc**
   - Set the **Payment amount** field to **200**
   - Set the **Currency** field to **USD**
   - Set the **Tender Type** field to **Direct Deposit**

   > As we receive the payment directly to our bank account, we can use **Direct Deposit** here. You can use any other **Tender Type** depending on the mode of payment.

4. Save and complete this document.

## Accounting facts

Press *F5* repeatedly, until you get a **Posted** status for this document. The general accounting facts/GL journal entry generated has the following format:

| Window  | Document   | Sign | Description                   | Posting Type |
|---------|------------|------|-------------------------------|--------------|
| Payment | AR Receipt | Db   | Checking In Transfer          | Actual       |
|         |            | Cr   | Checking Unallocated Receipts | Actual       |

The following screenshot shows the accounting fact generated:

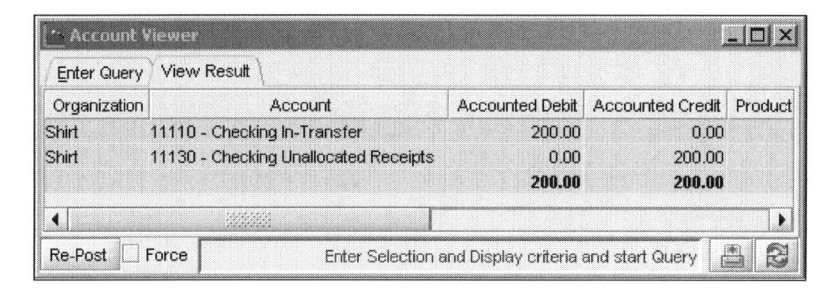

| Organization | Account | Accounted Debit | Accounted Credit | Product |
|---|---|---|---|---|
| Shirt | 11110 - Checking In-Transfer | 200.00 | 0.00 | |
| Shirt | 11130 - Checking Unallocated Receipts | 0.00 | 200.00 | |
| | | **200.00** | **200.00** | |

As you can see in the above screenshot, accounts **11110** and **11130** belong to the **Asset** type of account. The total value for the **Asset** transaction is zero (nothing).

> Although these accounting facts are not reflected in our bank accounts and account receivable entries yet, they are worth noting down.

## Payment allocation

*Payment from Liz has not been reflected in the Account Receivable entry yet. How do we allocate this payment to the related account receivable entry?*

We can perform payment allocation to the related invoice as follows:

1. Navigate to the **Menu | Open Items | Payment Allocation** window.
2. Set the following information fields:
   - Set the **Business Partner** field to **Liz Claiborne Inc**
   - Set the **Currency** field to **USD**

> After entering the business partner information, press the *Tab* key to move out of the **Business Partner** field, the system will generate an information in both the **Payment** grid and the **Invoice** grid automatically.

3. Ensure that you select the **Select** checkbox in a proper **Account Receivable** payment records available in the **Payment** grid record.
4. Allocate the payment to the Invoice. With the available invoice records in the **Invoice** grid, select the proper invoice by selecting the **Select** checkbox, in order to allocate the account receivable payment document to the selected invoice document.
5. Click on the **Process** button.

This is shown in the following screenshot:

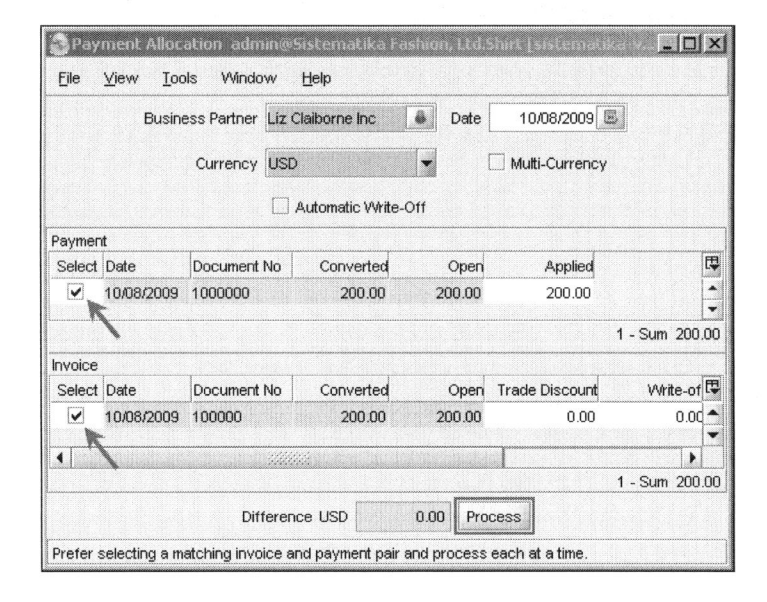

## View allocation

Based on the payment allocation, ADempiere internally creates records in the **View Allocation** window. Navigate to the **Menu | Open Items | View Allocation** window to find your records. You will find some information on the **Allocation** tab.

The most important information is present in the **Allocation Line** tab. This tab contains information regarding the relationship among **Sales Order**, **Invoice (Customer)**, and **Payment**. Refer to the following screenshot for details:

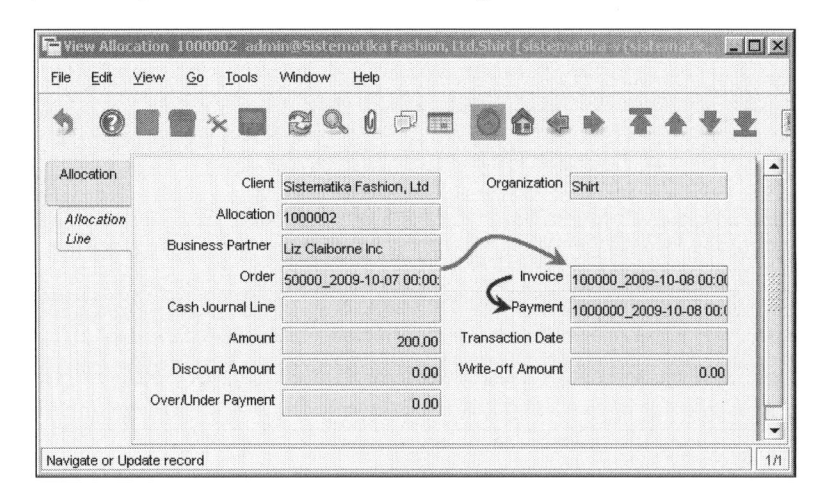

*So why bother ourselves with all of these allocation complexities?*

Well, this affords us great flexibility: many invoices for one order (which may come from partial shipments); many orders in one consolidated invoice (in case we deliver orders to one customer throughout the month and we send a single invoice at the end of the month); many payments for one invoice; and one payment for many invoices. The complex allocation is able to manage these many-to-many relationships!

## Accounting facts

Wait for a moment, and then press *F5* repeatedly until you get a **Posted** status for this document. The general accounting facts/GL journal format for account receivable payment allocation records is as follows:

| Sign | Description | Posting Type |
|---|---|---|
| Db | Checking Unallocated Receipts | Actual |
| Cr | Account Receivable - Trade | Actual |

The following screenshot shows the accounting facts for our sample transaction:

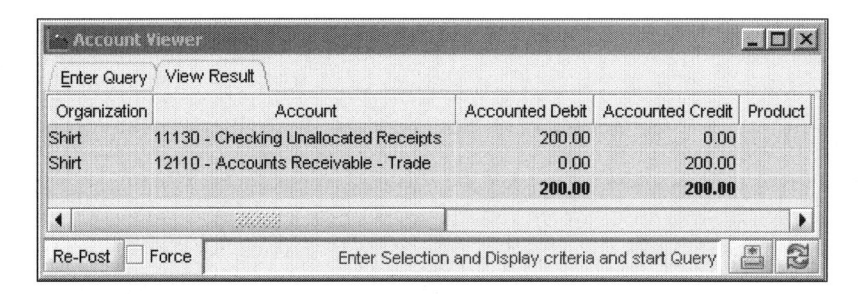

## Void and Reset allocation

*With increasing payments and invoices, it is possible that the accounting person performs a wrong allocation. For instance, the account receivable payment is allocated to the wrong invoices. How do we manage this situation?*

Yes, this is a common situation where hundreds of account receivable payment records are present. To revise or reset a previous payment allocation, ADempiere has features called **Reset Allocation** and **Void allocation**.

# Reset allocation

Access this feature by navigating to the **Menu | Open Items | Reset Allocation** window. Although you can proceed with blank information in the selection criteria (which means resetting all of the documents), it is suggested that you enter your related business partner information and specify the target allocation document that needs to be removed, as shown in the following screenshot:

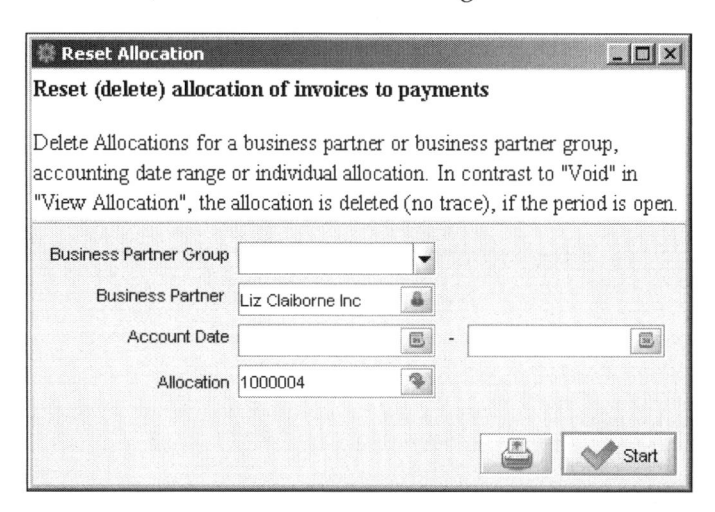

After performing these tasks, you can navigate back to the **Payment Allocation** window, and continue with your transaction.

> Due to these activities, the related **View Allocation** document and the accounting facts/GL journal entry will be deleted.

# Void allocation

The second method is to void the allocation. You can void the allocation document as follows:

1. Navigate to the **Menu | Open Items | View Allocation** window, and find your target allocation document.
2. Now that you have selected the allocation data, click on the **Close** button.

3. You will be prompted with the **Document Action** window. Select **Void** from the list in the **Document Action** field, and click on the **OK** button. A sample **Document Action** window is shown in the following screenshot:

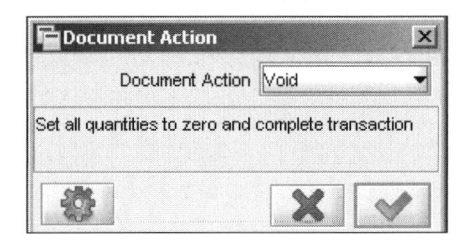

On completion, the selected view allocation data will have a **Voided** document status, and the accounting facts/GL journal entry will have been removed. You can continue with setting of correct payment allocation.

> In the **Void Allocation** method, we will have a **Voided** document that can still be used for document tracking, whereas in the **Reset Allocation** we will have nothing.

# Bank statement

We need to reconcile this payment with our bank transaction. Like in the previous procurement bank statement activity, we will get the copies of our bank statement from the bank officer or from the online banking facilities. The procedure for this bank statement activity is similar to the previous procurement bank statement activity.

Navigate to the **Menu | Open Items | Bank Statement** window. Complete the fields in the **Bank Statement** tab with the new data, and set the following information:

1. Set the **Organization** field to **Shirt**.
2. Set the **Bank Account** field to **USD-1-001-888888**.
3. Set the **Name** field to **Third Bank Statement**.
4. Set the **Statement date** field to *your working date*.
5. Set the **Beginning Balance** field to **520**.

After saving this information, navigate to the **Statement Line** tab, and set the following information:

1. Set the **Statement Line Date, Account Date,** and **Effective date** fields to **10/08/2009** (this date is subjective).
2. Set the **Statement amount** field to **200**.

We need to reconcile the **Statement amount** value with our ADempiere transaction. This is done in the following way:

1. Select the payment data by clicking on the **Payment** field.
2. In the upcoming **Payment Info** confirmation window, ensure that the **Receipt** checkbox is selected.
3. Click on the **ReQuery** button, in order to view the available account receivable payment list.
4. Select the appropriate record, and then click on the **OK** button.
5. If you wish, you can set up the **Reference No** and or **Memo** fields as well.

> Remember that this is only a simulation for a single bank statement. The actual company transaction will contain data from hundreds of bank statements that need to be reconciled.

6. Navigate to the **Bank Statement** tab, and then click on the **Complete** button.

## Accounting facts

Press *F5* repeatedly, until you get a **Posted** status for this document. The general accounting fact/GL journal format for reconciling the account receivable payment transaction is:

| Sign | Description | Posting Type |
|---|---|---|
| Db | Checking Account | Actual |
| Cr | Checking In-Transfer | Actual |

The following screenshot shows the accounting facts generated from our sample transaction:

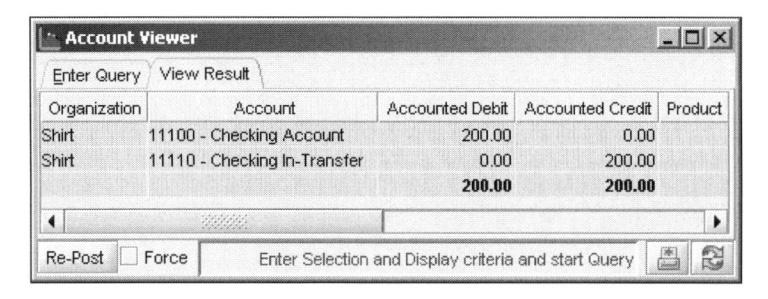

## Summary of Account receivable payment accounting facts

As you already know, the final journal for account receivable will have the same format as the debit checking, but account against credit account receivable trade. The following is a summary of the flow of accounting facts/GL journal created:

| Document | Dr/Cr | Description | Value | |
|---|---|---|---|---|
| Bank Statement | Dr | Checking Account | 200 | |
| | Cr | Checking in Transfer | | 200 |
| Payment | Dr | Checking In Transfer | 200 | |
| | Cr | Checking Unallocated Receipts | | 200 |
| View allocation | Dr | Checking Unallocated Receipts | 200 | |
| | Cr | Account Receivable - Trade | | 200 |

With this journal, you know that the final result of the accounting facts is **debit Checking Account** *against* **credit Account Receivable - Trade**.

## Managing direct sales

> *Our company wants to have a store that can be used for direct selling, so that, anybody can come to our store, look for a product, and buy the required products. How do we manage these types of sales?*

Yes, ADempiere can handle direct sales activities. In a supermarket, you must have noticed customers who want to buy some products go to the cashier and set a payment. No proposal or quotation is involved. Although you can create direct sales using modes of payment other than cash a (credit card, for example), here we will practice direct sales using only cash as the payment rule.

## Preparing cash books

In order to use cash as a payment method or rule, we need to prepare and set up ADempiere cash books. All of the cash transactions should be transferred directly to these cash books. Currently, we have two default cash books in the system: **USD Cash book** and **IDR Cash book**. Take a detailed look at both of these cash books. They use **Dress** as their **Organization** information.

> When you perform a *point of sales* activity in the Shirt organization, it will be mandatory to use a cash book that belongs to the Shirt organization only.

To comply with this requirement, we need to create a **USD Point of Sales** cash book. Navigate to the **Menu | System Admin | Organization Rules | Cashbook** window, and then complete and save the following information fields in the **Cashbook** tab:

1. Set the **Organization** field to **Shirt**.
2. Set the **Name** field to **USD Point of Sales Cash Book**.
3. Set the **Currency** field to **USD**.

The cash book is now ready for use, and we can proceed with creating the sales order document.

## Entering a sales order

There is no special window to book a direct sales transaction. You can simply navigate to the **Menu | Quote-to-Invoice | Sales Orders | Sales Order** window. Instead of using the **Standard Order** document type, we can specify **POS Order** as the document type for direct sales activities.

Assuming that we do not have enough stock of Shirt Finished Goods, you need to manufacture one Shirt Finished Goods product through the **Production** window (refer to the *Production* section of Chapter 6, *Landed Cost, Production, and Sales Activities*, for details of how to manufacture a product). Navigate to the **Sales Order** window, and complete the following information fields in the **Order** tab:

1. Set the **Organization** field to **Shirt**.
2. Set the **Target Document Type** field to **POS Order**.
3. Set the **Business Partner** field to **Standard**. Here, you can create your own business partner. Generally, we define this type of customer as a *walk in customer* (a special business partner) and use this business partner when handling the direct sales activities.
4. Set the **Warehouse** field to **1st Shirt W/h**. In general, you need to create a special warehouse that indicates your store.
5. Set the **Price List** field to **Sales PL**. This price list uses USD as its currency.

As a sales transaction standard, the **POS Order** document type uses **Cash** as its default payment rule. Examine the button below the **Price List** field information.

Assuming that the *walk in customer* buys one shirt, you can enter the following information on the **Order Line** tab:

1. Set the **Product** field to **Shirt Finished Goods**.
2. Set the **Quantity** field to **1**.

Navigate back to the **Order** tab to complete this document.

## Unveiling POS Order transaction workflow

After completing this document, you will see a message at the bottom left-hand side of the window (status bar), as shown in the following screenshot:

> Shipment/Receipt: 550000 - Invoice: 150000 (Cash Journal: 10/08/2009 USD Point of Sales Cash Book #10)

When completing a **POS Order** document, ADempiere automatically creates an extra document behind the scenes. The explanation for the messages in the above screenshot is that the system will create the following documents:

- An **MM Shipment Indirect** document in the **Shipment (Customer)** window. In this example, this document has 550000 as its document number.
- An **AR Invoice Indirect** document in the **Invoice (Customer)** window. In this example, this document has 150000 as its document number.
- **Cash Journal** entries in the **Menu | Open Items | Cash Journal** window. In the **Cash Line** tab, the contained transaction uses **Invoice** as its **Cash Type**, and has positive values.

You can examine both of the documents in their respective windows.

## Accounting facts

There is no difference between the accounting facts/GL journal entries generated in the shipping and the invoice document. The **MM Shipment Indirect** document generates accounting facts just like the **MM Shipment** document does, and the **AR Invoice Indirect** document generates accounting facts just like the **AR Invoice** does.

When entering the transaction in the **Cash Journal** by using **Invoice** as its **Cash Type** and having a positive value, the accounting facts/GL journal entry format should be as follows:

| Sign | | Description | Posting Type |
|------|------|-------------|--------------|
| Db | | Petty Cash | Actual |
| | Cr | Petty Cash In-Transfer | Actual |

The following screenshot shows the accounting facts/GL journal entries generated by our sample transaction:

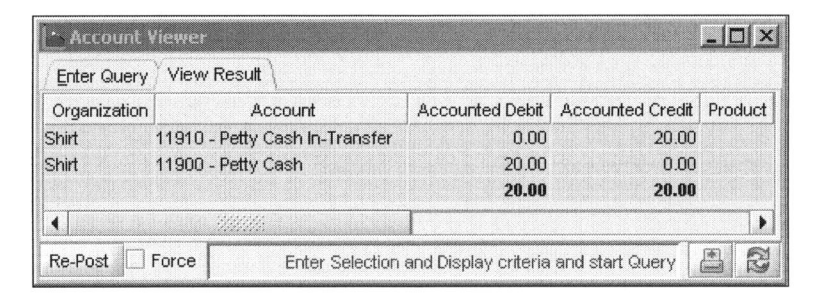

## Summary

In this chapter, you have learned more about the sample business process cycle.

We started our discussion by looking at how to book charges that are incurred during procurement activities. To accomplish this task, we learned how to create a new instance of a cost element, saw an example of how to distribute these expenses by using the available cost distribution types, and also learned the distribution of expenses in detail.

We continued our discussion by looking at how to manufacture a product in this version of ADempiere by using the **bill of material** feature, involving both item and expenses type of products. After manufacturing the products, we created an offer letter for the customers. On receiving their confirmation, we raised a sales order document, delivered the product to the customer, and finally invoiced them. After performing these activities, we learned how to manage the payment (account receivable payment) and reconcile the transaction with our bank statement.

Towards the end of this chapter, we learned how ADempiere manages direct sales—a type of sales transaction. In this type of transaction, ADempiere generates both shipment and invoice documents behind the scenes.

In the next chapter, we will take a look at the accounting configuration parts of ADempiere. We will learn how to define our own account, what an accounting dimension is, and will discuss the Accounting Schema. You will also be introduced to a sample implementation for Commitment accounting and General Ledger distribution.

# 7
# Accounting Information and Configuration

The heart of ADempiere ERP is accounting. The power behind its accounting engine is its accounting configuration. There are some areas that need your attention. They are the areas in which accounting configuration drives the accounting behavior when implementing the ADempiere system. Moreover, once you are familiar with the flexibility of the accounting configuration, you can configure it to suit your needs.

In this chapter, we will take a look at what can be done with the help of ADempiere accounting configuration. This includes the following parts:

- Chart of accounts
- Accounting dimensions
- Accounting schema
- Commitment accounting
- General Ledger distribution
- Product costs

From the previous chapters, we have learned what standard accounting facts and GL journal entries are generated when performing the sample business cycle activities. After completing this chapter, and after you have an idea of the ADempiere accounting behavior, you need to configure ADempiere in the actual implementation, after performing the initial client setup.

# Managing ADempiere accounts

Managing a chart of accounts for an organization is usually an accountant's responsibility. Although most of us are not accountants, we can try to understand what an account is, what a chart of accounts is, and how to map an organization's accounts through ADempiere. We will discuss these topics in the upcoming sections.

## Chart of accounts

A **Chart of accounts** is a list of the names of the accounts that an organization has accredited for recording transactions. This list of accounts can be numeric, alphabetic, or even alpha-numeric.

In standard accounting, the term **Account** is defined as a unique identifier that is used to retrieve and store information in the General Ledger. As you have seen in our previous transaction example, an organization will have an 'account receivable' account that is used when creating an invoice for a customer and/or when receiving a payment from the customer.

Throughout our examples in ADempiere, we will use numbers to identify an organization's accounts, and alphabets to identify account names. With the sample chart of accounts provided in the ADempiere binary installation, you have the flexibility to rebuild your own chart of accounts to suit your organization's needs.

In the chart of accounts, we can typically classify accounts as:

- Balance sheet accounts
  - Assets
  - Liabilities
  - Owner's equity
- Income statement accounts
  - Operating revenues
  - Operating expenses
  - Non-operating revenues and gains
  - Non-operating expenses and losses

All of the above types will influence the creation of a financial statement. With the help of a general ledger, which contains account transactions, you can generate periodic financial statement reports, such as the extraction of account balances from the Trial Balance reports, measuring the performance of the organization through Profit and Loss statements, and so on.

# A journey through the ADempiere list of accounts

When creating the **Sistematika Fashion, Ltd** client, we will require a predefined chart of accounts. In Chapter 3, *Exploring Company Structures and the Initial Client Setup*, we discussed the standard ADempiere format for charts of accounts and imported a sample chart of accounts during the initial client setup.

The entire list of accounts from the sample chart of accounts that is imported can be accessed through the **Menu | Performance Analysis | Accounting Rules | Account Element** window. This window contains three tabs: **Element**, **Element Value**, and **Sub Account**.

The **Element** tab contains one record, which mentions a standard account type as the primary natural account being used in the ADempiere system, while the **Element Value** tab lists all of your existing accounts (in area number 1) and the details of the account definition (in area number 2, below), as shown in the following screenshot:

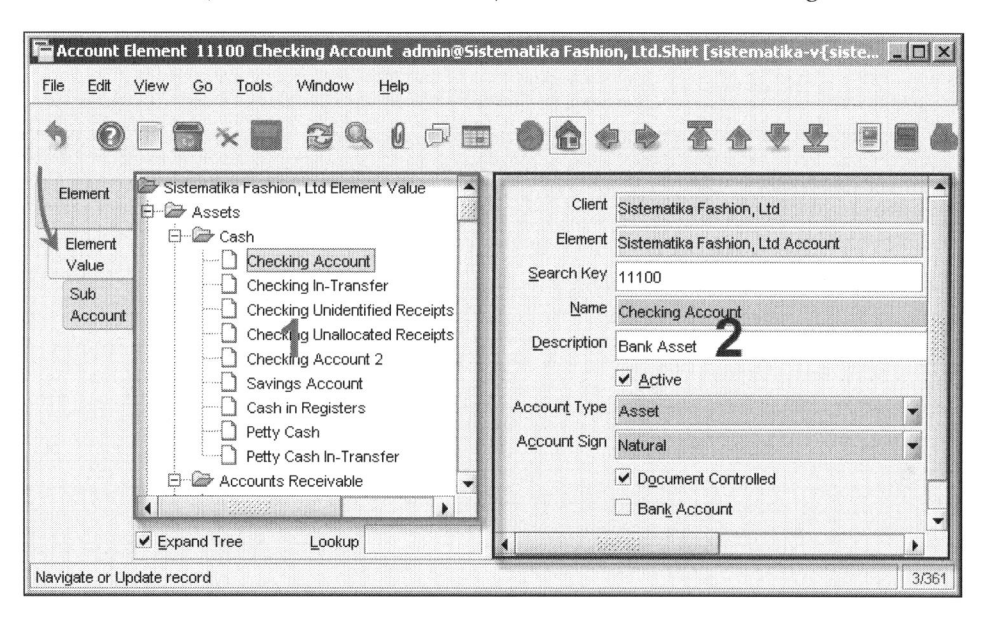

When using `AccountingUS.csv` files, we assume that the chart of accounts is a complete list of accounts. You will be able to edit or add to this account listing to suit your organization's accounting requirements.

# Adding more accounts

In a real organization, sooner or later, you will need to add more accounts.

*I need to enter a new account. Can you assist me with this task?*

Suppose you want to add your own deposit account. Click on the **New** button, and in area number 2 of the **Element Value** tab, complete the following information fields:

1. Set the **Organization** field to **\***.
2. This account should be accessible to all other organizations in this client.
3. Set the **Search Key** field to **19500**.
4. Set the **Name** field to **Deposit Account**.
5. Set the **Account Type** field to **Asset**.
6. Here, you can set your account type. In this case, we will use the Asset type of account.
7. Set the **Account Sign** field to **Natural**.
8. This field indicates whether the expected balance for this account should be a **Debit** or a **Credit**. If we set it to **Natural**, the account sign will follow the default expected balance for that account type.
9. Deselect the **Summary Level** checkbox.
10. A transaction can be posted to any account that is not summary level. A **Summary Level** account is an account whose balance represents the total balance of other account balances.
11. Select the **Post Actual** and **Post Budget** checkboxes.
12. This means that we can use and post this account in the *actual* and *budget* posting type. You are also free to set this account up as a *statistical* posting type.

After saving the new deposit account, the account does not, by default, have an account parent. Take a look at the previous screenshot. An example of an account that has an account parent is **11100 (Checking Account)**. This, in turn, has **Cash** as its account parent. The **Cash** account itself has **Assets** as its account parent.

Now that we have decided to set **19 (Other Assets)** as the created account's parent, all we need to do is drag-and-drop this newly-created account in area number 1 of the previous screenshot from **Assets** to the **Other Assets** summary account. The **Other Assets** total balance will thus contain the sum of all of the account balances that have **Other Assets** as its account parent, including our newly-created **Deposit Account**'s account.

# Summary accounts option

Now, we have an account **19500 (Deposit Account)**. This account is not set up as a **Summary Level** account. Without this attribute, we can post a transaction by using this account as a *posting* account. This means that we can use this account to post our transactions that come from Material Receipt, Invoice (Customer), or GL Journal, or other type of transactions.

Have a look at the **19 (Other Assets)** account. This is an example of a **Summary Level** account. This account is a *non-posting* account, having summary level account attributes. We cannot use this account in the transactions that are aimed to be a summary entity to all accounts having **19 (Other Assets)** account as their account parent.

In a hierarchy, a **Summary Level** account can contain:

- One or more non-posting or summary accounts
- One or more posting or transaction accounts

Check out the following screenshot:

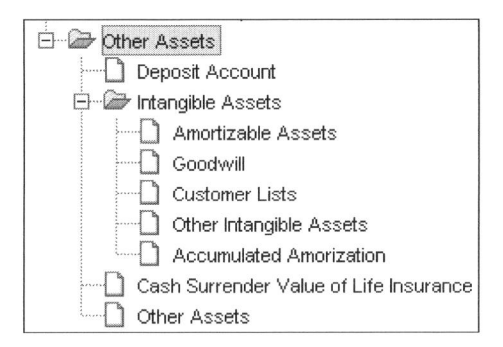

```
├─ 📂 Other Assets
│   ├─ 📄 Deposit Account
│   ├─ 📂 Intangible Assets
│   │   ├─ 📄 Amortizable Assets
│   │   ├─ 📄 Goodwill
│   │   ├─ 📄 Customer Lists
│   │   ├─ 📄 Other Intangible Assets
│   │   └─ 📄 Accumulated Amorization
│   ├─ 📄 Cash Surrender Value of Life Insurance
│   └─ 📄 Other Assets
```

The **Other Assets** sample posting account contains:

- One summary: **Intangible Assets**, which contains several posting accounts.
- Three posting accounts: **Deposit Account, Cash Surrender Value of Life Insurance**, and **Other Assets**.

You can examine **Accounts Receivable** as another example of a **Summary Level** account.

Accounting Information and Configuration

# Document Controlled option

The other option available when we set up or alter an account is the **Document Controlled** attribute. This option will appear when the account is not set as a **Summary Level** account.

When we set an account as **Document Controlled**, it means that we prepare this account to use as a target default account for ADempiere documents like the following target 'default' account:

- **MM Receipt**: This document is in use in the **Material Receipt** window
- **AR Invoice**: This document is in use in the **Invoice (Customer)** window

When account is selected as **Document Controlled**, we cannot use this account in a non-document driven (non-document related) transaction, such as the direct GL Journal transaction.

For example, the **14120 (Product Asset)** and **21190 (Not invoiced receipts)** accounts have been flagged as **Document Controlled** accounts, and will be used internally to generate accounting facts/GL journal entries when posting a document, such as the **MM Receipt** document in the **Material Receipt** window.

If you have a GL journal transaction with an account having the **Document Controlled** attribute, then you will get an error message when you try to post this transaction. To simulate this case, navigate to the **Menu | Performance Analysis | GL Journal** window, and carry out the following procedure:

1. In the **Batch** tab, set the **Organization** field to **Shirt**.
2. Set the **Description** field to **Test document controlled**.
3. Set the **Posting Type** field to **Actual**.
4. Set the **Document Type** field to **GL Journal**, and then click on the **Save** button.
5. Navigate to the **Journal** tab, set the **Description** field to **Journal Test**, and then click on the **Save** button.
6. Navigate to the **Line** tab. In the **Combination** field, click on the small red button. This will display a **Combination** form. Enter **14120** in the **Alias** field, and click on the **ReQuery** button (in the top right-hand side of the form). Now that the **14120 - Product Asset** account is available, click on the **OK** button.
7. Set the **Source Debit** field to **100**, and then click on the **Save** button.
8. We will now enter our credit journal. Click on the **New** button, and navigate to the **Combination** field. Double-click on it, and ensure that you are using the **73100 – Postage Expense** account.
9. Set the **Source Credit** field to **100**, and then click on the **Save** button.
10. Navigate back to the **Batch** tab, and click on the **Complete** button.

In the window's status bar, you will get a red-colored error message—**Account used is Document Controlled – Do not use for manual Journals**.

## Post Actual, Budget, and Statistical options

Like **Document Controlled**, the **Post Actual**, **Post Budget**, and **Post Statistical** checkboxes are shown or available only when an account is not set as **Summary Level**.

When entering a GL journal transaction, we can set up a **Posting Type** for any transaction. The available Posting types are:

- Actual
- Budget
- Statistical
- Commitment
- Reservation

> *We have a stationery budget of IDR 5,000,000 for our office operations. Can you explain to me how our example budget (stationery budget) and this topic are related?*

One of the targets of a company's performance evaluation purpose is comparing the actual expenditure with the budget. In ADempiere, we will enter our budget transaction through the **GL Journal** window, and you will have to use **Budget** as its **Posting Type**. When entering the real or actual expenses, we will use one of the following two options:

- Book this transaction within **GL Journal** and use **Actual** as its **Posting Type**

or

- Post an ADempiere document that affects the expenses type of account

With existing budget and actual transaction records, the manager can create reports to compare account balances between them, and can take appropriate action with the help of this information.

You can create a GL journal transaction for any posting type, but you can only use the **Actual** posting type to post a document-driven transaction. If we set this account without the **Post Actual** attribute, then when posting a document-driven transaction that uses this account, you will get a red-colored error message in the window's status bar—**Account does not have Post Actual attribute**, as shown in the following screenshot:

Account does not have Post Actual attribute - Line No=20 - 19500 - Deposit Account

> To avoid any issues, you can set all of the accounts to have a **Post Actual** attribute

# Introducing accounting dimensions

You may have experienced that when managing and analyzing your outstanding Account Receivable trade account, you needed to create a special account in the chart of accounts for each of your customers, in order to capture and show the customer's AR trade balances, as shown in the table below:

| Account | Customer name | Balance |
|---|---|---|
| 12110 | Customer A | 1000 |
| 12111 | Customer B | 1500 |
| 12112 | Customer C | 1750 |

Even though you can use this approach when implementing ADempiere in your organization, it is suggested that you create only one Account Receivable trade account in the system.

*If we use only one Account Receivable trade account, then how do we know the Account Receivable balances of each of our customers?*

When posting a document, there is some information that gets recorded, in addition to the account information itself. Take a look at one of the examples from the available **AR Invoice** posting documents in the **Invoice (Customer)** window. This gives you the accounting entries information in the **Account Viewer** window, as shown in the following screenshot:

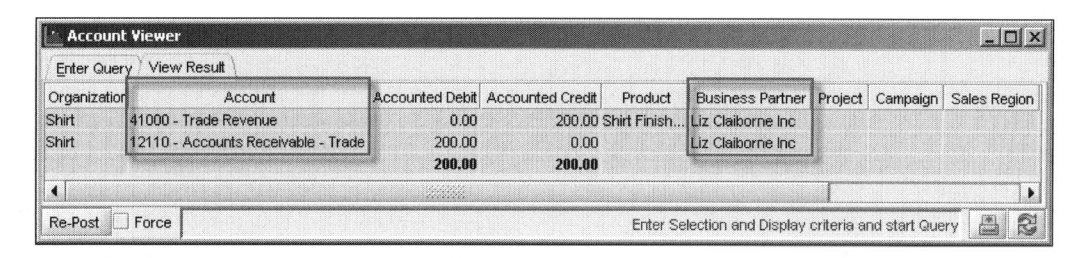

ADempiere automatically inserts additional **Business Partner**'s information in these accounting entries! Therefore, even if you have hundreds or thousands of AR trade accounting entries, they will appear as shown in the table below:

| Account | Customer Name | Amount |
|---------|---------------|--------|
| 12110   | Customer A    | 1000   |
| 12110   | Customer B    | 1500   |
| 12110   | Customer C    | 1750   |

With that information, you can create the outstanding Account Receivable trade balances by grouping the information on the business partner column.

In addition to the **Account** and **Business Partner** information, as seen in the previous screenshot, ADempiere will also give us the **Organization** and **Product** information. This will be generated automatically, based on the configuration and the available information in the document.

When receiving material, ADempiere generates the **Product** information in its accounting entries. This is another example of **Product** information that is generated automatically. Thus, there is no need to set a different **Product Asset** account for each of your products, as the information is already present.

Through this example, we have seen that there is information available for several entities such as **Organization**, **Account**, **Product**, **Business Partner**, **Project**, **Campaign**, and **Sales Region**. These are known as **accounting dimensions**. These accounting dimensions, containing unique information, join together to construct accounting facts or GL journal entries, and can be used to create a complex analysis according to your needs.

# Re-posting a document

Before we discuss the accounting configuration, you need to know about a special feature related to the document posting behavior. In ADempiere, we can force the system to re-post a document.

When re-posting a document, ADempiere will:

- Drop the existing accounting facts or GL journal entries belonging to this document
- Re-read all of the accounting configuration and accounting information involved
- Generate new accounting facts or GL journal entries based on the new accounting configuration information

> Re-posting a document should only be done for open accounting periods.

After changing the accounting configuration in the **Accounting Schema** window, we need to force the ADempiere system to get the latest configuration, by performing the following tasks:

1. Log out from the ADempiere client application.
2. Shut down the ADempiere application server.
3. Re-start the ADempiere application server.
4. Log in again to the ADempiere client application.

    In this case, we will *log in with the user ID admin*, using **Sistematika Fashion, Ltd Admin** as the role, **Shirt** as the organization, and **1st Shirt W/h** as the warehouse.

5. Re-post your document.

*How do we re-post the document?*

Because you have the rights to access the **Posted** button in the window (actually, the **Sistematika Fashion, Ltd Admin** role has these accounting rights), just click on this button. In the upcoming **Account Viewer** window, as shown in the following screenshot, find the **Re-Post** button, and click on it:

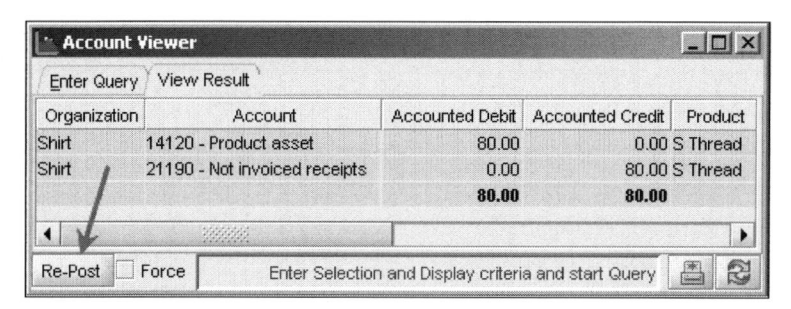

| Organization | Account | Accounted Debit | Accounted Credit | Product |
|---|---|---|---|---|
| Shirt | 14120 - Product asset | 80.00 | 0.00 | S Thread |
| Shirt | 21190 - Not invoiced receipts | 0.00 | 80.00 | S Thread |
|  |  | 80.00 | 80.00 |  |

You will be prompted with a confirmation window, stating **Post now and create Accounting entries**. Click on the **OK** button to finalize the re-posting document activities.

# A walkthrough of the Accounting Schema

The mother of all accounting configuration setups is the **Accounting Schema** window. Here, you can determine the behavior of the accounting entries in your own ADempiere installation by changing the default configuration. Navigate to the **Menu | Performance Analysis | Accounting Rules | Accounting Schema** window. This window contains four tabs: **Accounting Schema**, **Account Schema Element**, **General Ledger**, and **Defaults**. We will discuss these in more detail, with regard to what information is provided in each of tabs, in the following sections.

## Exploring the Accounting Schema tab

There are some configurations available in this tab, which include how to make our system an accrual- or cash-based accounting system, the **Commitment Type**, the **Costing Method** to be used, and so on.

The complete list of configurations that can be managed is shown in the following screenshot:

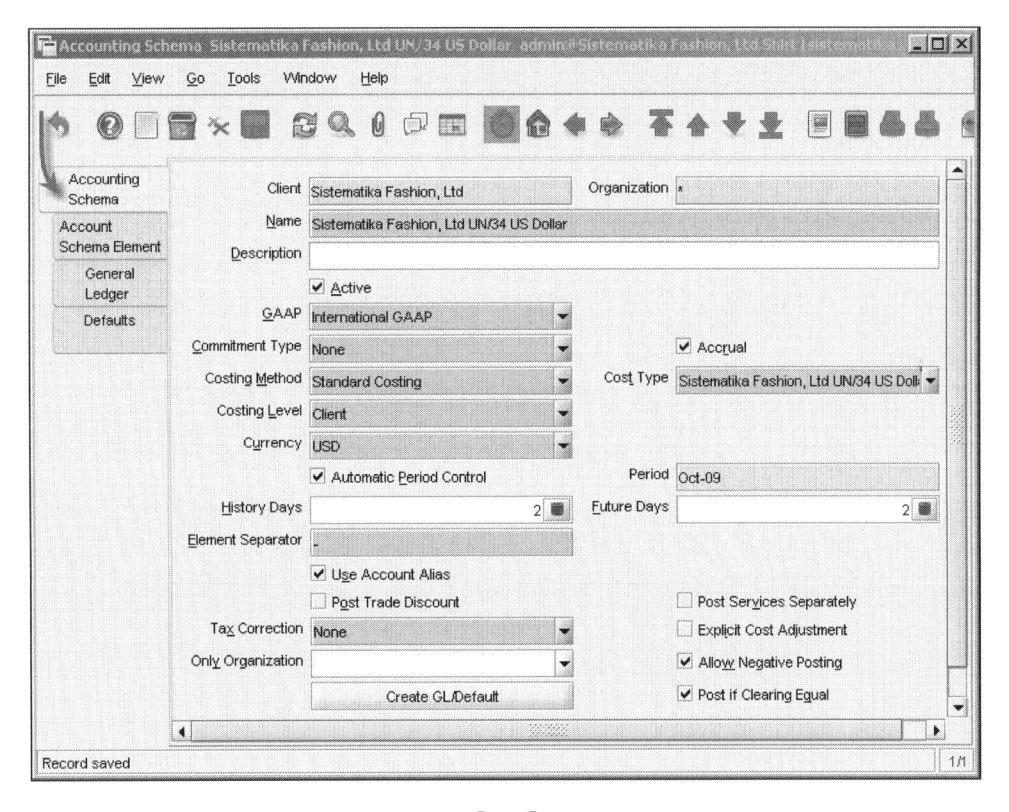

We will explain each of the available options in the following sections.

## GAAP

**GAAP (Generally Accepted Accounting Principles)** is a collection of methods used to process, prepare, and present public accounting information. Each country may have its own methods to achieve its accounting standards.

In ADempiere, the options for the **GAAP** field are: **Custom Accounting Rules**, **International GAAP**, **German HGB**, and so on.

By default, during client creation, **Generally Accepted Accounting Principles (GAAP)** would be set to **International GAAP**. Up to the current version of ADempiere, the value in this field does not affect the ADempiere accounting engine, and is preserved for future use.

## Commitment Type

Commitment accounting allows the posting of expenses prior to the creation or collection of the underlying documents, such as invoices, purchase orders, and so on, and before these committed funds are paid out. This allows the accounting entries to reflect in the allocation of budgetary resources when they are committed, instead of when they are paid out, thus providing earlier financial information than the 'budget and actual' reports and preventing budget overruns. We can set commitment accounting through the **Commitment Type** field.

Standard ADempiere configuration sets **Commitment Type** to **None** as the default value. We can set this value to **PO/SO Commitment/Reservation**, or any combination of PO, SO, Commitment, and Reservation. This configuration will determine the additional accounting facts or GL journal entries, that are generated when posting a requisition, purchase order, sales order, and invoice transaction. These additional accounting fact entries use **Reservation** and/or **Commitment** as their posting type, instead of **Actual**. We will practice these parts later.

## Accrual- or cash-based accounting

**Accrual-based accounting** is an accounting method where revenues and expenses are recognized when they are accrued, that is, accumulated (earned or incurred), regardless of whether the actual cash has been received or paid out.

As a default, ADempiere uses accrual-based accounting, instead of cash-based accounting, when creating a new client.

# Costing method and costing level

Cost accounting is an approach to evaluating the overall cost to run a business. Based on standard accounting practices, cost accounting is one of the tools that can be used by the manager to support decision making, in order to cut a company's cost and improve profitability.

In ADempiere, we use **Costing Method** to set up our cost accounting model. The standard used in ADempiere is the **Standard Costing** costing method. This is set as default for all new client creations. The following is a list of available costing methods:

- **Standard Costing**
- **Average PO**
- **Average Invoice**
- **FIFO**
- **LIFO**

Although there are many more costing methods available, up to the current ADempiere version, the most implemented features are **Standard Costing** and **Average PO**.

> **Standard Costing** means the amount the company thinks a product should cost for a period of time, based on economic conditions, certain assumed conditions, and other factors.

Another part of cost accounting determination in ADempiere is the **Costing Level**. As a default value, **Costing Level** is set to **Client**. The options for **Costing Level** are:

- **Client**
- **Organization**
- **Batch/Lot**

When we set the costing method to **Standard Costing** and the costing level to **Client**, throughout this book, it means that we need to set a standard cost for each of the products in the **Sistematika Fashion, Ltd** client level (only once).

Using **Organization** as the costing level means that we need to set a standard cost for each of the products in all of the organizations available in a certain **Client**. You need to set up a standard cost for each of the products in the **Dress**, **Shirt**, and **Jacket** organizations, in this case.

> In addition to **Standard Costing**, another cost accounting method type available in the standard accounting term is Actual Costing. **Actual Costing** is the actual amount paid or incurred. Unfortunately, there are no actual costing methods within ADempiere. Although there are no options to set this type of costing, we can acquire actual costing by setting **Costing Method** to **Average PO** and **Costing Level** to **Batch/Lot**.

The costing method and costing level configuration in **Accounting Schema** is the mother of all cost accounting calculations and implementations for all of our products. However, this costing method can be overridden by costing methods and costing levels, which are configured at the **Product Category** level. If there are no costing models and costing levels specified at the **Product Category** level (both of the **Costing Method** and **Costing Level** fields are blank) then all the products belonging to this **Product Category** will use the costing model and costing level information from the **Accounting Schema** level. However, if costing models and costing levels are specified, then use the **Product Category** configuration instead.

## Currency

During client creation, there is an option to set up the main currency. You can set it up in the **Currency** field. This currency will be used as the main currency for our accounting schema. Using USD as our main currency does not mean that we cannot use a currency other than USD in a transaction.

In our example for managing landed costs in Chapter 6, *Landed Costs, Production, and Sales Activities*, we used IDR as our transaction currency. If we have a multi-currency transaction like this one, then ADempiere should keep the original transaction values in the **Source Debit** or **Source Credit** fields, and the converted USD values are stored in the **Accounted Debit** or **Accounted Credit** parts, through the accounting facts or GL journal entries generated. Generally, we can use this *accounted* information when generating a financial statement for analysis purposes.

## Periods controlling

For controlling the periodic parts, by default, there is an **Automatic Period Control** checkbox, in a selected state. With this configuration, ADempiere will automatically check for the active periods (via the **Periods** field), and the criteria of **History Days** and **Future Days**, when completing a document.

With **Oct-09** as the active period (refer to the **Periods** field from the **Accounting Schema** tab), **2** as history days, and **2** as future days information, and let's say that it is Oct 12, 2009; then system will allow the posting of documents for the Oct-09 period, while the document date or account date can be between two days before and two days after Oct 12, 2009. When performing a transaction outside of these dates, the system will generate a **Period Closed** error message.

## Use Account Alias

When working with a GL journal transaction, or altering default account information, we will use an account combination. By determining what kind of account combination will be used for these activities, it will be easier to perform a search of this account combination by using the alias of this account combination.

The **Use Account Alias** checkbox is in a selected state by default. With this configuration, you can set an alias for each of the account combinations registered in the **Account Combination** window, and use its alias to identify the account combination.

Do you remember that you have already created a **Shirt-14120-_-_-_-_-_** account combination, and specified **14120** as its alias? When using this account combination in your transaction, you need to do the following in the **Account Dialog** window:

1. Click on the **Undo Changes** button.
2. Set your account combination **Alias**.
3. Click on the **ReQuery** button to get your account combination.
4. Click on the **OK** button to finalize, as shown in the following screenshot:

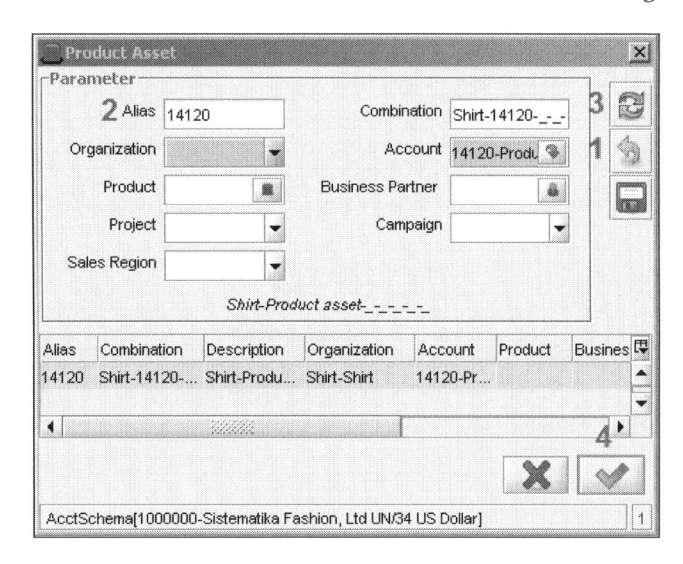

*Accounting Information and Configuration*

## Post Trade Discount

The ADempiere system does not select the **Post Trade Discount** option by default. In case you want to post a discount value that is reflected in the accounting facts or GL journal entries, then you need to select this option. The transaction for trade discount will be booked when posting an **AR Invoice** or **AR Credit Memo** document through the **Invoice (Customer)** window.

In our test case chart of accounts, the accounts related to discount are:

- **Trade Discount Received (59100)**
- **Trade Discount Granted (49100)**

To support our further example assuming that you do not have enough stock of Shirt Finished Goods, you need to:

1. Manufacture 1 Shirt Finished Goods product through the **Production** window (refer to the *Production* section of Chapter 6, *Landed Cost, Production, and Sales Activities* for details of how to manufacture a product).
2. Next, you need to select the **Post Trade Discount** option, and save your changes. Log off from the ADempiere client, re-start your ADempiere server, and then re-login to the ADempiere client.

We will give you an example of the impact of selecting the **Post Trade Discount** option, by examining the accounting fact/GL journal entry generated. Create more instances of **Sales Order** and finalize them with an **AR Invoice** document through the **Invoice (Customer)** window, as follows:

1. Navigate to the **Menu | Quote-to-Invoice | Sales Orders | Sales Order** window. If this does not show an inserted status in the **Order** tab, click on the **New** button, and then set the following information:
    - Set the **Organization** field to **Shirt**
    - Set the **Target Document Type** field to **Standard Order**
    - Set the **Date Ordered** and **Date Promised** fields to today's date
    - Set the **Business Partner** field to **Liz Claiborne**
    - Set the **Warehouse** field to **1st Shirt W/h**
    - Set the **Invoice Rule** field to **Immediate**
    - Set the **Price List** field to **Sales PL**, and then click on the **Save** button

*Chapter 7*

2. Navigate to the **Order Line** tab, and do the following:
   - Set the **Product** with **Shirt Finished Goods**, the **Qty** field to **1**, and the **UOM** field to **Piece**.
   - Set the **Price** and **Unit Price** fields to **18**, and the **List Price** field to **20**. Then we will have a **10** percent of discount value (automatically calculated).
   - Set the **Tax** field to **Standard** (there is no need to generate tax during this test case), and then click on the **Save** button. We will thus have a document with a total value of $18.

3. Navigate back to the **Order** tab, and complete this document.

4. Assuming that we are bypassing the shipment processes, we will directly generate invoices. Navigate to the **Menu | Quote-to-Invoice | Sales Invoices | Generate Invoices (manual)** window.
   - Set the **Organization** field to **Shirt**, the **Document Type** field to **Order**, and there will be a list of **Standard Order** document available (showing our previously-created **Standard Order** document).
   - Select the required records, and finalize the document by clicking on the **OK** button, as shown in the following screenshot:

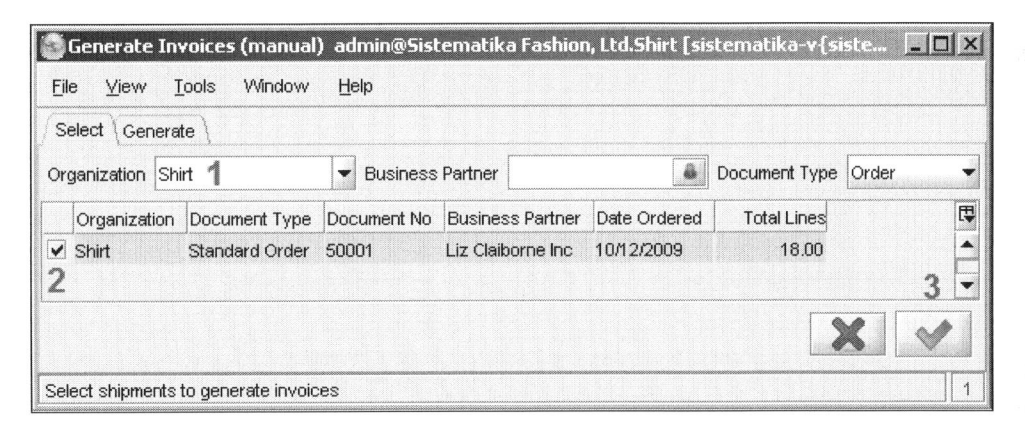

5. Now, navigate to the **Menu | Quote-to-Invoice | Sales Invoices | Invoice (Customer)** window. Find your newly-generated invoice. It will have a complete document status.

6. Press the *F5* key repeatedly, until you get a **Posted** status for this document. Check out the accounting facts or GL journal entry generated by this invoice, as shown in the following screenshot:

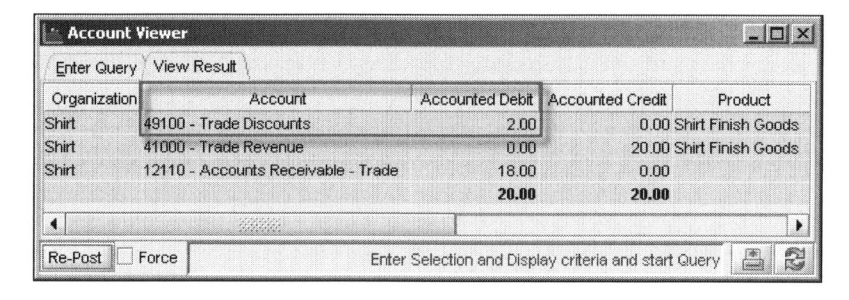

There are additional **49100 – Trade Discount** journal entries! The **Accounted Debit** trade discount value (which is **2**) is a result of the following equation:

$$( \text{List Price} - \text{Unit Price} ) * \text{Qty}$$

## Post services separately

When creating a product through the **Product** window, you need to specify the **Product Type** information. As you already know, product type options are: **Expense Type**, **Item**, **Resource**, and **Service**.

If we set the product type to **Service** and select the **Post Service Separately** option, then when posting our **AR Invoice** document, it will be posted to the **Receivable Services** default account (**12115**), instead of the **Customer Receivables** default account (**12110**).

You can examine the **Receivable Services** standard default account being used, through the **Business Partner** window, navigating to the **Customer Accounting** tab, as shown in the following screenshot:

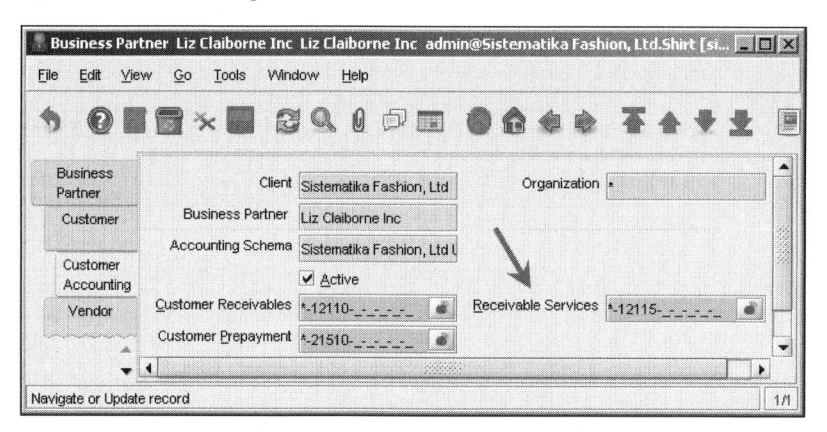

# Explicit Cost Adjustment

This option will generate optional accounting facts or GL journal entries when posting our invoice document through the **Invoice (Vendor)** window under following conditions:

- It has **AP Invoice** or **AP Credit Memo** as its **Target Document Type**
- The invoice is a landed cost type of transaction

For our example, revisit the *Landed cost* discussion in Chapter 6, *Landed Costs, Production, and Sales Activities*. In that section, we had assigned a transportation cost to our raw material. When we select the **Explicit Cost Adjustment** option and re-post this document, the accounting facts/GL journal entries generated are as shown in the following screenshot:

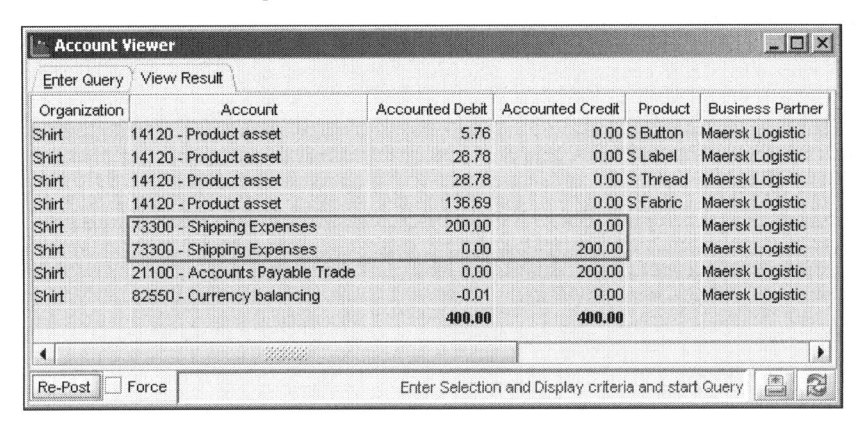

| Organization | Account | Accounted Debit | Accounted Credit | Product | Business Partner |
|---|---|---|---|---|---|
| Shirt | 14120 - Product asset | 5.76 | 0.00 | S Button | Maersk Logistic |
| Shirt | 14120 - Product asset | 28.78 | 0.00 | S Label | Maersk Logistic |
| Shirt | 14120 - Product asset | 28.78 | 0.00 | S Thread | Maersk Logistic |
| Shirt | 14120 - Product asset | 136.69 | 0.00 | S Fabric | Maersk Logistic |
| Shirt | 73300 - Shipping Expenses | 200.00 | 0.00 | | Maersk Logistic |
| Shirt | 73300 - Shipping Expenses | 0.00 | 200.00 | | Maersk Logistic |
| Shirt | 21100 - Accounts Payable Trade | 0.00 | 200.00 | | Maersk Logistic |
| Shirt | 82550 - Currency balancing | -0.01 | 0.00 | | Maersk Logistic |
| | | 400.00 | 400.00 | | |

If we compare these with the original accounting facts, we will find that there are some additional accounting facts/GL journal entries: **Dr 73300 – Shipping Expenses** and **Cr 73300 – Shipping Expenses**.

Because this landed cost transaction uses **Transportation** as its type of charge, the additional **73300 – Shipping Expenses** account journal entries are taken from the **Charge Expense** default account of the **Transportation** type of charges (refer to the *Setting transportation charges* section of Chapter 6, *Landed Costs, Production, and Sales Activities*).

# Allow Negative Posting

When entering a transaction such as a GL Journal transaction, ADempiere can and will proceed with both positive and negative amounts, by default. Deselecting this option does not mean that we are able to set a positive amount only. Whatever the configuration of this option is, it will still allow us to enter both positive and negative amounts.

## Accounting Information and Configuration

The impact of selecting this option is seen in the journal position of its accounting facts entries. Suppose we have the following GL journal entries transaction:

| Sign | Description | Amount |
|---|---|---|
| Dr | 71200 – Subscription Fees | -100 |
| Cr | 73100 – Postage Expenses | -100 |

Then the accounting facts/GL journal generated will look like the ones shown in the following screenshot:

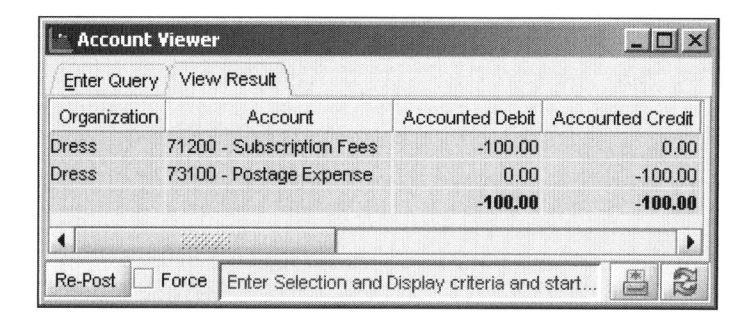

| Organization | Account | Accounted Debit | Accounted Credit |
|---|---|---|---|
| Dress | 71200 - Subscription Fees | -100.00 | 0.00 |
| Dress | 73100 - Postage Expense | 0.00 | -100.00 |
| | | -100.00 | -100.00 |

Otherwise, if we deselect the **Allow Negative Posting** option and re-post this document, then the accounting facts or GL journal entries generated will look like the ones shown in the following screenshot:

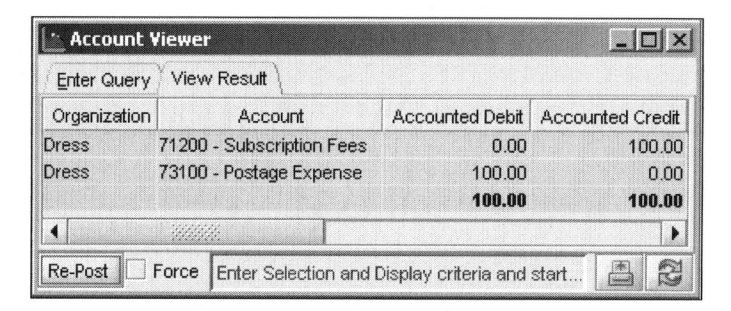

| Organization | Account | Accounted Debit | Accounted Credit |
|---|---|---|---|
| Dress | 71200 - Subscription Fees | 0.00 | 100.00 |
| Dress | 73100 - Postage Expense | 100.00 | 0.00 |
| | | 100.00 | 100.00 |

In short, this option will either allow or disallow negative posting of accounting facts and journal entries. If we deselect the **Allow Negative Posting** option, then when posting a negative amount, the journal created is the opposite of the original debit or credit transaction, and is accompanied by a positive amount.

> It is recommended that you deselect this option in the configuration.

## Post if Clearing Equal

If you do not need the *Product Inventory Clearing* journal entries in the **Matched Invoices** records and **AP Invoice** document, then you should deselect the **Post if Clearing Equal** option.

The decision to select this option or not depends on your business requirements. If you need to trace the relationship between the invoice and your material receipt, based on the accounting information generated from the AP Invoice and MM Receipt documents, then the credit journal or credit amount of the *Product Inventory Clearing* accounting entries can be used for this purpose.

> *Based on accounting entries, how do we know the relationship between the invoice and our material receipt?*

So far, you have accessed the accounting facts or GL journal entries through the **Account Viewer** window. The complete list of accounting facts/GL journal entries is accessible through the **Menu | Performance Analysis | Accounting Fact Details** window. Navigate to this window, and locate the **51290 – Product Inventory Clearing** account that has a credit journal or credit amount. The following screenshot example is taken from the author's ADempiere records:

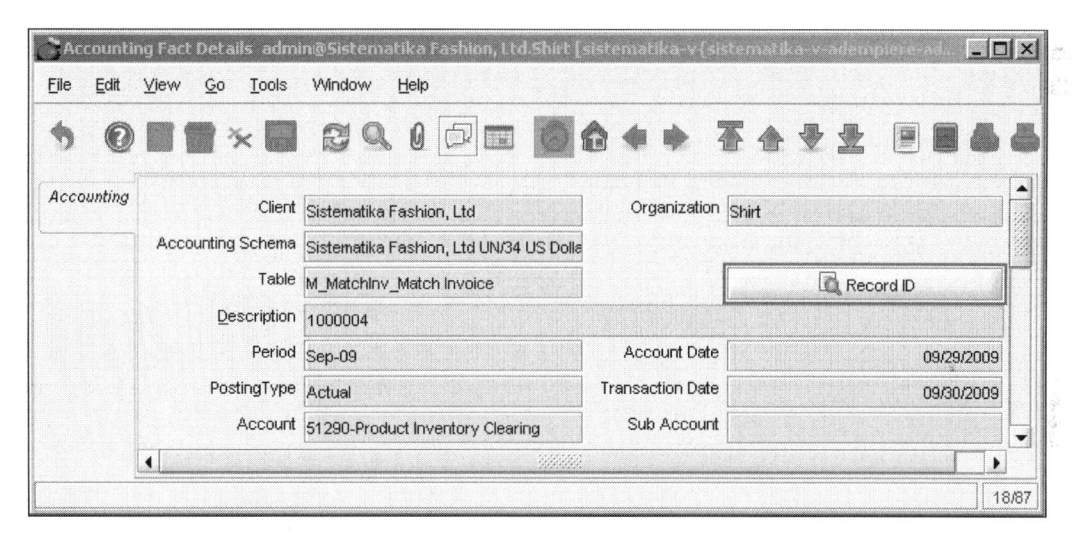

If you click on the **Record ID** button, then the system will show you a **Matched Invoices** window that shows the relation between the AP Invoice and the MM Receipt document.

# The Account Schema Element tab

When creating a new **Client** (refer to the section *Creating a new ADempiere client* of Chapter 3, *Exploring Company Structures and Initial Client Setup*), there are **Optional** checkboxes that need to be set up. In Chapter 3, we selected the **Business Partner**, **Product**, **Project**, **Campaign**, and **Sales Region** options.

After selecting these options, all of the optional parts are saved on the **Account Schema Element** tab, as shown in the following screenshot:

| Accounting Schema | Name | Active | Type |
|---|---|---|---|
| Sistematika Fashion, Ltd UN/34 US Dollar | Organization | ✔ | Organization |
| Sistematika Fashion, Ltd UN/34 US Dollar | Account | ✔ | Account |
| Sistematika Fashion, Ltd UN/34 US Dollar | Product | ✔ | Product |
| Sistematika Fashion, Ltd UN/34 US Dollar | BPartner | ✔ | BPartner |
| Sistematika Fashion, Ltd UN/34 US Dollar | Project | ✔ | Project |
| Sistematika Fashion, Ltd UN/34 US Dollar | Campaign | ✔ | Campaign |
| Sistematika Fashion, Ltd UN/34 US Dollar | Sales Region | ✔ | Sales Region |

Other than the **Business Partner**, **Product**, **Project**, **Campaign**, and **Sales Region** account schema elements, this tab also has **Organization** and **Account** as mandatory account schema elements.

> Throughout this book, we have seen that the ADempiere system has seven account schema elements available. For the minimum of ADempiere account schema elements registered, ADempiere requires at least the **Organization**, **Account**, **Product**, and **BPartner** account schema elements.

As you have seen in the *Introducing the accounting dimensions* section earlier in this chapter, the seven active options from the list of account schema elements should be used to activate and generate Accounting Dimension information that is taken from available data in the document (**Standard Order**, **AR Invoice**, and so on), and actualize this information in the accounting fact/GL journal entries generated.

# Adding campaign information

To improve our sales and profitability, we need to set a marketing campaign for promoting our products. From this marketing campaign's activities, the company expects more sales, which will improve its profitability. To measure the effectiveness of this marketing campaign, we can activate a **Campaign** accounting schema element, and assign the campaign information to all of the documents related to this campaign (for example, purchases, sales, total expenses incurred, and so on). As a result, we will be able to analyze the contribution of this campaign, in an effort to improve our sales and profitability.

Let us create an **AP Invoice** document, and set the **Campaign** information in this document by performing the following steps:

1. First, we need to set up additional campaign information, let's say for the **Anniversary Campaign**. Navigate to the **Menu | Quote-to-Invoice | Sales and Marketing | Marketing Campaign** window.

2. Click on the **New** button, and set the following information:
   - Set the **Organization** to *
   - Set both the **Search Key** and **Name** fields to **Anniversary Campaign**

3. Click on the **Save** button.

> In our campaign activities, we still need to create the **Purchase Order** and **MM Receipt** documents before proceeding with the **AP Invoice**. As we are here to see the impact of account element configuration, we will only create an **AP Invoice** document, to simplify things.

4. Navigate to the **Menu | Requisition-to-Invoice | Invoice (Vendor)** window. Set the following information on the **Invoice** tab:
   - Set the **Organization** field to **Shirt**
   - Set the **Target Document Type** field to **AP Invoice**
   - Set the **Date Invoice** and **Account Date** fields to today's date
   - Set the **Business Partner** field to **Hempel China Limited**
   - Set the **Campaign** field to **Anniversary Campaign**, and then click on the **Save** button

5. Navigate to the **Invoice Line** tab, and set the following information:
   - Set the **Product** field to **S Fabric**, the **Qty** field to **80**, and the **UOM** field to **Meter**
   - Set the **Price** field to **3.80**
   - Set the **Tax** field to **Standard**
   - Set the **Campaign** to **Anniversary Campaign**, and then click on the **Save** button

6. Navigate back to the **Invoice** tab, and complete this document. Wait for a moment, press the *F5* key repeatedly, until you get a **Posted** status for this document, click on the **Posted** button, and then check the details of the accounting facts/GL journal entry generated. This will contain the campaign information, taken from the **Campaign** accounting dimension, as shown in the following screenshot:

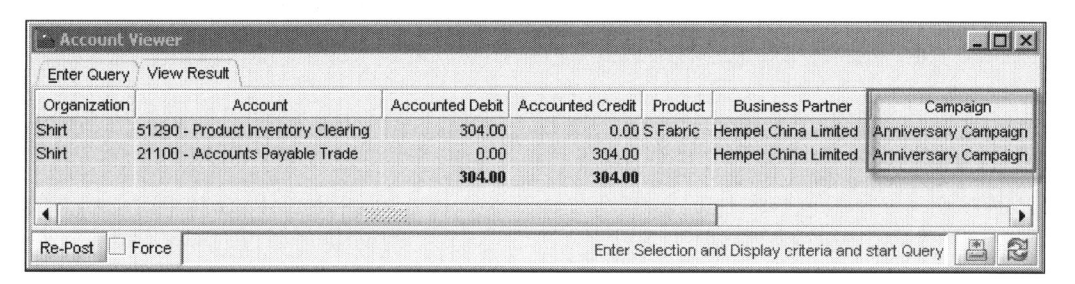

| Organization | Account | Accounted Debit | Accounted Credit | Product | Business Partner | Campaign |
|---|---|---|---|---|---|---|
| Shirt | 51290 - Product Inventory Clearing | 304.00 | 0.00 | S Fabric | Hempel China Limited | Anniversary Campaign |
| Shirt | 21100 - Accounts Payable Trade | 0.00 | 304.00 | | Hempel China Limited | Anniversary Campaign |
| | | 304.00 | 304.00 | | | |

# Registering another account schema element

ADempiere has the ability to add additional account schema elements. By using this capability, we can add built-in account schema elements that are not yet registered on the **Account Schema Element** tab. For example, the **Activity** account schema element. We will practice how to register **Activity** as a member of our account schema element. Perform the following steps:

1. Navigate to the **Menu | Performance Analysis | Accounting Rules | Activity (ABC)** window. On the **Activity** tab, set and save the following information:
   - Set the **Organization** field to *
   - Set the **Search Key** and **Name** field to **Our Sample Activity**

2. Navigate to the **Menu | Performance Analysis | Accounting Rules | Accounting Schema** window. In the **Account Schema Element** tab, add and save the following information:
   - Set the **Name** field to **Activity**
   - Set the **Type** field to **Activity** (choose from the available list)
   - Set the **Activity** field to **Our Sample Activity**

3. When saving information in the **Accounting Schema** window, you will be prompted by a confirmation window, as shown in the following screenshot:

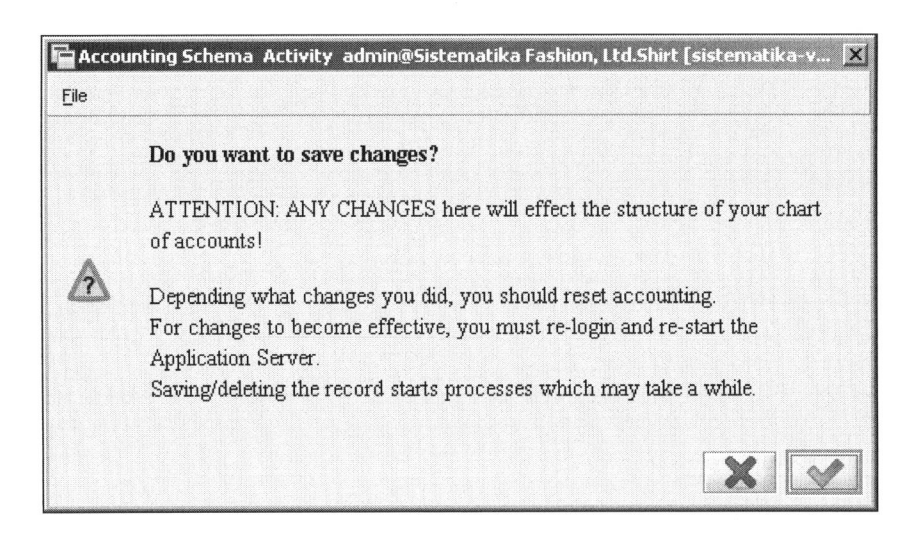

As mentioned, to make your changes effective, you need to restart your application server, and then re-login with your ADempiere user ID.

With your new configuration, navigate to the **Invoice (Vendor)** window. The **Invoice** tab will contain additional **Reference** information, **Activity**, as shown in the following screenshot:

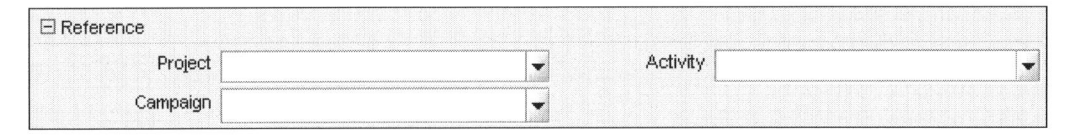

Next time, when you are entering **Activity** information at the document level, such as for an **AP Invoice** document, when posting this document, ADempiere will insert the **Activity** information into the accounting facts/GL journal entries generated.

## Deactivating the account schema element

If our business does not require information such as **Activity**, **Project**, **Campaign**, and **Sales Region** in its generated accounting facts/GL journal entries, then we can make this account schema element inactive.

> Although we are able to delete this account schema element directly, it is recommended that you set this account schema element as inactive.

After restarting your application server and logging in to the application, again your changes will be effective. Again, check your **Invoice (Vendor)** window. It will not contain **Reference** any more! Create your own new AP Invoice document and **Complete** the document. Examine the accounting fact/GL journal entries generated.

# Avoiding the Intercompany Due From/To journal entries

When explaining accounting facts/GL journal entries generated, in the *Cash Payment Allocation* section in Chapter 5, *Procurement Activities*, we came across additional journal entries when we had a transaction that used multiple organizations, as shown in the following screenshot:

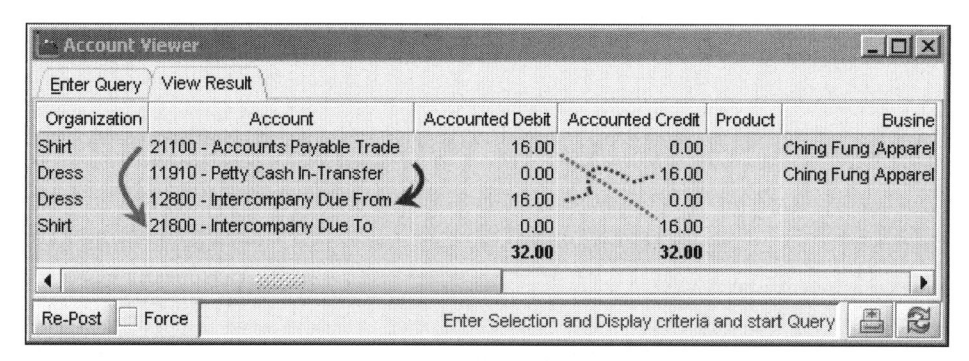

| Organization | Account | Accounted Debit | Accounted Credit | Product | Busine |
|---|---|---|---|---|---|
| Shirt | 21100 - Accounts Payable Trade | 16.00 | 0.00 | | Ching Fung Apparel |
| Dress | 11910 - Petty Cash In-Transfer | 0.00 | 16.00 | | Ching Fung Apparel |
| Dress | 12800 - Intercompany Due From | 16.00 | 0.00 | | |
| Shirt | 21800 - Intercompany Due To | 0.00 | 16.00 | | |
| | | 32.00 | 32.00 | | |

As you can see from the previous screenshot, the **Intercompany Due To** account is designed to set a journal balance entry in the **Shirt** organization, whereas **Intercompany Due From** sets a journal balance entry in the **Dress** organization. With this journal, if you create financial statement reports for a certain organization, these reports will give you a balance of the total debit against the total credit amount.

If needed, we can avoid the Intercompany journal entries. This can be done by deselecting the **Balanced** checkbox in the **Organization**'s account schema element, as shown in the following screenshot:

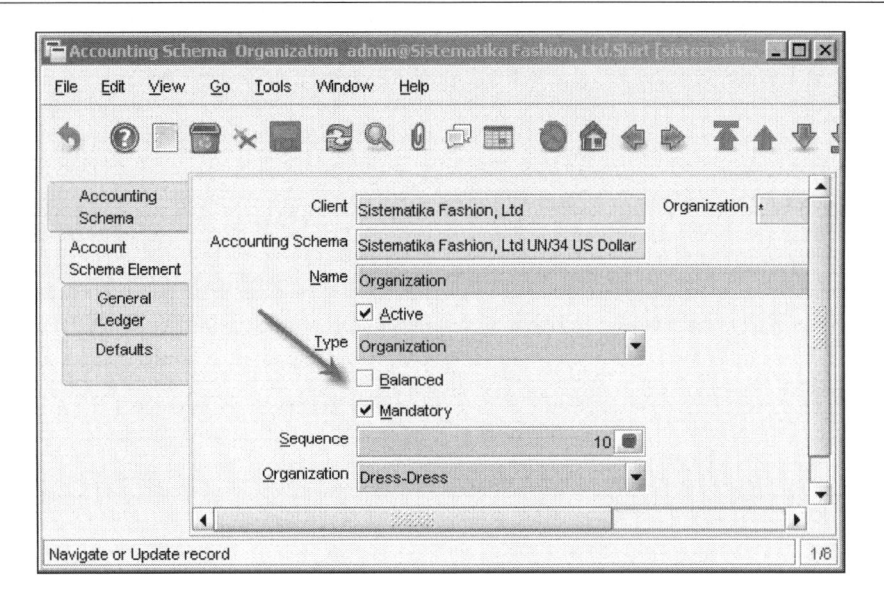

By re-posting the **View Allocation** document, both of the Intercompany journal entries are gone!

## The General Ledger and Defaults tabs

The **Defaults** tab carries a list of the ADempiere default accounts. These entries are based on the AccountingUS.csv default account, which was explained in Chapter 3, *Exploring Company Structures and Initial Client Setup*, in the *Managing Chart of accounts template* section.

On the **General Ledger** tab, it's recommended that you select **Use Suspense Balancing**, **Use Suspense Error**, and **Use Currency Balancing**. Furthermore, you can alter the account combination for the list of available default accounts, to suit your needs.

On the **Defaults** tab, the default accounts will be grouped according to their own purpose/target/reference, such as:

- Business Partner
- Product
- Warehouse
- Project
- Bank
- Tax
- Cash book

[ 245 ]

The **Charge Expense** and **Charge Revenue** default accounts in the **General** group will be used for the **Charge** document.

When creating a new **Business Partner Group**, **Product Group**, **Warehouse**, **Project**, **Bank Account**, **Tax Rate**, or **Cashbook** reference record, the list of default accounts configuration, which is available in the **Accounting** tab for each of those entities, will be copied from the standard default account available on the **Defaults** tab of **Accounting Schema** window.

For example, when creating a new **Business Partner Group**, the default account listed in the **Accounting** tab was taken from the **Accounting Schema** default account for **Business Partner**. As another example, when creating a new **Product Category**, the default account listed in the **Accounting** tab was taken from **Accounting Schema** default account for **Product**.

# Avoiding Product Inventory Clearing journal entries

As shown in the *Managing vendor invoices* section of Chapter 5, *Procurement Activities*, when posting a document in the **Matched Invoices** and **Invoice (Vendor)** window, ADempiere generates the *Product Inventory Clearing* journal. There is an option to eliminate the Product Inventory Clearing journal entries when posting an **AP Invoice** document in the **Invoice (Vendor)** window, and **Match Invoice** document in the **Matched Invoices** window.

## Prerequisites

There is some configuration that needs to be done to achieve these tasks:

1. Deselect the **Post if Clearing Equal** checkbox:

   Open the **Menu | Performance Analysis | Accounting Rules | Accounting Schema** window. In the **Accounting Schema** tab, you will find a **Post if Clearing Equal** checkbox. Deselect this checkbox.

2. Create a new **21190 - Not invoiced receipts** account combination:

   In the **Account Combination** window, enter a new account combination record with:

   - **Alias** field set to **21190**
   - **Organization** field set to **Shirt**
   - **Account** field set to **21190**

3. Set the **Not-invoiced Receipts** default account of the targeted **Business Partner Group** to the newly-created **21190-Not invoiced receipts** account combination:

   In the **Menu | Partner Relations | Business Partner Rules | Business Partner Group** window, find the **Import** business partner group for our example. Go to the **Accounting** tab and find its **Not-invoiced Receipts** field. Change the account combination value to the newly-created **21190** account combination.

4. Set the **Product Inventory Clearing** default account of the targeted product to the newly-created **21190-Not invoiced receipts** account combination:

   In the **Menu | Material Management | Material Management Rules | Product** window, create your new product, named **S Testing** products (refer to the *Product management* section of Chapter 4, *Setting up Master Data and Knowing its Accounting Configuration* for details on registering new products), and set the following information:

   - Set the **Product Category** to **Raw Material.**
   - Set the **Locator** to **Loc S1A.**
   - Deselect the **Sold** checkbox.
   - On the **Price** tab, create new records, and set the **Price List Version** to **Purchase PL March version**, and enter **100** in the **List Price**, **Standard Price** and **Limit Price** fields.
   - Navigate to the **Accounting** tab, and find the **Inventory Clearing** field. Change the account combination value to the newly-created **21190** account combination.

## Testing the configuration

You can create the **Purchase Order**, **MM Receipts** (through **Material Receipt** window) and **AP Invoice** document, using the **S Testing** product and **Hempel China Limited** as its business partner, in order to test this configuration.

## Accounting facts

With this configuration, when posting both the **AP Invoice** and **Match Invoice** documents, the system does not generate *Product Inventory Clearing* journal entries if it meets the following conditions:

- **S Testing** products are used in both the **Purchase Order** and **AP Invoice** documents
- It uses business partners that use **Import** as its business partner group in both the **Purchase Order** and **AP Invoice** documents (here we are using **Hempel China Limited**)

- There is no product price variance between the **Purchase Order** and the **AP Invoice** document

- Both the **Purchase Order** and the **AP Invoice** document use the same Organization

The general journal entry format is shown in the following table:

| Window | Document | Sign | Description | Posting Type |
|---|---|---|---|---|
| Material Receipt | MM Receipt | Dr | Product Asset | Actual |
| | | Cr | Not invoiced receipts | Actual |
| Invoice (Vendor) | AP Invoice | Dr | Not invoiced receipts | Actual |
| | | Cr | Account Payable Trade | Actual |

And yes, there are no accounting facts/GL journal entries generated for the document available in the **Matched Invoices** window!

# Practicing commitment accounting

As previously mentioned in the *Commitment Type* section of this chapter, we can use commitment type accounting as a tool to provide financial information before "budget to actual" reports, and prevent budget overrun. In the following sections, we will implement commitment accounting and analyze the accounting facts/GL journal entries generated.

## Prerequisites

We can activate commitment accounting through the **Accounting Schema** window. There is a list of options that can be used to enable commitment accounting. The options are:

- **PO Commitment only**
- **PO Commitment & Reservation**
- **SO Commitment only**
- **SO Commitment & Reservation**
- **PO;SO Commitment**
- **PO;SO Commitment & Reservation**

*Chapter 7*

For our reference, monitoring the expenses incurred in the purchase activity can be done by enabling **PO Commitment & Reservation** in our accounting engine, which we can do by performing the following steps:

1. In the **Accounting Schema** window, navigate to the **Accounting Schema** tab, and set the **Commitment Type** field to **PO Commitment & Reservation**.
2. Log off the ADempiere client application.
3. Restart the ADempiere application server by shutting down the server and then starting the server again.
4. Log in to the ADempiere client application again.

With the help of the accounting facts or GL journal entries that will be generated, we can create reports that show a prediction of *expenses progression*.

# Requisition reservation

Monitoring budget activities can be initiated at the time of creating a purchase requisition document. Here, we will utilize the existing **Purchase Requisition** document in the **Requisition** window, which we saw in the *Completing the replenish information* section of Chapter 5, *Procurement Activities*.

## Accounting facts

The general journal entry format is shown in the following table:

| Window | Document | Sign | Description | Posting Type |
|---|---|---|---|---|
| Requisition | Purchase Requisition | Db | Product Expense | Reservation |
| | | Cr | PO Commitment | Reservation |

We need to re-post this document, in order to show the accounting facts/GL journal entry generated. The following is a sample journal entry for our **Purchase Requisition** document:

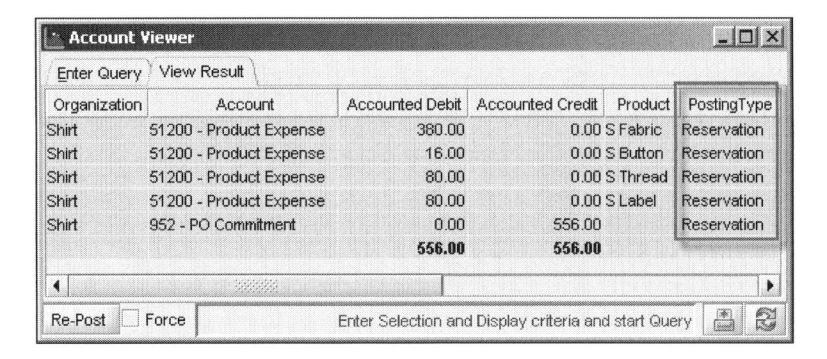

*Accounting Information and Configuration*

# Purchase Order Commitment and Reservation

In the previous **Purchase Requisition** document, the purchasing manager could monitor whether the expenses that were generated by this document exceeded a predetermined purchase budget. He or she could use the **Product Expense** account's outstanding balance in the active accounting periods (which uses both **Reservation** and **Commitment** as its posting type) as one of the many factors when making this decision. When we pass this condition, we can continue to generate a **Purchase Order** document based on this **Purchase Requisition**.

We will use the existing **Purchase Order** document that we obtained from the activities performed in the *Creating a Purchase Order from a Purchase Requisition* section of Chapter 5, *Procurement Activities*. Select the purchase order document that contains **S Fabric** in its ordered products.

## Accounting facts

After reposting this **Purchase Order** document, the general entry journal format will be as follows:

| Window | Document | Sign | Description | Posting Type |
|---|---|---|---|---|
| Purchase Order | Purchase Order | Db | PO Commitment | Reservation |
| | | Cr | Product Expense | Reservation |
| | | Db | Product Expense | Commitment |
| | | Cr | PO Commitment | Commitment |

When re-posting our **Purchase Order** document, the system will:

- Generate a journal entry using the **Reservation** posting type (aiming to reverse the **Reservation** journal entries generated during the posting of the **Purchase Requisition** document)
- Create another journal entry by using the **Commitment** posting type.

The following screenshot shows a sample of the journal entries generated for our **Purchase Order** document:

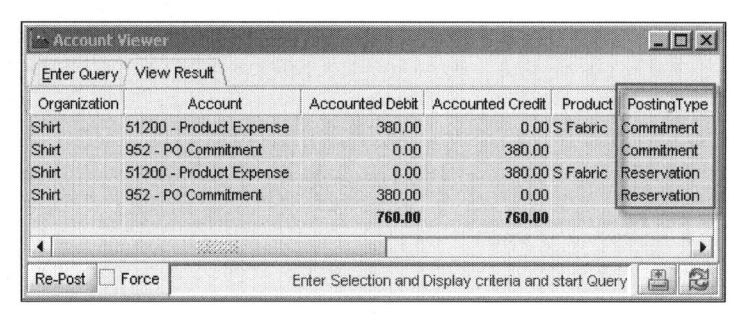

| Organization | Account | Accounted Debit | Accounted Credit | Product | PostingType |
|---|---|---|---|---|---|
| Shirt | 51200 - Product Expense | 380.00 | 0.00 | S Fabric | Commitment |
| Shirt | 952 - PO Commitment | 0.00 | 380.00 | | Commitment |
| Shirt | 51200 - Product Expense | 0.00 | 380.00 | S Fabric | Reservation |
| Shirt | 952 - PO Commitment | 380.00 | 0.00 | | Reservation |
| | | 760.00 | 760.00 | | |

# Matched Invoices commitment release

While invoicing this **Purchase Order** document, and after setting a connection between the **Purchase Order**, **MM Receipt**, and **AP Invoice** documents (via the **Matching PO-Receipt-Invoice** form), you will have **Matched Invoices** records. Find your appropriate **Matched Invoices** record related to the previous **Purchase Order** document.

## Accounting facts

When re-posting the **Matched Invoices**, the system will generate additional journal entries to reverse the **Commitment** journal entries generated when posting the **Purchase Order** document. These additional accounting facts/GL journal entries are as follows:

| Window | Document | Sign | Description | Posting Type |
|---|---|---|---|---|
| Matched Invoices | | Db | PO Commitment | Commitment |
| | | Cr | Product Expense | Commitment |

The following is a sample of the accounting facts/GL journal generated when re-posting **Matched Invoices**:

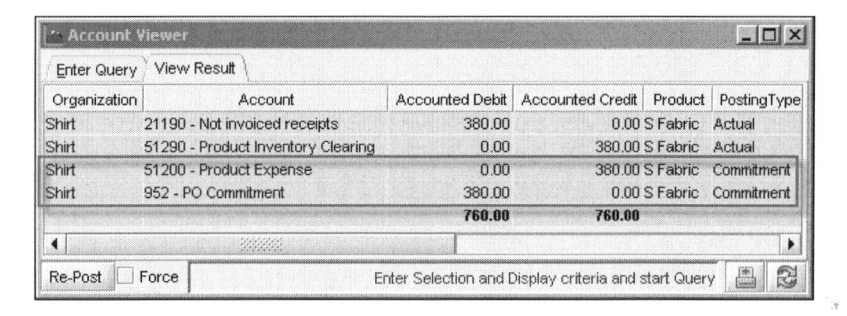

| Organization | Account | Accounted Debit | Accounted Credit | Product | PostingType |
|---|---|---|---|---|---|
| Shirt | 21190 - Not invoiced receipts | 380.00 | 0.00 | S Fabric | Actual |
| Shirt | 51290 - Product Inventory Clearing | 0.00 | 380.00 | S Fabric | Actual |
| Shirt | 51200 - Product Expense | 0.00 | 380.00 | S Fabric | Commitment |
| Shirt | 952 - PO Commitment | 380.00 | 0.00 | S Fabric | Commitment |
| | | 760.00 | 760.00 | | |

Whereas this journal aims to reverse the **Commitment** journal entries generated when posting a **Purchase Order** document, the real bill (booked through account payable trade entries in this case) will be booked when posting an **AP Invoice** document!

# General Ledger distribution

*We had an electricity bill of USD 1,500 this month. This bill covered electricity consumption for the Dress, Jacket, and Shirt organizations. Previously, we just entered these transactions one-by-one depending on the organization's allocation. Can ADempiere help us in such cases?*

Yes, of course, ADempiere can help you with this issue. You can enter your total bill in a single transaction itself, and this amount will be distributed or allocated by ADempiere based on a predefined configuration. All you need to do is to configure your distribution percentage to all of the available organizations once, and then ADempiere will take care of the rest of the transaction.

## Concept of GL distribution

There is some basic information that needs to be known, such as how to configure such a distribution. Navigate to the **Menu | Performance Analysis | Accounting Rules | GL Distribution** window. This contains two tabs: **Distribution** and **Line**. The important configuration of the **Distribution** tab is shown in the following screenshot:

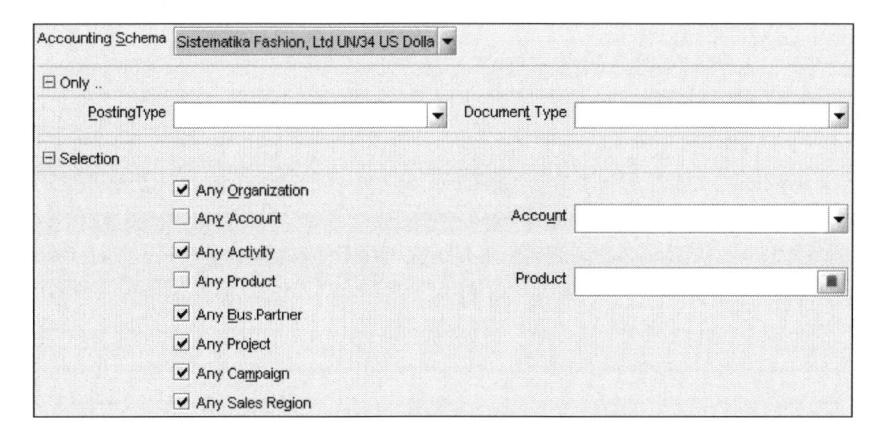

## Distribution tab configuration

The following is a list of the configuration elements of the **Distribution** tab:

- **Organization** field

    You need to define on which organization this configuration should be applied. Here, we put *, which means that this configuration should be applicable to all of the available organizations.

- **Accounting Schema** field

    If you have more than one accounting schema, then you can define to which **Accounting Schema** this configuration should be applied. As we only have one accounting schema registered, this configuration will be applied to the default **Sistematika Fashion, Ltd UN/34 US Dollar** accounting schema only.

- **Posting Type** field

    There are five available posting types. They are: **Actual**, **Budget**, **Commitment**, **Reservation**, and **Statistical**. If you select one of these, for example the **Actual** posting type, then this configuration will be applied to the **Actual** transaction type only. If there are no values in this field, then this configuration will be applicable to all posting types.

- **Document Type** field

    There are many document types available. The list of document types is available in the **Menu | Performance Analysis | Accounting Rules | Document Type** window. As for posting type, you can pick one of the document types to work with. If there are no values in this field, then this configuration will be applicable to all document types.

- **Account Schema Element Selection**

    The list of **Selection** values is taken from the **Account Schema Element** tab of the **Menu | Performance Analysis | Accounting Rules | Accounting Schema** window. In the **Selection** section, we can define that the distribution should be applied to:

    ○ **Any Organization** or a specific **Organization**

    ○ **Any Account** or a specific **Account**

    ○ **Any Activity** or a specific **Activity**

    And so on.

    If we select the **Any Account** checkbox, then the configuration will be applied to all **Account**s. Otherwise, if you deselect this option, then you have to set an **Account** value to work with, and this configuration will affect the selected **Account** only. This behavior is also applicable to the rest of the account schema element members (**Organization**, **Activity**, **Product**, **Business Partner**, **Project**, **Campaign**, and **Sales Region**).

Now, all of the information has been configured in the **Accounting Schema**, **Posting Type**, **Document Type**, and **Account Schema Element Selection**. If any transaction occurs that meets this configuration, then this transaction will be routed or distributed to the information in the **Line** tab.

## Line tab configuration

When performing distribution tasks on the **Line** tab, you can set up many conditions here. When entering a configuration, you need to define the following parts:

- **Percent** field

    What percentage of the available amount or value should be allocated.

- Overwrite target Account Schema Element or not

    In the Account schema element parts, there are options to:

    ○ **Overwrite Organization** or not
    ○ **Overwrite Account** or not
    ○ **Overwrite Activity** or not

    And so on.

    If you deselect the **Overwrite Organization** checkbox, then we will leave the available organization information as it is. If you select the **Overwrite Organization** checkbox, you can define the new target organization in the **Organization** field. This behavior is also applicable to the rest of the account schema element members (**Account**, **Activity**, **Product**, **Business Partner**, **Project**, **Campaign**, and **Sales Region**).

With the available records in the **Line** tab, ADempiere sets an internal check and verifies if the sum of the **Percent** field for all of the records registered in this **Line** tab is 100.

You can check the following screenshot for the configuration available in the **Line** tab:

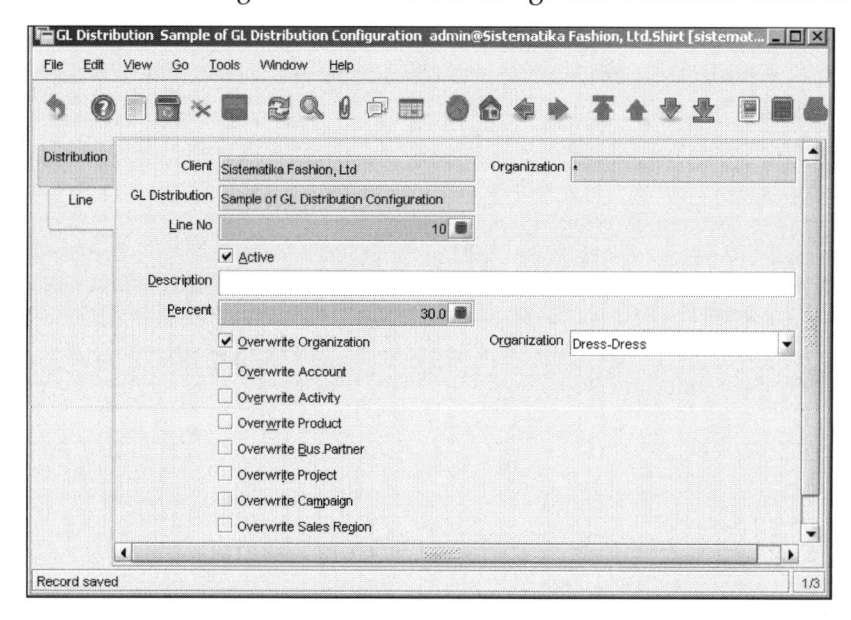

# Sample of GL distribution case

As previously mentioned, there is a case where we distributed the electricity bill worth US$ 1,500 to all of the available organizations. In our example, the distribution percentage will have the following format:

| Field\Org  | Dress | Jacket | Shirt | Total |
|------------|-------|--------|-------|-------|
| Percentage | 30    | 30     | 40    | 100   |

# Configuring GL distribution

With this information, navigate to the **Distribution** tab in the **GL Distribution** window, and set the following data in the available fields:

- Set the **Organization** field to *
- Set the **Name** field to **Sample of GL Distribution configuration**
- Set the **Posting Type** field to **Actual**
- Set the **Document Type** field to **GL Journal**

By default, all account schema elements in the **Selection** area are in the selected state. Deselect the **Any Account** field, set **82900 – Other Expense** in the **Account** field, and then continue by clicking on the **Save** button.

> As we did not have a special electricity account in this case, we used the **Other Expenses** account.

Navigate to the **Line** tab, and set the following information:

| Field\Data            | 1st Data | 2nd Data | 3rd Data |
|-----------------------|----------|----------|----------|
| Line                  | 10       | 20       | 30       |
| Percent               | 30       | 30       | 40       |
| Overwrite Organization| *select* | *select* | *select* |
| Organization          | Dress    | Jacket   | Shirt    |

If there are no changes in your requirement (such as the allocation percentage among organizations) then this configuration will be set only once, and all transactions that meet this criteria will automatically use this distribution.

Navigate back to the **Distribution** tab, and find and click on the **Verify** button, to ensure that we have a total of 100 percent in the **Line**.

## Sample transactions and accounting facts

In accordance with the configuration above, we will practice the impact of this GL Distribution on the GL Journal transaction.

### Creating a new account combination

When using the **Other Expense** account against the **Cash In Registers** account in a GL journal transaction (this is just an example), and because we do not have this account combination for both of the accounts, we need to create a new **Account Combination**. Navigate to the **Menu | Performance Analysis | Accounting Rules | Account Combination** window, and set and save the following information on the **Combination** tab:

| Field\Data | 1st Data | 2nd Data |
|---|---|---|
| Alias | 82900 | 11800 |
| Organization | Shirt | Shirt |
| Account | 82900 – Other Expense | 11800 – Cash in Registers |

### Creating a new General Ledger Journal transaction

For this sample testing transaction, navigate to the **Menu | Performance Analysis | GL Journal** window. As you know, this window contains three tabs: **Batch**, **Journal**, and **Line**. In the **Batch** tab, set and save the following information:

1. Set the **Organization** field to **Shirt**.
2. Set the **Description** field to **Testing GL distribution**.
3. Set the **Posting Type** field to **Actual**.
4. Set the **Document Type** field to **GL Journal**.
5. Set the **Document Date** and **Account Date** fields to today's date.
6. Set the **Currency** field to **USD**.
7. Set the **Control Amount** field to **1500**.

Navigate to the **Journal** tab, and set and save the following information:

1. Set the **Description** field to **Electricity bill for this period**.
2. Set the **Control Amount** field to **1500**.

Leave the remaining fields with their default values.

Navigate to the **Line** tab. On this tab, you may enter multiple records. First you need to enter your GL debit transaction information, and then continue by entering your GL credit transaction information. For our test case, you need to enter the following transactions:

| Field\Data | 1st Data (Debit transaction) | 2nd Data (Credit transaction) |
|---|---|---|
| Organization | Shirt | Shirt |
| Line | 10 | 20 |
| Currency | USD | USD |
| Combination | Shirt-82900-_-_-_-_-_ | Shirt-11800-_-_-_-_-_ |
| Source Debit | 1500 | — |
| Source Credit | — | 1500 |

After saving both the debit and credit transactions, we need to complete this document. Navigate to the **Batch** tab, complete this GL document, and then press the *F5* key repeatedly, until you get the **Posted** status for this document.

Click on the **Posted** button, and the accounting facts generated are as shown, as in the following screenshot:

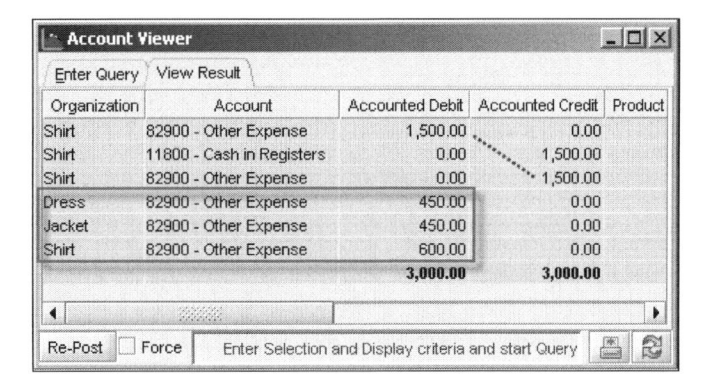

| Organization | Account | Accounted Debit | Accounted Credit | Product |
|---|---|---|---|---|
| Shirt | 82900 - Other Expense | 1,500.00 | 0.00 | |
| Shirt | 11800 - Cash in Registers | 0.00 | 1,500.00 | |
| Shirt | 82900 - Other Expense | 0.00 | 1,500.00 | |
| Dress | 82900 - Other Expense | 450.00 | 0.00 | |
| Jacket | 82900 - Other Expense | 450.00 | 0.00 | |
| Shirt | 82900 - Other Expense | 600.00 | 0.00 | |
| | | 3,000.00 | 3,000.00 | |

As you can see from these accounting facts, the first **Other Expense** journal (debit) is the original GL transaction, the second **Other Expense** journal (credit) is the reverse of the first journal entry, and in the third, fourth, and fifth **Other Expense** journal entries are allocated or distributed to each of the organizations.

> Remember that this journal involves multi-organization transactions and has no **Intercompany Due** journal. This happened because we previously deselected the **Balanced** field in the **Organization**'s account schema element, in the *Avoiding the Intercompany Due From/To journal entries* section.

# Product costs information

We have practiced procurement/material receiving, invoicing raw materials, recording transportation costs (as landed costs), production (making finished goods from raw materials), and finally selling the finished goods. All of these activities or events have financial information that is recorded in the **Product Costs** window.

Navigate to the **Menu | Performance Analysis | Costing | Product Costs** window. This contains five tabs. The most accessed information is in the first three tabs: **Select Product**, **Product Costs**, and **Cost Details**. In our example, navigate to the **Select Product** tab, set **S Thread** as an active record, and then navigate to the **Cost Details** tab. You can see the details of all of the transactions involved for this material, as shown in the following screenshot:

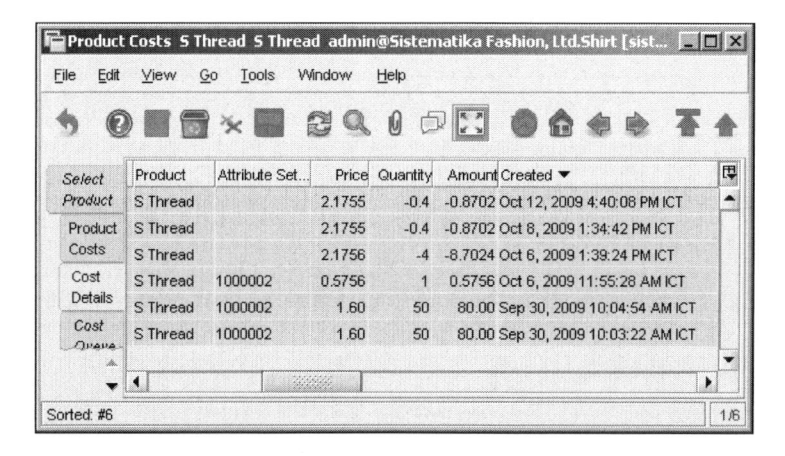

| Product | Attribute Set... | Price | Quantity | Amount | Created |
|---|---|---|---|---|---|
| S Thread | | 2.1755 | -0.4 | -0.8702 | Oct 12, 2009 4:40:08 PM ICT |
| S Thread | | 2.1755 | -0.4 | -0.8702 | Oct 8, 2009 1:34:42 PM ICT |
| S Thread | | 2.1756 | -4 | -8.7024 | Oct 6, 2009 1:39:24 PM ICT |
| S Thread | 1000002 | 0.5756 | 1 | 0.5756 | Oct 6, 2009 11:55:28 AM ICT |
| S Thread | 1000002 | 1.60 | 50 | 80.00 | Sep 30, 2009 10:04:54 AM ICT |
| S Thread | 1000002 | 1.60 | 50 | 80.00 | Sep 30, 2009 10:03:22 AM ICT |

Click on the **Created** column, and these records are sorted based on the **Created** field, as you can see in the above screenshot. The last record, created on **Sep 30, 2009**, is the result of the **Material Receipt** activity. System records have received **50 Quantity** of **S Thread**, having **1.60** as the **Price**. The next record created on **Sep 30, 2009** is a result of the **Invoice (Vendor)** activity. The next record, created on **Oct 6, 2009**, results from the cost allocation of the transportation cost (landed costs) for this material. The last three records are created due to **Production** activities.

All of the information related to this material in the **Cost Details** tab will be summarized based on the **Cost Element** specified on the **Product Costs** tab, as shown in the following screenshot:

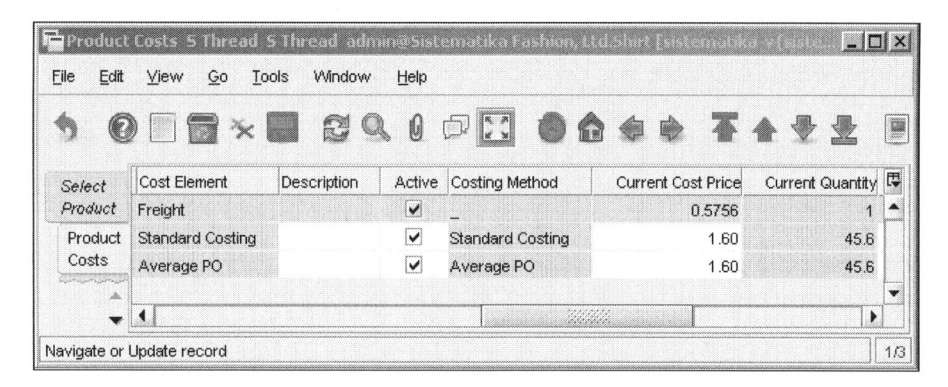

As we set up the **S Thread** costing method as **Average PO**, we need to pay attention to the **Freight** and **Average PO** cost elements information. The sum value of the **Current Cost Price** of **Freight** and the **Average PO** cost elements is used for producing **Shirt Finished Goods** during the **Production** activity (**0.5756 + 1.6 = 2.1756**).

# Summary

In this chapter, we saw the major accounting parts of configuration for ADempiere.

First, we discussed about the Account Element. During the initial client creation in the previous chapters, we had already configured a list of accounts in the chart of accounts file. All of these preconfigured accounts can be accessed from the **Account Element** window. You are free to add an additional account when needed. In this section, we also discussed the functions of the summary account and of the document controlled, post actual, budget, and statistical parts of an account.

The account itself is used when generating accounting facts/GL journal entries. In addition to the account, there are many other dimensions (such as product, business partner, and so on) involved, and these are all joined together to construct accounting facts and GL journal information.

Then we discussed the heart of ADempiere accounting configuration, that is, the Accounting Schema. In this, we covered the configuration for commitment type, accrual and cash-based accounting, costing method and costing level for products valuation, main currency, periods controlling, using account alias, impact of post trade discount when we activate this option, posting services separately, additional accounting facts while activating explicit cost adjustment, disallowing negative posting in its accounting facts, and the reasons for using the post if clearing equal option.

We continued our discussion with the account schema element. Our initial client creation consisted of organization, account, product, business partner, project, campaign, and sales region account schema element. We saw how all of these entities can be inserted as information while posting the documents. We saw an example of activating or just de-activating the unnecessary account schema elements. We concluded this section by learning how to avoid the Intercompany journal entries.

In the end, we discussed about avoiding product inventory clearing journal, the implementation of commitment accounting, implementing GL Distribution, and also a short introduction about product costs, which record all of the financial product activities.

In the next chapter, we will experiment with managing inventory activities in ADempiere. We will also take a look at material management, especially on product attributes, internal use inventory, physical inventory, inventory movement, and movement confirmation.

# 8
# Managing Inventory

So far in this book, you have learnt how to operate ADempiere effectively during procurement, sales, and have seen some of the accounting configuration parts. In continuing, we need to know how we can manage our inventory.

In your company, your warehouse staff manages the inventory stock, identifies and issues material, moves material among locations, handles scrap material, and so on. In this chapter, we will show you how ADempiere can help you with these activities. We will be discussing the following features:

- Product Attributes
- Internal Use Inventory
- Inventory Movements
- Physical Inventory

By understanding these topics, in the end, your warehouse staff will have sufficient knowledge to manage their inventory. In addition, your accounting staff or accountant will be aware of the accounting impact of these activities (if applicable).

## Introducing Product Attributes

Upon receiving material from your vendor (for example, **S Fabric**), your warehouse staff may need information that has a direct relation with his or her job such as:

- What is the fabric's color?
- What is the fabric's pattern?
- Is there any serial number identification available (a unique identity from your vendor) in each of the fabric rolls received?

*Managing Inventory*

All of this available information can help your warehouse staff to identify a material. It is really important to keep, let's say, a serial number or any other identity that comes from your vendor. If we need to send a material replacement request (due to the unacceptable quality of material, different fabric pattern, and so on), we can make a reference to this serial number as an identity when communicating with our vendors or suppliers.

For our internal warehouse references, with the various materials available in the warehouse, we need to think of how to identify our material. It will help us if we can identify these materials by our own codification standards and can find, track, and get the latest status of these materials as fast as possible, when required.

On the other hand, for our Shirt finished goods, which we need to ship to our customer, we need to set up unique information for our reference.

> *The question is how will ADempiere help us manage the task of including this additional information into our products?*

ADempiere can manage these requirements and can address them through the availability of the **Product Attributes** feature.

When using this feature, you need to create an attribute set. Each attribute set can include:

- A "non-instance" attribute—a static product attribute (such as the Shirt's color and size) that can be set up when registering (creating) the product in the Product window.
- An "instance" attribute—additional information or attributes, which could be set up when receiving raw materials or shipping finished goods. Information such as vendor serial number, additional notes, and so on are available at this point of time.

Each unique instance of a product in your current inventory is known as "Attribute Set Instance" in ADempiere.

> When you do not want to track each unique instance of your inventory (that is, you do not define any instance attributes), a special Attribute Set Instance (known as the "Standard Attribute Set Instance") is used for the products.

# Attributes for a raw material's product

We will practice setting up the product attributes for a raw material that has the following details:

- **Color**: It has two colors—red and white
- **Serial Number**: Saves the serial number information from vendors
- **Lot Number**: Generates a number for internal references
- **Description**: Saves any additional information that needs to be entered

This information should be used to identify both the instance and non-instance product attributes. Now, *log in with user ID admin* using **Sistematika Fashion, Ltd Admin** as the role, **Shirt** as the organization, and **1st Shirt W/h** as your **Warehouse**.

We will now guide you through how to set up a color, vendor serial number, lot number, description attributes, and bind these attributes to a product.

## Registering color attribute configuration

In our example, we can register the **Red** and **White** color attributes using the **Attribute** window. Open your **Menu | Material Management | Product Attributes | Attribute** window. This window contains two tabs: **Attribute** and **Attribute Value**. In the **Attribute** tab, you can set and save the following information:

1. Set the **Organization** field to *.
2. Set the **Name** field to **Color (R-W)**.
3. Set the **Attribute Value Type** field to **List**.
4. *Deselect* both the **Mandatory** and **Instance Attribute** checkboxes.

Leave the other fields unchanged. With this information, we are setting up a non-instance type of attribute.

After saving this information, while using **List** as **Attribute Value Type**, you need to register your own list (in this case, **Red** and **White**). Go to the **Attribute Value** tab, and set the following information:

| Field\Data  | 1st Data   | 2nd Data    |
|-------------|------------|-------------|
| Search Key  | Red        | White       |
| Name        | Red        | White       |
| Description | Red color  | White color |

*Managing Inventory*

## Registering the vendor serial number configuration

Next, we need to enter the vendor unique ID or serial number into our products. As we do not know exactly what information is provided until we perform the material receipt, we will set this attribute as an instance attribute.

In the **Attribute** tab, you can set and save the following information:

1. Set the **Organization** field to **\***.
2. Set the **Name** field to **Vendor Serial Number/Id**.
3. Set the **Attribute Value Type** field to **String (max 40)**.
4. *Deselect* the **Mandatory** checkbox.
5. *Select* the **Instance Attribute** checkbox.

Leave the other fields unchanged.

> When defining the **Attribute Value Type**, we have the option to define it as:
> - List,
> - String (max 40)
> - Numeric
>
> You need to define the **Attribute Value** if you are using the **List** type of data. Later, this list value will be used as an option to enter information. Otherwise, there is no need to set up the **Attribute Value**.

## Registering additional information (description)

You might need to register additional short information when receiving your material, which can help to easily identify this material. As this information should be available on receiving the material, we will set this configuration as instance attributes.

Go to the **Attribute** tab, and set and save the following information:

1. Set the **Organization** field to **\***.
2. Set the **Name** field to **Description**.
3. Set the **Attribute Value Type** field to **String (max 40)**. With this option, you can enter any characters to define information, with a maximum length 40.
4. *Deselect* the **Mandatory** checkbox.
5. *Select* the **Instance Attribute** checkbox.

Leave the other fields unchanged.

## Registering internal number references (lot number)

ADempiere can help identify products in your warehouse by using Lot Control. This feature can help you separate one set of balance identities from the other balance identities of the same products. We can define this identity manually or let the system automatically generate a number for us. As the last option is a better alternative for our purpose, we can utilize the **Menu | Material Management | Product Attributes | Lot Control** window.

Upon opening this window, we see that it contains two tabs: the **Lot Control** and **Exclude** tabs. In the **Lot Control** tab, you can specify and save the following information:

1. Set the **Organization** field to *****.
2. Set the **Name** field to **Internal lot numbering**.
3. You can specify any value for **Start Number**. The default value is **100**.
4. Set the **Increment** field to **1**.
5. The **Current Next** value is the same value as the **Start Number** value.
6. You can specify the **Prefix** and **Suffix** information if required. In our case, it will be a blank value.

For our examples throughout this chapter, there is no need to set up any information on the **Exclude** tab.

## Binding raw material attributes into an Attribute Set

Previously, we created a list of attributes that we need to bind into our raw material product. Prior to binding these attributes to our raw material, we need to register our previous attributes as a single **Attribute Set**. This **Attribute Set** will then be bound to our product.

Open the **Menu | Material Management | Product Attributes | Attribute Set** window. This window contains three tabs: **Attribute Set**, **Attribute Use**, and **Exclude**. In the **Attribute Set** tab, you can set and save the following information:

1. Set the **Organization** field to *****.
2. Set the **Name** field to **Attribute for raw material**.
3. *Select* the **Lot** checkbox.
4. *Select* the **Mandatory Lot** checkbox.
5. Set the **Lot Control** field to **Internal lot numbering** (pick from the options).
6. Set the **Mandatory Type** field to **Always Mandatory**.

After saving this data, the **Instance Attribute** checkbox will be selected automatically, as shown in the following screenshot:

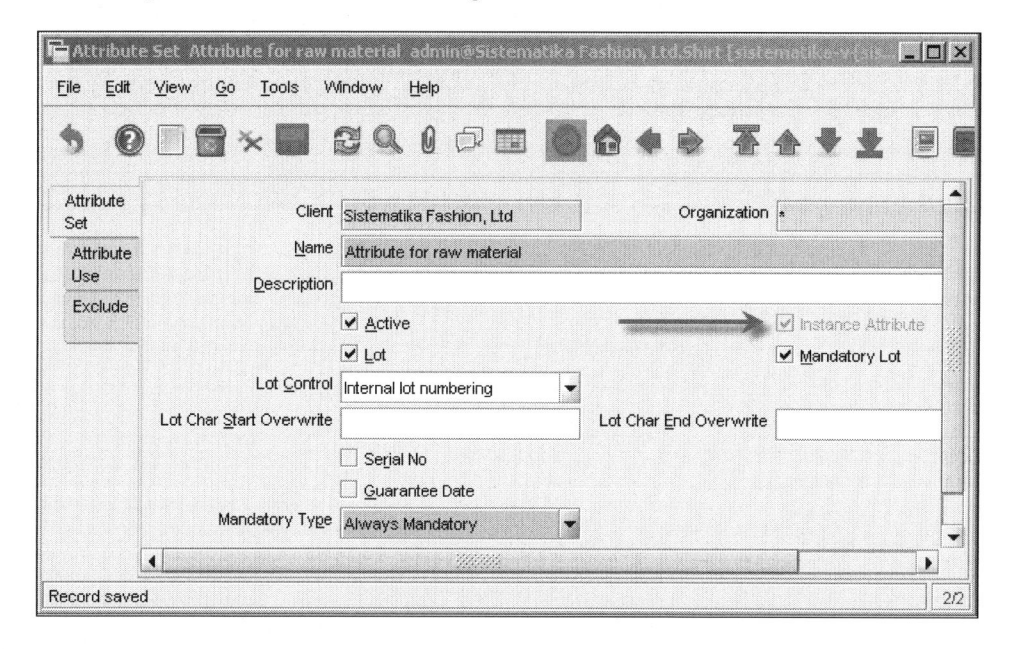

Now, navigate to the **Attribute Use** tab. We need to register our:

- Color attribute
- Vendor serial number
- Description

into this attribute set. Set and save the following information:

| Field\Data | 1st Data | 2nd Data | 3rd Data |
| --- | --- | --- | --- |
| Organization | * | * | * |
| Attribute | Color (R-W) | Vendor Serial Number/Id | Description |
| Sequence | 10 | 20 | 30 |

With all of these activities, we have the complete attribute configuration for our example.

# Registering attributes for a raw material product

Next, we need to create a sample product and bind this product to our newly created **Attribute Set**. Here, we can also define the **Attribute Set Instance** in which we define our color information (information which is already known when identifying your upcoming product).

Open the **Menu | Material Management | Material Management Rules | Product** window. On the **Product** tab, set and save the following information:

| Field\Data | 1st Data | 2nd Data |
|---|---|---|
| Organization | * | * |
| Search Key | PA Fabric Red | PA Fabric White |
| Name | PA Fabric Red | PA Fabric White |
| Product Category | Raw Materials | Raw Materials |
| UOM | Meter | Meter |
| Product Type | Item | Item |
| Stocked | select | select |
| Locator | Loc S1A | Loc S1A |
| Purchased | select | select |
| Sold | deselect | deselect |
| Attribute Set | Attribute for raw material | Attribute for raw material |
| Attribute Set Instance | Red | White |

> The optional values of **Attribute Set Instance** (in this case **Red** or **White**) are available when we set up the **Attribute for raw material** in the **Attribute Set** field. The **Red** or **White** options are available because we *deselect* the **Instance Attribute** field when defining the color attribute configuration.

For our newly-created product, we need to set up the price for our procurement purposes. Click on the **Price** tab, and set the following price information:

| Field\Data | PA Fabric Red | PA Fabric White |
|---|---|---|
| Price List Version | Purchase PL March version | Purchase PL March version |
| List Price | 4.00 | 4.00 |
| Standard Price | 3.80 | 3.80 |
| Limit Price | 3.60 | 3.60 |

# Example of using raw material product attributes

To understand the exact impact of defining product attributes (as our previous configurations are applicable to our sample raw material), we need to create a purchase order and record material receipt.

## Creating a new Purchase Order using a material that uses attributes

You can create a Purchase Order document as was done previously. There is no special or additional activity required during the creation of a Purchase Order document that uses a material that uses attributes.

Open the **Menu | Requisition-to-Invoice | Purchase Order** window. In the **Purchase Order** tab, enter the following information:

1. Set the **Organization** field to **Shirt**.
2. Set the **Target Document Type** field to **Purchase Order**.
3. Set the **Business Partner** field to **Hempel China Limited**.
4. Set the **Price List** field to **Purchase PL**.

Navigate to the **PO Line** tab, and then set and save the following information:

| Field\Data | 1st Data | 2nd Data |
| --- | --- | --- |
| Organization | Shirt | Shirt |
| Line No | 10 | 20 |
| Product | PA Fabric Red | PA Fabric White |
| Quantity | 100 | 120 |
| UOM | Meter | Meter |

Leave the other fields unchanged. Click on the **Purchase Order** tab, and complete this document.

## Entering attribute information during Material Receipt

On receiving a material, our warehouse staff has information such as the vendor serial number available to them. We can also define our internal lot number and set an extra description if needed.

Now, open the **Menu | Requisition-to-Invoice | Material Receipt** window. In the **Material Receipt** tab, set the following information:

1. Set the **Organization** field to **Shirt**.
2. Set the **Document Type** field to **MM Receipt**.
3. Set the **Business Partner** field to **Hempel China Limited**.

After saving this information, and while we have information on the related Purchase Order, we can copy the information from the purchase order line by clicking on the **Create lines from** button. In the upcoming window, pay attention to the **Purchase Order** field. Select our previously-created **Purchase Order** document, and then select both of the raw materials, as shown in the following screenshot:

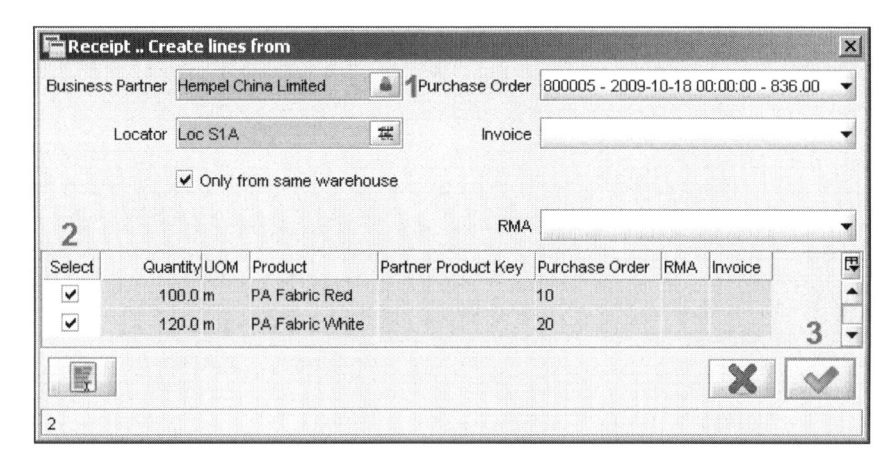

Click on the **OK** button to copy the **Purchase Order** records to our **Material Receipt** document.

> The important point to note when entering our **Material Receipt** document is that we need to define the attribute information. If you forget to set the attribute information, then when completing this document, you will get an **Attribute Set Mandatory (Line No #10, Product= PA Fabric Red)** error message, as we have set our **Mandatory Type** to **Always Mandatory** in our **Attribute for raw material** attribute set.

Go to the **Receipt Line** tab. Find a line with **PA Fabric Red** as the **Product**. You need to click on a button inside the **Attribute Set Instance** field, and it will show a window. In this window, we can enter the **Vendor Serial Number/Id** and **Description**.

*Managing Inventory*

The **Lot No** will be used for our internal reference. To generate a lot sequence number, all you need to do is click on the **New Record** button on the right-hand side of the **Lot** field. Finalize this procedure by clicking on the **OK** button, as shown in the following screenshot:

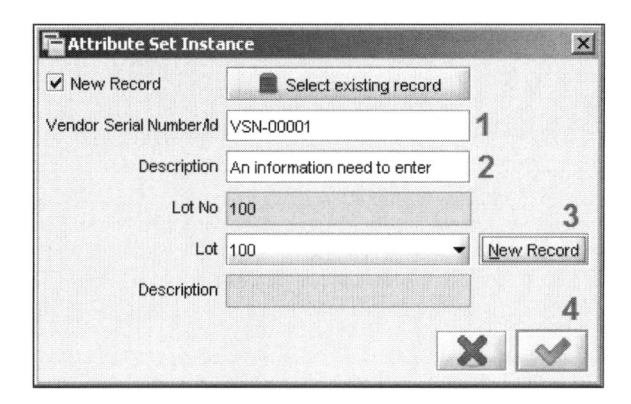

You need to perform the same procedure to define an **Attribute Set Instance** for your second product, **PA Fabric White**.

> If a document is not yet completed, then you are able to edit any information in the **Attribute Set Instance**. Just click on the button in the **Attribute Set Instance** field, and alter the information.

After entering the **Attribute Set Instance** for both of our products, you can complete this document.

# Tracking raw material related information using its attribute information

After completing a document that has specific information in an **Attribute Set Instance** for the products, you can access related information (such as vendor serial number and lot number) and track your products using the **Attribute Set Instance** window.

## Tracking using the Attribute Set Instance window

For this example, you can access your product in a previous **MM Receipt** document that contains the Attribute Set Instance information, by opening the **Menu | Material Management | Attribute Set Instance** window.

This window contains four default tabs: **Instance**, **Shipment**, **Receipt**, **Movement**, and **Invoice**. Within this window, if you select a product's attribute set instance, you can access the receipt, movement, and invoice related information for this product's attribute set instance. An example of the data taken from the **Instance** tab is shown in the following screenshot:

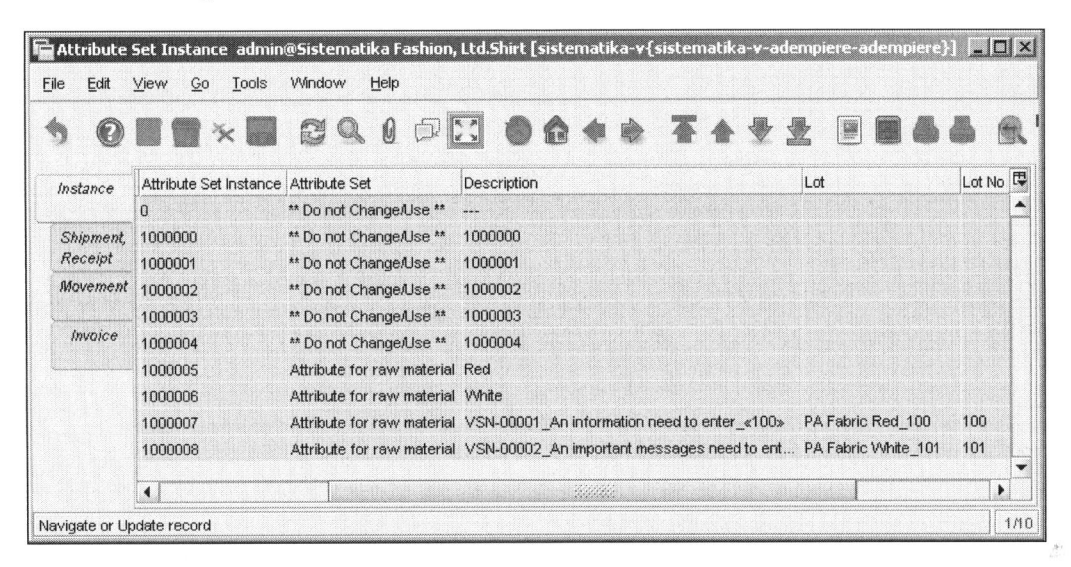

In the previous screenshot, a small set of records has been shown. In a real production environment, the list might contain thousands or even millions of records.

In case you need to search your specific attribute set instance products records, then you can click on the **Lookup Record** button that shows a search dialog window, and enter the information in the **Description** field, or use the **Advanced** tab to fulfill your searching criteria.

## Defining additional search criteria

*The Lookup Record just performs a search using only the Description field. Shouldn't a system be able to also search using the Lot No or Serial No information?*

Yes, you can find an **Attribute Set Instance** record based on the **Lot No** and also the **Serial No** information. You can define additional search criteria by accessing the ADempiere System client.

[ 271 ]

*Managing Inventory*

In the **Instance** tab of the **Attribute Set Instance** window, search on **Record Info** by clicking on the bottom right-hand side of its window. This will display the table name used by this tab (in this case, it shows the **M_AttributeSetInstance** table).

*Log in to System*, and set the role to **System Administrator**. Then open the **Menu | Application Dictionary | Table and Column** window. Find the **M_AttributeSetInstance** table by specifying this table name in the **DB Table Name** field in **Lookup Record** (search dialog window), as shown in the following screenshot:

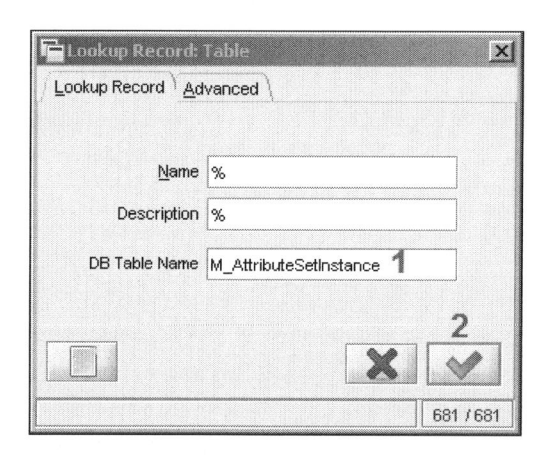

Click on the **OK** button. Now, ensure that you have an active record with **M_AttributeSetInstance** in the **DB Table Name** column. With this record, navigate to the **Column** tab. Find both, the **Lot No** and **Serial No** value in the **Name** field. In both of these records, click on the **Grid Toggle** button to show the detailed information for this column. Find and select the **Selection Column** attribute checkbox.

After completing this procedure, you can log off and *log in with user ID admin* using **Sistematika Fashion, Ltd Admin** as the role. Open the **Menu | Material Management | Attribute Set Instance** window, and click on the **Lookup Record** button. Now, the search dialog window will also provide the ability to search via the **Lot No** and **Serial No** fields.

# Attributes for Shirt finished goods products

Basically, there are no differences when defining an attribute for both your raw materials and Shirt finished goods. It just depends on your decision on how to map all of the attributes needed for your specific products.

For our example, we will define a special attribute for our Shirt finished goods, and it will have at least:

- Size and color
- Lot number to identify the production number
- Serial Number to identify the shipment identity
- Description

With the requirements listed, we will now create the size, lot, and serial number attributes. By re-using the existing color and description attributes, we will bind all of these attributes into a new attribute set, and attach this attribute set into your product.

## Registering size attribute configuration

For the Shirt finished goods, the size and color attribute is a common requirement. For example, when you go shopping and want to buy a shirt, you could choose a color and size that suits your needs. It could be a **Large** size and **White** in color.

Because we already have a color attribute, we only need to create the size attribute. Open the **Menu | Material Management | Product Attributes | Attribute** window. In the **Attribute** tab, set and save the following information:

1. Set the **Organization** field to **\***.
2. Set the **Name** field to **Size (S-M-L)**.
3. Set the **Attribute Value Type** field to **List**.
4. *Deselect* both, the **Mandatory** and **Instance Attribute** checkboxes.

After saving this information, go to the **Attribute Value** tab, and set the following information:

| Field\Data  | 1st Data   | 2nd Data    | 3rd Data   |
|-------------|------------|-------------|------------|
| Search Key  | S          | M           | L          |
| Name        | Small      | Medium      | Large      |
| Description | Small Size | Medium Size | Large Size |

Leave the other fields unchanged.

# Registering a lot number to identify production identity

If massive production begins, you should be able to identify your production identity in your products. This identity will be helpful while tracking the production history. Here, we can use a lot number for this purpose.

As mentioned previously in the *Registering internal number references (lot number)* section, access the **Menu | Material Management | Product Attributes | Lot Control** window**.** Create a new record, and then set and save the following information:

1. Set the **Organization** field to **\***.
2. Set the **Name** field to **Production Lot Number**.
3. Set the **Prefix** field to **PLN-**.

Leave the other fields unchanged.

# Registering the internal number for shipment references

We can use the serial number option for our own and customer references, for finished goods, during the shipment activities. For our example, we need to set up a serial number and configure its attributes in the **Menu | Material Management | Product Attributes | Serial No Control** window. This window will contain two tabs: **Serial No Control** and **Exclude**.

Within the **Serial No Control** tab, set and save the following information:

1. Set the **Organization** field to **\***.
2. Set the **Name** field to **Shipment Serial Number**.
3. Set the **Start No** field to **10000** (it has 100 as a default value).
4. Set the **Increment** field to **1**.
5. Set the **Current Next** field to **10000**.
7. Set the **Prefix** field to **SIN-** (**SIN** stands for **Shipment Identity Number**).

With this configuration, the number generated will be SIN-10000, SIN-10001, SIN-10002, and so on.

As we already have a **Description** attribute, in our case, there is no need to set up another description attribute here.

# Creating an Attribute Set for the Shirt product

We need to create an Attribute Set that will be used with our finished goods product. We need to combine our previously-created attributes into another new **Attribute Set**. This **Attribute Set** will then be set to our finished goods product.

Open the **Menu | Material Management | Product Attributes | Attribute Set** window. In the **Attribute Set** tab, set and save the following information:

1. Set the **Organization** field to *.
2. Set the **Name** field to **Attribute for finished goods products**.
3. *Select* the **Lot** checkbox.
4. Set the **Lot Control** field to **Production Lot Number**.
5. *Select* the **Serial No** checkbox.
6. Set the **Serial No Control** field to **Shipment Serial Number** (pick from option).
7. Set the **Mandatory Type** field to **Always Mandatory**.

On saving this data, the **Instance Attribute** checkbox will be automatically selected.

Now, navigate to the **Attribute Use** tab. We need to register our:

- Size attribute
- Color attribute
- Description attribute

Set and save the following information:

| Field\Data | 1st Data | 2nd Data | 3rd Data |
|---|---|---|---|
| Organization | * | * | * |
| Attribute | Size (S-M-L) | Color (R-W) | Description |
| Sequence | 10 | 20 | 30 |

Now that the attribute set has been properly configured. You need to attach this attribute set to your target product.

*Managing Inventory*

# Attaching an attribute set to finished goods products

We can create a new finished goods product and attach the attribute set that we have just created to it. For simplicity, we will just attach our **Attribute for finished goods products** to our existing finished goods product, **Shirt Finished Goods**.

Open the **Menu | Material Management | Material Management Rules | Product** window. Click on **Lookup Record**, and find your **Shirt Finished Goods** product by entering **Shirt%** in the **Name** field and then clicking on the **OK** button. In this record, enter the following information:

1. Set the **Attribute Set** field to **Attribute for finished goods products** (pick from the option list).
2. Click on the button inside the **Attribute Set Instance** field, and it will show a confirmation window. Set the **Size** as **Medium** and the color as **White**, and then click on the **Save** button.

If you get a message such as **No Product Attribute Set defined** when you click in the **Attribute Set Instance** field, you need to click on the **Save** button after first setting the **Attribute Set** info. Then you will be able to set the information in the **Attribute Set Instance** field.

On being successfully set up, your record will have an attribute, as shown in the following screenshot:

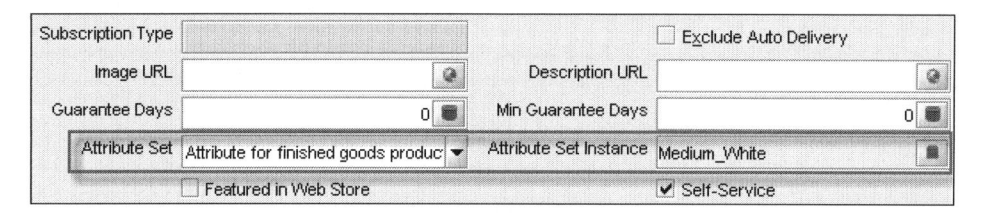

# Example of using product attributes on the Shirt finished goods product

Setting our attributes to our finished goods product should be done during the **Production** and **Shipment (Customer)** processes.

## Attaching attributes during production activities

We will now create a new Production activity and set the "attribute set instance". Open the **Menu | Material Management | Production** window. In the **Production Header** tab, set and save the following information:

1. Set the **Organization** field to **Shirt**.
2. Set the **Name** field to **Manufacture Shirt FG #4**.
3. Set the **Movement Date** field to *today*.

Navigate to the **Production Plan** tab, set and save the following information:

| Field\Data | 1st Data | 2nd Data |
|---|---|---|
| Line | 10 | 20 |
| Product | Shirt Finished Goods | Shirt Finished Goods |
| Production Qty | 2 | 3 |
| Locator | S1A | S1A |

> When defining the locator, the default locator may be J1A. In this book, it is important to set it to the S1A location.

Navigate back to the **Production Header** tab, and click on the **Create/Post Production** button. In the upcoming confirmation window, you do not need to alter any information, but can just finalize the process by clicking on the **OK** button. The read only **Records created** checkbox will then be selected.

To set an **Attribute Set Instance**, you have to:

1. First, navigate to the **Production Plan** tab, and select the first record.
2. Then navigate to the **Production Line** tab.

*Managing Inventory*

In the **Production Line** tab, make sure that your active record is in the **Shirt Finished Goods** products, as shown in the following screenshot:

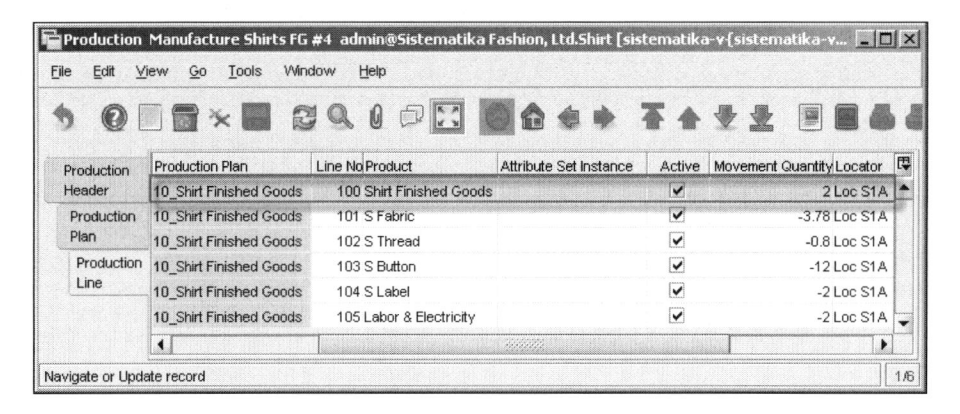

In this window, click on the **Grid Toggle** button to display the detailed information of the **Shirt Finished Goods** product. In this record, click on the button inside the **Attribute Set Instance** field, and set the **Description** and **Lot** information, as shown in the following screenshot:

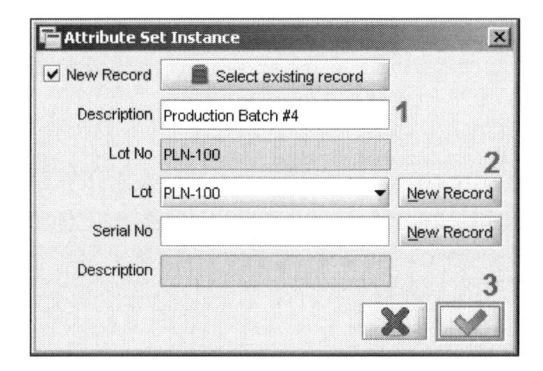

> Click on the **New Record** button to generate the **Lot No** automatically.

Right now, there is no need to set a **Serial No**. Click on the **OK** button, and then proceed by clicking on the **Save** button on the **Production Line** tab.

Navigate back to **Production Plan** tab, and select your next record. Navigate to the **Production Line** tab, find the **Shirt Finished Goods** product, and set the product's attribute set instance.

Now, navigate to the **Production Header** tab, and then finalize the task by clicking on the **Create/Post Production** button once again. Finally click on the **OK** button in the upcoming confirmation window.

You are free to open the **Menu | Material Management | Attribute Set Instance** window, and check that your newly-created records are available in the **Instance** tab.

## Searching for the Shirt product by its attributes

Now, we can access the **Product Info** for searching purposes. To access the **Product Info**, from the main menu you can point your mouse to **View | Product Info**, or just press *Alt + I*, as shown in the following screenshot:

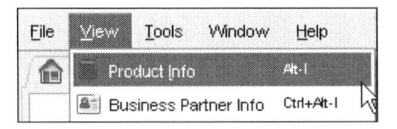

In the **Product Info** window, make sure that you set your **Pricelist Version** field to *blank* and the **Warehouse** field to **1st Shirt W/h**. In the top right-hand side of this window, you will see a **Product Attribute Info** button, as shown in the following screenshot:

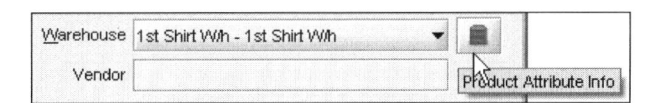

When you click on this button, you will be prompted with the **Product Attribute Info** confirmation window. In the **Size (S-M-L)** field, you can set the value as **Medium**, and click on the **OK** button. This will show data, as shown in the following screenshot:

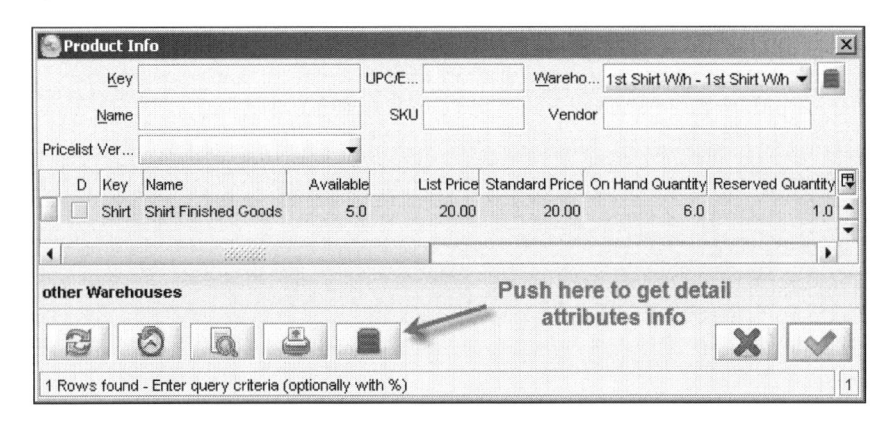

[ 279 ]

*Managing Inventory*

> *Previously, we have performed two production activities, with a quantity of 2 (production line 1) and a quantity of 3 (production line 2), for production batch #4. Here, using this information, why can I not see the break down and attribute information?*

Using this record (with a **Name** field value of **Shirt Finished Goods** and an **Available** field value **5.0**), click on the second **Product Attributes** button (as shown in the previous screenshot). It will show you the detailed attributes and the detailed quantity break down information.

## Assigning information during shipment activities

The next important point is assigning an identity to your products during shipment activities. For example, this information can be used for the after sales process or providing product support such as warranty claims.

Prior to the shipment activities, we need to prepare the Sales Order document. In the **Menu | Quote-to-Invoice | Sales Orders | Sales Order** window, set and save the following information in the **Order** tab:

1. Set the **Organization** field to **Shirt**.
2. Set the **Target Document Type** field to **Standard Order**.
3. Set the **Business Partner** field to **Standard** (Yes, **Standard**. Actually, you could setup any type of business partner).
4. Set the **Price List** to **Sales PL**.

Leave the other fields unchanged. Navigate to the **Order Line** tab, and then set and save the following information:

1. Set the **Product** field to **Shirt Finished Goods**.
2. Set the **Quantity** to **3**.

Leave the other fields unchanged. Go back to the **Order** tab, and click on the **Complete** button to complete this document.

Next, we can generate the Shipment document by using **Menu | Quote-to-Invoice | Shipments | Generate Shipments**. In the upcoming confirmation window, set the following information:

1. Set the **Business Partner** field to **Standard**.
2. Set the **Document Action** field to **Prepare**.

Finalize this task by clicking on the **OK** button. Note down the generated Shipment number.

*Chapter 8*

Now, you can open your shipment document through the **Menu | Quote-to-Invoice | Shipments | Shipment (Customer)** window. Open the target shipment document. Navigate to the **Shipment Line** tab, and you will have one record. Here, you can set a shipment identity number by using the following procedure:

1. Click on the button in the **Attribute Set Instance** field.
2. In upcoming window, set the **Description** and **Serial No**, and click on the **OK** button. For an example, refer to the following screenshot:

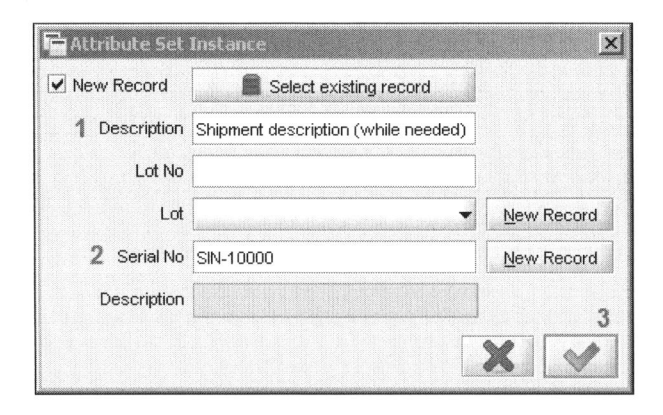

After saving this record in the **Shipment Line** tab, navigate to the **Shipment** tab, print out this document (it should contain an identity (**Serial No**) in its description). Now, you will be able to complete this document.

# Managing internal use of inventory

> *Sometimes, our company organizes exhibitions to show off our finished goods products and our raw materials to our prospective customers or even to the public. In such exhibitions, the company takes a small amount of our existing raw material. As it takes the pieces of raw material from our warehouses, could we book this type of transaction as our advertising and/or promotion costs?*

Another example that can be considered is where you have broken or damaged inventory—you would also need to book this transaction. This is just an example of the cases that are handled by warehouse staff, which could be solved by using the **Internal Use Inventory** feature. You can use this feature by accessing the **Menu | Material Management | Internal Use Inventory** window. This window contains two tabs: **Internal Use** and **Internal Use Line**.

*Managing Inventory*

In manual activities, the warehouse staff simply takes a piece of material or product out of the warehouse and notes this activity in their log book. At the end of the accounting period, they summarize all of the transactions related to material consumption, create a report, and send it to all of the concerned departments in the company (including the accounting department). Using this report, the accounting staff can follow up on this transaction. They can book this transaction and create a cost allocation to compensate for the material reduced.

When using **Internal Use Inventory**, we will map a cost allocation using the ADempiere **Charge**. The warehouse staff just picks a Charge option and does not care about what accounting parts are related to this. Behind the scenes, upon completing and posting this document, this transaction will instruct the system to reduce the material and increase the cost.

To support our upcoming sample transaction, we need to create the advertising and promotion charges.

# Creating advertising and promotion types of charge

As you know, we can create a new Charge directly by using the **Menu | Performance Analysis | Accounting Rules | Generate Charges** form. In the upcoming form, perform the following tasks:

1. Find and *select* the **62800 – Other Advertising & Promotion** account in the **Create Charge from Account** area.
2. Click on the **Create from Account** button. With the upcoming **Charge created** confirmation window, now you have a new **Charge** in your system.

Check your newly-created charge in the **Menu | Performance Analysis | Accounting Rules | Charge** window.

# Sample usage of Internal Use inventory

We will practice with our **S Fabric** raw material. In your **Internal Use Inventory** window, ensure that you are now on the **Internal Use** tab. Set and save the following information:

1. Set the **Organization** field to **Shirt**.
2. Set the **Warehouse** field to **1st Shirt W/h**.
3. Set the **Movement Date** field to *today*.
4. Set the **Document Type** field to **Physical Inventory**.

Navigate to the **Internal Use Line** tab, and then set and save the following information:

1. Set the **Locator** field to **Loc S1A**.
2. Set the **Product** field to **S Fabric**.
3. Set the **Internal Use Qty** field to **10**.
4. Set the **Charge** field to **Other Advertising & Promotion** (select from the options).

> There is no Unit of Measurement (UOM) information here. The system will use the default UOM, which is configured in the **Product** window.

Go back to the **Internal Use** tab, and complete this document.

## Accounting facts

From the accounting perspective, the default accounting facts/GL journal entry has the following format:

| Window | Document | Sign | Description | Posting Type |
|---|---|---|---|---|
| Internal Use Inventory | Physical Inventory | Db | Charge | Actual |
|  |  | Cr | Product Asset | Actual |

Check the posting status of this document; it will show you a **Non Posted** status. Wait for a moment, and then refresh this document by pressing the *F5* key or by clicking on the **ReQuery** button. With this activity, the system will read the latest status of the document. Behind the scenes, the accounting processor should, periodically, post this document automatically for us.

Assuming that this document has already been posted by the system, the accounting staff or accountant can click on the **Posted** button, and the accounting facts/GL journal entries generated by the system should be as follows:

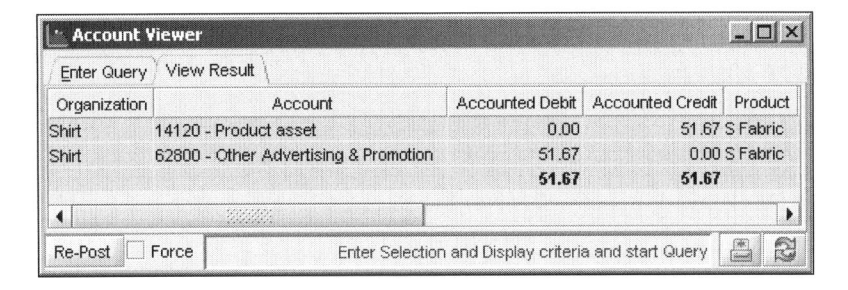

| Organization | Account | Accounted Debit | Accounted Credit | Product |
|---|---|---|---|---|
| Shirt | 14120 - Product asset | 0.00 | 51.67 | S Fabric |
| Shirt | 62800 - Other Advertising & Promotion | 51.67 | 0.00 | S Fabric |
|  |  | 51.67 | 51.67 |  |

> This journal amount comes from the product cost of **S Fabric**. Access the **Menu | Performance Analysis | Costing | Product Costs** window, and you will find that both Average Cost (**3.80**) and Freight allocation cost (**1.3669**) belong to **S Fabric**. Multiply both of these costs by the material consumption (**10**), and you will get **51.67**.

## Tracking inventory transactions

After issuing the material, the warehouse staff can check to ensure that the system has been cleaned out of the material from the warehouses. ADempiere provides a **Menu | Material Management | Material Transactions** form to check or monitor inventory activities.

For your reference, we will monitor our **S Fabric** inventory activities. Open the **Material Transactions** form, and set the following information:

1. Set the **Organization** field to **Shirt**.
2. Set the **Locator** field to **Loc S1A**.
3. Set the **Product** field to **S Fabric**.
4. Click on the **ReQuery** button.

As a result, the system should give you information similar to what is shown in the following screenshot:

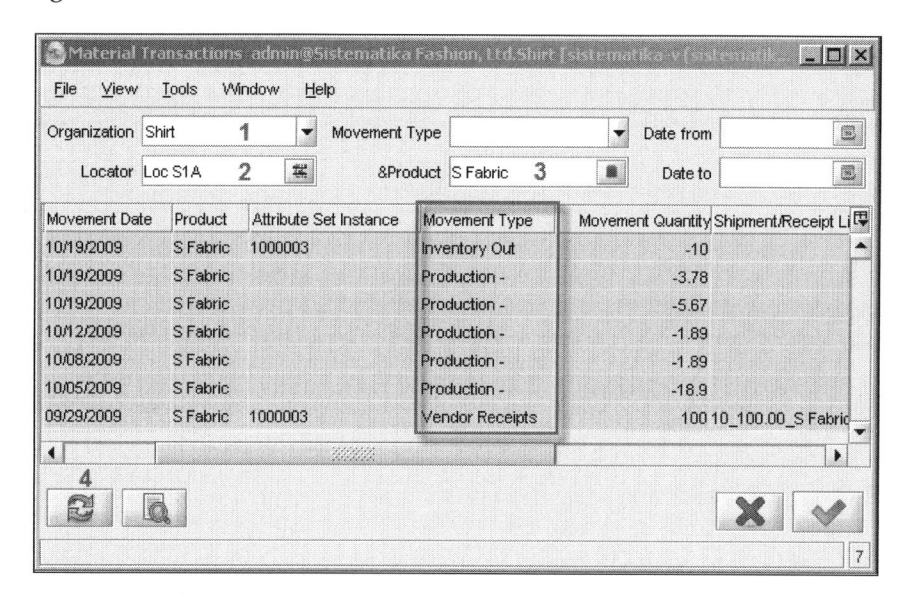

During examining a movement quantity, you should also be aware of the **Movement Type** information. The meaning of the information in the **Movement Type** field is as follows:

- **Vendor Receipts** means that we are receiving a material from your vendor, and as we have a positive value in the movement quantity, it will increase your stock
- **Production** tells us that this material is used during production activities, and it reduces your stock
- The **Inventory Out** is a transaction taken from our **Internal Use Inventory**, and it reduces your stock

# Managing Physical Inventory

In an effort to start an ADempiere implementation in the company, your warehouse manager might think of:

- How to perform stock counting. This is important to know what is the latest outstanding balance status of our material. With this information, we can perform stock reconciliation between system and actual stock.
- Whether there is any difference between system and actual stock levels, and how to book this variance in the system.
- A way to migrate our existing raw material records into ADempiere.

These are just a couple of issues that might occur during the implementation of a new system such as ADempiere in your company.

Fortunately, ADempiere can help us to resolve these issues by using its **Physical Inventory** feature. We will go through the process of how to resolve these issues in detail in the following sections.

## Stock counting and reconciliation

At the end of a month (or at the end of an accounting period), a company may have a procedure to check their stock of goods to ensure that their physical stock is equal to the quantity recorded in their system. We will map this activity through the **Menu | Material Management | Physical Inventory** window.

*Managing Inventory*

In the following activity, we shall see an example on how to perform stock counting in the **Shirt** organization, especially in the **1st Shirt W/h**, which is targeted only at raw material. In the **Inventory Count** tab, you can set and save the following information:

1. Set the **Organization** field to **Shirt**.
2. Set the **Description** field to **End of month stock counting & reconciliation**.
3. Set the **Warehouse** field to **1st Shirt W/h**.
4. Set the **Movement** field to *today's date*.
5. Set the **Document Type** field to **Physical Inventory**.

Then, click on the **Create Inventory Count List** button. In the upcoming confirmation window, you can set the following information:

1. Set the **Locator** field to **Loc S1A**.
2. Set the **Product Category** field to **Raw Material**.

Leave the other fields unchanged, and then click on the **OK** button. Internally, the system will count the stock based on our selection criteria, and the results can be accessed in the **Inventory Count Line** tab. The results should be similar to the following screenshot:

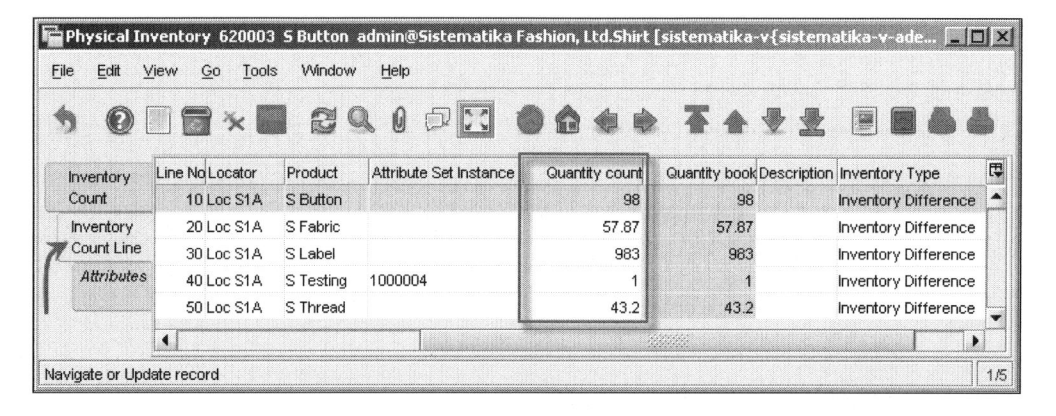

| | Line No | Locator | Product | Attribute Set Instance | Quantity count | Quantity book | Description | Inventory Type |
|---|---|---|---|---|---|---|---|---|
| Inventory Count | 10 | Loc S1A | S Button | | 98 | 98 | | Inventory Difference |
| Inventory Count Line | 20 | Loc S1A | S Fabric | | 57.87 | 57.87 | | Inventory Difference |
| | 30 | Loc S1A | S Label | | 983 | 983 | | Inventory Difference |
| Attributes | 40 | Loc S1A | S Testing | 1000004 | 1 | 1 | | Inventory Difference |
| | 50 | Loc S1A | S Thread | | 43.2 | 43.2 | | Inventory Difference |

Pay attention on the **S Fabric** record. In the author's installation, as per the system, it has a book quantity of **57.87** (quantity in the system). You can check the result of the balance quantity by examining the list of **S Fabric** movement activities through the **Menu | Material Management | Material Transactions** form.

[ 286 ]

If you were informed by your warehouse staff that the actual quantity remaining is only 57, based on this information, you could update the 57.87 quantity count to 57, by using the following procedure:

1. Navigate to an **S Fabric** active record, and click on the **Grid Toggle** button, in order to show detailed information for **S Fabric**.
2. Update the **Quantity count** field to **57**, and click on the **Save** button.

Examine the **Inventory Type** field in the **Inventory Count Line** tab. The available options are:

- Inventory Difference
- Charge Account

By default, the system will use **Inventory Difference**.

Make **Inventory Count** your active tab, and complete the document. Now, you can check your **Material Transactions** form again to get the latest **S Fabric** material movement activities.

## Accounting facts

> *What is the difference between Inventory Difference and Charge Account then?*

From an accounting perspective, we can use this inventory type as an alternative that can be used to map a cost allocation. When we use **Inventory Difference**, the system automatically uses **Warehouse differences** as the default account, which is configured in the **Defaults** tab of the **Accounting Schema** window, which is **56100 – Inventory Shrinkage**.

If you are using **Charge Account**, then you can define a target **Charge**, such as the one mentioned previously in the *Managing internal use of inventory* sections. Here, you will get the exact same results or behavior while using **Charge**.

Because the accounting processor runs behind the scenes, the system will automatically post this document for you. Wait a moment, and press the *F5* key, or click on the **ReQuery** button, until you see a **Posted** status for the document. As the quantity count value is below that of the quantity book, the following screenshot shows the accounting facts/GL journal entries generated:

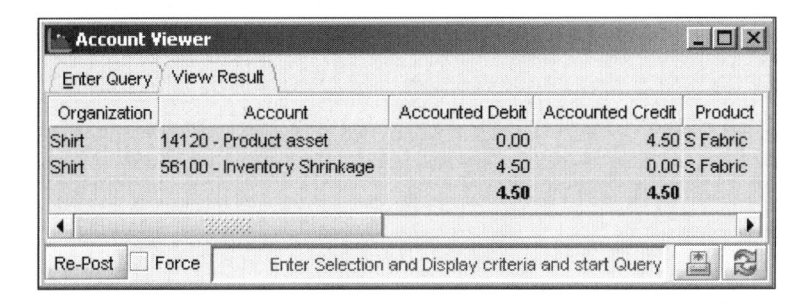

| Organization | Account | Accounted Debit | Accounted Credit | Product |
|---|---|---|---|---|
| Shirt | 14120 - Product asset | 0.00 | 4.50 | S Fabric |
| Shirt | 56100 - Inventory Shrinkage | 4.50 | 0.00 | S Fabric |
| | | 4.50 | 4.50 | |

The **4.50** value is derived from:

((Original Quantity count – New Quantity count) * **S Fabric** product costs)

=

( (57.87 – 57) * (3.8 + 1.3669) )

> If your new quantity count value is more than the original one (quantity count greater than quantity book), then the accounting facts/GL journal generated is an opposite format to the one shown in the previous screenshot.

# Migrating an existing raw material into ADempiere

Another example of utilizing the **Physical Inventory** feature is when you migrate your existing raw material into ADempiere:

Before performing the migration activities, the commonly-available information is:

- Description of raw material
- Quantity and its unit of measurement
- Price or latest material valuation

With this information, we can perform the data migration. The following is a list of tasks that need to be done:

- Create a **Product Category** for the material, and set the **Costing Method** to **Standard Costing**.
- Create a **Product**.
- Set the product cost for this product.
- Enter your raw material quantity in the **Physical Inventory** window.

Let say, we have data as listed in the following table:

| Description | UOM | Qty | Valuation |
|---|---|---|---|
| Hang Tag | Pieces | 100 | 0.2 |
| Carton Box | Pieces | 150 | 1.2 |

With this sample outstanding raw material, we will manually enter the **Hang Tag** data into our ADempiere environment.

## Creating a migration product category

We need to identify a special product category to differentiate from the available product category. For our example, we can create a **Migration RM** product category.

Open the **Menu | Material Management | Material Management Rules | Product Category** window. In the **Product Category** tab, set and save the following information:

1. Set the **Organization** field to *.
2. Set the **Search Key** and **Name** fields to **Migration RM**.

Leave the other fields unchanged.

Navigate to the **Accounting** tab, and then set and save the following information:

1. Set the **Costing Method** field to **Standard Costing**.
2. Set the **Costing Level** field to **Client**.

The process is now complete. Next, we need to create a new product.

# Creating a migration product

As per our requirement, we shall create the **Hang Tag** product, using **Migration RM** as its product category.

Open the **Menu | Material Management | Material Management Rules | Product** window. In the **Product** tab, set the following information:

1. Set the **Organization** field to *.
2. Set the **Search Key** and **Name** fields to **Hang Tag**.
3. Set the **Product Category** field to **Migration RM**.
4. Set the **Tax Category** field to **Standard**.
5. Set the **UOM** field to **Piece**.
6. Set the **Product Type** field to **Item**.
7. Set the **Locator** field to **S1A**.
8. *Deselect* both the **Purchase** and **Sold** checkboxes.

Furthermore, we need to create a product cost.

# Setting a product's product costs

As we are using **Standard Costing** as a costing method, we need to enter the latest material valuation, and set this amount or value as its product cost.

Open the **Menu | Performance Analysis | Costing | Product Costs** window. On the **Select Product** tab, ensure that **Hang Tag** is your active record. Navigate to the **Product Costs** tab. In this tab, there is a product cost record with **Standard Costing** as its **Cost Element** (if you cannot find this record, then you can add this record by yourself). You need to update the **Current Cost Price** field to **0.2**, as shown in the following screenshot:

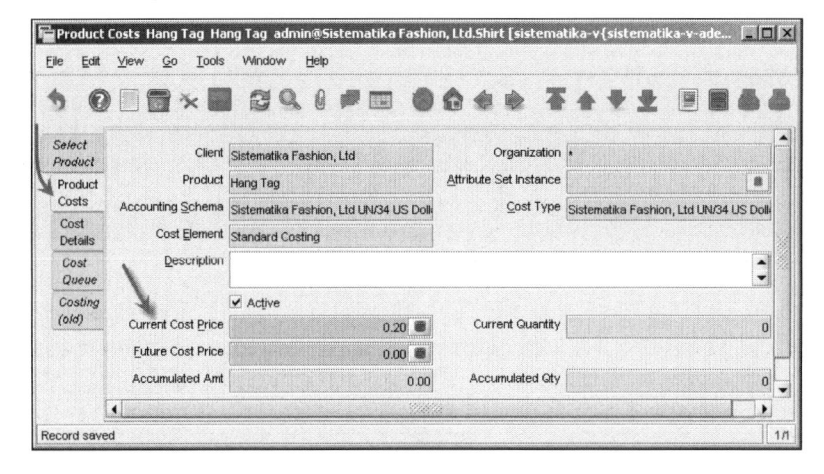

> Here, we have not set the currency information. The currency used for this record is taken from the default currency for the **Sistematika Fashion, Ltd UN/34 US Dollar** accounting schema.

## Performing migration activities

With the existing data and the preparation of the product category, product, and the set up of the products costs, we can create a migration transaction through the **Menu | Material Management | Physical Inventory** window. Open this window, and in the **Inventory Count** tab, you can set and save the following information:

1. Set the **Organization** field to **Shirt**.
2. Set the **Description** field to **Import legacy Raw Material data**.
3. Set the **Warehouse** field to **1st Shirt W/h**.
4. Set the **Movement** field to *today*.
5. Set the **Document Type** field to **Physical Inventory**.

Navigate to the **Inventory Count Line** tab, and then set and save the following information:

1. Set the **Organization** field to **Shirt**.
2. Set the **Locator** field to **S1A** (actually, you can define your own locator, which will be identified as the migration location).
3. Set the **Product** field to **Hang Tag**.
4. Set the **Quantity Count** field to **100**.
5. Set the **Inventory Type** field to **Inventory Difference**.

> If you need to set another target account despite having an **Inventory Difference**, then in the **Inventory Type** field, you can set the value as **Charge Account**. If you choose this type, then there will be a **Charge** field that can be set up.

Here, we are only entering the information related to **Hang Tag**. In a real-life scenario, you could enter all of your company's materials in this tab. Navigate back to the **Inventory Count** tab, and complete this document.

## Accounting facts

There is no significant difference between the general journal format created here and the previous stock counting activities. The only difference is in the journal position. In this activity, we can make an assumption that the count quantity is greater than the book quantity.

Wait for a moment, and then press the *F5* key or click on the **ReQuery** button, until the document shows a **Posted** status. An accounting facts/GL journal is generated, as shown in the following screenshot:

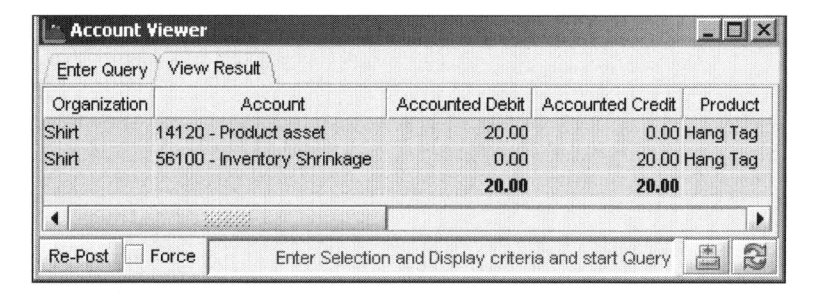

| Organization | Account | Accounted Debit | Accounted Credit | Product |
|---|---|---|---|---|
| Shirt | 14120 - Product asset | 20.00 | 0.00 | Hang Tag |
| Shirt | 56100 - Inventory Shrinkage | 0.00 | 20.00 | Hang Tag |
| | | 20.00 | 20.00 | |

## Moving Inventory

Moving the Inventory is a common task when managing our raw materials in a warehouse. In their daily activities, your warehouse staff might perform the following activities:

- Moving material between locations in different warehouses and different organizations
- Moving material between locations in different warehouses but in the same organization
- Moving material between locations in the warehouse

In these activities, if your warehouse staff is sending the material outside of the warehouse or location, the recipient (at the target warehouse) should record a confirmation when receiving the material.

ADempiere can help you manage these issues. You can use the **Menu | Material Management | Inventory Move** window to perform such an inventory movement. This window contains three tabs: **Move**, **Move Line**, and **Attributes**, and it should contain one document type to work on, that is, **Material Movement.**

We will use an example to practice all types of inventory movement and examine the generated accounting facts/GL journal entries.

# Movement between locations in different warehouses and / or different organizations

We will use our **S Label** raw material in our example. Currently, the **S Label** material resides in the **Loc S1A** location. This location is in the **1st Shirt W/h** in the **Shirt** organization. We will move a small quantity of the **S Label** material to **Loc D2B**, which is in the **1st Dress W/h** in the **Dress** organization. The following is a diagram of our source location and target location:

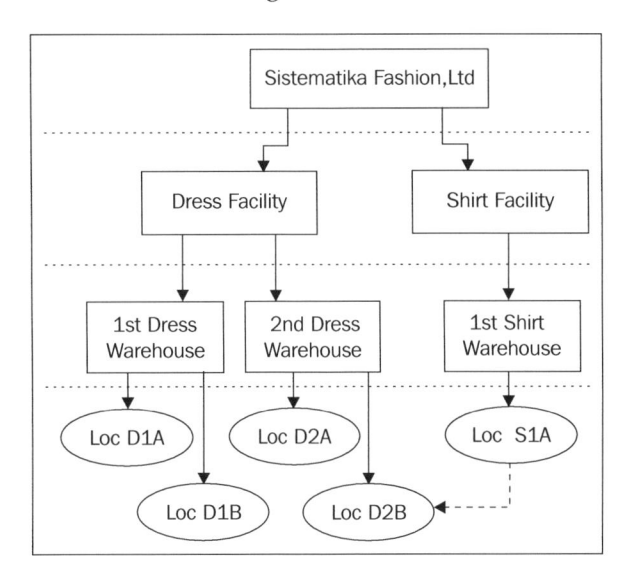

## Setting up the In-Transit Material Movement document

When performing an inventory move between locations and between warehouses, we usually need a confirmation from the people who receive the material. As per the standard configuration, ADempiere does not have the **In-Transit Material Movement** document.

We need to prepare this document type to accomplish our needs. You can open the **Menu | Performance Analysis | Accounting Rules | Document Type** window. Find the **Material Movement** document type by entering **Material Move%** in the **Name** field of the Lookup Record (search dialog) window. We need to copy this document type, and then alter some configuration.

*Managing Inventory*

Use the following procedure:

1. Press *Shift + F2* to create a new copy of the document type from the existing **Material Move** document type.
2. Change the **Name** field to **In-Transit Material Movement**.
3. *Select* the **In Transit** checkbox.
4. Save your record.

Leave the other fields unchanged. Save the record, and you will get a new document type, as shown in the following screenshot:

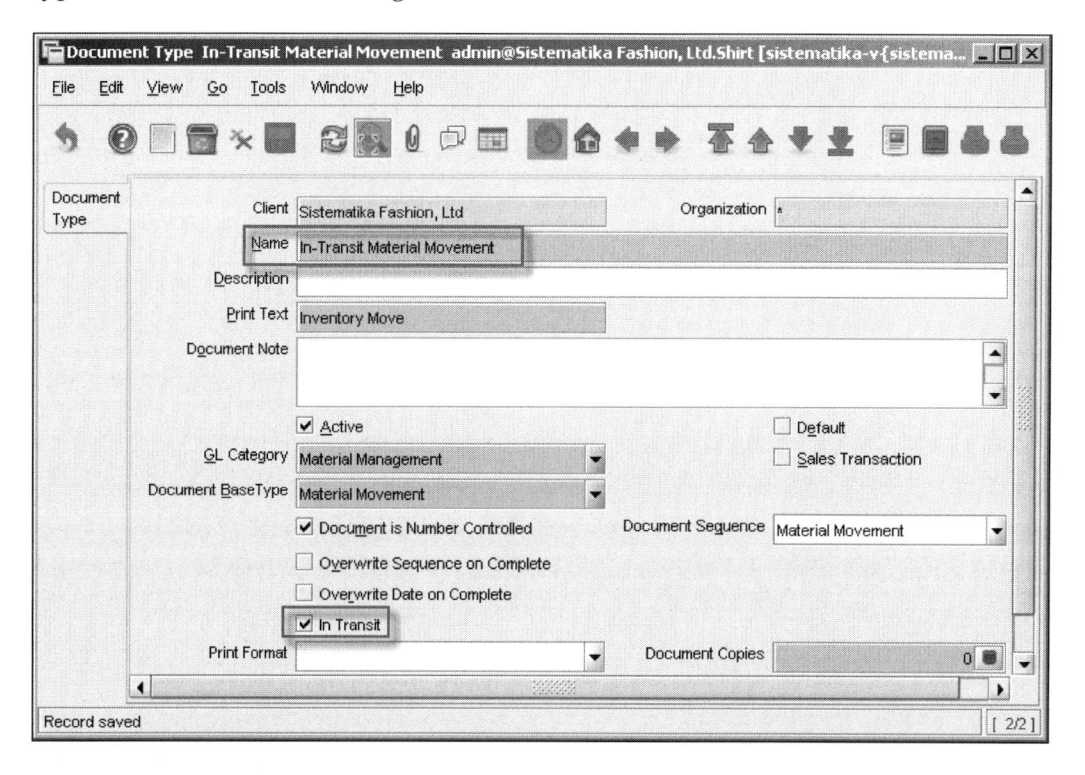

To ensure that our ADempiere client system will read our new configuration, you need to close all active ADempiere windows and reset the cache information by executing the **Menu | System Admin | General Rules | Cache Reset** process.

## Practising Moving Inventory with confirmation

Now, your warehouse staff, who have the authority for **Loc S1A**, should prepare a transaction through the **Inventory Move** window. In the **Move** tab, set and save the following information:

1. Set the **Organization** field to **Shirt**.
2. Set the **Movement Date** field to *today*.
3. Set the **Document Type** field to **In-Transit Material Movement** (now, you have two options for the document type).

Navigate to the **Move Line** tab, and then set and save the following information:

1. Set the **Product** field to **S Label**.
2. Set the **Locator** field to **Loc S1A** (this is source location).
3. Set the **Locator To** field to **Loc D2B** (this is target location).
4. Set the **Movement Quantity** field to **100**.

> If your product has attribute instance info, then you also need to set up the **Attribute Set Instance** and **Attribute Set Instance To** information.

Navigate back to the **Move** tab, and complete this document. Your document should now have an **In Progress** document status. Check your **Material Transactions** window related to the raw material. Currently, this transaction does not appear in this window.

## Confirming receipt of full material quantity

With the **In-Transit Material Movement** document type, ADempiere will automatically create a **Move Confirmation** document. Imagine that you are now acting as a warehouse person who has authority in the **Loc D2B** location of the **2nd Dress W/h** warehouse (the recipient), and you need to check the physical material that you have received, prior to creating a confirmation.

*Managing Inventory*

Suppose that you receive the same quantity, and that there is no broken material. You can make a confirmation by opening the **Menu | Material Management | Move Confirmation** window. Find the document, and examine the **Line** tab of the document, as shown in the following screenshot:

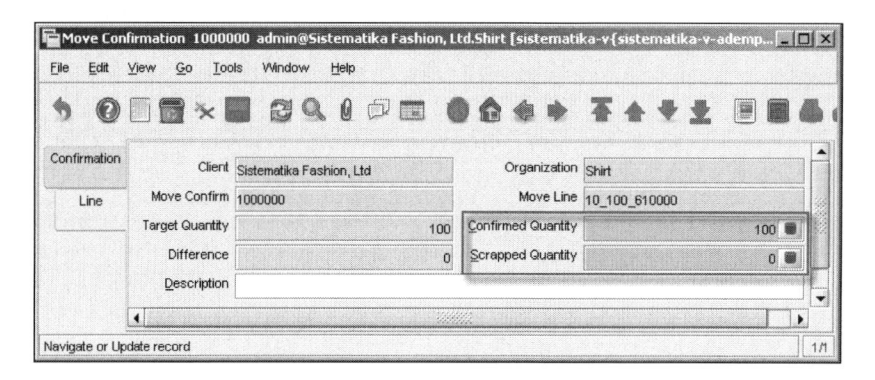

Okay, there is no variance in the quantity, and there is no broken material received. In such cases, the recipient needs to complete the **Move Confirmation** document in the **Confirmation** tab.

Upon this confirmation, the sender will be able to complete his or her **In-Transit Material Movement** document.

## Accounting facts

As an accounting staff member or an accountant, you can examine the generated accounting facts/GL journal entries. The standard journal format generated is:

| Window | Document | Sign | Description | Posting Type | Locator |
|---|---|---|---|---|---|
| Inventory Move | In-Transit Material Movement | Db | Product Asset | Actual | Locator to |
| | | Cr | Product Asset | Actual | Locator from |

Wait for a moment, and then press the *F5* key, or click on the **ReQuery** button, until the document has a **Posted** status. Now, examine the accounting facts/GL journal entries created for this transaction. We need to get more information related to the generated accounting facts/GL journal entries. In the **Account Viewer** window, select the **Enter Query** tab, select the **Display Document Info**, **Display Source Info**, and **Display Quantity** checkboxes, and then click on the **ReQuery** button. The output is shown in the following screenshot:

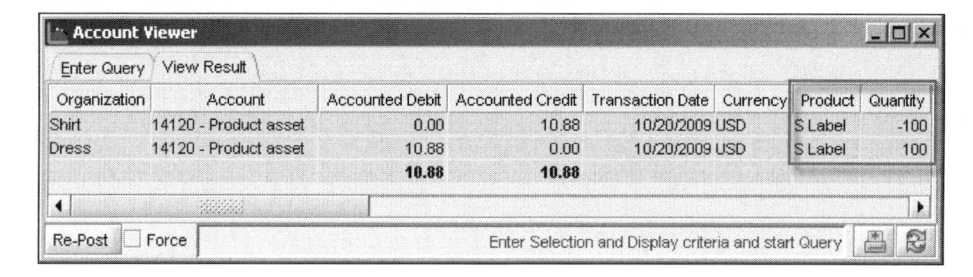

| Account Viewer | | | | | | | |
|---|---|---|---|---|---|---|---|
| Organization | Account | Accounted Debit | Accounted Credit | Transaction Date | Currency | Product | Quantity |
| Shirt | 14120 - Product asset | 0.00 | 10.88 | 10/20/2009 | USD | S Label | -100 |
| Dress | 14120 - Product asset | 10.88 | 0.00 | 10/20/2009 | USD | S Label | 100 |
| | | 10.88 | 10.88 | | | | |

> When comparing this with the results in your **Account Viewer** window, this screenshot will not look similar to your **Account Viewer** window. The fields have been rearranged in the screenshot (the **Product** and **Quantity** fields have been dragged and dropped onto the left-hand side of the **Currency** field).

Unfortunately, there is no **Locator** field information shown here. If you need the complete accounting facts/GL journal entries generated, then you need to access the information in the **Menu | Performance Analysis | Accounting Fact Details** window. Find the latest records in this window, and you (as the accounting staff or accountant) will get the complete journal information.

## Confirmation of receiving with scrapped material

During the process of transferring material, anything could happen. The material could break or, in the worst scenario, could be lost. If the warehouse staff (the recipient) receives broken material, he or she can create a confirmation by entering a scrapped quantity.

Create a new **In-Transit Material Movement** document, and set the same information mentioned in the *Practicing Moving Inventory with confirmation* section. These activities should be done by the sender.

Suppose you have five pieces of the **S Label** broken, in the **Line** tab of the **Move Confirmation** window, the target warehouse staff (the recipient) needs to enter the information mentioned as follows:

1. Set the **Confirmed Quantity** field to **95**.
2. Set the **Scrapped Quantity** field to **5**.

On completing this confirmation document, ADempiere will:

- Set a notification in the **Description** field, as shown in the following screenshot:

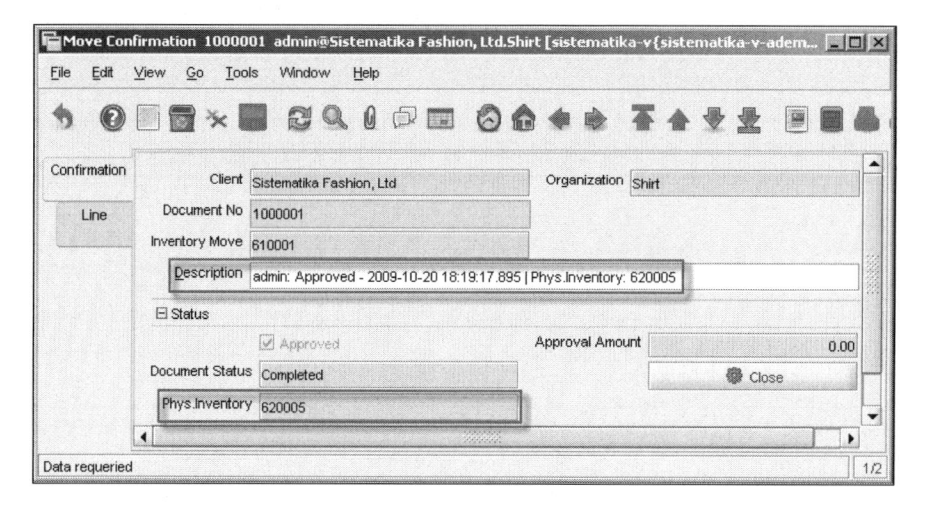

- Automatically create a **Physical Inventory** document in the **Physical Inventory** window. This document *belongs to organization in the target warehouse* (using **Dress** as the **Organization** and **2nd Dress W/h** as the **Warehouse**).

The purpose of this **Physical Inventory** document is to record the quantity variance. The recipient needs to go through this **Physical Inventory** document and check the results of the variance quantity. Furthermore, the recipient should use the **Inventory Difference** or **Charge Account** for the target **Inventory Type**.

After completing the confirmation window, the sender needs to complete the **In-Transit Material Movement**, whereas the recipient needs to complete the **Physical Inventory** document previously created.

## Confirmation of receiving with partial material

In our next case, if the target warehouse staff (the recipient) receives a partial quantity of material, we can create a confirmation by entering the quantity material as is.

Create another **In-Transit Material Movement** document, and set the information mentioned in the *Practicing Moving Inventory with confirmation* sections. These activities should be done by the sender.

Suppose your target warehouse staff (the recipient) receives 90 pieces of **S Label**, with the assumption that he or she lost 10 pieces of **S Label**. In the **Line** tab of the **Move Confirmation** window, he or she needs to enter the information mentioned as follows:

1. Set the **Confirmed Quantity** field to **90**.
2. Set the **Scrapped Quantity** field to **0**. The system will automatically set the value **10** in the **Difference** field.

On completing this confirmation document, ADempiere will automatically create a **Physical Inventory** document, and this document *belongs to the organization in the source warehouse* (using **Shirt** as the **Organization** and **1st Shirt W/h** as the **Warehouse**), as shown in the following screenshot:

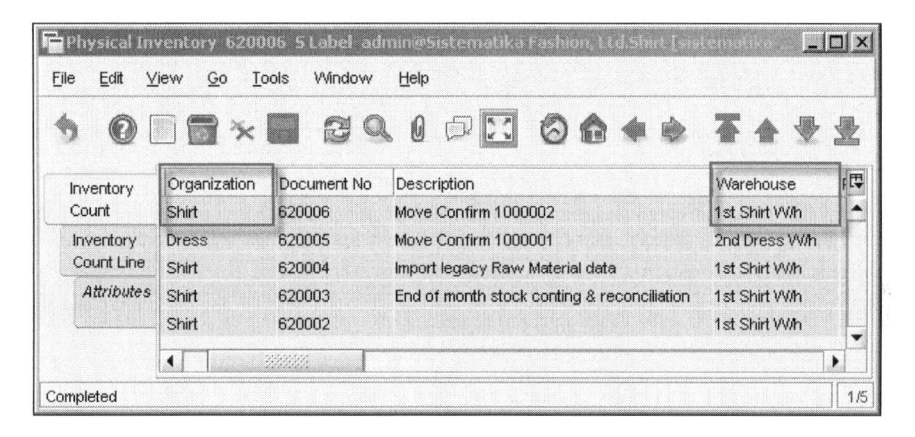

After completing the confirmation window, the sender needs to complete both, the **In-Transit Material Movement** and the **Physical Inventory** document previously created.

# Movement among locations in the same warehouse

Moving materials among locations within the same warehouse is the simplest of tasks for movement activities. Assuming that the target location is within the staff's authority, there is usually no need to create a confirmation. All of the material transferred will go to the target location without any problem.

Without confirmation, we can create a movement document by using the **Material Movement** document type instead of the **In-Transit Material Movement** document.

Let us practice by creating a **Material Movement** document. Suppose we need to transfer the **S Label** material from **Loc D2B** to **Loc D2A** (location in the same warehouse). In the **Move** tab, set and save the following information:

1. Set the **Organization** field to **Dress**.
2. Set the **Movement Date** field to *today*.
3. Set the **Document Type** field to **Material Movement** (Yes, **Material Movement**).

Navigate to the **Move Line** tab, and then set and save the following information:

1. Set the **Product** field to **S Label**.
2. Set the **Locator** field to **Loc D2B** (this is the source location).
3. Set the **Locator To** field to **Loc D2A** (this is the target location).
4. Set the **Movement Quantity** field to **100**.

Navigate back to the **Move** tab, and complete this document. You will now see your document showing a **Completed** status instead of **In Progress**. With this status, in the system, your material has been moved to the new location. You can check your movement activities by using the **Material Transactions** window.

# Summary

In this chapter, we have taken a deeper look at how to manage our inventory.

First, we played with the Product Attributes. In the Product Attributes, we could set additional information for all of our products. There are two types of attributes: non-instance attributes, and instance attributes. A "non-instance" attribute is a static product attribute such as the Shirt's color and size, and can be set up while registering (creating) the product in the **Product** window. An instance attribute is additional information or an attribute, and can be set up when receiving a raw material or when shipping finished goods. We have practiced how to set up information for both non-instance and instance attributes.

Then, we continued our discussion on how to book a material consumption for internal use (such as consuming material for an exhibition) and how to track this material movement using the **Material Transactions** window.

Later, we showed you how to perform stock counting and how to book any variance in quantity between system and physical stock by using the **Physical Inventory** window. The other feature that could be applied using this window is importing our legacy products. At the end of this chapter, we practiced inventory movements.

In the upcoming chapter, we will guide you through the concepts and implementation of the ADempiere workflow. We will try and explain the concept, configuration parts, and how to make the workflow work.

# 9
# ADempiere Workflow

*When creating a purchase requisition document, our company has a rule: if the total value reaches some amount, then it requires proper approval by management.*

In ADempiere, we identify this case as a process that requires a user's decision. This is a case that can be implemented with the help of a feature called ADempiere Workflow.

In this chapter, we will learn the concept and sample implementation of ADempiere Workflow types such as:

- General
- Document Process
- Document Value

We start our discussion by explaining the General type of workflow.

## Knowing the General workflow—a step-by-step guide

This type of workflow is aimed at providing guidance as well as step-by-step instructions to perform a task. This series of activities involves several ADempiere windows and/or forms or processes, which involve the user in each of the activities. You can access all of the preconfigured general workflow in the ADempiere Menu.

# Example of general workflow

One example form of standard general workflow available is **Product Setup**. *Log in with user ID admin,* using **Sistematika Fashion, Ltd Admin** as the role and **Shirt** as the organization. Access this workflow by clicking on **Menu | Material Management | Material Management Rules | Product Setup**. As you can see, this workflow is a sequential, or step-by-step activity, as shown in the following screenshot:

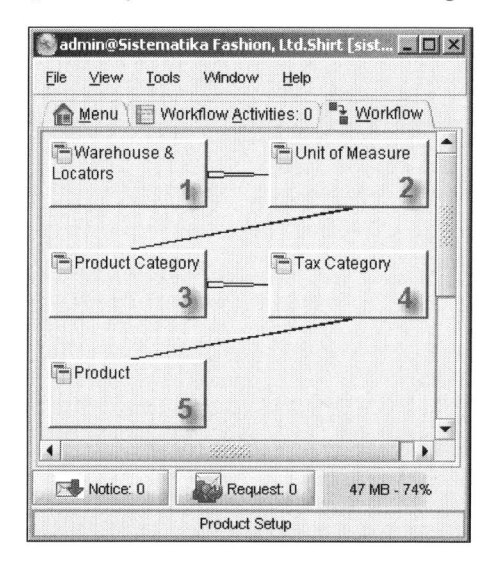

The activities related to setting up a **Product** are available in the **Workflow** tab. We need to open, review, and enter any information in the **Warehouse & Locators**, **Unit of Measure**, **Product Category**, **Tax Category**, and **Product** windows.

You will go to each of these windows one-by-one and perform the necessary activities.

# Constructing our own general workflow

*How is this type of workflow constructed?*

We will practice creating our own general workflow. We will create a short series of activities such as **Product Category → Unit of Measure → Product**. Log in to System (with the user ID **System** and **System Administrator** as the role). Open the **Menu | System Admin | General Rules | Workflow | Workflow** window, and set and save the following information in the **Workflow** tab:

1. Set the **Search Key** and **Name** fields to **Setup Product simplified version**.
2. Set the **Workflow Type** field to **General**.

3. Set the **Data Access Level** field to **Client + Organization** (select from the available options).
4. Set the **Author** field to *your name*.

   Navigate to the **Node** tab. Here, we need to register a series of activities. Enter and save the following information:

   | Field\Data | 1st data | 2nd data | 3rd data |
   |---|---|---|---|
   | Search Key | Product Category | Unit of Measure | Product |
   | Name | Product Category | Unit of Measure | Product |
   | Action | User Window | User Window | User Window |
   | Window | Product Category | Unit of Measure | Product |

   Leave the other fields unchanged.

We need to set the transition among registered windows. Ensure that you have **Product Category** in the **Search Key** field as the active record, navigate to the **Transition** tab, and then add and save the following information:

5. Set the **Next Node** field to **Unit of Measure**.

Go back to the **Node** tab and ensure that you have **Unit of Measure** in the **Search Key** field as your active record, navigate to the **Transition** tab, and then add and save the following information:

6. Set the **Next Node** field to **Product**.

Now, navigate back to the **Workflow** tab, and finalize this configuration by setting the **Start Node** field to **Product Category**. Save your changes.

This is just an example of building our own general workflow. You can build a series of tasks that might be unusual or non-daily tasks, such as a list of reports or processes to be carried out at month end or year end.

# Attaching general workflow to a menu

Now that the configuration has been done, we need to register our own new general workflow to the ADempiere menu, as this will make it accessible to the end-user.

Open the **Menu | System Admin | General Rules | System Rules | Menu** window. You need to enter and save the following information:

1. Set the **Name** field to **Sistematika Setup Product**.
2. Set the **Action** field to **Workflow**.
3. Set the **Workflow** field to **Setup Product simplified version**.

On the left-hand side of this window, you will see your newly-created menu. You can arrange the location of this menu by dragging and dropping it to the place that suits your needs.

In the last part of our activity, you need to register this menu to the roles that need to be able to access this menu. *Log in with user ID admin* with **Sistematika Fashion, Ltd Admin** as the role and **Shirt** as the organization, and then execute the **Menu | System Admin | General Rules | Security | Role Access Update** process. In the upcoming window, you should perform the following tasks:

1. Set the **Client** field to **Sistematika Fashion, Ltd**.
2. Set the **Role** field to *blank* (which means this menu will be accessible to all of the available roles).
3. Click on the **OK** button.

> We will discuss more detail about Role in the Chapter 12, *Implementing Security*

Re-log in with the user ID **admin**, and now you can see and access your own general workflow.

# Understanding ADempiere workflow

**Workflow** is defined as a step-by-step activity to complete a task that involves both the people and the system. As a default, all of the documents in ADempiere (for example, Purchase Requisition, Purchase Order, MM Receipt, and so on) are automatically workflow-enabled and are easy to extend or modify. Before we extend or modify anything, we need to know the details of how ADempiere Workflow works.

Now, log in to System (with the user ID **System** and **System Administrator** as the role), and open the **Menu | System Admin | General Rules | Workflow | Workflow** window. This window contains six tabs: **Workflow**, **Access**, **Node**, **Parameter**, **Transition**, and **Condition**.

# Knowing the workflow for an ADempiere document

The basic principle is that, the ADempiere **Document Process** and **Document Value** workflow will be configured based on table information.

*While all of the documents in ADempiere are workflow enabled, how do you know the relationship between ADempiere documents, workflow, and table information?*

All ADempiere documents (such as, **Purchase Order**, **MM Receipt**, **AR Receipt**, and so on) are entered through the relevant window. For example, **AR Receipt** documents will be entered in the **Payment** window. With this window, through its Record Info (refer to the section *More on Record Info*, in Chapter 2, *Exploring the ADempiere Client and Performing Tasks*), you will know which internal ADempiere table is being used to save the information. In this example, the **Payment** window is using the **C_Payment** table to store its information.

Knowing the table information, you can identify that we can create a workflow (both of **Document Process** or **Document Value** workflow) for payment purposes, defining C_Payment (**C_Payment_Payment** in the option) in the **Table** field, as shown in the following screenshot:

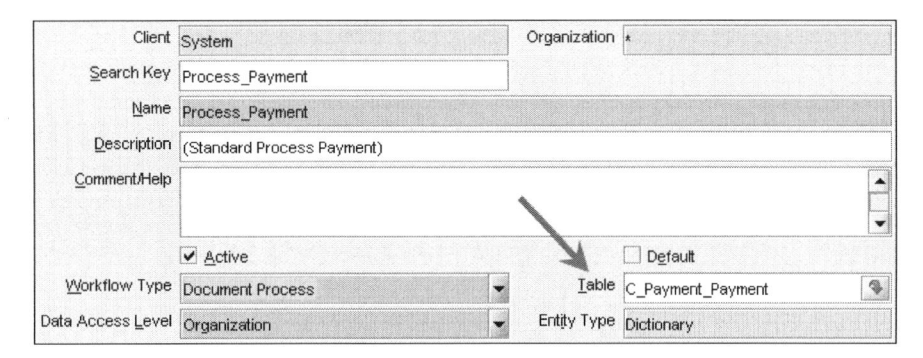

| Client | System | Organization | * |
|---|---|---|---|
| Search Key | Process_Payment | | |
| Name | Process_Payment | | |
| Description | (Standard Process Payment) | | |
| Comment/Help | | | |
| | ✓ Active | ☐ Default | |
| Workflow Type | Document Process | Table | C_Payment_Payment |
| Data Access Level | Organization | Entity Type | Dictionary |

As you can see, in this standard preconfigured **Process_Payment** workflow, ADempiere informs us that this **Document Process** workflow will be enabled if there are any activities that involve the C_Payment table, such as completing an **AR Payment** document.

*If we have two active Document Process workflows that use the C_Payment table in my configuration, then which one will be executed or processed by the ADempiere system?*

There is some additional configuration taking part in the process of knowing which Document Process workflow will be used in our ADempiere implementation.

Let us check the configuration through its internal Application Dictionary. Log in to System (with user ID **System** and **System Administrator** as the role). Open the **Menu | Application Dictionary | Table and Column** window. In the upcoming **Lookup Record** (search dialog) window, enter **C_Payment** in the **DB Table Name** field, and click on the **OK** button.

With the existing information in the **Table** tab, perform the following tasks:

1. Navigate to the **Column** tab. As per its Record Info, there will be 84 records available. Point your active records to the information having **DocAction** as its **DB Column Name**, as shown in the following screenshot:

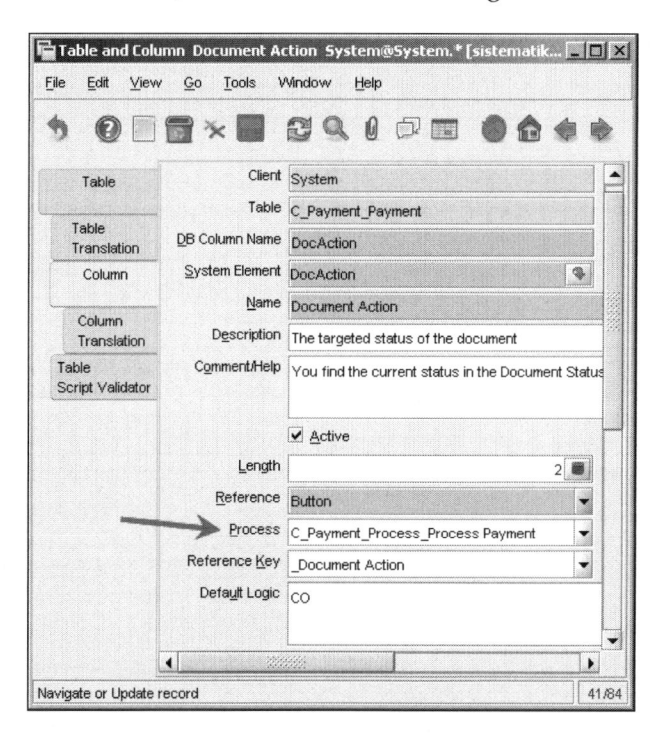

2. Check the **Process** field. It contains **C_Payment_Process_Process Payment**. Right-click on this field, and click on the **Zoom** button. You will be redirected to the **Report & Process** window that contains **C_Payment_Process** as its **Search Key** and **Process Payment** as its **Name**.

3. In the existing **Report & Process** tab, find the **Workflow** field. It has been set to the **Process Payment** workflow.

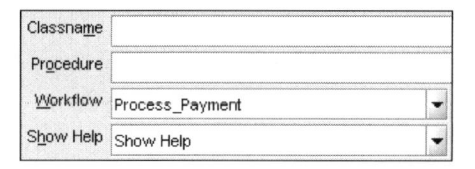

4. Right-click on this field, and click on the **Zoom** button. You will be directed to the **Workflow** window that contains **Process_Payment** in both the **Search Key** and the **Name** field

With this information, ADempiere tells us that while you click on the document action button (which is the **Complete** button in the **Payment** window), ADempiere will execute the **Process_Payment** workflow.

## Activity/Node flow

A workflow will contain more than one activity or step. In ADempiere, we will map our "activity" as a Node, and should register it in the **Node** tab.

If you go through all of the preconfigured workflow records in this **Workflow** window, you can divide all of these records into two types of *Workflow Types*:

- Document Process
- General

All of the workflow records that have the **Process_** prefix in their name are examples of the **Document Process** workflow, whereas workflow records which have the **Setup** prefix in their name are of a **General** type of workflow.

All of the workflows that have the prefix **Process_** in their name (such as **Process_Requisition**, **Process_Invoice** and so on) have a standard list of activity/nodes, as follows:

- (Start)
- (DocPrepare)
- (DocComplete)
- (DocAuto)

With the existing **Process_Payment** workflow, you can check all of these activities or nodes, on the **Node** tab.

Although it has four activities or nodes, actually ADempiere documents use a standard flow such as **(Start)** → **(DocPrepare)** → **(DocComplete)**. You may check the transition value among these activities on the **Transition** tab for each activity or node.

## Setting up transition among Activities/Nodes

When defining a workflow, it will contain a list of activities that need to be processed in the correct order. For example, suppose we have the following list of activities which needs to be executed in this order:

- Start
- Processing phase #1
- Processing phase #2
- End/Complete

# ADempiere Workflow

After registering a series of activities or nodes, the system needs some configuration about the sequence of activities to be followed.

With this sequence of activities, you need to setup the transition between activities or nodes in the **Transition** tab. In the *Start* activity, we need to set the next **transition** to *Processing phase #1*. In the *Processing phase #1* activity, we can set the next **transition** to *Processing phase #2*. Finally, the *Processing phase #2* activity will have the next **transition** set to *End/Complete*.

> *In some circumstances and conditions, we may need to bypass Processing phase #2. Thus, the sequence will be, Start → Processing phase #1 → End/Complete. Is this sequence possible?*

Of course, yes. Upon defining a next transition at the Processing phase #1 activity or node, you will define two types of transition as follows:

- In the first transition, set the next transition to *End/Complete*, and specify your condition.
- In the second transition, set the next transition to *Processing phase #2*.

> There are rules for defining more than one transition in the **Transition** tab. You need to specify the first transition record by entering a specific condition or criteria in the **Condition** tab. Next, enter another transition that has a more general condition.

## Node's Action

While registering an activity or node for the workflow, in the **Node** tab, there are multiple attributes, as shown in the following screenshot:

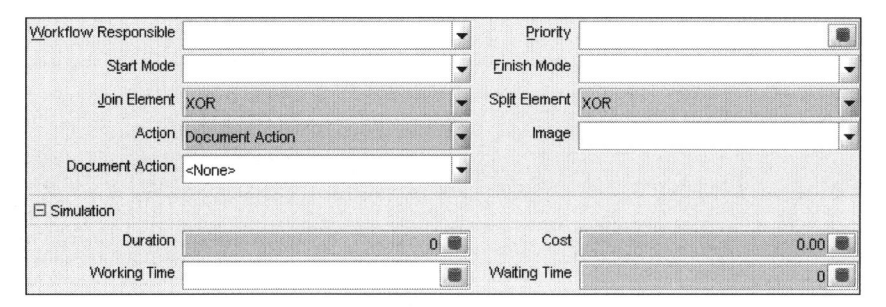

One of the types of available attributes is **Action**. The following is the list of available actions:

- **Wait (Sleep)**: We can specify a period of time (in minutes) before the system proceeds to the next activity or node.

- **User Choice**: This activity or node requires user interaction. The format of user choice can be a **Yes/No** decision or the selection of an option from a list of values (depending on the field type).
- **User Action:** This activity or node also requires user interaction. During processing of this node, the actions that need to be done are as follows: the user will open the Window (**User Window**) or Form (**User Form**), perform the necessary activities on this Window or Form, and then exit from the Window or Form, to complete the activity.
- **Automatic processes**: This type of action will execute any **Apps Process**, **Apps Report**, **Document Action** (Approve, Reject, Re-Activate, and so on), **Set Variable** which sets a constant value in the target column, and send an **Email**. Here, there is no user interaction needed to execute this activity or node.

Later, we will show you an example of using **Action**, when explaining the document process in more detail.

# Node's workflow responsible

Another attribute available when setting up a node is: **Workflow Responsible**. As indicated by the name itself, we can delegate the responsibility when executing or processing this activity or node to the **Workflow Responsible**.

To know the list of "workflow responsible" available in the system, *log in with user ID admin,* using **Sistematika Fashion, Ltd Admin** as the role, and * as the organization. Open the **Menu | System Admin | General Rules | Workflow | Workflow Responsible** window. In your ADempiere installation, there will be two default records, named **Invoker** and **Organization**.

## Responsible Type

In relation to with the records available in the **Workflow Responsible** window, there are three types of **Responsible Type** available during registration of the **Workflow Responsible**. These are as follows:

- **Human**: **Invoker** is an example of the workflow responsible that is created by using the **Human** responsible type. On registering the workflow responsible while using the **Human** responsible type, you can define the target user in the **User/Contact** field. Without setting up information in the **User/Contact** field, it means the person or user who starts the workflow will become a person who is responsible for the activity or node.

- **Organization**: When choosing the **Organization** as a responsibility type, this means that the person or user who was registered as a supervisor of the current transactional organization will become the person responsible. You can set up the supervisor of the organization in the **Menu | System Admin | Organization Rules | Organization** window, and navigate to the **Organization Info** tab. There you will find the **Supervisor** field.
- **Role**: All the people or users who are associated with this role will become responsible for this activity or node.

## Setting up a new workflow responsible

As required by our example, we will set up user **admin** as another instance of the **Human** workflow responsible, and will add two **Role** types of workflow responsible. In the **Workflow Responsible** window, set and save the following information:

| Field\Data | 1st data | 2nd data | 3rd data |
| --- | --- | --- | --- |
| Organization | * | * | * |
| Name | admin | admin role | user role |
| Entity Type | User Maintained | User Maintained | User Maintained |
| Responsible Type | Human | Role | Role |
| User/Contact | admin | - | - |
| Role | - | Sistematika Fashion, Ltd Admin | Sistematika Fashion, Ltd User |

Next, we will continue with our discussion of the document process workflow and an implementation example of this workflow type.

## Document process workflow

> *As discussed earlier, we need to implement the approval procedure if the requisition has reached some value. For our reference, could you show me how to configure this approval activity when we have a requisition value of more than US$ 100?*

Because we will work on the **Purchase Requisition** document, in which we are entering the information in the **Requisition** window, we know that this window uses the **M_Requisition** table for its Record Info. An available preconfigured workflow that uses the **M_Requisition** (shown **M_Requisition_Requisition** in the **Table** field) table is **Process_Requisition**.

Open the **Menu | System Admin | General Rules | Workflow | Workflow** window. Find a **Process_Requisition** record, and examine the **Table** field. In this record, the **Workflow Type** field contains **Document Process**, which indicates that we are working with the document process workflow.

We will extend this workflow to accomplish our requisition approval activities.

## Setting up User Choice actions

In this example, we will add a node using the **User Choice** action. Navigate to the **Node** tab, and then add and save the following information:

1. Set the **Organization** field to **\***.
2. Set the **Search Key** and **Name** fields to **(DocApproval)**.
3. Set the **Action** field to **User Choice**.
4. Set the **Column** field to **IsApproved**. This will show **IsApproved_Approved** in the option.

In this new active record, navigate to the **Transition** tab, and then add and save the following information.

5. Set the **Next Node** field to **(DocComplete)**

Now, navigate back to the **Node** tab, and find the **(DocPrepare)** record, and then navigate to the **Transition** tab again. You have one *transition default record*, with information such as:

- A **Node** field, set to **(DocPrepare)**
- A **Next Node** field, set to **(DocComplete)**
- A **Sequence** field, set to **100**

You need to enter additional transition records. Add and save the following information:

1. Set the **Organization** field to **\***.
2. Set the **Next Node** field to **(DocApproval)**.
3. Set the **Sequence** field to **10**.

> As we will set up a more detailed condition to compare with the default transition record, which does not have any condition; you must set this sequence number below the sequence number that belongs to *transition default records* (which was 100).

With this new transition record, navigate to the **Condition** tab, add and save the following information:

1. Set the **Sequence** field to **10**.
2. Set the **And/Or** field with **Or**.
3. Set the **Column** field to **TotalLines** (shown as **TotalLines_Total Lines** in the option).

    Note: **TotalLines** is a total amount from all of the lines. In this case, it is the total amount of all of the requisition lines.

4. Set the **Operation** field to **>**.
5. Set the **Value** field to **100**.

With this additional configuration, we have two standard flows, as follows:

1. If the total requisition value is > 100, the document flow will be:

    **Start → DocPrepare → DocApproval → DocComplete**

2. If the total requisition value is <= 100, the document flow will be:

    **Start → DocPrepare → DocComplete**

Now, we will see who is responsible for approving a document when the requisition value has an amount of more than 100.

# Finding the person with approval rights

*As per my understanding, if we have a total value of more than 100, the requisition needs approval. We have not assigned somebody to handle this approval. The question is, who is taking care of the approval processes?*

When configuring the **User Choice** action and using **IsApproved** as the column value, internally, ADempiere will find the person or user who has approval rights, in the following order:

1. First, the system will find the supervisor of this user. We can check the user's supervisor by opening the **Menu | System Admin | General Rules | Security | User** window. Find the target user in this window. In the **User Contact** tab, you will find the **Supervisor** field.

2. If no supervisor information is specified, then the system tries to find the supervisor of the **Organization**. You can check the organization's supervisor by opening the **Menu | System Admin | Organization Rules | Organization** window. Find and locate the organization (which is used in the target requisition document), navigate to the **Organization Info** tab, and then check the **Supervisor** field.

3. If no supervisor information is specified, then it will try to get the supervisor of the parent organization for this organization. We will get the parent organization in the **Parent Organization** field on the **Organization Info** tab.

After finding the user, the system will perform the following activity:

1. It will find all of the roles associated with this user. You can check this value by opening the **User** window and navigating to the **User Roles** tab. For the roles data itself, open the **Menu | System Admin | General Rules | Security | Role** window.

2. With those roles, the system tries to check the values in the **Approve own Documents** and **Approval Amount** fields. If the **Approve own Documents** is selected and the **Approval Amount** value is greater than the requisition value, then this user is eligible to process the document approval.

With this information, open the **User** window. Find user ID **admin**, and check the available roles associated with this user. In the **User Roles** tab, it has two roles associated: **Sistematika Fashion, Ltd Admin** and **Sistematika Fashion, Ltd User**. To support our example further, open the **Role** window. Set a proper change, and ensure that you have the following information:

| Field\Role | Sistematika Fashion, Ltd Admin | Sistematika Fashion, Ltd User |
| --- | --- | --- |
| Approval own Documents | *select* | *select* |
| Approval Amount | 1000 | 0 |

Next, you need to set up the supervisor for the user ID *user*. Perform the following activities:

1. Open the **User** window, and find the *user* records.
2. Set the **Supervisor** field to **admin**, and save this information.

# Sample of approval workflow implementation

As a common company requirement, we will create a purchase requisition document that has the user ID *user* who creates this document.

## Initiating a requisition document

We will create a purchase requisition document. *Log in with user ID user*, role **Sistematika Fashion, Ltd User**, and organization **Shirt**. Open the **Menu | Requisition-to-Invoice | Requisition** window. In the **Requisition** tab, enter and save the following information:

1. Set the **Organization** field to **Shirt**.
2. Set the **Document Type** field to **Purchase Requisition**.
3. Set the **Date Required** field to *today*.
4. Set the **Price List** field to **Purchase PL**.

Navigate to the **Requisition Line** tab, and then add and save the following information:

1. Set the **Product** field to **S Fabric**. After setting up this product, the **Price** field will be populated automatically by the price information taken from the **Product | Price** tab. You are still able to alter this price if necessary. For now, keep it as the standard price (3.80).
2. Set the **Quantity** field to **100**.

On saving this record, you will get a notice that your total value is 380. Complete this document. Instead of having a **Completed** document status, now the **Document Status** is **In Progress**.

Because the total value of this requisition document is more than 100, if you try to complete this document, the approval document process workflow procedure will be executed by the ADempiere system.

## Approving the requisition document

With our configuration, user ID **admin** is a person who is responsible for approving this document. *Log in with user ID admin,* using **Sistematika Fashion, Ltd Admin** as the role and **Shirt** as the organization. You can perform the approval by opening the **Menu | System Admin | General Rules | Workflow | Workflow Activities** window.

This window will contain all of the to-do lists or activity lists that need attention from this user. With the previous requisition processes, this window will now have information similar to that shown in the following screenshot:

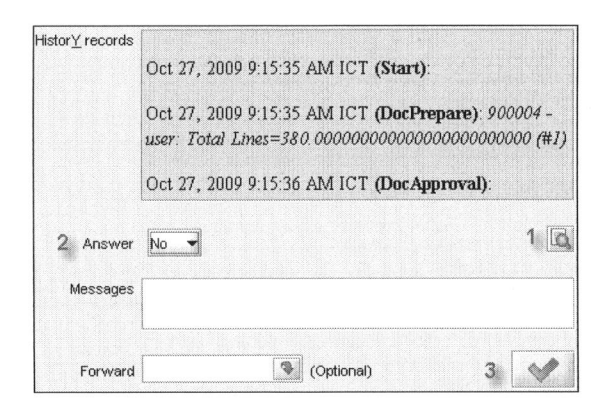

Before making a decision about this document, you should be able to access the original document by clicking on the **Zoom** button (**1**). If everything is OK, in the **Answer** field (**2**), you can select the **Yes** value, set some description in the **Messages** field, and then click on the **OK** button (**3**).

## Monitoring workflow progression

Both user ID **admin** and user ID **user** can monitor the progression of document workflow by using the **Menu | System Admin | General Rules | Workflow | Workflow Process** window. Open this window, and find your workflow processes. Here, you will get the latest status of the document workflow.

The following is the sample data for our workflow process, taken from the **Activity** tab:

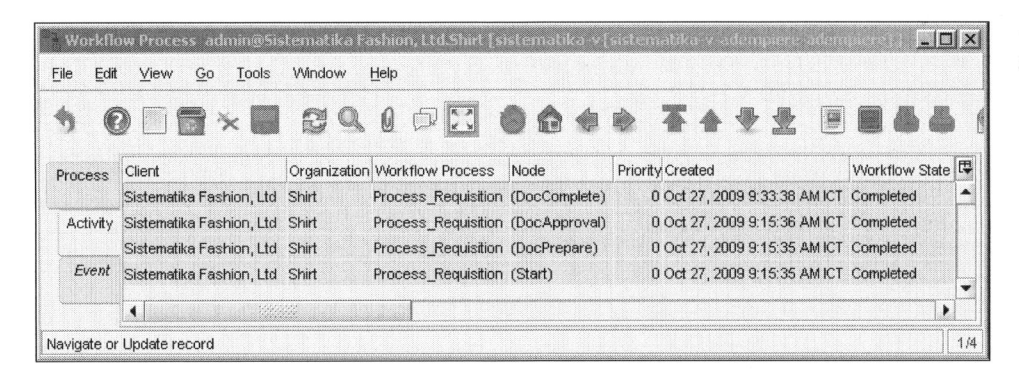

Next, we will continue our practice on how to cancel a workflow that is in progress.

## Cancelling a workflow in progress

*Prior to the approval processes, sometimes, we may need to cancel our document for some reason. And now, the status of document is waiting for approval. We need to cancel this document before our supervisor approves this requisition document.*

Yes, you can cancel this document. For our practice, create another purchase requisition document. *Log in with user ID user*, with **Sistematika Fashion, Ltd User** as the role, and **Shirt** as the organization. To enter a new purchase requisition document, follow the procedure mentioned in the *Initiating a requisition document* section, and finalize the requisition by completing this document.

Now, we are in the canceling stage. Open the **Workflow Process** window, and find your last **Workflow Process** record in the **Process** tab. Navigate to the **Activity**, and ensure that your active record is a **(DocApproval)** node with a **Suspended** workflow state. Change the view to detailed information by clicking on the **Grid Toggle** button. You will find the **Manage Activity** button in this window. Click on this button.

This will display a confirmation window, which has three options:

- Abort Process
- New User/Contact
- New Workflow Responsible

Select the **Abort Process** field, and then click on the **OK** button, and this **(DocApproval)** node is aborted.

## Setting up E-mail actions

*Our manager is not always connected to the ADempiere system. In his daily activity, he only regularly checks his e-mail to monitor and keep communicating with his staff. If there are any documents that need his approval, an automatic notification sent to his e-mail will be helpful.*

In the upcoming sections, we will set up an additional workflow configuration to send a notification e-mail to the Manager.

# Activating the e-mail feature

We need to find a way to enable our e-mail feature. *Log in with user ID admin,* with **Sistematika Fashion, Ltd Admin** as the role, and open the **Menu | System Admin | Client Rules | Client** window. In the **Client** tab, you will find some fields related to e-mail configuration. These fields need to be set up correctly.

An example of an e-mail configuration setup is as follows:

- **Mail Host** set to **127.0.0.1** (this is for the SMTP mail host set up)
- **Request Email** set to adempiere@sistematika.test
- **Request User** set to **adempiere**
- **Request User Password** set to **adempiere**

> All of these values depend on your mail server configuration. Contact your e-mail administrator for the information required to set up this e-mail configuration.

After saving this e-mail configuration, click on the **Test Email** button. Ensure that you get a successful test message as shown in the following screenshot:

## Setting up e-mail for end users

You need to set up e-mail addresses for all of the end users. With the e-mail address information, the system will send an e-mail to the users involved during running or executing a document workflow. Get the e-mail user ID and password information from your e-mail administrator. Open the **Menu | System Admin | General Rules | Security | User** window. In the **User Contact** tab, find and set the following information:

| Field\User-id | admin | user |
| --- | --- | --- |
| EMail User ID | admin@sistematika.test | user@sistematika.test |
| EMail User Password | adempiere | adempiere |

> All of these e-mail values depend on your e-mail configuration. Feel free to set up your own e-mail addresses.

## Setting up a mail template

We will set up a mail template for our requisition approval processes. In this template, we can define standard messages for delivering information via e-mail.

Open the **Menu | Partner Relations | Mail Template** window. In the **Mail Template** tab, add and save the following information:

1. Set the **Organization** field to **\***.
2. Set the **Name** field to **Requisition Approval**.
3. Set the **Subject** field to **Requisition Approval**.
4. Set the **Mail Text** field to **Dear manager, Need your help to review and approve the requisition document below**.

Next, we will bind this mail template to our **Process_Requisition** workflow.

## Altering workflow configuration

We will add a workflow activity/node, which will send an e-mail to certain users, and bind the mail template here.

Open the **Workflow** window, and find the **Process_Requisition** records in the **Workflow** tab. Navigate to the **Node** tab, and then add and save the following information:

1. Set the **Organization** to **\***.
2. Set the **Search Key** and **Name** field with **(EmailToManager)**.
3. Set the **Workflow Responsible** with **admin**.
4. Set the **Action** with **Email**.
5. Set the **EMail Recipient** with **WF Responsible**.
6. Set the **Mail Template** with **Requisition Approval**.

Navigate to the **Transition** tab, add and save the following information:

1. Set the **Organization** field to **\***.
2. Set the **Next Node** field to **(DocApproval)**.
3. Set the **Sequence** field to **10**.

We need to restructure our **(DocPrepare)** node. Previously, the next transition cycle was **(DocApproval)**. Navigate back to the **Node** tab, and find the **(DocPrepare)** record. Then navigate to the **Transition** tab, find the record which has a **Sequence** value of **10**, alter the existing **Next Node** information to be **(EmailToManager)**, and then save this information.

With this configuration, the flow is:

1. Total requisition value > 100

    **Start → DocPrepare → EmailToManager → DocApproval → DocComplete**

2. Total requisition value <= 100

    **Start → DocPrepare → DocComplete**

> We can set the **Workflow Responsible** to user, role, or organization. If set to **Organization**, then the e-mail will be sent to the supervisor for the organization.

## Testing the e-mail notification configuration

We need to test our configuration by creating a new **Requisition** document. *Log in with user ID user*, **Sistematika Fashion, Ltd User** as the role, and **Shirt** as the organization. Open the **Menu | Requisition-to-Invoice | Requisition** window. In the **Requisition** tab, enter and save the following information:

1. Set the **Organization** field to **Shirt**.
2. Set the **Document Type** field to **Purchase Requisition**.
3. Set the **Date Required** field to *today*.
4. Set the **Price List** field to **Purchase PL**.

In the **Requisition Line** tab, enter and save the following information:

1. Set the **Product** field to **S Fabric**.
2. Set the **Quantity** field to **115**.

Save this record. You will have the total value set to **437**. Complete this document, and the document status will be set to **In Progress**. You can check your workflow progression by watching the **Workflow Process** window.

The Manager is notified by e-mail, which contains a message, as shown in the following screenshot:

```
From:     adempiere@sistematika.test
To:       admin@sistematika.test
Date:     10/27/2009 11:50 AM
Subject:  Requisition 900007: Requisition Approval

Dear Manager, Need your help to review and approve the
requisition document below
-----
Requisition 900007
900007 - user: Total Lines=437.00000000000000000000000 (#1)
```

The information above the line is taken from the mail template, whereas the information under the line is the document information. The Manager can perform the approval activities based on this information.

## Setting up an application process's action

*After completing the requisition document, there is a feature to create a purchase order from a requisition. So, we manually execute this process to get our purchase order document. The question is, could we make it automatically?*

As mentioned in the *Creating a Purchase Order from a Purchase Requisition* section of Chapter 5, *Procurement Activities*, we can convert an existing purchase requisition into a purchase order by executing the **Menu | Requisition-to-Invoice | Create PO from Requisition** process. Behind the scenes, this process executes the internal ADempiere process, named **M_Requisition_POCreate**.

We can include this process into our workflow. So, when the Manager approves our requisition document, it will automatically create a purchase order document for us.

## Finding the internal ADempiere process identity name

At the moment, all you need to know is how to identify the name of the ADempiere process that performs the **Create PO from Requisition** activity, and what kind of information is needed when executing this process.

Log in to System (with the user ID **System** and using **System Administrator** as the role), navigate to the **Menu | Application Dictionary | Report & Process** window, and open this window. In the upcoming **Lookup Record** (search dialog) window, you need to enter **Create PO from%** in the **Name** field, click on the **OK** button, and you will be directed to a record that has **Create PO from Requisition** as the value in the **Name** field.

This window has three tabs: **Report & Process**, **Report Access**, and **Parameter**. To achieve our goal, we need to pay attention to the first and the third tab. With the **Report & Process** tab, just note down the value registered in the **Search Key** field. The value is **M_Requisition_POCreate**.

# Identifying a parameter for a certain ADempiere processes

When executing the **Create PO from Requisition** process manually, you will be prompted with a confirmation window in which you can specify specific information such as **Requisition** number, **Organization**, and so on, as shown in the following screenshot:

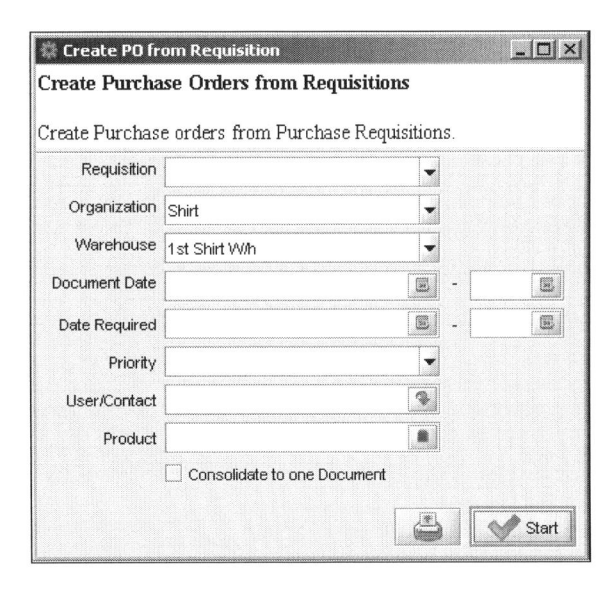

Actually, the list of available confirmation information is registered in the **Parameter** tab of the process. Navigate to the **Parameter** tab. Here, the **M_Requisition_POCreate** process contains nine parameters. The first parameter registered has **Requisition** in the **Name** field, and has **M_Requisition_ID** in the **DB Column Name** field. Keep in mind the **DB Column Name** field information.

> On entering and saving all of the documents, internally, ADempiere will generate a unique identity. In the case of the **Requisition** document, this unique identity information will be saved in the **M_Requisition_ID** field. We will use this field to identify the target Requisition document for our upcoming workflow configuration

Now, log out from the *System* user ID.

## Additional workflow configuration

We need to register a new workflow that creates a purchase order automatically. Because we need this workflow to work only for the **Sistematika Fashion, Ltd** client, we will add this workflow configuration by accessing ADempiere using the user ID **admin** (as administrator of the **Sistematika Fashion, Ltd** client).

*Log in with user ID admin* using **Sistematika Fashion, Ltd Admin** as the role, and * as the organization. Open the **Workflow** window, and find the **Process_Requisition** records in the **Workflow** tab. Navigate to **Node** tab, and then add and save the following information:

1. Set the **Organization** field to *.
2. Set the **Search Key** and **Name** fields to **(ConvertToPO)**.
3. Set the **Action** field to **Apps Process**.
4. Set the **Process** field to **M_Requisition_POCreate** (pick from the option list).

We need to inform this workflow about which requisition document needs to be processed. Navigate to the **Parameter** tab, add and save the following information:

1. Set the **Process Parameter** field to **Requisition** (pick from the available options).
2. Set the **Attribute Value** field to **@M_Requisition_ID@**.

> Because the **Process_Requisition** workflow should work for the **M_Requisition** table, if we define **@M_Requisition_ID@** in the **Attribute Value** field, ADempiere will take some value from the **M_Requisition_ID** field, and set this value as a parameter.

Move to the **Node** tab, and find the **(DocComplete)** record. We need to set the next transition of this node or activity to **(ConvertToPO)** node or activity. Navigate to the **Transition** tab, and then add and save the following information:

1. Set the **Organization** field to *.
2. Set the **Next Node** field to **(ConvertToPO)**.
3. Set the **Sequence** field to **10**.

With this configuration, the flow would be:

1. Total requisition value is > 100

   Start → DocPrepare → EmailToManager → DocApproval → DocComplete → ConvertToPO

2. Total requisition value is <= 100

   Start → DocPrepare → DocComplete → ConvertToPO

> Creating the purchase order document from a requisition will be done only if the requisition document has a **Complete** status. This is the reason for putting the **(ConvertToPO)** node or activity after the **(DocComplete)** node or activity.

## Testing the application process configuration

We can create a new requisition document to test our last configuration.

*Log in with user ID user*, **Sistematika Fashion, Ltd User** as the role, and **Shirt** as the organization. Open the **Menu | Requisition-to-Invoice | Requisition** window. On the **Requisition** tab, add and save the following information:

1. Set the **Organization** field to **Shirt**.
2. Set the **Document Type** field to **Purchase Requisition**.
3. Set the **Date Required** field to *today*.
4. Set the **Price List** field to **Purchase PL**.

On the **Requisition Line** tab, add and save the following information:

1. Set the **Product** field to **S Button**.
2. Set the **Quantity** field to **1500**.

On saving this record, you will have the total value set to 120. Complete this document, and the document status is **In Progress**. You can check your workflow progression by watching the **Workflow Process** window.

ADempiere Workflow

*Log in with user ID admin,* **Sistematika Fashion, Ltd Admin** as the role, and **Shirt** as the organization. Open the **Workflow Activities** window, and set the approval for this document. After this activity, ADempiere will proceed to convert our requisition document into a purchase order document. Check both the **Workflow Process** and the **Purchase Order** window.

The following screenshot shows a sample of the purchase order document, which is generated automatically when executing our **Process_Requisition** workflow:

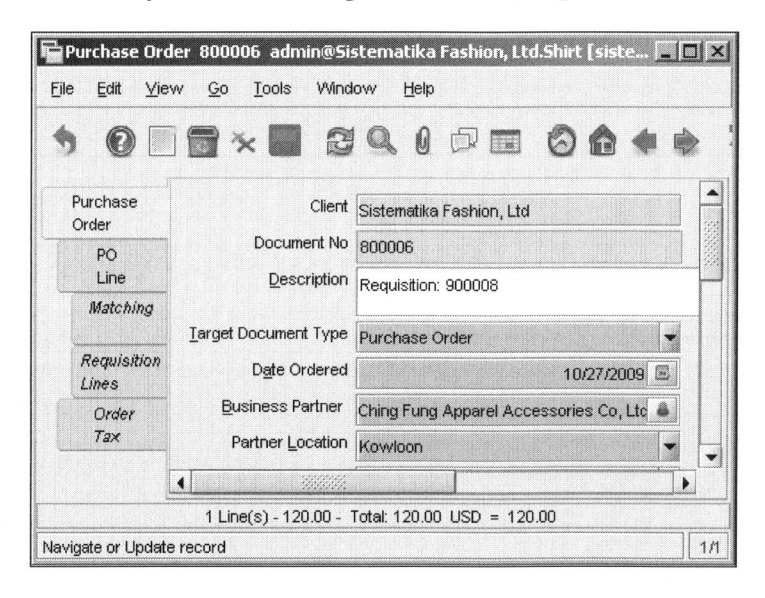

As you can see in the screenshot above, this purchase order document is created from requisition number 900008, as mentioned in the **Description** field.

## Setting up a Variable's action

You might need to automatically set the value of one or more available fields to your own value when processing your document. This condition applies when implementing the following action:

- Set a constant value (the only value) for a registered field

The list of available fields that can be set up are all of the fields that belong to the tables that are configured in the **Table** field located on the **Workflow** tab of the **Workflow** window. For example, the **Process_Requisition** workflow uses the **M_Requisition** table (shown as **M_Requisition_Requisition** in the **Table** field). You can set a constant value to all of the fields that belong to the **M_Requisition** table.

We will guide you through entering a constant value in the **Description** field when processing the **Process_Requisition** workflow.

## Configuring the set attribute action

We need to create a new activity or node in the **Process_Requisition** workflow that aims to set a variable or constant in the **Description** field.

*Log in with user ID admin,* **Sistematika Fashion, Ltd Admin** as the role, and * as the organization. Open the **Workflow** window, and find the **Process_Requisition** record on the **Workflow** tab. Navigate to the **Node** tab, and then add and save the following information:

1. Set the **Organization** field to *.
2. Set the **Search Key** and **Name** fields to **(SetVariable)**.
3. Set the **Action** field to **Set Variable**.
4. Set the **Column** field to **Description** (shown as **Description_Description** in the option list; here, you will see a list of available fields that belong to the **M_Requisition** table).
5. Set the **Attribute Value** with **Sample of constant text**.

Navigate to the **Transition** tab, and then add and save the following information:

1. Set the **Organization** to *.
2. Set the **Next Node** to **(ConvertToPO)**.
3. Set the **Sequence** with **10**.

We need to re-structure the next transition for the **(DocComplete)** node. Navigate to the **Node** tab, and find the **(DocComplete)** records. We need to set the next transition of this activity or node to **(SetVariable)**. Navigate to the **Transition** tab, alter the existing record, and then enter and save the following information:

- Set the **Next Node** field to **(SetVariable)**.

With this configuration, the flow would be:

1. Total requisition value is > 100

    Start → DocPrepare → EmailToManager → DocApproval → DocComplete → SetVariable → ConvertToPO

2. Total requisition value is <= 100

    Start → DocPrepare → DocComplete → SetVariable → ConvertToPO

> You can check this flow visually by opening the **Menu | System Admin | General Rules | Workflow | Workflow Editor** window and setting the **Process_Requisition** in the option list of the workflow.

## Testing the set variable workflow

Now, create a new requisition document to test our configuration.

*Log in with user ID user*, with **Sistematika Fashion, Ltd User** as the role, and **Shirt** as the organization. Open the **Menu | Requisition-to-Invoice | Requisition** window. On the **Requisition** tab, add and save the following information:

1. Set the **Organization** field to **Shirt**.
2. Set the **Document Type** field to **Purchase Requisition**.
3. Set the **Date Required** field to *today*.
4. Set the **Price List** field to **Purchase PL**.

On the **Requisition Line** tab, enter and save the following information:

1. Set the **Product** field to **S Button**.
2. Set the **Quantity** field to **1000**.
3. Save this record.

You will have the total value set to 80. With the current workflow configuration, this value is less than 100, so there is no need to get an approval from your manager. Just complete this document, and the document status will have **Complete** as its document status.

Now take a look at your **Description** field. It should automatically have the **Sample of constant text** value, as shown in the following screenshot:

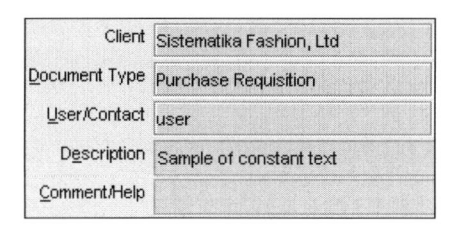

| | |
|---|---|
| Client | Sistematika Fashion, Ltd |
| Document Type | Purchase Requisition |
| User/Contact | user |
| Description | Sample of constant text |
| Comment/Help | |

Take a look at **Workflow Process** to examine the workflow steps. Ensure that you are in the last record (the requisition that has 80 as the total value), and navigate to the **Activity** tab. You will have a **(SetVariable)** node; find the **Text Message** field. This should contain **Description=Sample of constant text**, which makes sure that this text has come from workflow.

## Document value workflow

*Our Manager talked about a rule or condition. If there are any activities to cancel (void) an existing document (for example, a purchase order document related to a specific business partner), then the system should give us an alert that this document has been canceled. Could you help me to accommodate the manager's requirement?*

We will send the Manager a notification e-mail if there are any purchase order cancellations for a certain business partner. We will look at how ADempiere catches the condition itself.

ADempiere has a mechanism for monitoring a new value inserted or updated in its database table, when saving any information. This saving activity can be triggered by:

- **The user**: User clicks on the **Save** button.
- **Internal ADempiere system**: An internal ADempiere process and\or calculation inserts or updates any information.

Both of these conditions are monitored by default. In your case, we just need to tell ADempiere:

*Please help me in monitoring the purchase order document. If the document status becomes void or is canceled, and contains Hempel China Limited as the business partner, then please inform me via e-mail.*

## Setting up a new mail template

We need to set up a mail template, which can be used as a standard information header for this cancellation or for voiding purchase order activities.

*Log in with user ID admin*, using **Sistematika Fashion, Ltd Admin** as the role, and **\*** as the organization. Open the **Menu | Partner Relations | Mail Template** window. On the **Mail Template** tab, add and save the following information:

1. Set the **Organization** field to **\***.
2. Set the **Name** and **Subject** fields to **Canceling document information**.

3. Set the **Mail Text** field to **Dear manager, please be informed that the following document has been canceled**.

Next, continue with creating a new workflow.

## Defining configuration

We need to create a new workflow for our example. Open the **Workflow** window. On the **Workflow** tab, add and then save the following information:

1. Set the **Organization** field to **\***.
2. Set the **Search Key** and **Name** field to **PO_VoidingAlert**.
3. Set the **Workflow Type** field to **Document Value**.
4. Set the **Table** field to **C_Order**.
5. Set the **Document Value Logic** field to **@docstatus@=VO**.
6. Set the **Data Access Level** field to **Client+Organization**.
7. Set the **Author** field to *your name*.

> **@docstatus@=VO** means that ADempiere should take the value of the **docstatus** field of the **C_Order** table. If this value is VO (condition VO=VO is fulfilled), then this workflow will be executed.

Navigate to the **Access** tab. We will allow the **Sistematika Fashion, Ltd User** role to access this workflow. Add and save the following information:

1. Set the **Organization** field to **\***.
2. Set the **Role** field to **Sistematika Fashion, Ltd User.**
3. *Select* both, the **Active** and **Read Write** checkboxes.

Now, navigate to the **Node** tab. We need to set three workflows: **(Start)**, **(SendEmail)**, and **(End)**. You can add and save the following information:

| Field\Data | 1st data | 2nd data | 3rd data |
| --- | --- | --- | --- |
| Organization | * | * | * |
| Search Key | (Start) | (SendEmail) | (End) |
| Name | (Start) | (SendEmail) | (End) |
| Action | Wait (Sleep) | Email | Wait (Sleep) |
| EMail Address | - | admin@sistematika.test | - |
| Mail Template | - | Canceling document information | - |

> You need to specify your own target e-mail address for the 2nd data

Next, we need to set up the transition and the condition. On the **Node** tab, ensure that you are in the **(Start)** node or activity. Navigate to the **Transition** tab, and then add and save the following information:

| Field\Data | 1st data | 2nd data |
|---|---|---|
| Organization | * | * |
| Next Node | (SendEmail) | (End) |
| Sequence | 100 | 200 |
| Description | Hempel China cancellation docs | - |

We are now setting the condition. On the **Transition** tab, be sure to move your active record to the records that have **(SendEmail)** in their **Next Node** fields. We then need to navigate to the **Condition** tab. Add and save the following information:

| Field\Data | 1st data | 2nd data | 3rd data |
|---|---|---|---|
| Sequence | 10 | 20 | 30 |
| And/Or | Or | Or | Or |
| Column | C_BPartner_ID (Shown **C_BPartner_ID_Business Partner** in the option list) | IsSOTrx (Shown **IsSOTrx_Sales Transaction** in the option list) | C_DocType_ID (Shown **C_DocType_ID_Document Type** in the option list) |
| Operation | = | = | = |
| Value | 1000003 | N | 1000016 |

Note:

- In the author's ADempiere installation, the value **1000003** is the internal ID for **Hempel China Limited**. To determine this value, open the **Business Partner** window and point your record to **Hempel China Limited**. Double-click in the Record Info area, and you will get information such as **C_BPartner - C_BPartner_ID=1000003**.
- Internally, both the **Purchase Order** and **Sales Order** window persist its information in the **C_Order** table (check the **Record Info** in both of these windows). The internal difference between these windows is the information in the **IsSOTrx** field. With IsSOTrx = N (which means that this is not a sales transaction), we just instruct the system to process this workflow for the **Purchase Order** window only.

- **1000016** is the internal ID of the **Purchase Order** document type in the author's ADempiere installation.

Next, we need to set the transition from **(SendEmail)** to the **(End)** node. Go back to the **Node** tab, set your active record to **(SendEmail)**, and navigate to the **Transition** tab. Add and save the following information:

1. Set the **Organization** field to **\***.
2. Set the **Next Node** field to **(End)**.

With this configuration, the flow would be:

1. If the purchase order document is canceled in the purchase order window and the business partner is Hempel China Limited:

    **(Start)** → **(SendEmail)** → **(End)**

2. If the purchase order document is canceled and the business partner is not Hempel China Limited:

    **(Start)** → **(End)**

You are almost done. The last thing to do is to navigate to the **Workflow** tab, set the **Start Node** field to **(Start)**, and save it. Click on the **Validate Workflow** button, and ensure that you get an **OK** message on the bottom left side of this window.

## Testing the document value workflow

We need to create the purchase order document, and then complete and void this document.

Open the **Menu | Requisition-to-Invoice | Purchase Order** window. In the **Purchase Order** tab, add and save the following information:

1. Set the **Organization** field to **Shirt**.
2. Set the **Target Document Type** field to **Purchase Order**.
3. Set the **Date Ordered** and **Date Promised** field to *today*.
4. Set the **Business Partner** field to **Hempel China Limited**.
5. Set the **Price List** field to **Purchase PL**.

Navigate to the **PO Line** tab, then add and save the following information:

1. Set the **Product** field to **PA Fabric Red**.
2. Set the **Quantity** field to **500**.

Leave the other fields unchanged. On saving this PO Line record, the total value for this PO will be 1900. Finalize these tasks by completing this document.

To cancel this document, on the **Purchase Order** tab, click on the **Close** button. This will display a **Document Action** confirmation window. In the **Document Action** field, click on the option list, set it to **Void**, and then click on the **OK** button.

Take a look at your **Workflow Process** window. Check the, newest record, and then navigate to the **Activity** tab. The author's system showed the following output:

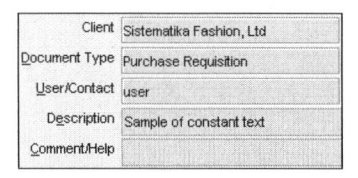

| | |
|---|---|
| Client | Sistematika Fashion, Ltd |
| Document Type | Purchase Requisition |
| User/Contact | user |
| Description | Sample of constant text |
| Comment/Help | |

We will also check the e-mail that was delivered to our manager. This e-mail will contain a notification and a PDF file attachment, which contains the voided purchase order document.

# Document value logic format

In the previous example, we put **@docstatus@=VO** in the **Document Value Logic** field. This is the basis of the document value logic format. We can divide this format into three parts, as follows:

- **Document Value**: In this example, the value is **@docstatus@**
- **Operator**: In this example, the value is **=**
- **Evaluation Value**: In this example, the values is **VO**

The following sections provide us with additional details.

## Document and Evaluation Value

When entering the condition in the logic format condition for both the Document Value and Evaluation Value parts, we can enter:

- A value taken from the ADempiere context (check all of the available context variables in the **Tools | Preference** window, and navigate to the **Context** tab) or a value taken from an ADempiere table field. In general, to get the value from the context, for example **#AD_Org_Name**, you will enter **@#AD_Org_Name@**. If you need to get a value from the **DocStatus** field from the **C_Order** table (check the Record Info in the Purchase Order window), you would enter **@docstatus@**.

- Constant value (like **VO** in our case).

Next, we will introduce you to the operator.

## Operator

Here, we can use several types of operands. The following is an operator list and the meaning of the operands:

| Operator | Description |
|---|---|
| ! | not equal |
| = | equal |
| ^ | not equal |
| > | bigger than |
| < | lesser than |

You can create your own logic format to suits your needs. You can familiarize yourself with these rules.

## Multiple logic

*In the previous example, it seems that we are only comparing two values (a single criterion). Does the document value logic support multiple logic, such as comparing more than one criterion?*

Yes, definitely. You need to use a logical operator between the logic, as shown in the following table:

| Operator | Description |
|---|---|
| \| | or |
| & | And |

If you need to fulfill a requirement such as: "*please execute this workflow while the document status is either complete or draft*", you would enter:

**@docstatus@=CO|@docstatus@=DR**

in the document value logic, and it will work for you.

## SQL document value logic format

Somebody from the class course just shouts out:

> *The previous format is not human-readable. I could misinterpret this format. An operand like @ and | could make me crazy. Is there any other easier format when writing document value logic?*

There is an alternative way of entering document value logic. This logic, has a clear enough format. For example, we were previously entering **@docstatus@=CO**. In addition to entering those phrases, you can enter it as **SQL=DOCSTATUS = 'CO'**. With this syntax, ADempiere executes this workflow into an active purchase order document that has a document status of **CO** (means Complete).

While writing this new format, you have to ensure the following things:

- Prefix your statement with **SQL=**
- You need to be aware of spaces when writing this phrase, especially if you have multiple logical statements

The format **@docstatus@=CO|@docstatus@=DR** can be replaced with:

**SQL=DOCSTATUS = 'CO' OR DOCSTATUS='DR'**

You can enter a complex criteria such as the following:

**SQL=(DOCSTATUS = 'CO' OR DOCSTATUS = 'DR') AND (TOTALLINES >= 500)**

This means that ADempiere will perform internal checks if this purchase order document has a draft or complete document status, and the total value of this purchase order is more than 500, and will execute this workflow only if all of these conditions are true.

## Summary

Workflow is defined as a step-by-step activity to complete a task that involves both, people and a system. As a default, all of the documents in ADempiere (for example, Purchase Requisition, Purchase Order, MM Receipt, and so on) are automatically workflow-enabled, and the standard workflow is easy to extend or modify.

To introduce you to the workflow, we worked on configuring a general type of workflow. Because all of the nodes executed in this workflow require user interaction, there was nothing to be done internally by ADempiere when processing this workflow.

We set activities via *nodes* in the ADempiere workflow. In this activity, we set up an action. When processing the nodes, we set up who is responsible for performing this activity.

We followed this with a case study, which showed you how to set up an approval workflow that utilizes the User Choice action. We provided information on how ADempiere finds a person who is responsible for setting the approval action.

We monitored the progress of the workflow. ADempiere provides a Workflow Process window, which shows the status of each of the nodes. When monitoring, we can also perform the cancellation of a running workflow.

Next, we extended our example, to utilize an e-mail notification, executing an application process type of node, and setting a variable. We revealed how to configure this type of node, and gave some examples of how these workflows work.

On saving any data or document in the ADempiere system, the system has a feature to monitor a new value that has been inserted or updated. Based on this value, we can initiate a workflow activity. We called this procedure the Document Value workflow. There are two ways of configuring the document value workflow, and we saw both of these.

We will discuss the Info and Reporting capabilities in our next chapter. That chapter will tell us how to get information and how to configure reports in ADempiere.

# 10
# Reporting Management

So far, you have practiced entering documents that simulate a common manufacturing business processes. After entering our documents, we could take a print-out and examine the results from the standard predefined reports provided by ADempiere. On producing reports, internally, ADempiere reads some configuration settings, retrieves information from databases, and then displays the requested reports.

Furthermore, with all of the accounting facts/GL journal entries generated, we can analyze the company's performance, by creating a financial statement such as a Balance Sheet, Profit and Loss statement, and other types of financial reports.

In this chapter, we will learn what type of configurations are involved in producing standard reports and financial reports, and provide you with some preliminary information on the Info window feature.

In this chapter, we will take a look at:

- Reports and printing
- Customizing reports
- Financial reporting
- The Info window

Based on this information, you can alter the standard reports provided and make them fit to your organization's needs.

*Reporting Management*

# Introduction to the ADempiere standard printing feature

For each of the standard ADempiere windows, you will see a standard toolbar, which contains icons such as the ones shown in following screenshot:

From the left-hand side to the right-hand side of the previous screenshot, the names of the buttons in the toolbar are:

- **Report**
- **Archived Documents/Reports**
- **Print Preview**
- **Print**

You can refer to the *Other tasks* section under the *Performing tasks* heading in Chapter 2, *Exploring the ADempiere Client and Performing Tasks*, for the preliminary explanation of these buttons. We will show examples of the use of these buttons in following sections.

# Accessing the Report button

The main purpose of this button is to display columnar information for a selected document in the window.

*Log in with user ID admin,* using **Sistematika Fashion, Ltd Admin** as the role, and **Shirt** as the organization. Open the **Menu | Requisition-to-Invoice | Purchase Order** window. Having performed the activities in the earlier chapters, you will already have a number of purchase order documents. Just select one of the available records (the first purchase order document is recommended), and then click on the **Report** button.

After clicking on the **Report** button, in the author's installation, we will get an *order header* report similar to the following screenshot:

| ADempiere | | | Order | | | | | Page 1(1,1) of 8(1,8) |
|---|---|---|---|---|---|---|---|---|
| **Parameter:** *Purchase Order = 800000* | | | | | | | | |
| Document No | Order Reference | Description | Target Doc Type | Self-Service | Date Ordered | Date Promised | Business Partner | |
| 800000 | | | Purchase Order | X | 09/29/2009 | 09/29/2009 | Hempel China Limited | |

## Working with the Drill down feature

The purpose of this feature is to provide detailed information about a certain column.

In the report in the previous screenshot, you can see underlined information in the **Target Doc Type** and **Business Partner** columns. Your own report may have a lot of underlined information.

Using the Drill down feature, you can double-click on the underlined information to see a report providing the detailed information for the selected information. For example, in the *order header* report that we have seen in the previous screenshot, the **Business Partner** column has **Hempel China Limited** underlined. Double-clicking this information will show you a report containing detailed information about the **Hempel China Limited** business partner.

> This feature is similar to the **Zoom** feature (refer to the *Field context menu* section of Chapter 2, *Exploring the ADempiere Client and Performing Tasks*). The difference is that the **Zoom** feature provides detailed information by opening a window, whereas Drill down provides detailed information by showing a report.

## Working with the Drill across feature

The purpose of this feature is to see the list of documents created, using, or having a reference to certain data.

For our example, open the **Menu | Partner Relations | Business Partner Rules | Business Partner** window and find **Hempel China Limited**. Click on the **Report** button. At the top of this report, you will have a drop-down of **Drill** options, as shown in the following screenshot:

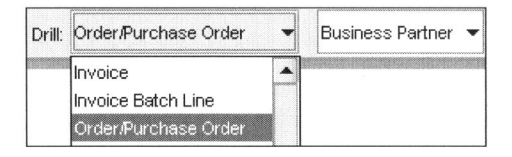

There are many options available in the **Drill** field. Select **Order/Purchase Order** for our example, and then double-click on the report line information. You will get a list of purchase order reports that were created using the **Hempel China Limited** business partner.

*Reporting Management*

> This feature is similar to the **Zoom Across** feature (refer to *More examples on the use of Zoom Across* section of Chapter 2, *Implementing the ADempiere Client and Performing Tasks*). The difference is that the Zoom Across feature provides a list of information by opening a window, whereas Drill Across provides a list of information by showing a report.

## Printing a report

Reopen the **Menu | Requisition-to-Invoice | Purchase Order** window. In this purchase order document, you can take a **Print preview** or **Print** of this document. We will take a look at the standard toolbar available in the Report form, and introduce you to the print format template, in the following sections.

## Introducing print format templates

The print format template is a feature for managing a template report in ADempiere.

Take a **Print preview** of the purchase order document. After the **Print preview**, there will be a Report form available. Check the available toolbar at the top of this report. On the right-hand side of the **Drill** field, a print format template, which is used to generate this report, will be shown, as follows:

Drill: ▼   Order_Header ** 1000000 ** &Copy Record 192611 ▼ 🛠

In the screenshot, from the left-hand side to the right-hand side are the:

- Drill across options
- Print format template
- Customize report button

In the author's installation, the print format template used to generate the purchase order report is **Order_Header ** 1000000 ** &Copy Record 192611**.

> The print format template shown in your installation will be different. It will show **Order_Header ** 1000000 ** &Copy Record** and a number other than **192611**.

Next, we will take a look at the **Order_Header ** 1000000 ** &Copy Record 192611** print format template in detail. We can open this print format template by clicking on the **Customize Report** button or by accessing the **Menu | System Admin | General Rules | Printing | Print Format** window. This window contains four tabs: **Print Format**, **Display Order**, **Sort Order**, and **Format Item**. The explanation of these tabs is as follows:

- **Print Format** tab contains the configuration for:
    - **Table**: This is the source table from the application dictionary.
    - **Form**: Select this checkbox for pre-formatted reports of documents. Any report that has master-detail information has this checkbox selected. Deselecting this checkbox means that a columnar list of reports is created.
    - **Print paper**: This defines the target paper for the reports.
    - **Font** and **Color**: This defines the fonts and color to be used in the reports.
    - **Copy/Create** button: This can be used to copy an existing print format, or create a new one from the existing **Table**.
- The **Display Order** tab contains all of the available fields, which come from the **Table** information in the **Print Format** tab. You can make a list of the fields that need to be shown, and create an order for these fields.
- The **Sort Order** tab defines the short order of the print format items when showing multiple records. Usually, this will be used in the detail parts of reports.
- The **Format Item** tab determines the detail format appearance when generating reports. The important points in this configuration are:
    - The **Sequence** field: The sequence not only determines the order of the on-screen appearance, but also the order in which the fields are processed for the report.
    - The **Format Type** field: You can set the following configuration:
        - **Field** information is taken from the application dictionary table column. When using **Field** as your format type, you can set a bar code format, where necessary, in the **Barcode Type** field.
        - **Image** can be used to define your own (company) logo. You can specify an image from a table column or uniform resource locator (URL).
        - **Rectangle** or **Line**.

- **Text** defines your own text. You can define standard variables to represent information. The list and the purpose of the standard variable format is as follows:
  - **@*Page@**: Current page number
  - **@*PageCount@**: Total number of pages in the report
  - **@*MultiPageInfo@**: If we have more than one page in the report, this will shown Page x of y
  - **@*ReportName@**: Print format template name
  - **@*Header@**: Print user, client and connection information
  - **@*CurrentDate@**: Print the current date
  - **@*CurrentDateTime@**: Print the current date with time
- **Print Format**. Here, you can insert another Print Format. During the display of **master-detail** information, like our Purchase Order document reports, we need to set up another print format. In the author's system, the **Order_Header ** 1000000 ** &Copy Record 192611** print format templates use the **Order_LineTax ** 1000000 ** &Copy Record 22157425** print format template as part of their report confguration. Refer to records that have **250** as their **Sequence** value. The **Order_LineTax ** 1000000 ** &Copy Record 22157425** should be used to generate order line information (detailed data of the purchase order).
- For the report's layout, you can determine the position when displaying information in the reports, by using the **Area**, **Relative Position**, **Set NL Position**, **Next Line**, **Next Page**, **Line Alignment**, **X Space** and **Y Space** fields.

## Sending e-mail, archiving reports, and exporting

After displaying the **Print Preview** for your document, you can:

- Send the report to your colleague by using the **Send Email** facility
- Make an archive of the report by using **Archived Documents/Reports**
- Export the report in various formats by using the **Export** feature

In the toolbar available, on the right-hand side of the **Customize Report** button, you can access these features by clicking on the buttons, as shown in the following screenshot:

# How the ADempiere window finds its print format templates

On executing the **Print preview** or **Print** button, internally, the ADempiere window has a mechanism to find the location of the print format templates being used, and will then produce a report using this print format template. Refer to the following sections to know which print format template is used for a certain ADempiere window.

## Purchase Order and Sales Order

In the default configuration, ADempiere windows such as Purchase Order and Sales Order will use the following procedure to find the print format template:

- *First*, it will check the **Print Format** field value in the **Menu | Performance Analysis | Accounting Rules | Document Type** window for the target document type.
- *Second*, if there is no print format found in the first step, it will check the value in the **Menu | System Admin | General Rules | Printing | Print Form** window. As a standard, this form shall contain two records. The first record has the value **System** in the **Client** field, and the second has **Sistematika Fashion, Ltd**. Ensure that your active records are for **Sistematika Fashion, Ltd**, click on the **Grid Toggle** button (to show a detailed record), and then find the **Order Print Format** field.
- If there is no value in the **Order Print Format** field, ADempiere will raise a **No Document Print Format defined** error message.

## Invoice

If you are working with an ADempiere window such as:

- Invoice (Vendor)
- Invoice (Customer)

*Reporting Management*

then the following procedure will be used to find the print format template:

- *First*, it will check the **Invoice Print Format** field value in the **Customer** tab of the **Menu | Partner Relations | Business Partner Rules | Business Partner** window.

- *Second*, if there is no print format available in the first step, it will check the **Print Format** field value in the **Document Type** window for the target document type.

- *Third*, if there is no print format found in the second step, then it will check for a value in the **Print Form** window. Ensure that your active record is for **Sistematika Fashion, Ltd**, and click on the **Grid Toggle** button to show the detail record, and then find the **Invoice Print Format** field.

- If there is no value in the **Invoice Print Format** field in the third step, ADempiere will raise a **No Document Print Format defined** error message.

# Payment

When working with the **Payment** window, the two fields (or information) that have a direct relationship with the printing process are:

- Bank Account
- Tender Type (such as Check, Credit Card, Direct Debit, or Direct Deposit)

On printing the document in this **Payment** window, ADempiere will check the **Check Print Format** field value in the **Menu | System Admin | Organization Rules | Bank** window. The following procedure will be used to find the print format template:

- Find the target bank information in the **Bank** tab, and choose your account number on the **Account** tab.

- In the existing record on the **Account** tab, navigate to the **Bank Account Document** tab, select the record that has the appropriate **Payment Rule** such as Check, Credit Card, Direct Debit, or Direct Deposit (as specified in the **Tender Type** field, when entering the payment information) and examine the **Check Print Format** field.

- If there are no values in these fields, then ADempiere will raise a **No Document Print Format defined** error message.

## Shipment (Customer) and Material Receipt

To take a print of this window, ADempiere will carry out the following procedure:

- *First*, it will check the **Print Format** field value in the **Document Type** window for the targeted document type.

- *Second*, if there is no print format found in the first step, then it will check for a value in the **Print Form** window. Ensure that your active records is for **Sistematika Fashion, Ltd**, click on the **Grid Toggle** button to show the detailed records, and then find the **Shipment Print Format** field.

- If there are no values in this field, ADempiere will raise a **No Document Print Format defined** error message.

## Customizing Reports

In the available print format template, we are free to modify the template to suit our needs. We will play with our **Purchase Order** document in the **Purchase Order** window, and customize the print format template, which finally shows a report similar to the following screenshot:

*Reporting Management*

Compare this report layout with the current, default print out of your purchase order document. There will be a difference in the appearance of the:

- Logo
- Header information composition
- Layout of the detailed order information
- Amount in words

We will try to alter the standard, default format and create a report in the format shown in the previous screenshot.

## Creating new print format templates

As mentioned previously, there were two print format templates involved while producing the Purchase Order document reports. In the author's installation, the templates were:

- **Order_Header ** 1000000 ** &Copy Record 192611**
- **Order_LineTax ** 1000000 ** &Copy Record 22157425**

Take a look at the following screenshot:

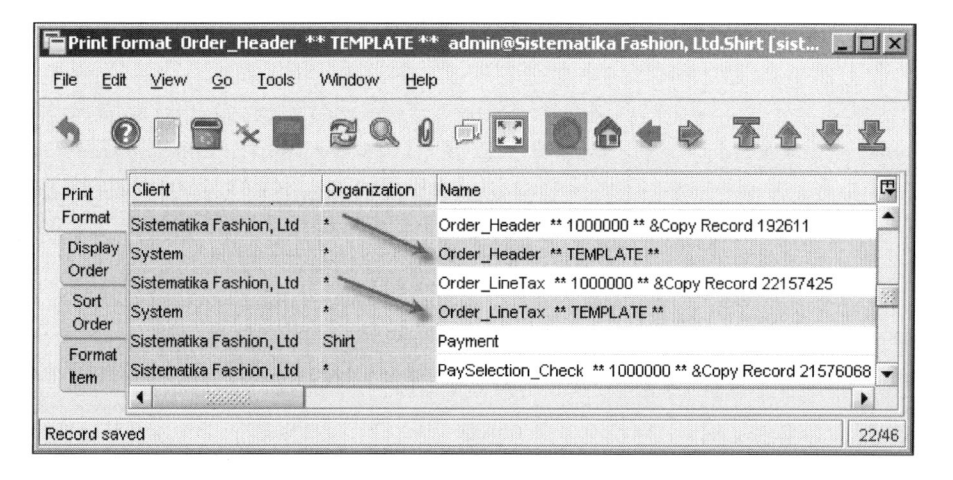

The first print format (**Order_Header ** 1000000 ** &Copy Record 192611**) is just a duplicate print format of **Order_Header ** TEMPLATE **,** whereas the third print format (**Order_LineTax ** 1000000 ** &Copy Record 22157425**) is a duplicate of **Order_LineTax ** TEMPLATE **.** We need to create another print format based on these templates.

## Duplicate Order Line print format

Open the **Menu | System Admin | General Rules | Printing | Print Format** window. In the **Print Format** tab, click on the **Lookup Record** button, enter **Order_LineTax ** TEMPLATE **** in the **Name** field, and click on the **OK** button. With the existing record, you need to:

1. Copy this available record to a new one by pressing the *Shift + F2* key combination.
2. Set the **Name** field to **Order Line Sistematika**, and then save this record.

With this activity, we just create duplicate information in the **Print Format** tab but not the configuration in **Display Order**, **Sort Order**, and **Format Item** tabs.

To duplicate all three of the tabs' information or configuration, in this **Order Line Sistematika** record, you need to perform the following:

1. Click on the **Copy/Create** button.
2. Enter **Order_LineTax ** TEMPLATE **** in the **Print Format** field, and then click on the **OK** button.
3. Upon processing this procedure, the **Name** field value will be overridden by the system, and we will need to re-enter a value in the **Name** field back to **Order Line Sistematika**.

We will continue our activity and create a duplicate order header print format.

## Duplicate Order Header print format

In the **Print Format** tab, click on the **Lookup Record** button, enter **Order_Header ** TEMPLATE **** in the **Name** field, and then click on the **OK** button. With existing records, you need to perform the following:

1. Copy the available record to a new one by pressing the *Shift + F2* key combination.
2. Set the **Name** field to **Order Header Sistematika**, and then click on the **Save** button.

Duplicate the remaining three tabs' information or configuration by performing the following:

1. Click on the **Copy/Create** button.
2. Enter **Order_Header ** TEMPLATE **** in the **Print Format** field, and then click on the **OK** button.
3. Change the value in the **Name** field to **Order Header Sistematika**.

The next important thing that we need to configure is to set up our new **Order Header Sistematika** template to use the **Order Line Sistematika** print format template. To achieve this, you need to perform the following:

1. Navigate to the **Format Item** tab, and find a record that has **250** in the **Sequence** field and **Order** in the **Name** field.
2. Click on the **Grid Toggle** button to show the detailed information, and change the **Included Print Format** configuration from **Order_LineTax ** TEMPLATE **** to **Order Line Sistematika**.
3. Finalize the task by clicking on the **Save** button.

> This **Order Header Sistematika** print format template requires the **Order Line Sistematika** print format template as a part of its configuration. That is why we need to create the **Order Line Sistematika** print format template first.

## Setting the purchase order default print format

We need to set the **Order Header Sistematika** print format as a default template for our Purchase Order document printing.

We can do this by opening the **Menu | System Admin | General Rules | Printing | Print Form** window (not the **Print Format** window). There will be two records available in this window. Make sure that your active record has **Sistematika Fashion, Ltd** as the **Client**, and select **Order Header Sistematika** in the **Order Print Format** field, as shown in the following screenshot:

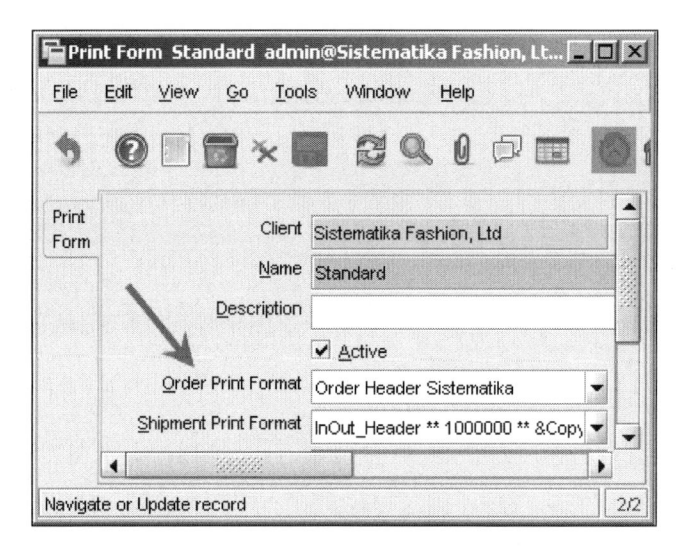

# Altering the logo

The default ADempiere installation comes with the `adempiere_5a.jpg` picture example. You can access this file in the `C:\Adempiere\images` folder. To practice, we will use this image for our company logo.

> ADempiere recognizes images that are in **JPG** or **GIF** file format.

Open the **Purchase Order** window. Select the first Purchase Order document, and click on the **Print Preview** button to create a report for this document. With this preview, click on the **Customize Report** button, and you will see **Order Header Sistematika** print format records in the **Print Format** window.

Navigate to the **Format Item** tab, and find the record with the following condition:

- **Sequence** of **10**
- **Name** of **Logo**

Actually, this is the first record in the **Format Item** tab. Click on the **Grid Toggle** button, and change the values of the following fields:

1. **Image URL** to `file:C://Adempiere//images//adempiere_5a.jpg`.
2. **Max Width** to **300**.
3. **Max Height** to **50**.

Note: The **Max Width** and **Max Height** configuration will depend upon the size (in pixels) of the image.

Save and close the **Print Format** window.

> After some modifications to the **Print Format**, you will be able to see the changes in your current print preview.

*Reporting Management*

# Altering another header layout

There are many things here that need to be done for our example. We shall divide these activities into several tasks. First, click on the **Customize Report** button. Navigate to the **Format Item** tab, and perform the following changes:

| Sequence and Name or Info | Activities and description |
| --- | --- |
| 20. Org Address | Deselect the **One Line Only** checkbox.<br>Note: We need to print addresses on a separate line. |
| 100. Invoice Name<br>110. Invoice Name 2<br>120. Invoice Title<br>130. Invoice Contact Name<br>140. Invoice Address | Deselected the **Active** checkbox.<br>Note: There is no need to show this invoice information for our practice example. |

We need to move the **Date Ordered** information, and set it after the **Invoice Address** information. Navigate to the **Display Order** tab. There will be two parts available: **Available Choices** and **Sequence**. Pay attention to the **Sequence** part, and move the **Date Ordered** by clicking on the green up arrow. Make sure that you get the final sequence shown in the following screenshot:

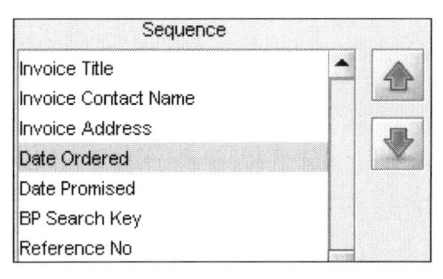

| Sequence |
| --- |
| Invoice Title |
| Invoice Contact Name |
| Invoice Address |
| Date Ordered |
| Date Promised |
| BP Search Key |
| Reference No |

Save the changes, and then navigate back to the **Format Item** tab.

| | |
| --- | --- |
| 150. Date Ordered | Set **Print Text** to **Date Order    :**<br>Deselect **Relative Position** checkbox<br>Select **Set NL Position** checkbox<br>Set **X Position** to **340**<br>Set **Y Position** to **100**<br>Set **Print Font** to *blank* (remove the contents)<br>Note: This activity is to print the **Date Ordered** information in the correct place |
| 160. Date Promised | Set **X Position** to **0**<br>Set **Y Position** to **0**<br>Deselect **Set NL Position** checkbox<br>Select **Relative Position** checkbox<br>Select **Next Line**<br>Note: This will instruct ADempiere to print this information below the **Date Ordered** information |

Navigate to the **Display Order** tab. Move the **Payment Term** information to after the **Sales Representative** information. Ensure that the **Sequence** is as shown in the following screenshot:

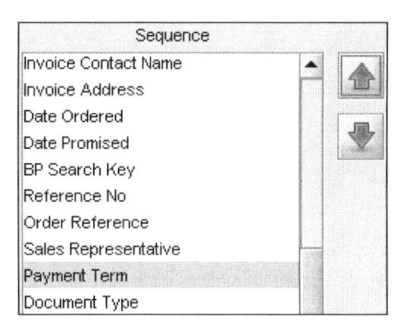

| Sequence |
|---|
| Invoice Contact Name |
| Invoice Address |
| Date Ordered |
| Date Promised |
| BP Search Key |
| Reference No |
| Order Reference |
| Sales Representative |
| Payment Term |
| Document Type |

Save this change and then navigate back to the **Format Item** tab.

| Sequence and Name or Info | Activities and description |
|---|---|
| 210. Payment Term | **Print Text** to **Payment Term** :<br>Set **Area** to **Header**<br>Set **X Space** to **0**<br>Select **Next Line** checkbox<br>Note: This will instruct ADempiere to print this information below the **Sales Representative** info in the header area |
| 230. Document No | Set **Print Text** to **No:**<br>Set **X Space** to **10**<br>Note: This will add a prefix to the document number |
| 270. Currency<br>280. Grand Total<br>290. Payment Term Note<br>300. Document Type Note | Deselect the **Active** checkbox<br>Note: There is no need to display this information |
| We need to set the amount in words information. In the **Format Item** tab, click on the **New** button and add this information | Set **Organization** to *<br>Set **Sequence** to **310** (default value)<br>Set **Name** to **Amount in words**<br>Set **Print Label Suffix** to **only**<br>Set **Format Type** to **Field**<br>Set **Column** to **AmtInWords**<br>Set **Area** to **Content**<br>Set **Field Alignment** to **Leading (left)**<br>Set **X Space** to **10**<br>Set **Print Font** to *blank* (remove the contents) |

## Altering the detailed purchase order layout

Next, we will continue with our activity to re-organize the detailed information. In the **Format Item** tab, navigate to the record that has **260** as the **Sequence** and **Order** as the **Name**.

> Initially, the **Sequence** for **Order** was **250**. Now, it has become **260** because of our previous activities to change the field ordering in **Display Order**.

Click on the **Grid Toggle** button to show the detailed information, and navigate to the **Included Print Format** field. Right-click on this field, and select the **Zoom** button. Now, you are already in the **Order Line Sistematika** print format.

Navigate to the **Display Order** tab. This tab contains the **Available Choices** and **Sequence** information. We need to include some information listed in the **Available Choices**, and then set the correct information ordering.

In the **Available Choices** list, move the **Line No** and **Product Key** to the **Sequence** area by clicking on the right green arrow ( ).

In the **Sequence** area, move the **Description** and **Name** field to **Available Choices**. There is no need to show this information. Perform the appropriate ordering, and ensure that the information is ordered as shown in the following screenshot:

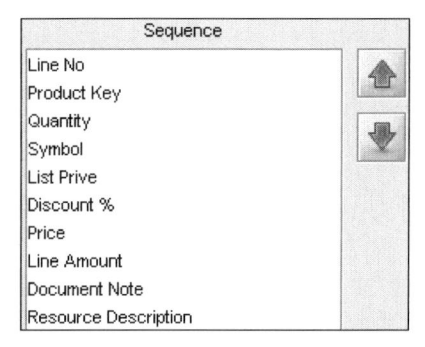

| Sequence |
| --- |
| Line No |
| Product Key |
| Quantity |
| Symbol |
| List Prive |
| Discount % |
| Price |
| Line Amount |
| Document Note |
| Resource Description |

Next, navigate to the **Format Item** tab, and deselect the **Suppress Null** checkbox for the record that has a **Sequence** of **60** and a **Name** of **Discount %**.

The task is now complete.

> Upon closing the **Print Format** window (for both **Order Line Sistematika** and **Order Header Sistematika**), you will not be able to see the recent changes (especially for changes in the **Order Line Sistematika** print format). You need to execute the **Menu | System Admin | General Rules | Cache Reset** process.

With all of the changes to both print format templates, you will now have the print preview report shown previously.

# Financial Reporting

Every organization needs some financial reports in order to analyze their business. Based on the available financial data in the system, ADempiere can help the organization by producing reports such as Balance Sheets, Profit and Loss Statements, Statements of Account, and other types of financial reports.

When creating the new Client, these types of reports are not available by default. This is because they are heavily dependent on the Chart of Accounts, which should be unique for each company. You need to perform some configuration to create your own financial reporting format.

ADempiere provides the following list of windows for working with financial reporting:

- Report Line Set
- Report Column Set
- Reporting Hierarchy
- Financial Report

When looking at financial reports, they generally have two-dimensional information. These dimensions are mapped into columns and lines (or rows), as shown in the following screenshot:

|   | A | B | C | D | E | F | G |
|---|---|---|---|---|---|---|---|
| 1 |   | Beginning Balance | Debit Transaction | Credit Transaction | Period Balance | Ending Balance | Growth |
| 2 | Asset | 100 | 10 | 5 |   |   |   |
| 3 | Liabilities | 200 | 20 | 10 |   |   |   |
| 4 | Owner Equity | 300 | 30 | 15 |   |   |   |
| 5 | Total | 600 | 60 | 30 |   |   |   |

*Reporting Management*

The **Asset** row (mentioned in row **2** in the previous screenshot) and the other row's information should be configured in the **Report Line Set** window, whereas the **Beginning Balance** column (which is mentioned in the **B** column in the above figure) and the other column's information should be configured in the **Report Column Set** window. Keeping this format in mind, we will now create some report configurations.

## Working with the Report Line Set window

You can create financial reports that contain information on your list of accounts, according to your needs. In our example, we will create a configuration to display only the **Asset**, **Liabilities**, **Owner Equity**, and **Total** report line information.

Open the **Menu | Performance Analysis | Financial Reporting | Report Line Set** window. This window has three tabs: **Report Line Set**, **Report Line**, and **Report Source**.

In the **Report Line Set** tab, click on the **New** button, and set the following information:

1. Set **Organization** to *.
2. Set **Name** to **Account Information**.

Navigate to the **Report Line** tab. Add and save the following information:

| Field\Data   | 1st data      | 2nd data      | 3rd data      |
|---|---|---|---|
| Organization | *             | *             | *             |
| Name         | Asset         | Liabilities   | Owner Equity  |
| Sequence     | 10            | 20            | 30            |
| Line Type    | Segment Value | Segment Value | Segment Value |
| Posting Type | blank         | blank         | blank         |
| Amount Type  | blank         | blank         | blank         |

> *Here we just set Asset, Liabilities, and Owner Equity as a name. There is no account (from chart of accounts) information connected with this information. Is there any other configuration required?*

Yes, we need to supply some configuration in the **Report Source** tab for *each record* in the **Report Line** tab. Add and save the following information:

| Reports Source Fields\ Report Line records | Asset      | Liabilities    | Owner Equity                   |
|---|---|---|---|
| Report Line    | Asset      | Liabilities    | Owner Equity                   |
| Type           | Account    | Account        | Account                        |
| Account Element | 1 – Asset | 2 – Liabilities | 3 – Owner's Equity/Net Worth |

> Here, if you set **1 – Asset** as an **Account Element**, you have just selected one account that has a Summary Account type. As you can see in our **Account Element** window, this **1 – Asset** account element has many summary accounts (non-posting) and transaction accounts (posting), that point to it. This account configuration means that the **1 – Asset** account shall contain a summed-up value taken from listed posting and non-posting accounts belonging to **1 – Asset**.

We need to set the **Total** information in the **Report Line** tab. This effort is designed to sum up the values of **Asset**, **Liabilities**, and **Owner Equity**. Add and save the following information:

| Field\Data | 4th data |
|---|---|
| Organization | * |
| Name | Total |
| Sequence | 40 |
| Line Type | Calculation |
| Calculation | Add Range (Op1 to Op2) |
| Operand 1 | Asset |
| Operand 2 | Owner Equity |

There is no need to configure the **Report Source** for this record.

# Working with the Report Column Set window

We now need to configure the Beginning Balance, Debit Transaction, Credit Transaction, and Ending Balance for our financial reports example. Open the **Menu | Performance Analysis | Financial Reporting | Report Column Set** window. This window contains two tabs: **Report Column Set**, and **Report Column**.

We create some configurations with the following conditions:

- Beginning Balance means the total balance in the previous period
- Debit Transaction means the total debit transaction in the active period
- Credit Transaction means the total credit transaction in the active period
- Period Balance means the total balance in the active period (net balance of Debit Transaction and Credit Transaction)
- Ending Balance means the ending balance up to and including active period (Beginning Balance plus Period Balance value)
- Growth means the percentage difference between the Ending Balance and the Beginning Balance

*Reporting Management*

With your **Report Column Set** as the active tab, add and save the following information:

1. Set **Organization** to **\***.
2. Set **Name** to **List of account balances**.

Navigate to the **Report Column** tab, add and save the following information:

| Field\Data | 1st data | 2nd data | 3rd data | 4th data | 5th data |
|---|---|---|---|---|---|
| Organization | * | * | * | * | * |
| Name | Beginning Balance | Debit Transaction | Credit Transaction | Period Balance | Ending Balance |
| Sequence | 10 | 20 | 30 | 40 | 50 |
| Posting Type | Actual | Actual | Actual | Actual | Actual |
| Amount Type | Total Balance | Period Debit Only | Period Credit Only | Period Balance | Total Balance |
| Column Type | Relative Period | Relative Period | Relative Period | Relative Period | Relative Period |
| Relative Period | -1 | 0 | 0 | 0 | 0 |

> The relative period **0** means the active period, and **-1** means 1 period prior to the active period. You can also specify **1**, which means 1 period after the active period.

We need to set up deviation and growth information. **Deviation** data is needed to calculate **Growth** information. The deviation itself is taken by subtracting the Ending Balance value from the Beginning Balance value. There is no need to print this deviation data within our reports.

In the **Report Column** tab, add the following data:

| Field\Data | 6th data | 7th data |
|---|---|---|
| Organization | * | * |
| Name | Deviation | Growth (%) |
| Printed | *deselected* | *selected* |
| Sequence | 60 | 70 |
| Posting Type | Actual | Actual |
| Amount Type | blank | blank |
| Column Type | Calculation | Calculation |

[ 356 ]

| Field\Data  | 6th data            | 7th data                 |
|-------------|---------------------|--------------------------|
| Calculation | Subtract (Op1-Op2)  | Percentage (Op1 of Op2)  |
| Operand 1   | Ending Balance      | Deviation                |
| Operand 2   | Beginning Balance   | Beginning Balance        |

> If you have the budget transaction, you could set the **Budget** posting type and create the actual against budget transaction comparison report.

# Creating a Financial Report

In the previous activities, we created one report line set in the **Report Line Set** window, and one report column set in the **Report Column Set** window. As per your requirements, you can create many report line sets (that use a certain account) and report column sets, to fulfill your financial analysis requirements.

Following these activities, you can create a financial report based on the combination of report line set and report column set.

For example, we can create an **Asset, Liabilities and Equity list** report. Open the **Menu | Performance Analysis | Financial Reporting | Financial Report** window. This window contains only one tab. Click on the **New** button, and then add and save the following information:

| Field             | Data                                      |
|-------------------|-------------------------------------------|
| Organization      | *                                         |
| Accounting Schema | Sistematika Fashion, Ltd UN/34 US Dollar  |
| Calendar          | Sistematika Fashion, Ltd Calendar         |
| Name              | Asset, Liabilities and Equity list        |
| Report Line Set   | Account Information                       |
| Report Column Set | List of account balances                  |

After saving this record, you can process the report immediately. Click on the **Create Report** button, and you will be shown a **Create Report** confirmation window. Proceed by clicking on the **OK** button.

In the author's installation, the report appears as follows (the actual numbers may vary with your installation, but the format generated should be the same):

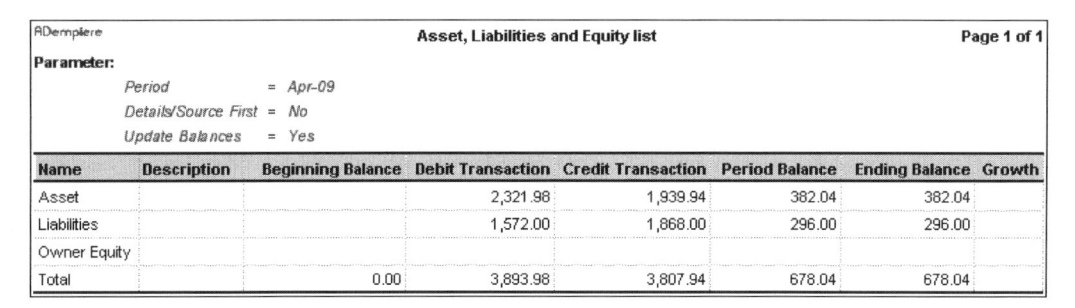

| ADempiere | | Asset, Liabilities and Equity list | | | | | Page 1 of 1 |
|---|---|---|---|---|---|---|---|
| **Parameter:** | | | | | | | |
| | Period | = Apr-09 | | | | | |
| | Details/Source First | = No | | | | | |
| | Update Balances | = Yes | | | | | |
| **Name** | **Description** | **Beginning Balance** | **Debit Transaction** | **Credit Transaction** | **Period Balance** | **Ending Balance** | **Growth** |
| Asset | | | 2,321.98 | 1,939.94 | 382.04 | 382.04 | |
| Liabilities | | | 1,572.00 | 1,868.00 | 296.00 | 296.00 | |
| Owner Equity | | | | | | | |
| Total | | 0.00 | 3,893.98 | 3,807.94 | 678.04 | 678.04 | |

Because we only have financial data for one accounting period in the author's example, there is no **Beginning Balance** or **Growth** information available. Once we have financial data for more than one accounting period, the information will be present.

> After saving this **Financial Report** record, we can utilize this record to create Asset, Liabilities, and Equity list reports in the future. There is no need to create a new Financial Report record again. Just select an available Financial Report record, click on the **Create Report** button, and you are done.

## Enabling the List Sources option

In the previous screenshot, the system has created summary reports for **Asset**, **Liabilities**, and **Owner Equity**. ADempiere has a feature to show the detailed sources of accounts involved when producing this report. In the **Asset, Liabilities and Equity list** financial report previously created, be sure to select the **List Sources** checkbox prior to executing the **Create Report** button, as shown in the following screenshot:

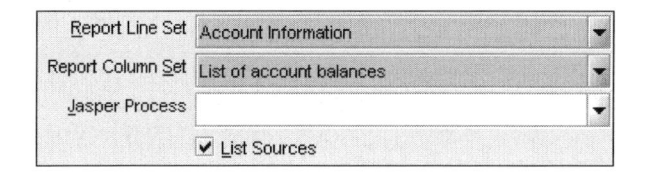

| Report Line Set | Account Information |
|---|---|
| Report Column Set | List of account balances |
| Jasper Process | |
| | ☑ List Sources |

Process the report, and you will be shown the list of posting accounts involved for the Asset, Liabilities, and Owner Equity.

# Reporting Hierarchy

Previously, we created a report summary by using all of the available financial data in the selected active periods. There are some questions raised during our implementation, such as: *how to produce this financial report for a specific business partner and/or product only?*

ADempiere has a feature to create summary reports based on the selection or criteria of available account schema element configuration. In order to determine your account schema element configuration, you can open the **Accounting Schema** window, and navigate to the **Account Schema Element** tab. In the author's ADempiere system, we get the following list of active account schema elements:

| Accounting Schema | Name | Active | Type |
|---|---|---|---|
| Sistematika Fashion, Ltd UN/34 US Dollar | Organization | ✔ | Organization |
| Sistematika Fashion, Ltd UN/34 US Dollar | Account | ✔ | Account |
| Sistematika Fashion, Ltd UN/34 US Dollar | Product | ✔ | Product |
| Sistematika Fashion, Ltd UN/34 US Dollar | BPartner | ✔ | BPartner |
| Sistematika Fashion, Ltd UN/34 US Dollar | Project | ✔ | Project |
| Sistematika Fashion, Ltd UN/34 US Dollar | Campaign | ✔ | Campaign |
| Sistematika Fashion, Ltd UN/34 US Dollar | Sales Region | ✔ | Sales Region |

You can create a summary of financial reports with a combination option of available account schema elements, such as **Organization** and **Product**. In the **Organization** and **Product** account schema element, we can determine the selection information required (such as **Shirt** for **Organization** and **S Fabric**, **S Button**, and **S Label** for **Product**).

For our example, we will create a summarized report based on only the **Product** account schema element, and involving the following list of products:

- S Fabric
- S Button
- S Label

# Configuring a specific financial report

We need to set a series of tasks (including new summary product creation, managing **Tree**, and setting up the reporting hierarchy) to fulfill this requirement. This will be explained in the subsequent sections.

## Setting up a new summary product

We need to create a summary product that is a summary of three products. Open the **Menu | Material Management | Material Management Rules | Product Category** window. Add and save the following information:

1. Set **Organization** to **\***.
2. Set **Search Key** and **Name** to **Products Summary**.

Leave the other fields unchanged. Then, add and save the following information in the **Menu | Material Management | Material Management Rules | Product** window:

| Field\Data | Data |
|---|---|
| Organization | * |
| Search Key | Summary of 3 products |
| Name | Summary of 3 products |
| Summary Level | *selected* |
| Product Category | Products Summary |
| UOM | piece |
| Product Type | Item |

Because this is a special product summary, there is no need to define the price information in the **Price** tab.

## Setting up a Summary of Products Tree

As a part of reporting configuration, we need to set up a special **Tree**. **Reporting Hierarchy** that will use this special **Tree**, while producing the summarized financial report.

Open the **Menu | System Admin | General Rules | System Rules | Tree** window. Add and save the following information:

1. Set **Organization** to **\***.
2. Set **Name** to **Summary of Products**.
3. Set **Type | Area** to **Product**.
4. Select the **All Nodes** checkbox.

We will include a list of products as a part of **Summary of Products** in the subsequent sections.

# Setting Tree Maintenance

The purpose of this effort is to include a list of products in the **Summary of Products** Tree, which was created previously. Open the **Menu | System Admin | General Rules | System Rules | Tree Maintenance** window.

Select **Summary of Products** in the **Tree** field. This window has two parts. The left-hand side is for the list of products already connected to this **Summary of Products** Tree, whereas the right-hand side is the list of available products.

The first thing that needs to be done is to move the **Summary of 3 products** to the left-hand side of this window. You can perform this task by selecting this product from the available products and then clicking on the **Add To Tree** button. Do the same thing for the **S Fabric**, **S Button**, and **S Label** products.

Next, we need to include the **S Fabric**, **S Button**, and **S Label** products in this **Summary of 3 products** product. You can perform drag-and-drop activities here. Be sure that you complete this setup, and the left-hand side must be as shown in the following screenshot:

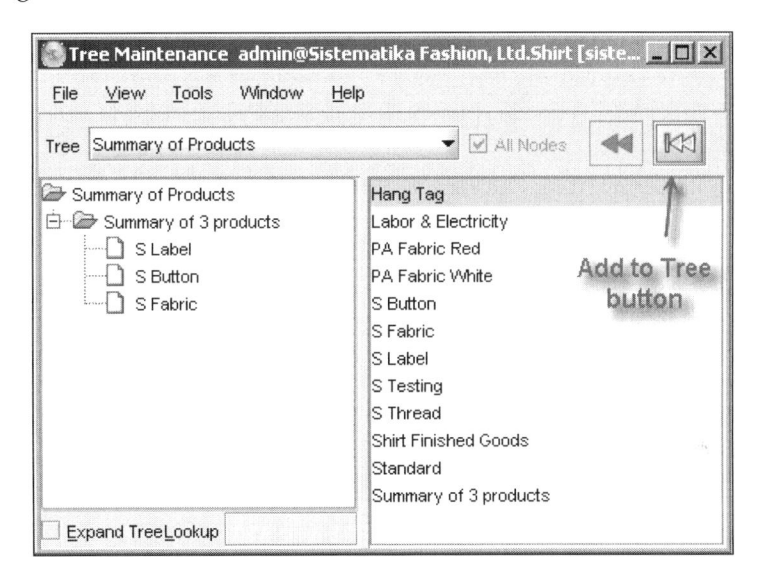

## Verifying the Summary of Products Tree

After inserting some value for the tree maintenance, you need to verify the **Summary of Products** Tree itself. Navigate to the **Tree** window, and point your records to the **Summary of Products**. Click on the **Verify Tree** button, and then click on the **OK** button in the upcoming confirmation window.

Upon successfully verifying your configuration, in the author's installation (it could vary with your installation), the following message is displayed:

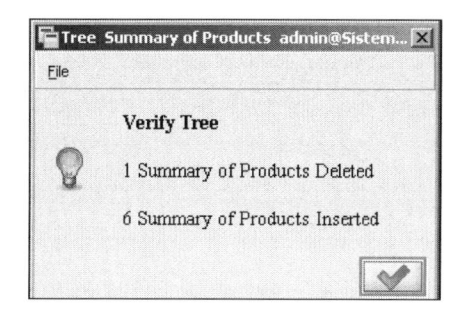

## Setting up the Summary of certain products reporting hierarchy

The last required piece of configuration is to create the Reporting Hierarchy records. The aim of this task is to configure the *tree combination* of the account schema element and apply this specific hierarchy, while creating our reports later.

Open the **Menu | Performance Analysis | Financial Reporting | Reporting Hierarchy** window. This window contains only one tab. You could add and save the following information:

1. Set **Organization** to **\***.
2. Set **Name** to **Summary of certain products**.
3. Set **Organization Tree** to **Sistematika Fashion, Ltd Organization**.
4. Set **Account Tree** to **Sistematika Fashion, Ltd Element Value**.
5. Set **Activity Tree** to **Sistematika Fashion, Ltd Activity**.
6. Set **BPartner Tree** to **Sistematika Fashion, Ltd BPartner**.
7. Set **Product Tree** to **Summary of Products**.
8. Set **Project Tree** to **Sistematika Fashion, Ltd Project**.
9. Set **Campaign Tree** to **Sistematika Fashion, Ltd Campaign**.
10. Set **Sales Region Tree** to **Sistematika Fashion, Ltd Sales Region**.

*Chapter 10*

The completed window is shown in the following screenshot:

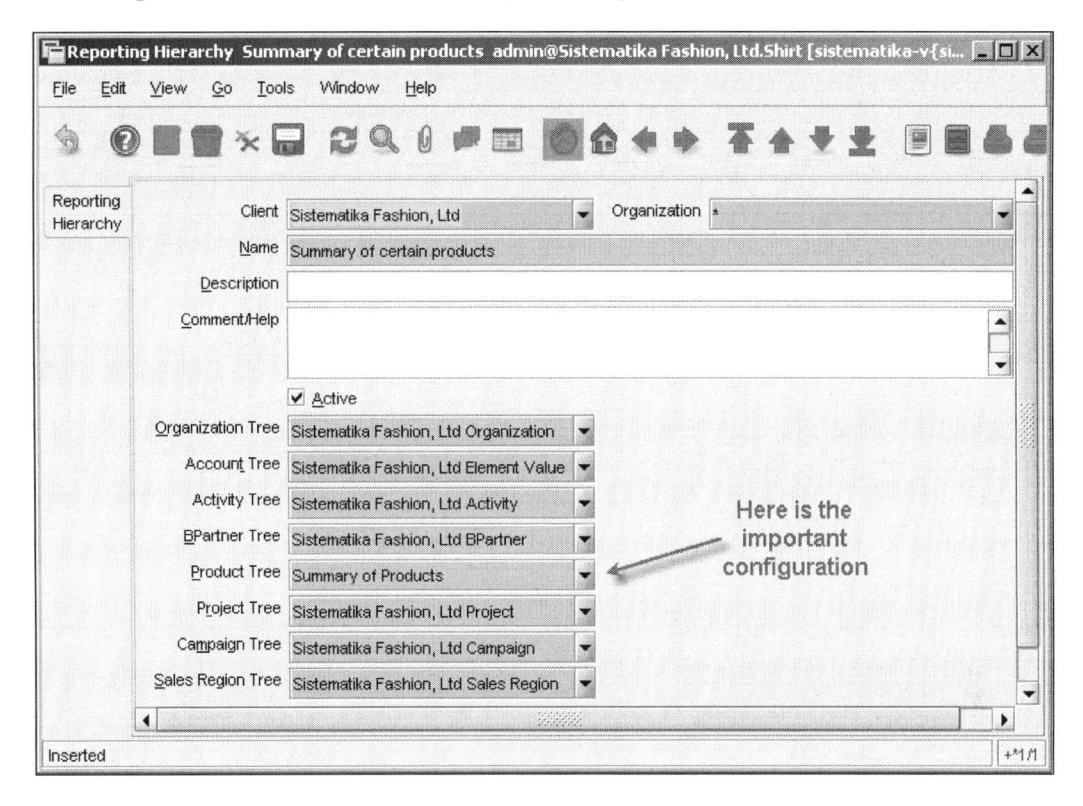

[Screenshot of Reporting Hierarchy window showing fields: Client: Sistematika Fashion, Ltd; Organization: *; Name: Summary of certain products; Description; Comment/Help; Active (checked); Organization Tree: Sistematika Fashion, Ltd Organization; Account Tree: Sistematika Fashion, Ltd Element Value; Activity Tree: Sistematika Fashion, Ltd Activity; BPartner Tree: Sistematika Fashion, Ltd BPartner; Product Tree: Summary of Products (← Here is the important configuration); Project Tree: Sistematika Fashion, Ltd Project; Campaign Tree: Sistematika Fashion, Ltd Campaign; Sales Region Tree: Sistematika Fashion, Ltd Sales Region]

> With the exception of **Product Tree**, there is only one option available when setting up these fields. When setting up the **Product Tree**, ensure that you select the correct one.

## Testing our sample reporting hierarchy reports

Well, the configuration is done. We now need to create a sample report with this new configuration.

Open the **Financial Report** window. We will use our **Asset, Liabilities and Equity list** report. Deselect the **List Sources** checkbox, and then click on the **Create Report** button. In the upcoming **Create Report** confirmation window, make the following changes:

1. Set **Product** to **Summary of 3 products**.
2. Set **Reporting Hierarchy** to **Summary of certain product**.

*Reporting Management*

> When creating the **Summary of certain products** reporting hierarchy information, we specify **Summary of products** in the **Product Tree** field, and keep the other tree fields as default. With this configuration, the summary reports will be processed correctly when you enter the correct information in the **Product** and **Reporting Hierarchy** fields in the **Create Report** confirmation window.

In the author's installation (the numbers might vary with yours), the resulting reports are as follows:

**ADempiere** — Asset, Liabilities and Equity list — Page 1 of 1

**Parameter:**

| | |
|---|---|
| Product | = Summary of 3 products |
| Period | = Apr-09 |
| Details/Source First | = No |
| Reporting Hierarchy | = Summary of certain products |
| Update Balances | = Yes |

| Name | Description | Beginning Balance | Debit Transaction | Credit Transaction | Period Balance | Ending Balance | Growth |
|---|---|---|---|---|---|---|---|
| Asset | | | 647.23 | 105.27 | 541.96 | 541.96 | |
| Liabilities | | | 476.00 | 476.00 | 0.00 | 0.00 | |
| Owner Equity | | | | | | | |
| Total | | 0.00 | 1,123.23 | 581.27 | 541.96 | 541.96 | |

You can compare this report against the financial reports previously generated without applying a specific product and reporting hierarchy in the **Create Report** confirmation window.

# More details on the summary financial report

> *Well, we need to create this summary report for those three products and using both Hempel China Limited and Coats and Clarks (business partner), could you show me how to create this report?*

With this new requirement, you need to perform the tasks described in the following sections.

## Setting up a new summary business partner

We need to create a summary business partner that will summarize the two business partners. Open the **Business Partner** window, and then add and save the following information:

1. Set **Organization** to *.
2. Set **Search Key** and **Name** to **Summary of 2 BP**.
3. Select the **Summary Level** checkbox.

> Here, we have no additional **Business Partner Group** information. You can define a new **Business Partner Group** and attach this newly-created information into the appropriate field when needed.

Leave the other fields unchanged. Next, we need to configure a special Tree, as explained in the next section.

## Setting up a Summary of BP Tree

Open the **Tree** window. Add and save the following information:

1. Set **Organization** to **\***.
2. Set **Name** to **Summary of BP**.
3. Set **Type | Area** to **BPartner**.
4. Select the **All Nodes** checkbox.

We need to include the list of business partners as part of the **Summary of BP**, as explained in the next section.

## Setting Tree Maintenance

Open the **Tree Maintenance** window. Choose **Summary BP** in the **Tree** field, move **Summary of 2 BP**, **Hempel China Limited**, and **Coats and Clarks** to the left-hand side of this window, and perform the appropriate drag-and-drop activities. These activities should give you the final result shown in the following screenshot:

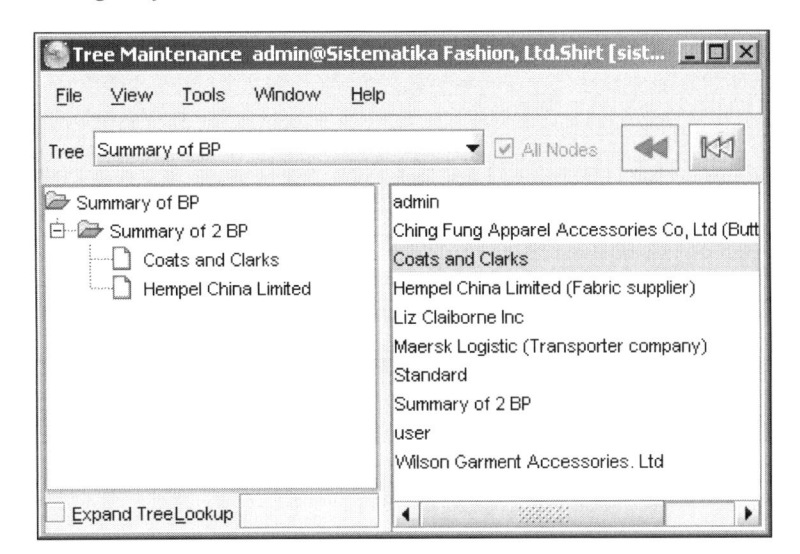

## Verifying the Summary of BP Tree

Once the Tree has been created, you need to verify the **Summary of BP** Tree. Navigate to the **Tree** window, and point your records to **Summary of BP**. Click on the **Verify Tree** button, and then click on the **OK** button in the upcoming confirmation window.

Next, we need to set up a more specific reporting hierarchy, as explained in the next section.

## Setting up a more specific reporting hierarchy

Open the **Reporting Hierarchy** window. Add and save the following information:

1. Set **Organization** to *.
2. Set **Name** to **Summary of certain products and BP**.
3. Set **BPartner Tree** to **Summary of BP**.
4. Set **Product Tree** to **Summary of Products**.

Set another tree field with their default option value. For example, set **Organization Tree** to **Sistematika Fashion, Ltd Organization** and so on.

## Executing a more specific financial report

Open the **Financial Report** window, and use our **Asset, Liabilities and Equity list** of reports. Click on the **Create Report** button. In the **Create Report** confirmation window, enter the following:

1. Set **Business Partner** to **Summary of 2 BP**.
2. Set **Product** to **Summary of 3 products**.
3. Set **Reporting Hierarchy** to **Summary of certain product and BP**.

Based on the author's installation, the results were as follows:

| ADempiere | | Asset, Liabilities and Equity list | | | | | |
|---|---|---|---|---|---|---|---|
| **Parameter:** | | | | | | | |
| | Business Partner | = Summary of 2 BP | | | | | |
| | Product | = Summary of 3 products | | | | | |
| | Period | = Apr-09 | | | | | |
| | Details/Source First | = No | | | | | |
| | Reporting Hierarchy | = Summary of certain products and BP | | | | | |
| | Update Balances | = Yes | | | | | |
| **Name** | **Description** | **Beginning Balance** | **Debit Transaction** | **Credit Transaction** | **Period Balance** | **Ending Balance** | **Growth** |
| Asset | | | 380.00 | 0.00 | 380.00 | 380.00 | |
| Liabilities | | | 380.00 | 380.00 | 0.00 | 0.00 | |
| Owner Equity | | | | | | | |
| Total | | 0.00 | 760.00 | 380.00 | 380.00 | 380.00 | |

# Info window

ADempiere comes with built-in real-time information for product, business partner, account info, and so on. You can access this information in the **View** main menu. The list of information available in the **View** menu is shown in the following screenshot:

Open **Product Info**. This will show you a list of products available, and their outstanding balances. Open **Account Info**, and it will show you the available accounting facts. You can get the data that is needed, based on the available criteria. Play with all of the available Info windows, and review the information available in each of these Info windows.

# Integration with JasperReports

JasperReports (http://jasperforge.org) is a powerful open source Java reporting tool that has the ability to deliver rich content. With this tool, the report's results can be exported into PDF, HTML, XLS, CSV, and XML file formats. JasperReports allows you to generate wonderful reports, including reports with sub-reports in them.

Fortunately, we can integrate JasperReports into ADempiere. For further reading, we advise you to take a look at:

http://www.adempiere.com/index.php/ADempiere/Compiere_JasperReports_Integration_HowTo

and practice, in order to examine the power of JasperReports.

## Summary

This chapter introduced you to the print feature, which comes with the standard ADempiere window. You can perform a Report, Print Preview and Print, or Archive and Export your document.

The standard features, such as drill down and drill across, which are used when previewing our reports, were explained. To print a document, there are some print format templates that are used to produce a document report. We introduced what a print format template is, and how to find the print format template used for a certain document.

After introducing the concept of the print format template, we then created a new print format template, based on the existing templates, and modified this template to suit our needs.

We covered Financial Reports and how these reports are produced. With these Financial Reports, we produced a summary report with all of the available financial data in a certain accounting period. For specific analysis, we saw how to create a summary of reports for a specific product and business partner.

At the end of this chapter, we covered another feature wherein ADempiere can provide light information. This feature is called the Info Window. A lot of information can be accessed through the Info Window (which is accessed from the View main menu).

At the beginning of an ADempiere implementation, there is a lot of data available that needs to be entered into the ADempiere system. This could be lots of products, business partners, currency rates, and so on. In the next chapter, we will show you how to import this data in to the ADempiere system, by using the import feature.

# 11
# Importing Data

During the implementation of, or migration to, a new ERP system such as ADempiere, there will be existing data that will need to be entered into ADempiere. This existing data can be entered item-wise, one-by-one. Entering a small amount of data would not be a problem, but when working with a large amount of data, the process is time-consuming and error-prone. Recovering from incomplete data will be an exhausting and costly affair. We need effective and efficient ways to input such data into the system.

By default, ADempiere provides us with an import feature. Before we proceed to the import processes, we will discuss the following:

- Import Loader Format
- Import File Loader

After understanding these features, we will continue on to practicing how to import data, which includes importing:

- Business Partners
- Products
- Currency Rates
- GL Journal entries
- Orders (both Purchase Order and Sales Order)
- Invoices (both Invoice (Vendor) and Invoice (Customer))
- Inventory
- Statements

We will start by discussing how ADempiere's import mechanism functions internally.

## ADempiere's import mechanism

To speed up data entry, we often find that some people use **Structured Query Language (SQL)** to enable direct **Data Manipulation Language (DML)** to inject information directly into ADempiere databases (this is not a healthy practice!). This method does not include validation of data, or data integrity checking. It is advisable to perform data import using ADempiere's import features.

ADempiere has a methodology to accomplish data import. This is as follows:

- First, we need to configure a template that will read and capture data through the **Import Loader Format** window. To do so, we prepare a columnar format of template, which is flexible. To fulfill our needs, we can add, alter, or amend a column at any point in time.
- Continuing this activity, we need to prepare text file data sources that comply with the pre-configured **Import Loader Format** template.
- Next, we load the text file data sources into the system.
- Finally, we execute the import procedure. ADempiere will check and validate data at this stage. If the data has not passed the data integrity test, then the system will display a message, and we can take action accordingly.

We will work with this standard approach and show you the details later.

## Determining the Import Loader Format

Prior to learning about import processes, we need to know what kind of information can be processed and supported by ADempiere's import feature. We can use the **Import Loader Format** window to know about the available structure or template (including table and column) that can be used for importing.

In the current version of ADempiere, we find the following Imported Table Format methods that can be used for importing:

- **I_BankStatement**, a mediator table for importing bank statements
- **I_BPartner**, a mediator table for importing business partners
- **I_Conversion_Rate**, a mediator table for importing exchange rates
- **I_ElementValue**, a mediator table for importing accounts
- **I_GLJournal**, a mediator table for importing GL journals
- **I_InOutLineConfirm**, a mediator table for importing shipped or receipt confirmations
- **I_Inventory**, a mediator table for importing inventories (including physical inventory)

- **I_Invoice**, a mediator table for importing invoices
- **I_Order**, a mediator table for importing orders
- **I_Payment**, a mediator table for importing payments
- **I_Product**, a mediator table for importing products
- **I_ReportLine**, a mediator table for importing report line sets

We log in with the user ID **admin**, using **Sistematika Fashion, Ltd Admin** as a role and **Shirt** as the organization. To see this list of tables, we can:

1. Navigate to the **Menu | System Admin | Data | Data Import | Import Loader Format** window. This window contains two tabs: **Import Format** and **Format Field**.

2. On the **Import Format** tab, click on the **New** button, and jump to the **Table** field. There is a list of tables available, as shown in the following screenshot:

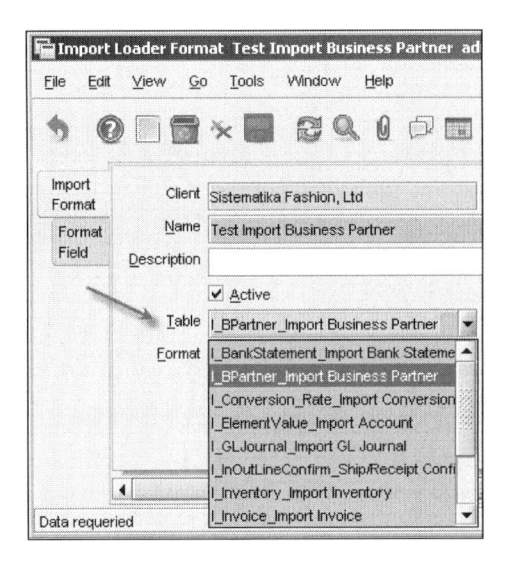

This **Import Format** tab is aimed at defining:

- The Imported Table Format (for example, **I_BPartner** for importing business partner). We can define this table in the **Table** field.
- The format of source data in a text file, which includes comma separation, fixed positioning, or tab separation to distinguish an element of information. This format can be defined in the **Format** field.

Each of the Imported Table Formats contain a predefined column that can be used to store information.

*Importing Data*

For example, we can use **I_BPartner** Imported Table Format to import customer, vendor, or employee information. This table has a collection of columns that could be used to capture any type of information. To see this collection of columns, you can:

1. Set information in the **Name** field (for example, **Test Import Business Partner**).
2. Select the **I_BPartner_Import Business Partner** in the **Table** field.
3. Set the **Format** type (for example, **Comma Separated**).
4. Click on the **Save** button.

Now, navigate to the **Format Field** tab in this window. We click on the **Column** field to display information, as shown below:

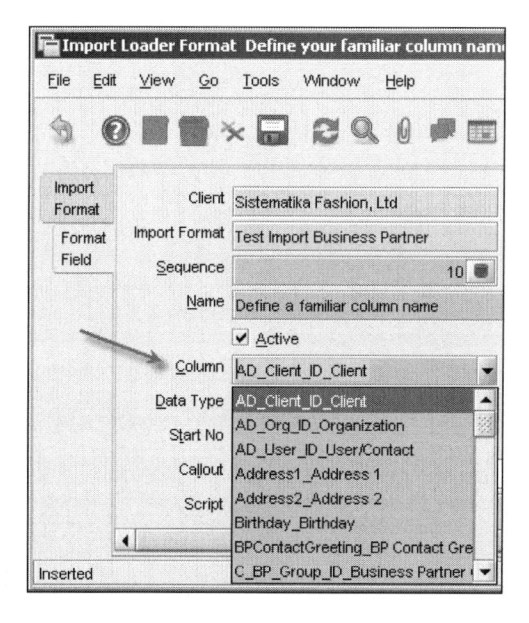

As we scroll down through the option list, we can see that **I_BPartner** table contains nearly 44 options that can be used to set information!

Summarizing the **Format Field** tab, it is aimed at defining a list of columns that are needed to capture information, set a data type, and define the position of this information. We can pick either all, or parts, of the available predefined columns for the import process.

> We can create a list of the most needed columns. Through the subsequent sections, we will learn how to set up most columns used when importing data.

Once we have defined the table and column as per our requirements, we can use and reuse this preconfigured Import Loader Format for your importing activities.

## Preparing the data source

Once we define the **Import Loader Format** templates, we can then prepare our source text data files. We store the data in a simple-to-read format (such as comma-separated values (CSV file)), based on the Import Loader Format structure.

When preparing the text file data source for documents such as GL journal, Order, Invoices, Inventory, and Bank Statement, we have the opportunity to provide the `Accounting Date`, `Movement Date`, or `Effective Date` information. When entering these dates, we need to check whether the date is outside the permitted date range, and whether or not it's in the ADempiere active period. For example, while the active accounting period is December 2009, we cannot create a GL journal document with an `Accounting Date` before or after December 2009.

## Loading data with the Import File Loader

With the available data sources, we need to load the data. On completion, the system places the data into the relevant Imported Table Format.

We can use the **Menu | System Admin | Data | Data Import | Import File Loader** window to load the data. At this stage, it loads the data and places it into the relevant import table.

## Import activities

Once the data is available in the internal ADempiere import table, we will process it. All we need to do is click on a button to execute the import task. We don't need to worry about the type of button being clicked at this point of time.

When executing this task, ADempiere will:

- Verify and validate the data
- Create default data for other values (related to this data) based on the provided data
- Transfer the data to the correct target table. One example of a target table, when importing business partner information, is **C_BPartner**

*Importing Data*

If there are some errors when validating the data, the system displays a message in the **Import Error Message** field. Accordingly, we can take action based on the information provided, and continue to re-import the data.

In the following section, we will learn how to import the Business Partner information.

# Import the Business Partner information

To import Business Partner information, we need to perform the following tasks:

## Creating the BPartner Import Loader Format

Here, we create a structure and declare .csv files as data sources in the **Import Loader Format** window. We add and save the following information in the **Import Format** tab:

1. Set the **Organization** field to **\***.
2. Set the **Name** field to **Import BPartner**.
3. Set the **Table** field to **I_BPartner** (shown as **I_BPartner_Import Business Partner** in the option).
4. Set the **Format** field to **Comma Separated**.

Next, we proceed to the **Format Field** tab. The **I_BPartner** table contains 44 columns that can be used to construct an import structure. You can see all of the available column options in the **Column** tab.

Here, we can see the nine most commonly-used columns for importing the Business Partner purposes. We can add and save this information.

| Field\Data | 1st data | 2nd data | 3rd data | 4th data | 5th data |
|---|---|---|---|---|---|
| Sequence | 10 | 20 | 30 | 40 | 50 |
| Name | Search Key | Name | Address | City | Country Codes |
| Column | Value_Search Key | Name_Name | Address1_Address 1 | City_City | CountryCode_ISO Country Code |
| Data Type | String | String | String | String | String |
| Start No | 1 | 2 | 3 | 4 | 5 |

| Field\Data | 6th data | 7th data | 8th data | 9th data |
|---|---|---|---|---|
| Sequence | 60 | 70 | 80 | 90 |
| Name | Contact Name | Email | BP Group | Organization |
| Column | ContactName_Contact Name | Email_Email Address | C_BP_Group_ID_Business Partner Group | AD_Org_ID_Organization |
| Data Type | String | String | String | Constant |
| Start No | 6 | 7 | 8 | |
| Constant Value | | | | 0 |

> In Sequence 90, when loading the data sources, the system automatically defines the **Organization** information as a constant, with a value of 0. This means that all business partners should be set up using * organization as a default. Thus, this data could be accessible to all of the available organizations.

## Preparing the Business Partner data files

We need to create sample data, based on our **Import Loader Format** definition. As per the **Import BPartner** structure or configuration, we will need to set up eight elements of information from a total of nine registered elements. We don't need to set up **Organization** information. According to the **Import BPartner** structure, it will be inserted automatically by the system.

While entering data, we should follow the **Start No** sequence. In our **Import BPartner** structure, **1** should be occupied with the **Search Key** information, **2** should be occupied with the **Name**, and so on.

We open our editor (Notepad, ConTEXT, vi, or anything else). Add and save the following information (without spaces between a comma and the next element):

- Andi Store,Andi Book Store,Sudirman street,Kab. Ungaran,ID,Andi, andi@gmail.com,1000002
- Dewa Stationery,Dewa Book Store,Patimura street,Kab. Ungaran,ID,Budi,budi@gmail.com,1000002

For example, we can name this file `sample_bpartner.csv`, and save it as `C:\sample_bpartner.csv`.

*Importing Data*

> We can prepare the data using Microsoft Excel or Open Office SCalc, and save it as `Text CSV (.csv)` file format.

In this example, **1000002** is a record ID (taken from `Record Info`) for the **Local** business partner group in the author's ADempiere installation. We can refer to the *More on Record Info* section of Chapter 2, *Exploring the ADempiere Client and how to Perform Tasks*, to learn more about record IDs.

## Loading the Business Partner data

We need to load the `C:\sample_bpartner.csv` sample data. Based on the **Import BPartner** configuration, this data will be loaded into our **I_BPartner** Imported Table Format.

We open the **Import File Loader** window. In this window, we:

1. Click on the **<Select File to Load>** button, and browse to the `C:\sample_bpartner.csv` files.
2. In the drop-down list next to the button, we select **UTF-8**.
3. Set the **Import Format** field to **Import BPartner**.

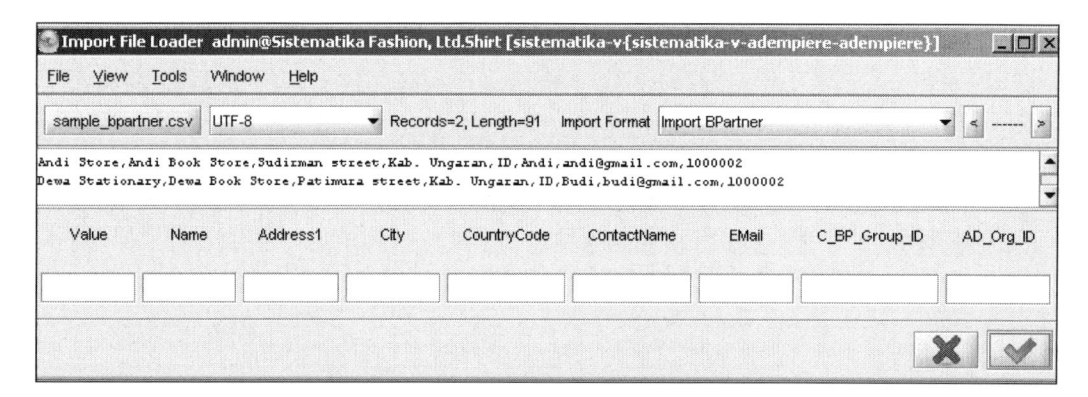

We'll finalize everything by clicking on **OK**. Upon completion, a message will be displayed, which contains information such as **Rows in file / loaded and ready to import : 2 / 2#**.

## Importing the Business Partner data

Now, we need to import data from **I_BPartner**; the system will verify and validate the data, and set it into a proper table. We'll open the **Menu | System Admin | Data | Data Import | Import Business Partner** window.

This window will contain two records, for further processing. We'll click on the **Import Business Partner** button. In the upcoming confirmation window, we'll click on the **OK** button. Upon importing successfully, a confirmation message such as **2 Business Partner: Inserted** will be displayed. The **Business Partner** window can be checked to verify the imported Business Partner information.

By default, those two Business Partner records will contain the following information:

- Flag **Prospect** checkbox selected (on the **Business Partner** tab)
- Flag **Customer** checkbox selected (on the **Customer** tab)
- Flag **Vendor** checkbox deselected (on the **Vendor** tab)
- Flag **Employee** checkbox deselected (on the **Employee** tab)

> At the time of import, we included a contact name and e-mail ID. With this existing information, ADempiere inserts the data in the **User** window automatically.

## Import Error Message sample

While entering data in the data sources, sometimes we supply incorrect references. For example, we may write the country ID for Indonesia as IA, instead of ID. As you would already know, the system will reject this record during the import process.

A sample of the message displayed when an incorrect country code is entered, is shown in the following screenshot:

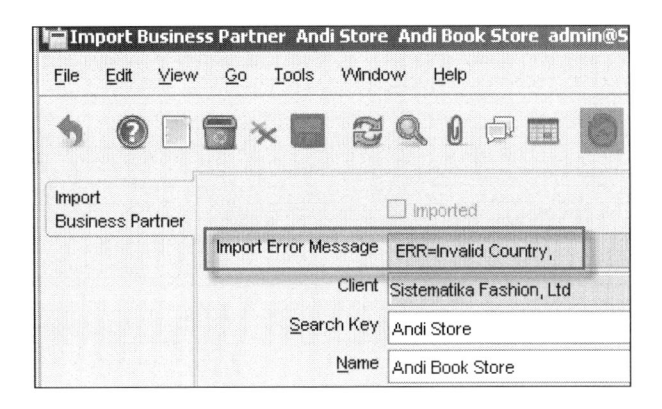

*Importing Data*

We need to find the **ISO Country Code** field in the **Import Business Partner** window, rectify its value, and save our changes. We'll finalize our process by clicking on the **Import Business Partners** button once again, and now the Business Partners will be successfully imported.

# Importing Products

Similar to importing Business Partners, this procedure also involves four steps, which are outlined in the subsequent sections.:

## Creating the Product Import Loader Format

In the **Import Loader Format** window, we add and save the following information on the **Import Format** tab:

1. Set the **Organization** field to **\***.
2. Set the **Name** field to **Import Product**.
3. Set the **Table** field to **I_Product** (shown as **I_Product_Import Product** in the option).
4. Set the **Format** field to **Comma Separated**.

Next, we proceed to the **Format Field** tab. The **I_Product** table contains 50 columns that can be used to construct an import structure. The available column option can be found in the **Column** tab.

For the purposes of our example of importing Products, we will use the nine most commonly-used columns. We can add and save the following information:

| Field\Data | 1st data | 2nd data | 3rd data | 4th data | 5th data |
|---|---|---|---|---|---|
| Sequence | 10 | 20 | 30 | 40 | 50 |
| Name | Search Key | Name | Category ID | Product Type | List Price |
| Column | Value_Search Key | Name_Name | M_Product_Category_ID_Product Category | ProductType_Product Type | PriceList_List Price |
| Data Type | String | String | String | String | String |
| Start No | 1 | 2 | 3 | 4 | 5 |

[ 378 ]

| Field\Data | 6th data | 7th data | 8th data | 9th data |
|---|---|---|---|---|
| Sequence | 60 | 70 | 80 | 90 |
| Name | Standard Price | Limit Price | UOM Id | Organization |
| Column | PriceStd_Standard Price | PriceLimit_Limit Price | C_UOM_ID_UOM | AD_Org_ID_Organization |
| Data Type | String | String | String | Constant |
| Start No | 6 | 7 | 8 | – |
| Constant Value | – | – | – | 0 |

> With Sequence 90, we define **Organization** as a constant with a value of 0. This means that all products should be set up at the * organization as a default, and thus will be accessible to all of the available organizations.

## Preparing Product data files

As per the **Import Product** structure of configuration, we shall have eight elements of information. We'll open our editor, and add and then save the following information (without spaces between a comma and the next element):

- Books,Books,1000000,Item,30,30,30,1000001
- Pencil,Pencil,1000000,Item,5,5,5,1000001

We'll name this file `sample_product.csv`, and save it at `C:\sample_product.csv`.

> Here, **1000000** is a Record ID (taken from Record Info) for **Standard** of **Product Category**, while the last **1000001** is a Record ID (taken from Record Info) for **Piece** of unit of measurement in the author's installation.

## Loading Product data

Next, we need to load this `C:\sample_product.csv` data file. Based on the previous **Import Product** configuration, this data will be loaded into the **I_Product** imported table format.

Navigate to the **Import File Loader** window. In this window, we:

1. Click on **<Select File to Load>**, and select the `C:\sample_product.csv` file.
2. In the drop-down list next to the button, select **UTF-8**.
3. Set the **Import Format** field to **Import Product**.

*Importing Data*

Next, we'll finalize the file by clicking on the **OK** button. Upon completion, ADempiere will display the message: **Rows in file / loaded and ready to import : 2 / 2#**.

## Importing Product data

Navigate to the **Menu | System Admin | Data | Data Import | Import Product** window.

This window contains two records, ready to be imported, by clicking on the **Import Product** button. The **Import Product** confirmation window will contain important information that needs to be set up. Here, we will be able to set up the **Price List Version** information, as shown in the following screenshot:

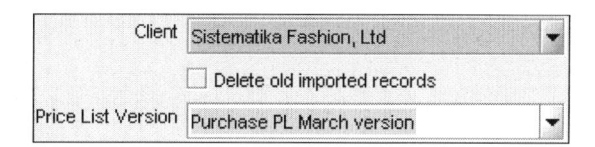

In this case, we'll select the **Purchase PL March version** price list, and click on the **OK** button.

> With this information, it is advisable to import a product based on **Price List Version**.

Upon successful completion, the system will show a confirmation message: **2 Product: Inserted**. The **Product** window can be checked to examine the imported product, along with its price. If you have not supplied the **List Price**, **Standard Price**, and **Limit Price** information, you need to manually set up this information through the **Price** tab of the **Product** window.

With the available imported product, and because we did not set up any **Locator** information, we need to define the **Warehouse Standard Locator** information manually.

## Importing currency rates

When working with multiple currencies, we need to set up exchange rates, for example, IDR against USD. With our existing configuration, we will try to import currency rates for the **Daily** currency type.

# Creating the Daily currency rates Import Loader Format

In the **Import Loader Format** window, we'll add and save the following information on the **Import Format** tab:

1. Set the **Organization** field to **\***.
2. Set the **Name** field to **Import Daily currency rates**.
3. Set the **Table** field to **I_Conversion_Rate** (shown as **I_Conversion_Rate_Import Conversion Rate** in the option).
4. Set the **Format** field to **Comma Separated**.

Next, we'll proceed to the **Format Field** tab. The **I_Conversion_Rate** table contains 21 columns that can be used to construct an import structure.

In our example, we will use the eight most commonly-used columns to import currency rates. We'll add and save the following information:

| Field\Data | 1st data | 2nd data | 3rd data | 4th data | 5th data |
|---|---|---|---|---|---|
| Sequence | 10 | 20 | 30 | 40 | 50 |
| Name | Currency From | Currency To | Currency Type | Multiply Rates | Valid From |
| Column | ISO_Code_ISO Currency Code | ISO_Code_To_ISO Currency To Code | ConversionTypeValue_ Currency Type Key | MultiplyRate_ Multiply Rate | ValidFrom_ Valid from |
| Data Type | String | String | String | Number | Date |
| Data format | — | — | — | — | ddMMyy |
| Start No | 1 | 2 | 3 | 4 | 5 |

| Field\Data | 6th data | 7th data | 8th data |
|---|---|---|---|
| Sequence | 60 | 70 | 80 |
| Name | Valid To | Create reciprocal | Organization |
| Column | ValidTo_Valid to | CreateReciprocalRate_ Create Reciprocal Rate | AD_Org_ID_Organization |
| Data Type | Date | Constant | Constant |
| Data format | ddMMyy | — | — |
| Start No | 6 | — | — |
| Constant Value | — | Y | 0 |

*Importing Data*

> In Sequence 70, we supply **Create reciprocal** with the default value. We don't need to define a value for this column, as we make it default to **Y** (which means Yes).

## Identifying Search Key information

We have two options for identifying a record identity during data import in ADempiere:

- Getting the record identity from Record Info.
- Getting the record identity from its Key

We already know about how to identify a record identity via the Record Info. Refer to the *More on Record Info* section of Chapter 2, *Exploring the ADempiere Client and How to Perform Tasks*, to know more about the record identity.

*What about knowing an identity from its Key?*

For example, when creating currency rates with the **Import Loader Format**, one column being used is the **ConversionTypeValue_Currency Type Key**. With this information, the system tells us to set a **Search Key** value of currency conversion type when writing in data sources.

In the upcoming example, we will use **D** as **Search Key** information to identify the **Daily** currency type. We'll navigate to the **Menu | Performance Analysis | Accounting Rules | Currency Type** window. We will find out the **D** information, as shown in the following screenshot:

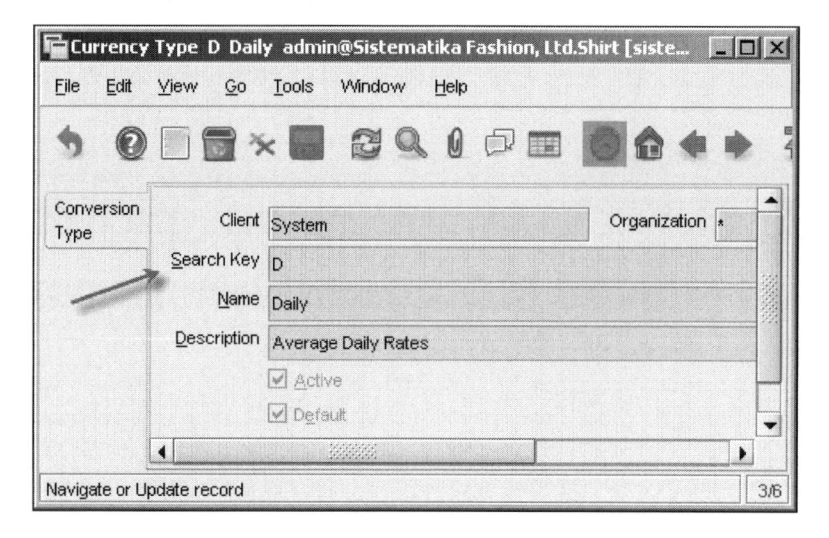

[ 382 ]

This guidance is applicable to all columns that have **Key** in their name. For example, when using the **ProductCategory_Value_Product Category Key** column at the time of constructing the **Import Product** structure or configuration, we can find a **Search Key** value from the related products in the **Product Category** window, and place it in our data sources.

## Preparing Currency rates data files

We need to define at least six elements of information. We'll open the editor, and then add and save the following information (without spaces between a comma and the next element):

- IDR,USD,D,9970,280709,280709
- IDR,USD,D,9975,290709,290709
- IDR,USD,D,9990,300709,300709
- IDR,USD,D,9920,310709,310709

We'll name this file sample_rates.csv, and save it at C:\sample_rates.csv.

> In the author's ADempiere installation, **D** is a **Search Key** value for the **Daily** type of **Currency Type**.

## Loading Currency rates data

Next, we'll need to load the C:\sample_rates.csv data file into our **I_Conversion_Rate** Imported Table Format.

We'll open the **Import File Loader** window, in which we:

1. Click on the **<Select File to Load>**, and navigate to and select the C:\sample_rates.csv file.
2. In the drop-down list next to the button, select **UTF-8**.
3. Set the **Import Format** field to **Import Daily currency rates**.

We'll finalize the definition by clicking on the **OK** button. Upon completion, ADempiere will display a message such as **Rows in file / loaded and ready to import : 4 / 4#**.

[ 383 ]

*Importing Data*

## Importing Currency rates data

We'll navigate to the **Menu | System Admin | Data | Data Import | Import Currency Rate** window; it will contain four records, which need to be processed. We'll click on the **Grid Toggle** button to view the details, where we'll find and click on the **Import Conversion Rate** button.

Upon the **Import Currency Conversion Rate** confirmation, we'll have to set the following :

1. Set the **Client** field to **Sistematika Fashion, Ltd**.
2. Set the **Organization** field to *.
3. Set the **Currency Type** field to *blank*.
4. Set the **Valid from** field to *blank*.
5. Deselect the **Create Reciprocal Rate** checkbox. We read this information based on the default value provided in the import loader format.
6. Deselect the **Delete old imported records** checkbox.

We'll then click on the **OK** button. Based on our sample data, the message **8 Conversion Rate: Inserted** will be shown. This means that ADempiere successfully imported four records and automatically inserted an additional four reciprocal data records based on our sample data.

We can check the **Menu | Performance Analysis | Accounting Rules | Currency Rate** window to see imported currency rates data results.

## Importing General Ledger journal entries

To speed up our GL journal data entries, ADempiere provides an import GL journal feature. Here, we will practice how to perform GL journal import activities.

## Creating the GL journal Import Loader Format

In the **Import Loader Format** window, we'll add and save the following information on the **Import Format** tab:

1. Set the **Organization** field to *.
2. Set the **Name** field to **Import GL Journal**.
3. Set the **Table** field to **I_GLJournal** (shown as **I_GLJournal_Import GL Journal** in the option).
4. Set the **Format** field to **Comma Separated**.

Next, we go to the **Format Field** tab. The **I_GLJournal** table contains 66 columns that can be used to set up our information.

In our case, we'll use the 13 most commonly-used columns for importing GL journal examples. We'll add and save the following information:

| Field\Data | 1st data | 2nd data | 3rd data | 4th data | 5th data |
|---|---|---|---|---|---|
| Sequence | 10 | 20 | 30 | 40 | 50 |
| Name | Organization Key | Date Accounting | Posting Type | Doc Type | Category |
| Column | OrgValue_Org Key | DateAcct_Account Date | PostingType_PostingType | DocTypeName_Document Type Name | CategoryName_Category Name |
| Data Type | String | Date | String | String | String |
| Data format | | ddMMyy | | | |
| Start No | 1 | 2 | 3 | 4 | 5 |

| Field\Data | 6th data | 7th data | 8th data | 9th data | 10th data |
|---|---|---|---|---|---|
| Sequence | 60 | 70 | 80 | 90 | 100 |
| Name | Journal Doc No | Currency Codes | Line No | Account Key | Amt Source Dr |
| Column | JournalDocumentNo_Journal Document No | ISO_Code_ISO Currency Code | Line_Line No | AccountValue_Account Key | AmtSourceDr_Source Debit |
| Data Type | String | String | String | String | Number |
| Start No | 6 | 7 | 8 | 9 | 10 |

| Field\Data | 11th data | 12th data | 13th data |
|---|---|---|---|
| Sequence | 110 | 120 | 130 |
| Name | Amt Source Cr | Description | Conversion Type |
| Column | AmtSourceCr_Source Credit | Description_Description | ConversionTypeValue_Currency Type Key |
| Data Type | Number | String | String |
| Start No | 11 | 12 | 13 |

## Preparing GL journal data files

We need to define at least 13 elements of information. We'll open the editor, add and save the following information (without spaces between a comma and the next element):

- Shirt,310709,Actual,GL Journal,Manual,100,USD,10,73100,150,0,First journal,D
- Shirt,310709,Actual,GL Journal,Manual,100,USD,20,73100,0,100,Second journal,D
- Shirt,310709,Actual,GL Journal,Manual,100,USD,30,73100,0,30,Third journal,D
- Shirt,310709,Actual,GL Journal,Manual,100,USD,40,73100,0,15,Fourth journal,D
- Shirt,310709,Actual,GL Journal,Manual,100,USD,50,73100,0,5,Fifth journal,D

We'll name this file `sample_gljournal.csv`, and save it as `C:\sample_gljournal.csv`.

In this example, we tried to insert a journal with the **73100** Account Key (**Postage Expenses**). The first journal entry is for a debit transaction, while the rest (second to fifth journal) are for credit transactions.

## Loading GL journal data

Next, we'll need to load this `C:\sample_gljournal.csv` data file into our **I_GLJournal** Imported Table Format.

We'll open **Import File Loader** window, in which we'll:

1. Click on **<Select File to Load>**, and navigate to and select to the `C:\sample_gljournal.csv` file.
2. In the drop-down list next to the button, select **UTF-8**.
3. Set the **Import Format** field to **Import GL Journal**.

Next, we'll finalize our settings by clicking on the **OK** button. Upon completion, ADempiere will display a message that contains the following information: **Rows in file / loaded and ready to import : 5 / 5#**.

## Importing GL journal data

We'll open the **Menu | System Admin | Data | Data Import | Import GL Journal** window; this will contain five records, which need to be processed. We'll click on the **Grid Toggle** button to view the details, and then click on the **Import Journal** button.

Upon the display of the **Import Journal** confirmation window, we'll need to ensure that we complete the following:

1. Set the **Client** field to **Sistematika Fashion, Ltd**.
2. Set the **Organization** field to **Shirt** (the same org information that was supplied in the **sample_gljournal.csv**).
3. Pick and set **Accounting Schema** to the default one.
4. Set the **Account Date** field to **07/31/2009** (this is the same date as supplied in the **sample_gljournal.csv**).
5. Deselect the **Only Validate Data** checkbox.
6. Select the **Import only if No Errors** checkbox.
7. Deselect the **Delete old imported records** checkbox.

We'll click on the **OK** button, and if we are successful, then a message will be displayed, as shown in the following screenshot:

```
Import Journal

0 Source Debit - Source Credit

0.00 Accounted Debit - Accounted Credit
0 Errors
1 Journal Batch: Inserted
1 Journal: Inserted
5 Journal Line: Inserted
```

Next, we can go to the **GL Journal** window where we will find the imported GL journal records. The **Batch** tab does not contain the **Account Date** and **Period** information. We'll update this **Account Date** to **07/31/2009**, and then save and complete the document.

## Import Orders

We could perform data import for both Purchase Order or Sales Order documents. In terms of ADempiere, the difference between a Purchase Order and a Sales Order documents is the document type and the **Is Sales Transaction** flags. With this requirement, we shall include **Is Sales Transaction** flags in the Import Loader Format.

*Importing Data*

# Creating the Order Import Loader Format

In the **Import Loader Format** window, we'll add and save the following information on the **Import Format** tab:

1. Set the **Organization** field to **\***.
2. Set the **Name** field to **Import Order**.
3. Set the **Table** field to **I_Order** (shown as **I_Order_Import Order** in the option).
4. Set the **Format** field to **Comma Separated**.

Next, we go to the **Format Field** tab. The **I_Order** table contains 59 columns that can be used when constructing Order Import Loader Format.

We'll use ten of the most commonly-used columns for our example Order import loader. We can add and save the following information:

| Field\Data | 1st data | 2nd data | 3rd data | 4th data | 5th data |
|---|---|---|---|---|---|
| Sequence | 10 | 20 | 30 | 40 | 50 |
| Name | BPartner Key | Acct Date | Order Date | Product Key | Qty Ordered |
| Column | BPartnerValue_ Business Partner Key | DateAcct_ Account Date | DateOrdered_ Date Ordered | ProductValue_ Product Key | QtyOrdered_ Ordered Quantity |
| Data Type | String | Date | Date | String | Number |
| Data format | — | ddMMyy | ddMMyy | — | — |
| Start No | 1 | 2 | 3 | 4 | 5 |

| Field\Data | 6th data | 7th data | 8th data | 9th data | 10th data |
|---|---|---|---|---|---|
| Sequence | 60 | 70 | 80 | 90 | 100 |
| Name | Price List Id | Actual Price | UOM Id | Doc Type | Is Sales Trx |
| Column | M_PriceList_ ID_Price List | Price_ Actual_Unit Price | C_UOM_ID_ UOM | DocTypeName_ Document Type Name | IsSOTrx_ Sales Transaction |
| Data Type | String | Number | String | String | String |
| Start No | 6 | 7 | 8 | 9 | 10 |

[ 388 ]

# Preparing the Purchase Order data files

In this example, we'll insert a Purchase Order document, in which we will set the **Is Sales Trx** set to **N**.

We'll need to define at least ten elements of information. We'll open our editor, add and save the following information (without spaces between a comma and the next element):

- Andi Store,310709,310709,Books,10,1000001,25,1000001,Purchase Order,N
- Andi Store,310709,310709,Pencil,20,1000001,5,1000001,Purchase Order,N

We'll name this file `sample_order.csv`, and save it as `C:\sample_order.csv`.

In this case, the first **1000001** is a Record ID (taken from the Record Info) for **Purchase PL March version**, while the second **1000001** is a Record ID for **Piece**, a unit of measurement on the author's computer.

# Loading the purchase order data

Next, we'll need to load the `C:\sample_order.csv` data file into our **I_Order** imported table format.

We'll open the **Import File Loader** window, in which we'll:

1. Click on the button **<Select File to Load>** and navigate to and select the `C:\sample_order.csv` files.
2. In the drop-down list next to the button, select **UTF-8**.
3. Set the **Import Format** field to **Import Order**.

Next, we'll finalize our settings by clicking on the **OK** button. Upon completion, a message similar to: **Rows in file / loaded and ready to import : 2/2#** will be displayed.

# Importing Purchase Order data

We'll open the **Menu | System Admin | Data | Data Import | Import Order** window, which contains two records that need to be processed. While you are now in the grid mode, click on the **Grid Toggle** button to view the details, and then click on the **Import Orders** button.

*Importing Data*

When the **Import Orders** confirmation window is displayed, we'll ensure that we set the following information:

1. Set the **Client** field to **Sistematika Fashion, Ltd**.
2. Set the **Organization** field to **Shirt** (depends on your requirements).
3. Set the **Document Action** field to **Prepare**.

We'll click on the **OK** button, and when successful, a message (shown below) will be displayed:

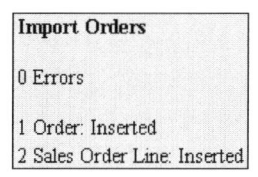

```
Import Orders

0 Errors

1 Order: Inserted
2 Sales Order Line: Inserted
```

We can view the **Purchase Order** window, and verify our document there.

## Sales Order data import sample

For our reference, we will prepare another sample .csv file, which contains the following information:

- Liz Claiborne Inc,310709,310709,Shirt,10,1000002,20,1000001,Standard Order,Y
- Liz Claiborne Inc,310709,310709,Shirt,15,1000002,20,1000001,Standard Order,Y
- Liz Claiborne Inc,310709,310709,Shirt,20,1000002,20,1000001,Standard Order,Y

In this case, **1000002** is a Record ID (taken from the Record Info) for **Sales PL March version**, while **1000001** is a Record ID for **Piece**, a unit of measurement in the author's computer

We can load, import, and examine the **Sales Order** window for verification.

> In this example, we've used the **Standard Order** document type. We could also use other document types, such as **Binding Offer** or **Non binding offer**.

# Importing Invoices

Both, the **Invoice (Vendor)** and **Invoice (Customer)** can be imported. Again, the **Is Sales Trx** will indicate the type of document. Here, we should practice creating both invoices, based on prior import order data activities.

## Creating the Invoices Import Loader Format

In the **Import Loader Format** window, we'll add and save the following information on the **Import Format** tab:

1. Set the **Organization** field to *.
2. Set the **Name** field to **Import Invoices**.
3. Set the **Table** field to **I_Invoice** (shown **I_Invoice_Import Invoice** in the option).
4. Set the **Format** field to **Comma Separated**.

Next, we jump to the **Format Field** tab. The **I_Invoice** table contains 58 columns that can be used during construction of the Invoice Import Loader Format.

In this example, we'll use the ten most commonly-used columns:

| Field\Data | 1st data | 2nd data | 3rd data | 4th data | 5th data |
|---|---|---|---|---|---|
| Sequence | 10 | 20 | 30 | 40 | 50 |
| Name | BPartner Key | Doc Type | Doc No | Currency Id | Date Invoiced |
| Column | BpartnerValue_Business Partner Key | DocTypeName_Document Type Name | DocumentNo_Document No | C_Currency_ID_Currency | DateInvoiced_Date Invoiced |
| Data Type | String | String | String | String | Date |
| Data format | — | — | — | — | ddMMyy |
| Start No | 1 | 2 | 3 | 4 | 5 |

*Importing Data*

| Field\Data | 6th data | 7th data | 8th data | 9th data | 10th data |
|---|---|---|---|---|---|
| Sequence | 60 | 70 | 80 | 90 | 100 |
| Name | Date Acct | Product Key | Qty Ordered | Actual Price | Is Sales Trx |
| Column | DateAcct_Account Date | ProductValue_Product Key | QtyOrdered_Ordered Qty | PriceActual_Unit Price | IsSOTrx_Sales Transaction |
| Data Type | Date | String | String | Number | String |
| Data format | ddMMyy | — | — | — | — |
| Start No | 6 | 7 | 8 | 9 | 10 |

## Preparing Invoice Vendor data files

In this example, we'll try to insert an **AP Invoice** document, which has **Is Sales Trx** set to N.

We need to define ten elements of information. We'll open our editor, and add the following information (without spaces between a comma and the next element):

- Andi Store,AP Invoice,100020,100,310709,310709,Books,10,25,N
- Andi Store,AP Invoice,100020,100,310709,310709,Pencil,20,5,N

We can name this file `sample_invoices.csv`, and save it as `C:\sample_invoices.csv`.

In this case, **100** is a Record ID (taken from Record Info) for **USD** currency, on the author's computer.

## Loading Invoice Vendor data

We'll need to load the `C:\sample_invoices.csv` data file into our **I_Invoice** Imported Table Format.

We'll open the **Import File Loader** window, in which we'll:

1. Click on the button **<Select File to Load>**, and navigate to and select the `C:\sample_invoices.csv` file.
2. In the drop-down list next to the button, select **UTF-8**.
3. Set the **Import Format** field to **Import Invoices**.

Then, we'll finalize our settings by clicking on the **OK** button. Upon completion, the message **Rows in file / loaded and ready to import : 2/2#** will be displayed.

## Importing Invoice Vendor data

We'll navigate to the **Menu | System Admin | Data | Data Import | Import Invoice** window; this contains two records that need to be processed. We'll click on the **Grid Toggle** button to view the details, and then click on the **Import Invoice** button.

Upon display of the **Import Invoice** confirmation window, we'll ensure that we set the following information:

1. Set the **Client** field to **Sistematika Fashion, Ltd**.
2. Set the **Organization** field to **Shirt** (as per our requirements).
3. Set the **Document Action** field to **Prepare**.

We'll click on **OK**, and upon successful completion, the following message will be shown:

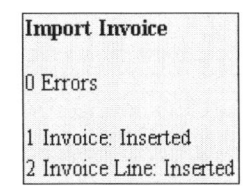

```
Import Invoice

0 Errors

1 Invoice: Inserted
2 Invoice Line: Inserted
```

We can view the **Invoice (Vendor)** window to examine the import results.

## Invoice Customer data import sample

For our exercise, we will prepare another sample `.csv` file, which contains the following information:

- Liz Claiborne Inc,AR Invoice,100010,100,310709,310709,Shirt,10,20,Y
- Liz Claiborne Inc,AR Invoice,100010,100,310709,310709,Shirt,15,20,Y
- Liz Claiborne Inc,AR Invoice,100010,100,310709,310709,Shirt,20,20,Y

We can load, import, and examine the results in the **Invoice (Customer)** window.

The Invoice import is handy for recurring overhead invoices that are similar every month. We just need to create a `.csv` file with various business partners and values, and then import this data once a month.

## Importing Inventory

At the end of the month, we can perform a physical stock check and then book this transaction in the **Physical Inventory** window. To speed up the entry process, we can use the **Import Inventory** feature.

As mentioned in the *Stock counting and reconciliation* section of Chapter 8, *Managing Inventory*, when utilizing Physical Inventory activities, we have two options for **Inventory Type**: **Inventory Difference** and **Charge Account**. Unfortunately, this Import Inventory feature is applicable only to the **Inventory Difference** option of **Inventory Type**. We cannot use the **Charge Account** option of **Inventory Type** here.

## Creating the Inventory Import Loader Format

In the **Import Loader Format** window, we'll add the following information in the **Import Format** tab:

1. Set the **Organization** field to *.
2. Set the **Name** field to **Import Inventory**.
3. Set the **Table** field to **I_Inventory** (it will appear as **I_Inventory_Import Inventory** in the option).
4. Set the **Format** field to **Comma Separated**.

Next, we move on to the **Format Field** tab. The **I_Inventory** table contains 27 columns that can be used to construct the Import Loader Format.

For our testing purposes, we use five of the most commonly-used columns:

| Field\Data | 1st data | 2nd data | 3rd data | 4th data | 5th data |
| --- | --- | --- | --- | --- | --- |
| Sequence | 10 | 20 | 30 | 40 | 50 |
| Name | Warehouse Key | Locator Key | Product Key | Movement Date | Qty count |
| Column | WarehouseValue_Warehouse Key | LocatorValue_Locator Key | Value_Search Key | MovementDate_Movement Date | QtyCount_Quantity Count |
| Data Type | String | String | String | Date | Number |
| Data format | — | — | — | ddMMyy | — |
| Start No | 1 | 2 | 3 | 4 | 5 |

## Preparing Inventory data files

Based on the Import Loader Format definition, we need to define five elements of information. We'll open our editor and add the following information (without spaces between a comma and the next element):

- 1st Shirt W/h,Loc S1A,Books,310709,20
- 1st Shirt W/h,Loc S1A,Pencil,310709,30

We'll name the file `sample_inventory.csv`, and save it as `C:\sample_inventory.csv`.

## Loading Inventory data

We need to load this `C:\sample_inventory.csv` data file into our **I_Inventory** imported table format.

We'll open the **Import File Loader** window, in which we'll:

1. Click on the button **<Select File to Load>**, and direct it to the `C:\sample_inventory.csv` file.
2. In the drop-down list next to the button, select **UTF-8**.
3. Set the **Import Format** field to **Import Inventory**.

We'll then finalize our settings by pressing **OK**. Upon completion, the message **Rows in file / loaded and ready to import : 2 / 2#** will be displayed.

## Importing Inventory data

Upon navigating to the **Menu | System Admin | Data | Data Import | Import Inventory** window, we'll see that it contains two records that need to be processed. For this, we'll click on the **Grid Toggle** button to view the details, where we'll click on the **Import Inventory** button.

Upon confirmation of the **Import Invoice**, we'll need to ensure that we set:

1. Set the **Client** field to **Sistematika Fashion, Ltd.**
2. Set the **Organization** field to **Shirt** (depending on our requirement; this should be the same value as specified in `sample_inventory.csv`).
3. Set the **Locator** field to **Loc S1A**.
4. Set the **Movement Date** field to today's date.

*Importing Data*

> As we already provide **Locator** and **Movement Date** information in the `sample_inventory.csv` files, the system should use a value taken from this file.

We'll press **OK**, and upon successful completion, the following message is displayed:

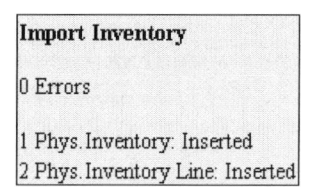

```
Import Inventory
0 Errors

1 Phys.Inventory: Inserted
2 Phys.Inventory Line: Inserted
```

We can check the **Physical Inventory** window to examine the imported inventory data.

# Importing a Bank Statement

If there are e-banking facilities available, we can get our bank statement online through websites. Unfortunately, with the default files provided, we generally cannot use this file directly as a data source. It still needs some touch-up and re-formatting the file to fulfill the Import Loader Format configuration, and only then can we import this data through ADempiere Bank Statement import. In this section, we will create a data source that complies with the Import Loader Format.

For our example, we will practice importing a bank statement that is targeted to a certain currency of the bank account.

# Creating the Bank Statement Import Loader Format

In the **Import Loader Format** window, we'll add and save the following information on the **Import Format** tab:

1. Set the **Organization** field to **\***.
2. Set the **Name** field to **Import Bank Statement for 1-001-888888**.
3. Set the **Table** field to **I_BankStatement** (shown as **I_BankStatement_Import Bank Statement** in the option).
4. Set the **Format** field to **Comma Separated**.

Next, we move to the **Format Field** tab. The **I_BankStatement** contains 55 columns that can be used to construct the Bank Statement Import Loader Format.

In this example, we use seven of the most commonly-used columns:

| Field\Data | 1st data | 2nd data | 3rd data | 4th data | 5th data |
|---|---|---|---|---|---|
| Sequence | 10 | 20 | 30 | 40 | 50 |
| Name | Bank Account Id | Currency Id | Statement Date | Statement Line Date | Effective Date |
| Column | C_BankAccount_ID_Bank Account | C_Currency_ID_Currency | StatementDate_Statement Date | StatementLineDate_Statement Line Date | ValueDate_Effective Date |
| Data Type | Constant | Constant | Date | Date | Date |
| Data format | — | — | ddMMyy | ddMMyy | ddMMyy |
| Constant Value | 1000000 | 100 | — | — | — |
| Start No | — | — | 1 | 2 | 3 |

| Field\Data | 6th data | 7th data |
|---|---|---|
| Sequence | 60 | 70 |
| Name | Statement Amount | Description |
| Column | StmtAmt_Statement Amount | LineDescription_Line Description |
| Data Type | Number | String |
| Start No | 4 | 5 |

Bank Account Id **1000000** is a Record ID (taken from the Record Info) for the **USD-1-001-888888** bank account, while **100** is a Record ID for **USD** currency in the author's installation.

## Preparing Bank Statement data files

Based on the Import Loader Format definition, we need to define five elements of information. We'll open our editor, and create and save the following information (without spaces between a comma and the next element:

- 290709,290709,290709,125,Payment from Liz
- 290709,290709,290709,-25,Payment to Andi Store

- 290709,290709,290709,-50,Payment to Hempel Limited
- 300709,300709,300709,-20,Payment to Andi Store

We'll name the file `sample_bankstatement.csv`, and save it as `C:\sample_bankstatement.csv`.

## Loading Bank Statement data

We need to load this `C:\sample_bankstatement.csv` data file into our **I_BankStatement** imported table format.

For that, we'll open the **Import File Loader** window, in which we'll:

1. Click on the **<Select File to Load>** button and navigate to and select the `C:\sample_bankstatement.csv` files.
2. In the drop-down list next to the button, select **UTF-8**.
3. Set the **Import Format** field to **Import Bank Statement for 1-001-888888**.

We'll then finalize these settings by pressing the **OK** button. Upon completion, **Rows in file / loaded and ready to import : 4 / 4#** is displayed.

## Importing Bank Statement data

We'll navigate to the **Menu | System Admin | Data | Data Import | Import Bank Statement** window, which contains four records that need to be processed. For this, we'll click on the **Grid Toggle** button to view the details, and then click on the **Import Bank Statement** button.

When we see the **Import Bank Statement** confirmation window, we'll need to ensure that we've set:

- The **Client** field to **Sistematika Fashion, Ltd**
- The **Organization** field to **Shirt**
- The **Bank Account** field to bank account information provided in the Import Loader Format

We'll press **OK**, and upon successful completion, the following message is displayed:

```
Import Bank Statement

0 Errors

2 Bank Statement: Inserted
4 Bank statement line: Inserted
```

> In this message, **2 Bank Statement: Inserted** was displayed as we had two different Statement Line Dates: **290709** and **300709**.

We proceed onto examining the **Bank Statement** window, finding the imported data, and setting additional information in the **Payment** or **Charge** fields to complete the transaction.

# Summary

In this chapter, we learned to perform most of the data import activities. We completed four common tasks. The first one was creating the Import Loader Format file. We did that just once, and this can be used for further transactions. Secondly, we prepared source text files based on the predefined Import Loader Format file. Then we learned about loading the data into the ADempiere Imported Table Format. Lastly, we moved the import data in its own windows (verifying and validating data).

During the creation of the Import Loader Format, we chose which import table was to be used, and defined the format for the source files. This was either comma separated, fixed positioned, or tab separated. We also defined what type of information is needed in the **Format Field** tab. We defined a list of columns required during the data import processes.

When setting up information in the **Format Field** tab, we can define both constant and variable information. For variable information, we can set date, string, or numeric data types.

Moving on, with the pre-formatted data available, we loaded it using the **Import File Loader**. We combined and matched information in source files with the target import format. We ensured that the load process was successful by examining the load confirmation messages.

Finally, we concluded this chapter by performing import activities. During this procedure, ADempiere took care of verifying and validating data.

So far in this book, we have had a basic knowledge of the implementation of ADempiere. With all of the basics clear, we need to plan and implement the security of our ADempiere installation, which we'll learn about in the next chapter.

# 12
# Implementing Security

So far in this book, almost all of our practical sessions used the user ID **admin**. With this user ID, we can perform activities such as creating an organization, registering and/or altering master data (such as business partner and products), configuring and watching accounting information, performing production activities, and so on.

In a real ERP implementation, there are many people (such as the General Manager, Accounting Manager, Warehouse Manager, Accounting staff, warehouse staff, shipping staff, and so on) involved in operating the system. Because every individual has his or her own responsibilities in the organization, the system should help the organization manage the access rights to information and perform activities in the system.

In this chapter, we will introduce you to what we can do to implement ADempiere security in your organization. We will discuss how to:

- Set up Users
- Create Roles and give access rights to end-users
- Record Access security rules

We will elaborate on these topics in the upcoming sections.

## Managing ADempiere user IDs

In our ADempiere implementation, we need to define a list of users in the system. A user could be the Accounting Manager, the Warehouse Manager, or any of the staff who need to access the system. Now, *log in with user ID admin,* using **Sistematika Fashion, Ltd Admin** as the role and **\*** as the organization. We will register a new user ID with the help of the ADempiere administrator.

# Creating a user ID in the system

In this example, we will create two additional user IDs. Open the **Menu | System Admin | General Rules | Security | User** window. On the **User Contact** tab, enter and save the following minimum requirement information:

| Field | 1st data | 2nd data |
|---|---|---|
| Client | Sistematika Fashion, Ltd | Sistematika Fashion. Ltd |
| Organization | * | * |
| Name | Daniel | Moses |
| Search Key | daniel | moses |
| Password | 123456 | 123456 |

An example of the first set of user ID data entered in the **User** window is shown in the following screenshot:

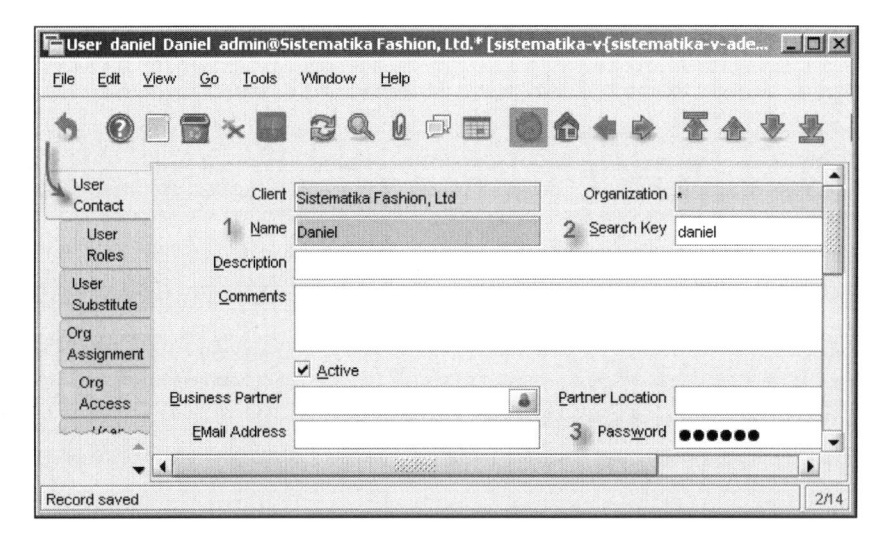

As these user IDs are not yet connected to any **Role**, they cannot currently access the ADempiere system.

> There are other tabs listed in the **User** window (for example, **User Roles**, **User Substitute**, **Org Assignment**, and so on). For our purpose, there is no need to set up any data here.

# Managing user ID access control

For a computer system's security, role-based access control is an approach to restricting system access to authorized users. ADempiere uses this role-based access control approach for its internal security implementation.

In the subsequent sections, we will introduce you to creating and configuring role-based access control in the ADempiere system.

## Introduction to ADempiere roles

The ADempiere role is the place where we can define and configure the access rights for our authorized user ID. These access rights include access to:

- Organization
- Window
- Process
- Form
- Workflow
- Task
- Document Action

In our example, we will create two roles, which have the following behavior:

- The first role will have all access rights
- The second role will have restricted or limited rights

We will practice creating these sample roles and examine the impact of the security configuration.

## Creating a new ADempiere role

Open the **Menu | System Admin | General Rules | Security | Role** window, and then enter and save the following minimum requirements information on the **Role** tab:

| Field | 1st data | 2nd data |
|---|---|---|
| Client | Sistematika Fashion, Ltd | Sistematika Fashion, Ltd |
| Organization | * | * |
| Name | All Access | Restricted Access |
| User Level | Client + Organization | Organization |

*Implementing Security*

| Field | 1st data | 2nd data |
|---|---|---|
| Manual | *deselected* | *selected* |
| Preference Level | Client | Organization |
| Maintain Change Log | *selected* | *selected* |
| Show Accounting | *selected* | *deselected* |
| Access all Orgs | *selected* | *deselected* |
| Can Report | *selected* | *selected* |
| Can Export | *selected* | *selected* |

For the **All Access** role, select all of the checkboxes in the **Allow Info in Role** fields group.

An example for the information in the **Role** tab for **All Access** is shown in the following screenshot:

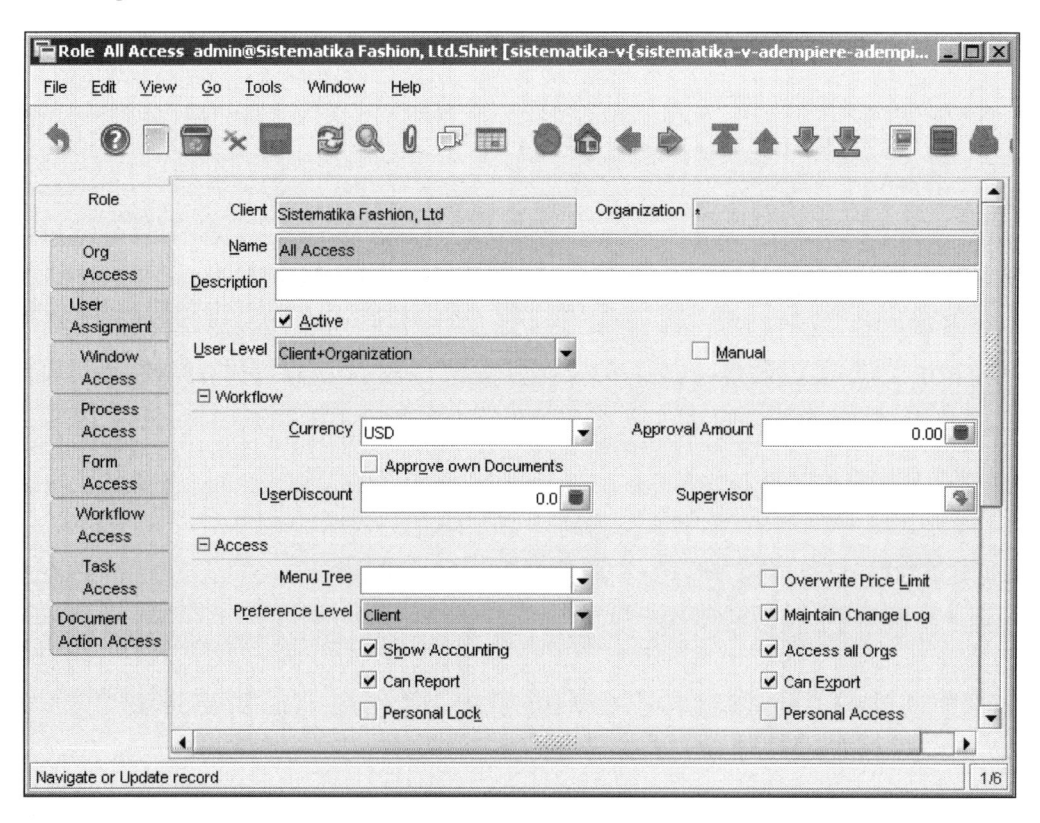

> On saving the **All Access** role (which has the **Manual** checkbox deselected), the **Window Access**, **Process Access**, **Form Access**, **Workflow Access**, **Task Access**, and **Document Action Access** will be granted automatically, based on **User Level** selection. Check it out in all of the available tabs in this **Role** window. This role has almost identical access rights when compared to the default **Sistematika Fashion, Ltd Admin** role.

## Attaching a user ID to a specific role

With our newly-created role, you need to assign a user ID to this role. Perform the following activities:

1. Assign user ID **Daniel** to the **All Access** role.

    Ensure that your active record in the **Role** tab of the **Role** window is **All Access**. Navigate to the **User Assignment** tab, and then click on the **New** button. Set the **Organization** to *, and the **User/Contact** field to **Daniel**, and then save this information.

2. Assign user ID **Moses** to the **Restricted Access** role.

    Ensure that your active record in the **Role** tab of **Role** window is **Restricted Access**. Navigate to the **User Assignment** tab, and then click on the **New** button. Set the **Organization** to *, and the **User/Contact** field to **Moses**, and then save this information.

With this configuration, user ID **Daniel** will be able to log in to the system and work in all of the available organizations. Organization assignment is automatically provided for the **All Access** role because, it has the **Access all Orgs** checkbox selected.

## Assigning organization access to a user ID

Unfortunately, although user ID **Moses** has already been assigned to the **Restricted Access** role, he will still not able to access and log in to the system. This is because the **Restricted Access** role has the **Access all Orgs** checkbox deselected.

With this configuration, we need to manually assign organization access to this role. For our example, we will assign the **Shirt** and **Dress** organization to this role. Perform the following tasks:

- Be sure that your active record in the **Role** tab of **Role** window is **Restricted Access**. Navigate to the **Org Access** tab, set the **Organization** to **Shirt**, and then click on the **Save** button.
- While still on the **Org Access** tab, click on the **New** button, set the **Organization** to **Dress**, and finalize the task by clicking on the **Save** button.

*Implementing Security*

The result is shown in the following screenshot:

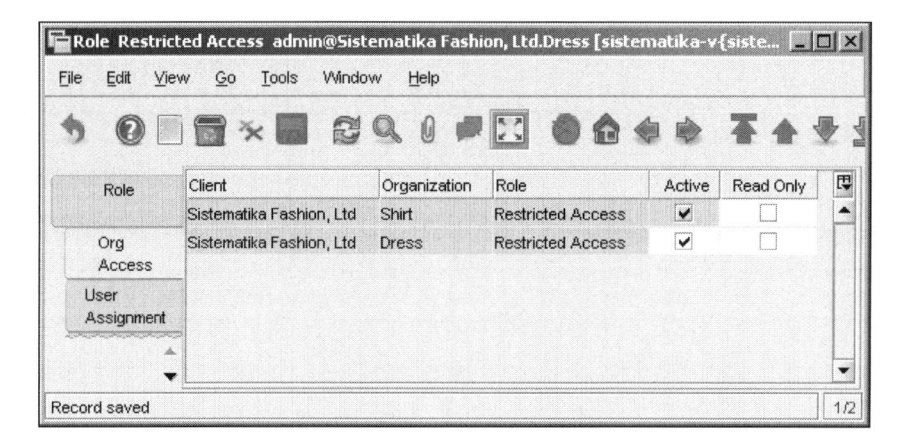

Now, user ID **Moses** will be able to log in and access the system.

## Working with the Access all Orgs option

If the **Access all Orgs** option is *selected*, your user ID will be able to access all of the organizations available in the client. If this option *deselected*, you have two options for assigning organization access to a certain user ID:

- *Select* the **Use User Org Access** checkbox. This option will appear if you *deselect* the **Access all Orgs** option. You need to register the organization access through the **Org Access** tab in the **User** window.
- If the **Use User Org Access** checkbox is *deselected*, you can register an organization through the **Org Access** tab in the **Role** window.

## Working with the Maintain Change Log option

As mentioned in the *Maintaining a log of data changes* and *More on Record Info* sections of Chapter 2, *Exploring the ADempiere Client and Performing Tasks* with the **Maintain Change Log** option enabled, the system will show the history of changes to our data.

To see the history of the data changes, launch another ADempiere client, log in with user ID **Daniel**, password **123456**, using **All Access** as a role, and **Shirt** as organization. As this feature is enabled for all of the available ADempiere windows, we can practice by working in the **Product** window. Open this window and find the **Standard** product. For this product, perform the following activities:

- Change the **UPC/EAN** field to **UPC-STD**, and click on the **Save** button
- Once again, change the **UPC/EAN** field to **UPC-STD001**, and click on the **Save** button

Now, click on **Record Info** in this window. This will show you the information shown in the following screenshot:

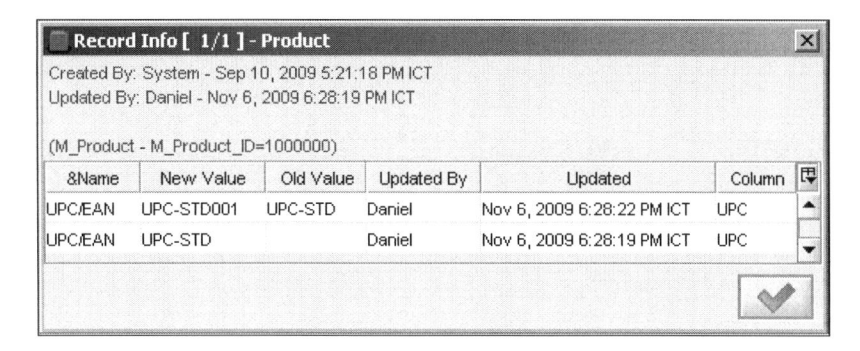

## Working with the Show accounting option

With this option *selected* (along with having the **Show Accounting Tabs** option in **Tools | Preference** selected), you will be able to read, modify, and execute processes related to accounting. If this option is *deselected*, you will *not be able* to:

- Access accounting facts/GL journal entries in any of the ADempiere documents such as **MM Receipt**, **AR Invoice**, and so on. The **Posted** or **Not Posted** button will not available in all of the documents.
- Access windows related to accounting (such as **Accounting Fact Details**, **Account Combination**, **Account Element**, **GL Journal** window, and so on).
- Access accounting configuration (such as the **Accounting** tab of **Product**, **Business Partner**, **Cashbook**, **Bank** window, and so on).

The last two types of access are basically configurable. When registering the tab as part of constructing the window in the **Window, Tab & Field** window, the tab has **Accounting Tab** attributes. With these attributes, you can define whether or not this tab will show information related to Accounting.

*Implementing Security*

To unveil this configuration, launch another ADempiere client, and log in with user ID **System**, password **System**, and the role **System Administrator**. Open the **Menu | Application Dictionary | Window, Tab & Field** window. In the upcoming **Lookup Record** window (search dialog window), enter **Accounting Fact Details** in the **Name** field and click on the **OK** button. In the **Accounting Fact Details** record, navigate to the **Tab** tab. You will see that the **Accounting Tab** checkbox is selected, as shown in the following screenshot:

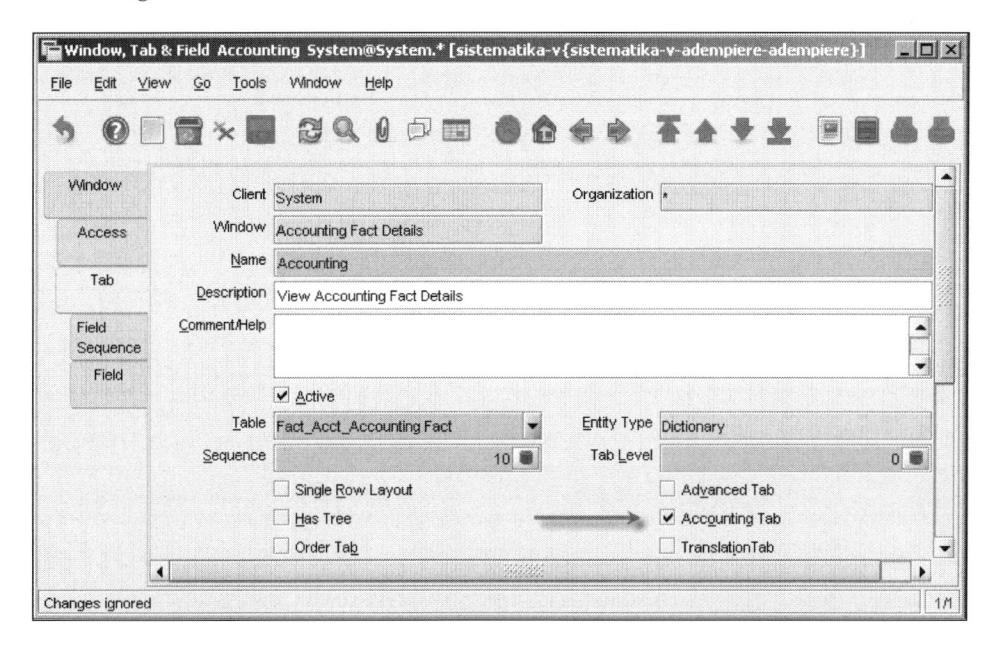

With this configuration, and while the **Show Accounting** checkbox is *deselected* for your role, you will not be able to access this tab. Because this is the only tab available in the **Accounting Fact Details** window, you cannot access the window. Try to access this window by using user ID **user** and **Sistematika Fashion, Ltd User** as the role. The system will display a message such as **With your current role and settings, you cannot view this information.** Now, log off from user ID **System**.

## Working with the Can Report option

As a default, the **Can Report** option is *selected*. With this option, you *can* generate a report by clicking on the **Report** button for any window that has the reports feature. If this option is *deselected*, you *cannot* generate a report for these windows. Refer to the *Accessing the Report button* section in the Chapter 10, *Reporting Management*, for details of how to create reports.

If the **Can Report** option is *deselected*, the user ID that is connected using this role will get the following error message while creating reports:

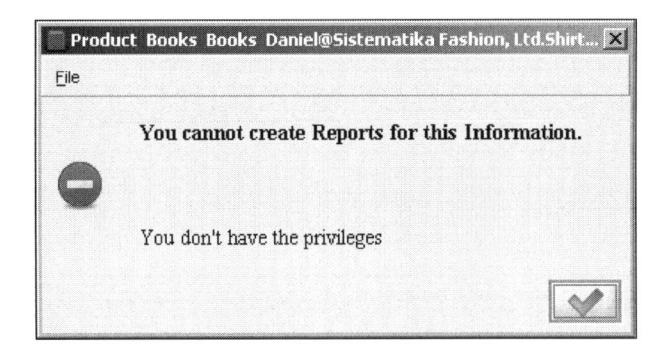

## Working with the Can Export option

After print previewing our reports using the **Print preview** or **Print** button, if the **Can Export** option is selected, we will be able to export our reports into various file formats (such as, XLS, PDF, and so on). Refer to the *Sending e-mail, archiving reports, and export* section in Chapter 10, *Reporting Management*, for the button related to export activity.

If this option is *deselected*, the **Export** button will not be available. Therefore, you cannot export your reports.

## Accessing Info Window

As already mentioned in the *Info window* section of Chapter 10, *Reporting Management*, ADempiere provides us with real-time information to assess product, business partner, account information, and so on. You will be able to control the availability of this information by selecting or deselecting the corresponding Info window in the **Role** tab of the **Role** window, as shown in the following screenshot:

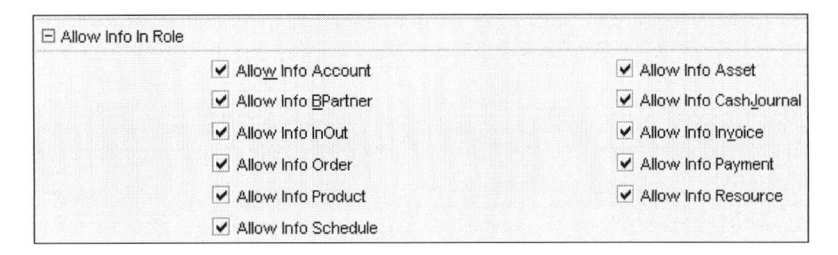

For example, if you *deselect* the **Allow Info BPartner** checkbox, the **Business Partner Info** will disappear from the **View** menu.

## Assigning Window Access

As described in the *Assigning organization access to user ID* section, user ID **Moses** will be able to log in, select **Restricted Access** as a **Role** and **Shirt** as the **Organization** to work in this environment. He can then start working with the available window.

> *"Available window? There is no window available in the main menu. I can not see any window after logging in!"*

Yes, there is no window available while accessing the system by using the Restricted Access role. We have not yet registered the list of windows in the **Window Access** tab. In our example, we will register two windows for this role: **Purchase Order** and **Material Receipt**. This user ID then will have the rights to perform activities in both of these windows.

Ensure that you are in the **Restricted Access** record in the **Role** tab of the **Role** window. Navigate to the **Window Access** tab, and then enter and save the following information:

| Field | 1st data | 2nd data |
| --- | --- | --- |
| Organization | * | * |
| Window | Purchase Order | Material Receipt |
| Read Write | selected | selected |

Launch another ADempiere client, and log in with the user ID **Moses** and use **123456** as the password. Set **Restricted Access** as the role, and **Shirt** as the organization. With a successful log in, you will see a menu such as the one shown in the following screenshot:

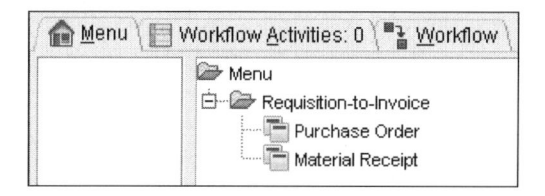

For the subsequent section, we need to enter sample Purchase Order data. Open the **Purchase Order** window, and in the **Purchase Order** tab, and then enter and save the following information:

1. Set the **Target Document Type** field to **Purchase Order**
2. Set the **Business Partner** field to **Hempel China Limited**
3. Set the **Price List** field to **Purchase PL**
4. Set the **Company Agent** field to **user**

Leave the other fields unchanged. Navigate to the **PO Line** tab, and then enter and save the following information:

1. Set the **Product** field to **S Fabric**
2. Set the **Quantity** field to **100**

Leave the other fields unchanged. Now, click on the **Print preview** button. It will perform nothing!

## Identifying Process Access

*Do you mean that user ID Moses, when connected using the Restricted Access role cannot make a print of this document?*

With the existing **Restricted Access** role configuration, the role does not have access rights to perform a purchase document print or print preview.

On launching your ADempiere client by using `Run_Adempiere.bat` when working with the Microsoft Windows operating system, there will be a small *DOS prompt* window created by default. This will contain a message such as the one shown in the following screenshot:

```
-----------> DB_PostgreSQL.getCachedConnection: # Connections: 10 , # Busy Conne
ctions: 10 , # Idle Connections: 0 , # Orphaned Connections: 0 [11]
-----------> ProcessCtl.process: ProcessInfo[Purchase Order   800013    Moses@Siste
matika Fashion, Ltd.Shirt [sistematika-v{sistematika-v-adempiere-adempiere}],Pro
cess_ID=110,Record_ID=1000022,Error=true,Summary=Cannot access Process 110 with
role: Restricted Access,Log=0] [12]
```

The system tells us that we **Cannot access Process 110 with role: Restricted Access**.

*What is process 110?*

To answer this question, we need to access the internal ADempiere configuration. Use the following procedure:

1. Launch another ADempiere client, and log in with the user ID **System**, password **System**, and **System Administrator** as the role.
2. Open the **Menu | Application Dictionary | Report & Process** window.

3. In the upcoming **Lookup Record** (search dialog) window, navigate to the **Advanced** tab, and set the **Column** to **Process (ID)**, the **Operator** to =, and the **Query Value** to **110**, as shown in the following screenshot:

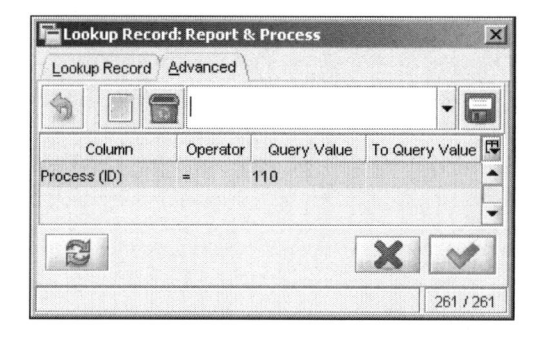

Click on the **OK** button.

4. After performing the above activities, you will be directed to a process having an identity of 110, which is a record that has **Rpt_C_Order** as its **Search Key** and **Order Print** as its process **Name**, as shown in the following screenshot:

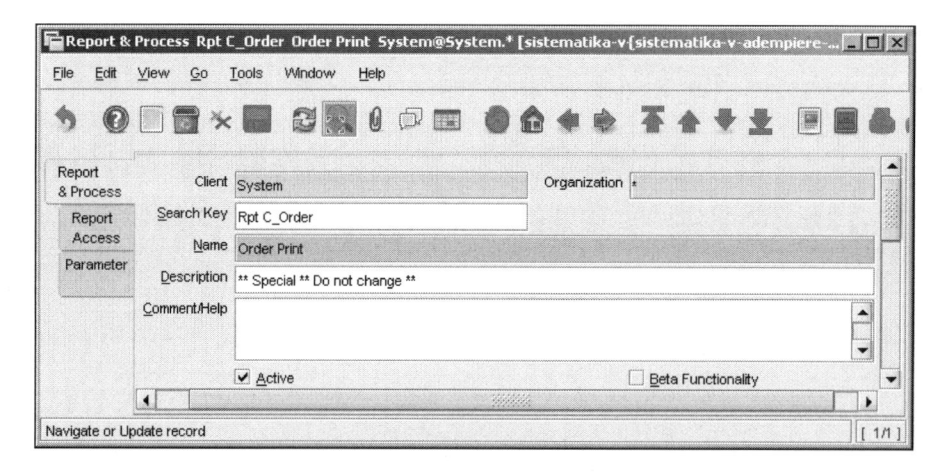

5. Now, log out from this ADempiere client.

With this information, we can register this process to the **Restricted Access** role.

## Registering Process Access

In the available ADempiere client, log in with the user ID **admin** and **Sistematika Fashion, Ltd Admin** as the role, and then open your **Role** window. In the **Role** tab, ensure that your active record is **Restricted Access**.

Navigate to the **Process Access** tab, and then enter and save the following information:

| Field | 1st data | 2nd data |
|---|---|---|
| Organization | * | * |
| Process | Rpt C_Order_Order Print | Rpt M_InOut_Delivery Note / Shipment print |
| Read Write | selected | selected |

> The second piece of information is to allow a user ID that is connected with the **Restricted Access** role, to print or print preview the document in the **Material Receipt** window.

Now, re-login with the user ID **Moses** and password **123456**. Open the **Purchase Order** window and you can then print or print preview a document in this window.

Next, you can try to **Complete** this document. Again, it does nothing! No problem, we will show you how to allow user ID **Moses** to complete this document, in the subsequent sections.

## Introduction to Document Action Access

In all of the ADempiere documents, such as Purchase Order, MM Receipt, AR Receipt, AP Payment, and so on, we can perform some actions for them. The standard actions available in the ADempiere system are listed (in alphabetical order) below:

| Number | Name | Description |
|---|---|---|
| 1 | <None> | No action. |
| 2 | Approve | Approve this transaction. |
| 3 | Close | Finally close this transaction. It cannot be re-activated. |
| 4 | Complete | Generate documents and complete transaction. |
| 5 | Invalidate | Invalidate the Document. |
| 6 | Post | Post a transaction. |
| 7 | Prepare | Check the Document consistency and check the Inventory. |
| 8 | Re-activate | Reopen a Document and Reverse automatically generated documents. You need to Complete the transaction after the change. |
| 9 | Reject | Reject the approval of the Document. |

| Number | Name | Description |
|---|---|---|
| 10 | Reverse - Accrual | Reverse by switching Dr/Cr with the current date. |
| 11 | Reverse - Correct | Reverse a Transaction (correction) by reversing the sign with the same date. |
| 12 | Unlock | Unlock a Transaction (process error). |
| 13 | Void | Set all quantities to zero and complete transaction. |
| 14 | Wait Complete | Wait Condition ok, Complete Document. |

With all of these available actions, we can select two of the most commonly used actions in the ADempiere document, namely:

- Prepare
- Complete

> These two document actions are used as a standard action when determining a document workflow. Refer to the *Activity/Node flow* section in Chapter 9, *ADempiere Workflow*, for more information. The **Prepare** action is used in the **(DocPrepare)** node, whereas **Complete** is used in the **(DocComplete)** node.

## Registering Document Action Access

Here, we need to assign both **Prepare** and **Complete** document access for both the Purchase Order and MM Receipt documents to the **Restricted Access** role. With the available ADempiere client that is connected to user ID **admin**, and using **Sistematika Fashion, Ltd Admin** as the role, you can open your **Role** window. In the **Role** tab, ensure that your active record is **Restricted Access**.

Navigate to the **Document Action Access** tab, and then enter and save the following information:

| Field | 1st data | 2nd data | 3rd data | 4th data |
|---|---|---|---|---|
| Organization | * | * | * | * |
| Document Type | Purchase Order | Purchase Order | MM Receipt | MM Receipt |
| Reference List | Prepare | Complete | Prepare | Complete |

Now, re-login with user ID **Moses** and password **123456**, and then open the **Purchase Order** window. Go to the newly-created purchase order document. When attempting to **Complete** this document, the option for **Document Action** will be as shown in the following screenshot:

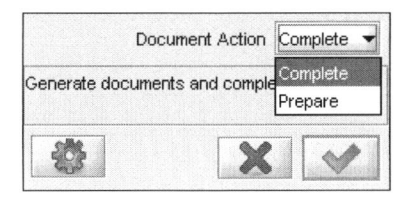

Select **Complete** from the list, and then click on the **OK** button to finalize this activity.

## Managing Form Access

If we need to grant the **Restricted Access** role to perform the import data activity, we could grant the **Import File Loader** form to this role. Using the existing user ID **admin** and the **Sistematika Fashion, Ltd Admin** role, you can open your **Role** window. On the **Role** tab, ensure that your active record is **Restricted Access**.

Navigate to the **Form Access** tab, and then enter and save the following information:

1. Set the **Organization** field to **\***.
2. Set the **Special Form** field to **Import File Loader**.
3. Select the **Read Write** checkbox.

On re-logging in with user ID **Moses** and password **123456**, the list of available menus should be as shown in the following screenshot:

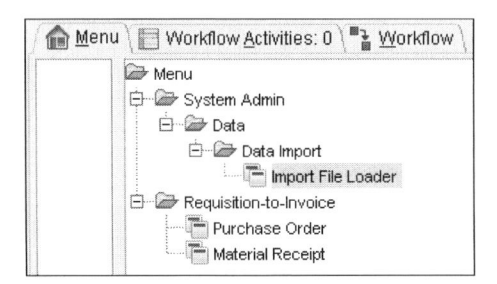

Related to the **Import File Loader** window, as explained in the Chapter 11, *Importing Data*, you need to add an access right to a certain import window (for example, **Import Product**, **Import Inventory**, and so on) to this role. You can access the **Window Access** tab and register this window there.

*Implementing Security*

# Recording access security rules

Currently, with our configuration, there are two warehouses available in the Dress organization. These are:

- 1st Dress W/h
- 2nd Dress W/h

By default, all users that have access rights to the **Dress** organization will be free to access these warehouses.

> *Do we have a requirement that allows just user Moses to access 2nd Dress W/h only? Is that possible?*

ADempiere has a feature to block users from accessing information in certain records. With this feature, the locking process is applied based on a **Role**, and not on a certain user ID.

# Enabling Personal Lock

There are some prerequisite activities required in order to be able to block access to certain records. This activity defines which **Role** has the rights to block access.

In our example, we will give the default **Sistematika Fashion, Ltd Admin** role this right. *Log in with user ID admin*, select **Sistematika Fashion, Ltd Admin** as the role. Open the **Role** window, and access the **Role** tab. Point your active records to **Sistematika Fashion, Ltd Admin**, and then find and select the **Personal Lock** checkbox, as shown in the following screenshot:

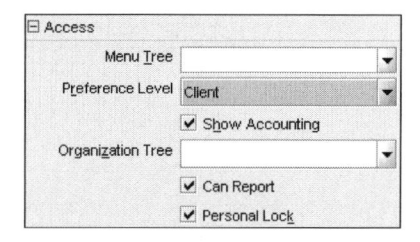

On enabling the personal lock, if you are logged in as user ID admin have **Sistematika Fashion, Ltd Admin** as an active **Role**, on opening all of the ADempiere windows, there will be an additional special **Private Record Lock** toolbar available, as shown in the following screenshot:

# Blocking access to certain records

With the previous requirement, we will block the user ID (which connects with the **Restricted Access** role) from accessing the **1st Dress W/h** warehouse.

This be done by using the following procedure:

1. Open the **Menu | Material Management | Material Management Rules | Warehouse & Locators** window.
2. In the **Warehouse** tab, find your **1st Dress W/h** record. Press the *Ctrl* key, and then click on the **Private Record Lock** button at the same time.
3. In the upcoming **Record Access Dialog** confirmation window, set the following information:
    - Set the **Role** field to **Restricted Access** (pick from the options available)
    - Select the **Active** checkbox
    - Select the **Exclude** checkbox

The following screenshot shows the completed window:

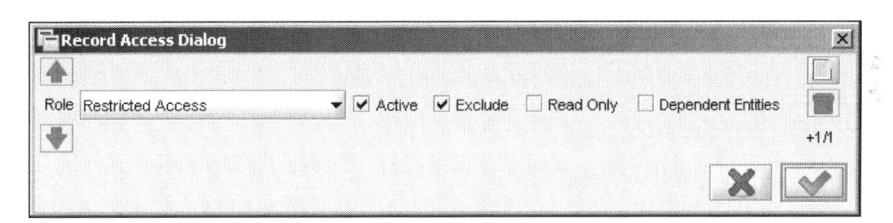

Finalize the process by clicking on the **OK** button.

Log in with user ID **Moses** and password **123456**, using **Restricted Access** as the role, and **Dress** as the organization. Open the **Purchase Order** window, and try to create a new document. Take a closer look at the available options in the **Warehouse** field. Now, it will only list **2nd Dress W/h**, as shown in the following screenshot:

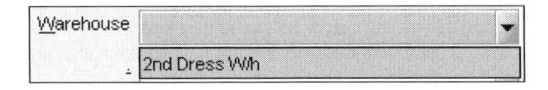

## Restoring access to certain blocked records

There are two way to restore user rights to certain blocked records.

*First*, if you know the blocked records and the Role to which these records are blocked (in our case, **1st Dress W/h** with **Restricted Access**), then you can open the **Warehouse & Locators** window, find your 1st Dress W/h record, press the *Ctrl* key, and then click on the **Private Record Lock** button. In the upcoming **Record Access Dialog** confirmation window, make sure that you set the **Role** to **Restricted Access**, and then click on the **Delete** record button.

> The **Delete** record button is a green recycle button on the right-hand side of the **Dependent Entities** checkbox.

*Second*, you can open the **Menu | System Admin | General Rules | Security | Role Data Access** window. Select the role that needs to be maintained in the **Role** tab. In our case, this is the **Restricted Access** role.

Navigate to the **Record Access** tab. This tab will contain all of the record restriction configuration. This is a sample record format, which contains blocking information for certain records, as shown in the following screenshot:

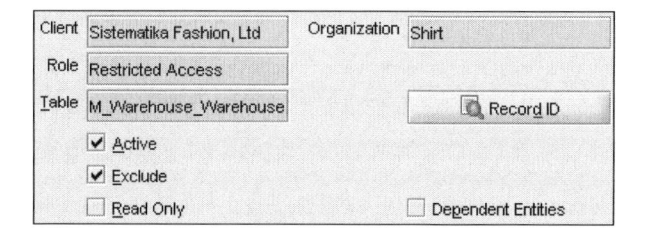

| Client | Sistematika Fashion, Ltd | Organization | Shirt |
|---|---|---|---|
| Role | Restricted Access | | |
| Table | M_Warehouse_Warehouse | | Record ID |
| | ✔ Active | | |
| | ✔ Exclude | | |
| | ☐ Read Only | | ☐ Dependent Entities |

Click on the **Record ID** button, to check what kind of record information is currently blocked. On confirmation, you can press the *F3* key to delete this record, and the access rights to this information will be restored.

## Using Dependent Entities

With the previous record access lock activity, the user who was connected to the ADempiere system using Restricted Access role could not use the 1st Dress W/h as their target warehouse when working with a new document (such as, **Purchase Order**, **Material Receipt**, and so on). They will still be able to access any existing document that uses 1st Dress W/h as part of their warehouse information references.

If you need to hide or restrict access to any document that has 1st Dress W/h as part of its document information, you can select the **Dependent Entities** checkbox.

# Working with Role Data Access in detail

In the **Menu | System Admin | General Rules | Security | Role Data Access** window, we can define an access right on both the ADempiere database **table** and **column**, which is registered in the ADempiere Application Dictionary. We will elaborate on a sample use of this data access in the subsequent sections.

## Restricting Table access

Suppose that you need to grant access to a role that can only read or view the **Material Receipt** window and cannot add or alter any information in this window. With User ID **admin** and using **Sistematika Fashion, Ltd Admin** as the role, you need to perform the following steps:

1. Find the document's target table. You can get this information by opening the **Material Receipt** window and clicking on **Record Info**. In this case, the table name is **M_InOut**.

2. Open the **Role Data Access** window, set your target role (for example, **Restricted Access**) in the **Role** tab, and then navigate to the **Table Access** tab. Enter and then save the following information:
   - Set the **Table** field to **M_InOut** (on the screen, it will show as **M_InOut_Shipment/Receipt**)
   - Select the **Exclude** checkbox
   - Set the **Access Type** field to **Accessing**
   - Select the **Read Only** checkbox

With this configuration, if the user is connected to the ADempiere system using the **Restricted Access** role, on opening their **Material Receipt** window they will have read-only access and will not be able to alter or add any information.

## Restricting Report access

Refer to the *Working with the Can Report option* section of this chapter. In this section, the option was to be able to create a report, and unfortunately, this configuration applies to all of the available windows.

*Implementing Security*

With the combination of the **Can Report** option and restricting report access, we have the option to give report access by first authorizing access to all of the available reports, and then restricting access to certain selected reports.

We will use this approach. Here, we will show you an example wherein a user ID connected using the **Restricted Access** role will not be able to access only the **Material Receipt** report. For this requirement, using user ID **admin** and **Sistematika Fashion, Ltd Admin** as the role you need to:

1. Access the **Role** tab in the **Role Data Access** window. Ensure that your active record is **Restricted Access**.
2. On the **Role** tab, select the **Can Report** option.
3. Navigate to the **Table Access** tab, add and then enter and save the following information:
    - Set the **Table** field to **M_InOut** (on the screen, it will show **M_InOut_Shipment/Receipt**)
    - *Select* the **Exclude** checkbox
    - Set the **Access Type** field to **Reporting**
    - *Deselect* the **Can Report** checkbox (this option will be available if the **Access Type** is set to **Reporting**)

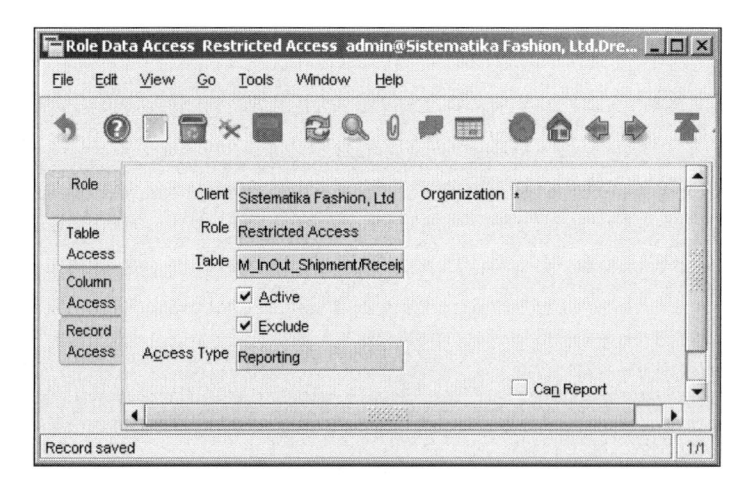

## Restricting Export access

So far, if user ID **Moses** is connected using the **Restricted Access** role, he can process a report, print preview, or print the **Purchase Order** data.

*"Okay, this role has rights to create a report, print preview, or print Purchase Order data through the Purchase Order window. For security reasons, could we ensure that the user ID connected to the system using the Restricted Access role cannot export this report?"*

Yes, this is possible with ADempiere. You can achieve this by carrying out the following steps:

1. Access the **Role** tab in the **Role Data Access** window. Ensure that your active record is **Restricted Access**.
2. In the **Role** tab, select the **Can Export** option.
3. Navigate to the **Table Access** tab, and then enter and save the following information:
    - Set the **Table** field to **C_Order** (on the screen, it will show as **C_Order_Order**)
    - *Select* the **Exclude** checkbox
    - Set the **Access Type** field to **Exporting**
    - *Deselect* the **Can Export** checkbox (this option will be available if the **Access Type** is set to **Exporting**)

If the user is connected to the ADempiere system using the **Restricted Access** role, when making a report and print previewing the document in the **Purchase Order** window, the **Export** button will not be available.

## Restricting Column Access

*Well, what we need is just to make sure that this role cannot alter the Purchase Order's Date Ordered only. We need anyone who is connected with this role to use a default Date Ordered.*

If this configuration should be applied to the **Restricted Access** role, you can do this by carrying out the following procedure:

1. Identify the table name of the targeted column with the Record Info.
2. Open the **Role Data Access** window, set your targeted role in the **Role** tab, and then go to the **Column Access** tab. Enter and then save the following information:
    - Set the **Table** field to **C_Order** (on the screen, it will show as **C_Order_Order**)
    - Set the **Column** field to **DateOrdered** (on the screen, it will show as **DateOrdered_Date Ordered**)
    - Select the **Exclude** and **Read Only** checkboxes

*Implementing Security*

After these changes, the user ID connected with this role will not be able to alter the **Date Ordered** field. The system sets this field as read-only information, as shown in the following screenshot:

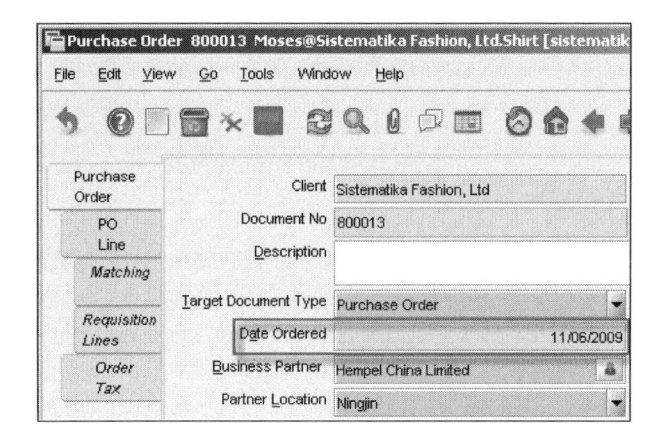

> If you have not selected the **Read Only** checkbox field, then this **Date Ordered** field information will completely disappear, or will be hidden in the document.

# Obscuring information

When working with a system that involves many people, we need to make sure that sensitive data, such as the user IDs password information, and financial information such as credit-card numbers, are secure.

As an ADempiere standard feature, the system has a mechanism to obscure information. We will elaborate on how ADempiere accomplishes this in the following sections.

## Enabling the encrypted feature

When we interact with the **Menu | System Admin | General Rules | Security | User** window, we can define the user ID information, including the **Password**. By default, the **Password** field does not show the actual password characters. The information in the **Password** field will be as shown in the following screenshot:

We will now take a look at the **Window, Tab & Field** window to understand how ADempiere makes this work:

1. Log in with user ID **System**, password **System** and using **System Administrator** as the **Role**. Open the **Menu | Application Dictionary | Window, Tab & Field** window. In the upcoming **Lookup Record** (search dialog) window, enter **User** in the **Name** field. With this activity, we will check the **User** window configuration.

2. In the **Window** tab, ensure that your active record has **User** in the **Name** field, and **Maintain Users of the system** in the **Description** field.

3. Navigate to the **Tab** tab. As per the default configuration, you are directed to the first record of the eight available records in this tab (which are displaying **User Contact** in the **Name** field).

4. Navigate to the **Field** tab. Here, there are many fields available, which construct your **User Contact** tab. Find your **Password** record, and click on the **Grid Toggle** button to show the detailed configuration for this field. Here, you will have the **Encrypted** checkbox selected, as shown in the following screenshot:

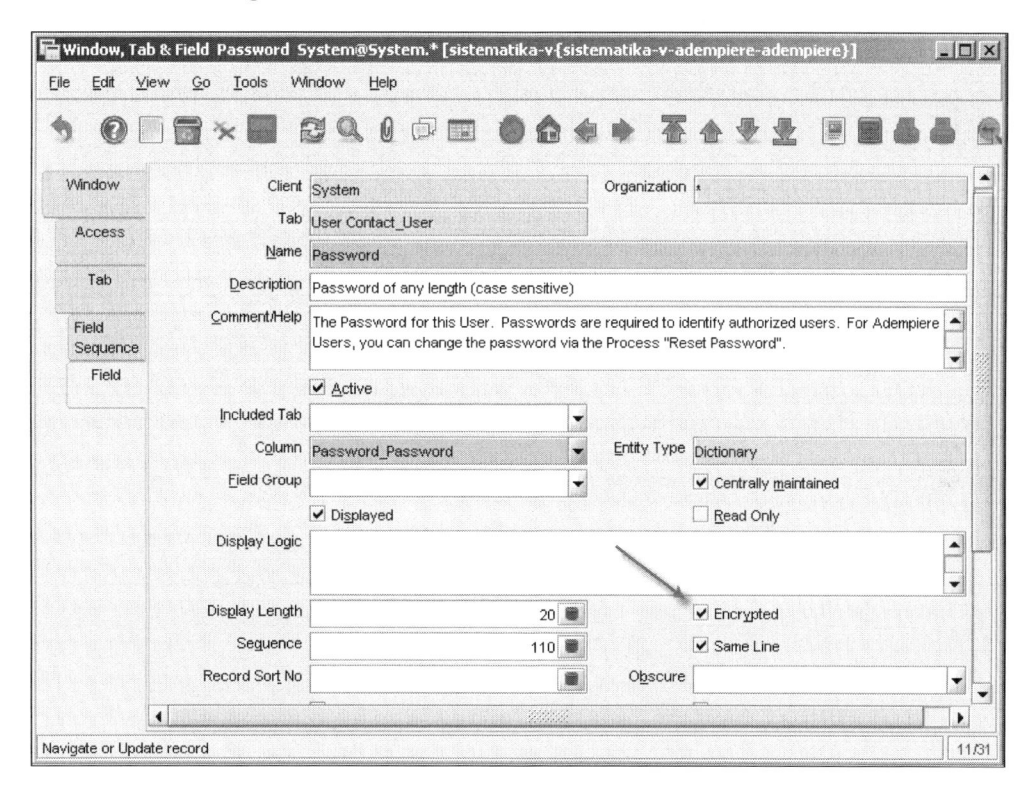

*Implementing Security*

With this configuration, the system tells us that any information entered in this field should be encrypted, and you will not be able to see the characters entered.

Deselect the **Encrypted** checkbox, and save your changes. Log in with the user ID **admin**, using **Sistematika Fashion, Ltd Admin** as the role. Open the **Menu | System Admin | General Rules | Security | User** window. Select the **Password** field in the **User Contact** tab. Now in the **User Contact** tab of the **User** window, the **Password** field will appear as plain text, as shown in the following screenshot:

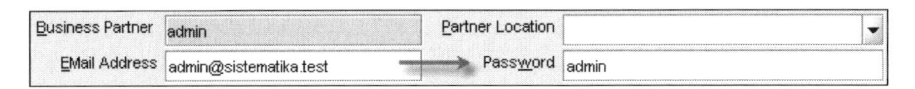

## Working with the Obscure feature

There is another option for obscuring information. Below the **Encrypted** checkbox, there is an **Obscure** field available. Here, you can select an option from the four available methods, as shown in the following screenshot:

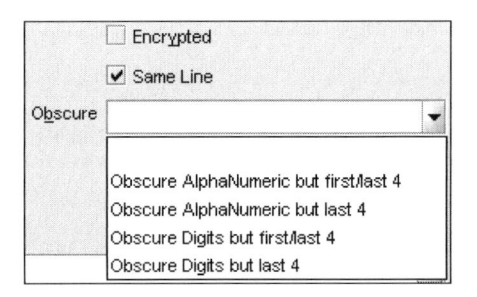

If you select the **Obscure AlphaNumeric but last 4** as your option, then the system will not obscure the last four characters when entering any data, but will obscure the rest. In this case, your **admin** user ID's **Password** field will appear as **\*dmin**. You can try any of the other available option that suits your needs.

> You need deselect the **Encrypted** checkbox when using the **Obscure** option.

# Summary

In this chapter, we have learnt how to implement security in ADempiere. We started with a discussion on how to create a new user ID in the system. With the new user ID available, we assigned a role.

When creating the role, we explained the important options, such as accessing all organizations, maintaining a change log, and showing accounting and other available attributes. We continued these activities and saw examples of how to grant access to the Info Window, Window, Process Access, Document Action Access, and Form Access.

We elaborated on how to restrict access to a certain record, and introduced you to table, report, export, and column access configuration. Finally, we showed you how ADempiere obscures information.

You now have a basic knowledge of how to implement ADempiere in your organization. We encourage you to join the ADempiere community and share your experience of using ADempiere on our forum. Visit us at `http://www.adempiere.org` and `http://www.adempiere.com` to learn more. For virtual chat, you can join and say hello to the community using **Internet Relay Chat (IRC)** at `irc.freenode.net`, channel room #adempiere. See you there!

# Index

## A

**Account**
  defining 220
**account combination, master data accounting configuration**
  account alias 98
  changing, for ADempiere default account 98
  creating 96, 98
  creating, common rules 95
  creating, ways 95
  product asset default account, altering 99
  Window Type attributes 96
**accounting dimensions** 227
**accounting processor**
  activating 172
  enabling 172
**accounting processor, configuration parts**
  common error, manual posting 88
  document, posting automatically 87, 88
**Accounting Schema**
  about 229
  Accounting Schema tab 229
  element tab 240
**Accounting Schema tab**
  about 229
  accrual-based accounting 230
  Actual costing 232
  Allow Negative Posting option 238
  Commitment Type field 230
  cost accounting 231
  Costing Level 231
  Costing Method 231
  Currency field 232
  Explicit Cost Adjustment option 237
  GAAP 230
  Periods field 233
  Post Service Separately option 236
  Post Trade Discount option 234-236
  Product Inventory Clearing accounting 239
  Standard Costing 231
  Use Account Alias checkbox 233
**account receivable payment**
  about 206
  allocation, viewing 209, 210
  bank statement 212, 213
  entering, in ADempiere 207, 208
  payment allocation 208
  reset allocation 211
  void allocation 211, 212
**accounts, ADempiere**
  adding 222-225
  balance sheet accounts 220
  Budget option 225
  chart of accounts 220
  deposit account, adding 222
  document controlled option 224
  income statement accounts 220
  list 221
  Post Actual option 225
  Statistical option 225
  summary account option 223
  Summary Level account 222
**Account schema**
  Defaults tab 245
  General Ledger tab 245
**Account schema element tab**
  about 240
  another account, registering 242, 243
  campaign information, adding 240, 242
  deactivating 244

Intercompany journal entries, avoiding  244
**Actual costing  232**
**additional organization, ADempiere client**
  creating  74
  information, updating  75
  setting  74
  type, creating  74
  type, Division  74
  type, Sub Unit  74
**additional warehouse, ADempiere client**
  existing default warehouse, altering  76
  extra locators, adding  78-80
  extra warehouse, adding  78-80
  locators, altering  76
  setting up  76
**ADempiere**
  3.4.2s release notes  35
  about  9
  accounts, managing  220
  account combination, changing  98
  Archived Documents/Reports button  338
  chart of account  66
  client, managing  42
  Client user  40
  client version, checking  38
  company hierarchy  65
  company structure, mapping  63
  connection aspect  38
  databases, installing  16
  document, re-posting  227
  features  9
  GardenAdmin user ID  40
  hardware, requirements  10
  import mechanism  370
  Info window  367
  installing, at client side  33
  installing, at server side  21
  operating system, requirements  10
  predefined user ID  39
  predefined user password  39
  Print button  338
  Print Preview button  338, 340
  product attributes  262
  product type  119
  purchase requisition, creating  131
  Report button  338
  server connection, changing  40
  System user  40
  user ID, managing  401
  users, grouping  40
  version used  41
  Workflow  303
**ADempiere 3.4.2s release notes  35**
**ADempiere client**
  city field  72
  client field  71
  country field  72
  creating  70-72
  currency field  71
  data changes log, maintaining  50
  data changes log, role-based  50
  data changes log, table-based  51
  menu, working with  43
  menu tab  43
  new creation, reviewing  73
  optional field  72
  organization field  71
  performance tab  43
  region field  72
  reviewing  73-83
  standard window fields  51
  tasks, performing  52
  User/Contact Client field  71
  User/Contact Organization field  71
  user preference  46
  window, parts  49
  Workflow Activities  43
**ADempiere client, reviewing**
  additional organization, setting  74
  additional warehouse, setting up  76
  chart of account, Import Account  81-83
  chart of account, Import File Loader  81
  chart of account, reimporting  80
  general workflow  73
  list, accessing  73
  login  73
**ADempiere company structures**
  client  65
  mapping  66
  organization  65
  warehouse  65
**ADempiere database**
  database migration script, applying  31
  importing  30

**ADempiere document**
    about  129
    diagrammatic representation  130
**ADempiere installation**
    application patch files, applying  25
    application server, starting up  32
    at client side  33
    at server side  21
    binary files, verifying  23, 24
    core installation files, extracting  25
    PostgreSQL databases, creating  26
    server, configuring  27-29
**ADempiere installation, at client side**
    steps  33
    verifying  34
    WebStart client, installing  34
**ADempiere installation, at server side**
    about  21
    core files, downloading  21
    database, importing  30
    patch files, downloading  21
    server memory management  32
**ADempiere role, role-based access control**
    about  403
    Access all Orgs option, working with  406
    Can Export option, working with  409
    Can Report option, working with  409
    creating  403-405
    Document Action Access, registering  414
    Form access, managing  415
    Info window, accessing  409, 410
    Maintain Change Log option, working with  406, 407
    organization access, assigning to userID  405, 406
    process access, identifying  411, 412
    process access, registering  413
    user ID, attaching  405
    window access, accessing  410, 411
    Working with the Show accounting option  407, 408
**ADempiere Workflow**
    about  303, 306
    Document Process workflow  309
    for ADempiere documents  306-308
    general workflow  309
    node's actions  310, 311

node's workflow responsible  311
transition, setting up  310
**AP Credit Memo  148**
**API  10**
**application process, document process workflow**
    additional workflow configuration  324
    configuration, setting up  325, 326
    internal process name, identifying  322
    parameters, identifying  323
    setting up  322-324
**Application Programming Interface.** *See* API
**approval workflow implementation, document process workflow**
    document, cancelling  318
    progression, monitoring  317
    requisition document, approving  316, 317
    requisition document, initiating  316

# B

**bank information, company financial management**
    account document, registering  108
    bank accounting, configuring  108
    entering  107
    registering  107
**Bank statement, importing**
    data, importing  398, 399
    data, loading  398
    data files, preparing  397
    Import Loader Format, creating  396, 397
    steps  396-398
**bill of material.** *See* BOM
**BOM**
    about  183
    electricity products, creating  185
    electricity products, registering  187
    information, entering  183
    labor products, creating  185
    labor products, registering  187
    overhead product category, creating  184
    product's standard cost, setting up  186, 187
    products default account, altering  185
    raw materials  183

**Business Partner**
  about 100, 103
  Customer Accounting, configuring 106
  group 100
  new Customer, registering 105, 106
  new Vendor, registering 103, 104
  vendor accounting, configuring 105
**Business Partner, importing**
  data, importing 377
  data, loading 376, 377
  data files, preparing 375
  Import Error Message sample 377
  Import Loader Format, creating 374, 375
  steps 374-377
**Business Partner group**
  about 100
  accounting configuration, defining 101, 102
  criteria 100, 101
  new group, creating 102

## C

**Calendar Year.** *See* **period, configuration parts**
**cash book, company financial management**
  about 110
  accounting, configuring 110
  configuring 109
  General receipts transaction 110
  managing 109
**cash payment**
  cash type, Bank Account Transfer 165
  cash type, Charge 165
  cash type, Difference 165
  cash type, General Expenses 165
  cash type, Invoice 165
  Invoice cash payment 166, 167
**charge, company financial management**
  new account combination, preparing 111
  new type, charging 111
**chart of accounts**
  account editor tools 66, 69, 70
  account editor tools, downloading 69
  accounting format file template, exploring 67, 68
**COGS** 203

**comma separated values.** *See* **csv files**
**commitment type accounting**
  about 248
  Matched Invoices records 251
  Matched Invoices records, GL journal entries 251
  prerequisites 248
  Purchase Order Commitment 250
  Purchase Order document, journal format 250
  Purchase Requisition document 249
  Purchase Requisition document, journal format 249
  Reservation 250
**company financial management**
  about 106
  bank information, managing 107
  cash book, managing 109
  charge 111
**configuration parts**
  accounting processor 87
  accounting schema 84, 85
  Calendar Year, creating 85
**configuration prerequisites, landed cost**
  additional business partner, entering 173, 174
  new account combination, creating 174
  new cost element, setting 176
  Price List, creating 177
  product cost adjustment default account, altering 176, 177
  setting up 173
  transportation charges, registering 178
  transportation charges, setting 174-176
**Cost of Goods Sold.** *See* **COGS**
**csv files** 69
**currency rate, multiple currencies**
  entering 115
  reciprocal rates, entering 116
**currency rates, importing**
  data, importing 384
  data, loading 383, 384
  data files, preparing 383
  Import Loader Format, creating 381
  record identity, identifying 382, 383
  steps 381-384

customer invoices
  generating, Generate Invoices (manual) used  203, 204
  generating, methods  203
  Invoice (Customer) window, examining  204-206

# D

data, importing
  Business Partner  374
  currency rates  380
  General Ledger journal  384
  inventory  394
  invoices  391
  Product  378
  purchase order  387
  sales order  387
databases installation
  about  16
  additional PostgreSQL path, verifying  18
  firewall, configuring  20
  PostgreSQL, configuring  19
  PostgreSQL databases, obtaining  16
  PostgreSQL path, adding  17, 18
Data Manipulation Language. *See* DML
Defaults tab, Account schema
  grouping  246
direct sales
  accounting facts  216
  cash books, preparing  214
  managing  214-216
  POS Order transaction workflow, unveiling  216
  sales order, entering  215
DML  370
document, re-posting
  steps  227, 228
document process workflow
  about  312
  application process  322
  approval workflow implementation  316
  e-mail's action  319
  User Choice action, approval rights  314, 315
  User Choice action, setting up  313, 314
  variable, setting up  326

document value workflow
  about  329
  configuration, defining  330-332
  logic format, document value  333
  logic format, evaluation value  333
  logic format, operands  334
  multiple value  334
  new mail template, setting up  329
  SQL document logic format  335
  testing  332, 333

# E

email, document process workflow
  activating  319
  notification configuration, testing  321, 322
  setting up, for end users  319
  template, setting up  320
  workflow configuration, altering  320
Enterprise Resource Planning. *See* ERP
ERP  9
Excel format. *See* xls format
existing raw material migration, Physical Inventory
  accounting facts  292
  activity, performing  291
  migration product, creating  290
  migration product category, creating  289
  product's cost, setting  290
  tasks  289

# F

field context menu
  ReQuery  59
  Value preference  60
  Zoom  59
Financial Reporting
  about  353, 354
  creating  357
  List Sources option, enabling  358
  Report Column Set, working with  355, 356
  Report Column Set window  353
  Reporting Hierarchy window  353
  Report Line Set window  353
  Report Line Set window, working with  354, 355

**finished goods, manufacturing**
  prerequisites, BOM  183
  prerequisites, production  188-191
**finished goods, products attributes**
  attributes, attaching  277, 278
  Attribute Set, attaching  276
  Attribute Set, creating  275
  examples  277-280
  identity, assigning  280, 281
  internal number, registering  274
  Product Info, accessing  279, 280
  production identity, identifying  274
  size attribute configuration, registering  273

# G

**GAAP**  84
**General Ledger, Account schema**  245
**General Ledger distribution**
  about  252
  configuring  252, 255
  Distribution tab, configuring  252, 253
  Line tab, configuring  254
  new account combination, creating  256
  new General Ledger Journal transaction,
      creating  256, 257
  Product costs information  258
  sample case  255
  sample transactions  256
**General Ledger journal, importing**
  data, importing  387
  data, loading  386
  data files, preparing  386
  Import Loader Format, creating  384, 385
  steps  385-387
**Generally Accepted Accounting Principles.**
      *See* **GAAP**
**general workflow**
  attaching, in menu  305, 306
  constructing  304, 305
  examples  304

# H

**HQ-14120-_-_-_- format**
  about  93
  dimensions  94

# I

**Import Loader Format**
  about  370, 371
  Import Format tab  371
  Import Format tab, defining  372
**import mechanism, ADempiere**
  about  370
  activities  374
  data loading, Import File Loader used  373
  data source, preparing  373
  Imported Table Format, methods  370, 371
  Import Loader Format  370-373
  steps  370
**Info window**
  view menu  367
**internal use, Inventory**
  accounting facts  283
  transaction, tracking  284, 285
  using  282
**Inventory**
  charge, creating  282
  importing  394
  internal use  282
  internal use line  281
  moving  292
  Physical Inventory  285
**Inventory, importing**
  data, importing  395
  data, loading  395
  data files, preparing  395
  Import Loader Format, creating  394
  steps  394, 395
**Inventory movement**
  along different warehouse  293
  among same warehouse locations  299, 300
**Inventory movement, along different
      warehouse**
  accounting facts  296, 297
  diagrammatic representation  293
  In-Transit Material Movement document,
      setting up  293, 294
  Inventory Move window, using  295
  material quantity, confirming  295, 296
  partial material confirmation  298, 299
  scrapped material confirmation  297, 298

invoice 147
invoices, importing
   customer data import sample 393
   Import Loader Format, creating 391
   steps 391-393
   Vendor data, importing 393
   Vendor data, loading 392
   Vendor data files, creating 392

# J

JasperReports
   features 367
Java Development Kit. *See* JDK
Java Runtime Environment. *See* JRE
Java Virtual Machine. *See* JVM
JDK 10
JDK installation
   at the ADempiere client computer 13
   at the ADempiere server computer 12
   Java system variables, configuring 14
   Java system variables, verifying 15
   JDK/JRE, installing 11, 12, 13
   JDK/JRE, obtaining 11
   Windows path, setting up 14
   Windows path, verifying 15
JRE 10
JVM 10

# K

key
   BP Partner key 388
   Business Partner key 388
   Organization key 385
   Org value_org key 385
   Product key 388

# L

landed cost
   about 173
   prerequisites, configuring 173
   raw material, handling expenses 172
lookup records, task performance
   about 55
   additional search criteria, searching 56, 57

# M

master data accounting configuration
   about 92
   account combination 94
   HQ-14120-_-_-_-_format 93
   product's account configuration,
      example 92, 93
   product account configuration, example 93
Material Requirement Planning. *See* MRP
menu, ADempiere client
   General Workflow icon 44
   icon 44
   Lookup feature, accessing 45
   Normal ADempiere Window icon 44
   Process icon 44
   Reports icon 44
   shortcuts, creating 45
   working with 44, 45
MM Shipment 200
MM Shipment Indirect. *See* MM Shipment
MRP 134
multiple currencies
   accessing 113
   Currency conversion rate type 114
   Currency conversion rate type, creating 114
   currency rates 115
   unneeded currencies, deactivating 113
   using 112

# N

new print format templates, report
   creating 346
   Duplicate Order Header print format 347
   Duplicate Order Line print format 347
   purchase order default print format,
      setting 348
node workflow responsible, ADempiere
      Workflow
   about 311
   Responsible Type, human 311
   Responsible Type, role 312
   setting up 312

## O

**obscure information**
  encrypted feature, enabling 422-424
  Obscure feature, working with 424
**order, importing**
  Import Loader Format, creating 388
  purchase order data, importing 389, 390
  purchase order data, loading 389
  purchase order data files, creating 389
  sales order data import sample 390
  steps 388-390

## P

**patch files, ADempiere**
  database migration script, obtaining 23
  obtaining 22
**payment, making to vendor**
  Account Payment document 160
  allocation, viewing 161
  Bank Statement document 162
  Bank Statement information, entering 162
  Bank Statement line, accounting facts 164
  Bank Statement line, entering 163
  cash payment 165
  cash payment allocation, accessing 167, 168
  Invoice cash payment 166
  outstanding liabilities 156
  selecting 157
**period, configuration parts**
  creating 85
  document types, opening 85, 86
  Period closed error message 86, 87
**Physical Memory (K) information 32**
**Physical Inventory**
  existing raw material, migrating 288
  reconciliation 285-287
  stock counting 285-287
**PostgreSQL, configuring**
  client authentication configuration file, modifying 19, 20
  configuration file, verifying 20
**PostgreSQL databases, ADempiere installation**
  ADempiere database, creating 27
  creating 26
  new login role, creating 26, 27

**PostgreSQL databases installation**
  steps 17
**price list, price management**
  creating 118
  registering 118
  version, creating 118, 119
**price list schema, price management**
  managing 117
  registering 117
**price management**
  about 116
  Limit Price 116
  List Price 116
  price list, creating 118
  price list schema, managing 117
  prices, configuring 117
  Standard Price 116
**price tab, product**
  about 124-127
  Automatic processes 125
  Limit Price 126
  List Price 126
  manual process 124
  Price List Version 126
  Standard Price 126
**print format template**
  Display Order tab 341
  finding 343
  Format Item tab 341
  Format Type field 341, 342
  Print Format tab 341
  Sort Order tab 341
**print format template, finding**
  Invoice 344
  Material Receipt 345
  payment 344
  Purchase Order 343
  Sales Order 343
  Shipment 345
**product, creating**
  new measurement unit, preparing 122, 123
  price tab 124
  product tab 123
  purchasing tab 124
**Product, importing**
  data, importing 380
  data, loading 379

data files, preparing 379
Import Loader Format, creating 378
steps 378-380
**product attributes**
about 261, 262
finished goods, attributes 272
instance attribute 262
raw material, setting up 263
raw material related information, tracking 270
**Product Inventory Clearing journal entries, eliminating**
about 246
accounting facts 248
configuration, testing 247
prerequisites 246
**product management**
about 119
product, configuring 120
product, creating 122
product category, accounting part 121, 122
product category, creating 121
product category, Finished Goods 121
product category, Raw Material 121
product type 119
**product type**
effects, on General Ledger posting 120
expense type 119
item 119
resource 120
service 120
**proposal**
about 191
document, entering 193-195
**purchase order**
about 136
creating, from purchase requisition 137
creating, manually 136
creating, ways 136
document types 136
**purchase requisition**
accounting facts 134, 135
creating, manually 131, 132
creating, ways 131
Replenish reports, working with 132

## Q

**Quotation**
about 191
document, entering 193-195
product's sales price, setting up 192, 193

## R

**raw material's product attribute**
additional information, registering 264
attributes, registering into 267
binding, into Attribute Set 265, 266
color 263
color attribute configuration, registering 263
description 263
internal number references, registering 265
local number 263
serial number 263
setting up 263
using, example 268
vendor serial number configuration, registering 264
**raw material's product attribute, example**
attribute information, entering 269
purchase document, creating 268
**raw material related information, product attributes**
additional searching criteria, defining 271, 272
Attribute Set Instance window, using 270
tracking 270
**receiving materials**
accounting facts 141
error, posting 143
Matched Purchase Order 145
Matched Purchase Order, accounting facts 147
Matched Purchase Order, aim 146
Purchase Order - Receipt, accounting facts 145
Purchase Order - Receipt, matching 143, 144
without purchase order reference 141, 142

with purchase order reference 139, 140
working with 138
**record access security rule**
  about 416
  blocking, to certain records 417
  Dependent Entities, using 419
  Personal Lock, enabling 416
  restoring, to certain blocked records 418
**Replenish report, purchase requisition**
  default price list, setting up 133
  information, setting up 132
  replenish information, completing 134
**report**
  archiving 342
  customizing 345
  export feature 343
  print format template 340
  Print preview, using 340
  Send Email facility 342
**report, customizing**
  another header layout, altering 350, 351
  comparing, with other document 346
  detail purchase order layout,
    altering 352, 353
  logo, altering 349
**Report button**
  accessing 338, 339
  Drill across feature 339
  Drill down feature 339
**reporting hierarchy**
  about 359
  specific financial report, configuring 360
  summary financial report 364
**role-based access control 403**
**Role Data Access**
  Column access, restricting 421, 422
  Export access, restricting 421
  Report access, restricting 420
  Table access, restricting 419
  working with 419

# S

**Sales Order**
  Delivery Rule 197
  Invoice Rule 197
  proposal conversion, to Standard order 196

**sample apparel company structure**
  about 64
  simulation 64
**shipment**
  accounting facts 202, 203
  automatic 198
  confirmation 200
  document, accessing 199, 200
  finished goods standard cost,
    updating 201, 202
  generating 198, 199
  manual 198
  semi automatic 198
**Sistematika Fashion Ltd.** *See* **sample apparel company structure**
**specific financial report configuration**
  new summary product, setting up 360
  reporting hierarchy records,
    creating 362, 363
  sample reporting hierarchy, testing 363, 364
  Summary of Products Tree, setting up 360
  Summary of Products Tree, verifying 362
  Tree Maintenance, setting 361
**SQL 370**
**standard window fields, ADempiere client**
  Active checkbox field 51
  client field 51
  organization field 51
**Structured Query Language.** *See* **SQL**
**summary financial report**
  about 364
  business partner, setting up 364
  business partner summary, verifying 366
  business partner tree summary 365
  specific financial report, executing 366
  specific reporting hierarchy, setting up 366
  Tree Maintenance, setting up 365

# T

**task performance, ADempiere client**
  data management, icons 52
  data navigation, icons 53
  field context menu 58
  lookup records 55
  other tasks 54
  Zoom Across usage, examples 57

**transportation charges, registering**
   accounting facts  181
   cost distribution types  179
   expected distribution value  179
   transportation cost, entering  179-181

# U

**user ID, ADempiere**
   entering, in system  402, 403
   managing  401
**user preference, ADempiere client**
   Cache Windows field  48
   Context  48
   Errors  48
   Info  48
   preference tab, field recommended
       values  46, 47
   User Interface Theme  48

# V

**variable, document process workflow**
   set attribute action, configuring  327
   setting up  326, 328
   set variable workflow, testing  328
**vendor invoice**
   about  147, 148
   accounting facts  152
   Matched Invoices, accounting facts  154, 155
   Matched Invoices, evaluating  153, 154
   matching, to material receipt  152
   material receipt reference, not
       using  150, 151
   material receipt reference, using  148, 149
**vendor payment**
   selecting  157
**vendor payment selection**
   about  157
   payment proposal, creating  157-159
   Print/Export  159
   unpaid invoices reports list, creating  157

# W

**window, ADempiere client**
   Cancel button  50
   Ok button  50
   parts  49
   Record Info  49
**Workflow**
   defining  306

# X

**xls format  66**

# Z

**Zoom Across usage, example  57**

# Thank you for buying
# ADempiere 3.4 ERP Solutions

## Packt Open Source Project Royalties

When we sell a book written on an Open Source project, we pay a royalty directly to that project. Therefore by purchasing ADempiere 3.4 ERP Solutions, Packt will have given some of the money received to the ADempiere project.

In the long term, we see ourselves and you—customers and readers of our books—as part of the Open Source ecosystem, providing sustainable revenue for the projects we publish on. Our aim at Packt is to establish publishing royalties as an essential part of the service and support a business model that sustains Open Source.

If you're working with an Open Source project that you would like us to publish on, and subsequently pay royalties to, please get in touch with us.

## Writing for Packt

We welcome all inquiries from people who are interested in authoring. Book proposals should be sent to author@packtpub.com. If your book idea is still at an early stage and you would like to discuss it first before writing a formal book proposal, contact us; one of our commissioning editors will get in touch with you.

We're not just looking for published authors; if you have strong technical skills but no writing experience, our experienced editors can help you develop a writing career, or simply get some additional reward for your expertise.

## About Packt Publishing

Packt, pronounced 'packed', published its first book "Mastering phpMyAdmin for Effective MySQL Management" in April 2004 and subsequently continued to specialize in publishing highly focused books on specific technologies and solutions.

Our books and publications share the experiences of your fellow IT professionals in adapting and customizing today's systems, applications, and frameworks. Our solution-based books give you the knowledge and power to customize the software and technologies you're using to get the job done. Packt books are more specific and less general than the IT books you have seen in the past. Our unique business model allows us to bring you more focused information, giving you more of what you need to know, and less of what you don't.

Packt is a modern, yet unique publishing company, which focuses on producing quality, cutting-edge books for communities of developers, administrators, and newbies alike. For more information, please visit our website: www.PacktPub.com.

## EJB 3 Developer Guide

ISBN: 978-1-847195-60-9　　　Paperback: 259 pages

A Practical Guide for developers and architects to the Enterprise Java Beans Standard

1. A rapid introduction to the features of EJB 3
2. EJB 3 features explored concisely with accompanying code examples
3. Easily enhance Java applications with new, improved Enterprise Java Beans

## JBoss AS 5 Development

ISBN: 978-1-847196-82-8　　　Paperback: 496 pages

Develop, deploy, and secure Java applications on this robust, open source application server

1. A complete guide for JBoss developers covering everything from basic installation to creating, debugging, and securing Java EE applications on this popular, award-winning JBoss application server
2. Master the most important areas of Java Enterprise programming including EJB 3.0, web services, the security framework, and more
3. Starts with the basics of JBoss AS and moves on to cover important advanced topics with the help of easy-to-understand practical examples
4. Written in a very simple and readable style, this book includes essential tips and tricks that will help you master JBoss AS development

Please check **www.PacktPub.com** for information on our titles

Printed in Germany
by Amazon Distribution
GmbH, Leipzig